Introduction to Money and Banking

Oliver G. Wood, Jr.
University of South Carolina

D. Van Nostrand Company
New York   Cincinnati   London   Melbourne   Toronto

In memory of my grandmother,
Grace d'Alvigny McBrayer

Her intellect, class, pride, and determination
were an inspiration to her family and friends.

D. Van Nostrand Company Regional Offices:
New York   Cincinnati

D. Van Nostrand Company International Offices:
London   Toronto   Melbourne

Library of Congress Catalog Card Number: 79-65818
ISBN: 0-442-25787-2

Published by D. Van Nostrand Company
135 West 50th Street, New York, N.Y. 10020

10 9 8 7 6 5 4 3 2 1

Preface

This book is designed as a basic textbook in the undergraduate course in money and banking. The author's aim is to provide students with a concise, up-to-date, and balanced treatment of institutional, theoretical, and policy-related material.

Over the years, the traditional money and banking course developed into a course in macroeconomics. More recently, however, there has been a movement toward emphasizing once again the basic concepts of money and banking. This book was written with this new emphasis in mind.

The concept of money provides the common thread integrating the various subareas of money and banking. Most of the textual discussion is involved with answering five broad questions:

1. What are the nature and functions of money?
2. What are the mechanics of money production?
3. What are the framework for and techniques involved with control of money production?
4. How do changes in the money supply affect income, employment, and prices?
5. What are the goals and alternative strategies of money supply management?

To deal with these questions, the seventeen chapters are organized into five parts:

1. Introduction to Money, Financial Institutions, and Markets (3 chapters)
2. Commercial Banking (3 chapters)
3. Central Banking (3 chapters)
4. Monetary and Income Theory (4 chapters)
5. Monetary Policy (4 chapters)

Part 1, Chapter 1, in addition to the traditional discussion of the nature and functions of money, examines the evolution of our payments system—from barter to EFT—and shows the student how to find the real value of money with examples from both the lending and borrowing side of the market. Chapter 2 is devoted to the "Basics of Deposit Creation and Destruction." Chapter 3 looks at the broad subject of "Financial Intermediation in the Economy," with emphasis on the growing similarity among financial intermediaries.

Part 2 deals with commercial banking. Too often this subject gets short shrift in the money and banking course. For many students, however, this course offers the only opportunity to study commercial banks—the most important financial institution in the economy and a place where many students will look for employment. The three chapters dealing with commercial banking look at the structure and regulation of the banking industry and examine in detail the sources and uses of bank funds.

Part 3, (Central Banking), begins with a chapter on the structure and operation of the Federal Reserve System. The next chapter is devoted to the "Framework for Monetary Control." Here, the aim is to develop the student's understanding of the bank reserve equation and the monetary base-multiplier approach to monetary control. There is no substitute for extensive work with T-accounts to illustrate the factors that supply and absorb bank reserves. The final chapter in this part examines the "Techniques of Monetary Control" and shows how each relates to the monetary base-multiplier framework for monetary control.

Part 4 contains four chapters on monetary and income theory. A major objective of this part is to provide a balanced treatment of traditional and modern theories. The first two chapters are devoted to the classical and Keynesian theories, respectively. The Keynesian presentation, along with the IS-LM synthesis is condensed into one chapter. For most students, this chapter will be a review of material learned in basic economics courses.

The third chapter in the theory section deals with modern theories of the demand for money. The student is shown that each "modern" theory is grounded in the classical and/or Keynesian theories of the demand for money. Major topics covered in this chapter include the refinements to the Keynesian liquidity preference theory, the neo-Keynesian portfolio-balances approach, and the modern quantity-theory approach to the demand for money. Each of these topics is developed in an intuitive manner that should promote comprehension.

The last chapter in the theory section is entitled "Channels of Monetary Influence: Relative Price Effects and Wealth Effects." Scenarios are developed to show that, under each of the major theories of the demand for money, changes in the money supply influence the economy through relative price or substitution effects in a portfolio of assets. Moreover, wealth effects such as the Pigou effect and equity effect are explained as reinforcing relative price effects.

Part 5 deals with monetary policy. The first two chapters examine the domestic goals and international aspects of monetary policy. The next chapter presents alternative strategies for monetary policy, including the priorities and conflicts involved with the formulation of monetary policy. Following an examination of the natural rate of unemployment and accelerationist hypotheses, the rational expectations hypothesis is discussed. The last two parts of this chapter look at the monetarist-Keynesian debate and the Federal Reserve's current strategy for monetary policy that reflects both monetarist and Keynesian influences. A final chapter traces the history of monetary policy: 1941–present.

The book is short enough to be completed in one semester. For convenience, a short list of "Suggestions for Additional Reading" is offered at the end of each chapter.

Writing this book was a challenging and enjoyable experience. The author wishes to thank Professors Charles M. Neufeld and William S. Rawson for their helpful comments. The author benefited greatly from his discussion with Professor John M. Harris, Jr. concerning matters of organization and from the comments and suggestions of Professors John A. Halloran, University of Notre Dame; Lee R. McPheters,

Arizona State University; Crumpton Farrell, St. Cloud State University; William J. Swift, Pace University; and James J. Clarke, University of Delaware. Maggie Schwarz, of D. Van Nostrand, offered excellent assistance and was a pleasure to work with. Gloria Nicholson's cheerful and professional typing of the manuscript is most appreciated. Finally, my greatest debt is to my wife, Patricia, for her encouragement and hard work in helping to see the book through to its completion.

Oliver G. Wood, Jr.

Contents

1

Introduction to Money, Financial Institutions, and Markets

Money

Money ranks as one of the greatest inventions of all time. Outside of some monumental discoveries in physics, chemistry, and medicine, perhaps no other invention has had a greater positive impact on overall welfare. But like nuclear fission, money serves people best when it is controlled. This book is about money, how it is produced, how it affects our economic welfare, and the institution we have created to control its production.

In this chapter we will (1) define money, (2) answer the question "Who produces money?" (3) look at various measures of the money supply, (4) outline the evolution of the payments system, (5) describe the functions of money, and (6) show how to find the real value of money.

Definition of Money

If you go to the library and examine other material on money and banking, you will find that there is no universal definition of money. But this should not cause you a great deal of trauma. As a veteran of at least two economics courses and having read the newspaper for many years, you must have surmised by now that "if you laid all economists end to end, you still would not reach a conclusion!" Nevertheless, it would be helpful to have a good definition of money in mind before we tackle some of the problems ahead. Let's try this one.

Money is anything commonly used and generally accepted as a medium of exchange and as a unit of account. This is a functional definition of money because it embodies the two most important functions of money. The word "anything" is used to avoid restriction. Throughout history many things in local economies have been used as money—cattle, stones, tobacco, wampum, shark's teeth, woodpecker scalps. The term "commonly used" indicates that we do not wish to include items that are occasionally used, such as cigarettes. The term "generally accepted" is used because we wish to include only those items that people are always ready and willing to accept and accumulate in great quantity.

Who Produces Money?

What items meet the criteria imposed in our definition of money? Who produces these items? How does money get into circulation? Believe it or not, the first two questions really are difficult to answer, and have become more difficult in recent years because of the increasing "moneyness" of claims issued by nonbank financial intermediaries such as mutual savings banks, savings and loan associations, and credit unions. Let us begin by considering the three primary producers of money: (1) Federal Reserve banks, (2) the US Treasury, and (3) commercial banks.

Federal Reserve Banks

Each of the twelve Federal Reserve Banks **(FRBs)** issues **Federal Reserve notes** which comprise virtually all of the currency in circulation. At the end of 1978, Federal Reserve notes totaling $113 billion were in circulation in denominations of 1, 2, 5, 10, 20, 50, and 100. Get out a few Federal Reserve notes and see if you can determine which FRBs issued the notes. FRBs issue Federal Reserve notes to commercial banks which, in turn, exchange them for demand deposits of customers who wish to "cash checks."

US Treasury

The US Treasury is the sole issuer of coins and also, by law, maintains $320 million in US notes ($5 denominations only). In

Figure 1-1. Federal Reserve notes being engraved (*Courtesy of the United States Treasury*)

addition, small amounts of silver certificates, Treasury notes of 1890, and several other minor note issues are in circulation; however, these are in the process of retirement. The Treasury issues coin and currency to the FRBs and from there this money gets into circulation in the same manner as Federal Reserve notes. At the close of 1978, the Treasury had outstanding $12 billion in coins and currency.

Commercial Banks

Commercial banks produce **demand deposits.** At the end of 1978 these totaled $264 billion. Demand deposits simply are bookkeeping credits (liabilities) of commercial banks. Most demand deposits are *created* in the process of banks making loans and investments. Suppose you wished to buy a new Oldsmobile Cutlass and a bank agreed to lend you money to buy it. At the bank, you would

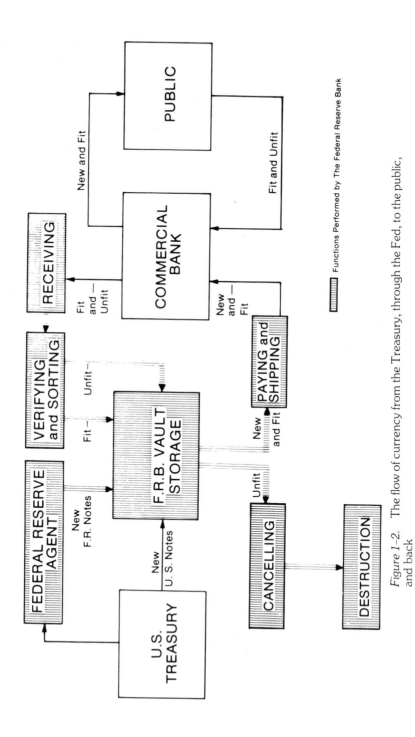

Figure 1-2. The flow of currency from the Treasury, through the Fed, to the public, and back

sign a note that specifies the terms of the loan. The amount of the note would be recorded on the asset side of the bank's balance sheet and, simultaneously, the bank would credit your demand deposit account with an equal sum. Two entries are made on the bank's balance sheet. You then may transfer these bookkeeping credits by means of a **check** to the Oldsmobile dealer. Note that checks are not demand deposits or money; checks are orders to your bank to transfer demand deposits to the payee designated by you on the check. After the loan is received, on your own balance sheet you would increase your assets (cash) and your liabilities (loan payable).

Demand deposits also originate in the banking system when currency and coin are deposited. Suppose you were the treasurer for a dorm party and collected a good many Federal Reserve notes. You might go to the bank and deposit the notes in the bank. In this case, the bank would increase your demand deposit account (its liability) and increase cash-in-vault (its asset).

Commercial banks also produce savings deposits, time deposits, and time **certificates of deposits (CDs)**. Each of these claims represents an interest-bearing deposit with various restrictions on withdrawal and the payment of interest. We will consider these sources of funds in more detail in Chapter 5. Each of these types of deposit differs with respect to the ease with which it can be converted into demand deposits. On November 1, 1978, banks were given authority to make transfers for their customers from savings deposits to demand deposit accounts to cover checks written on the latter. Thus, savings deposits no longer should be considered "near money"; they are demand deposits disguised as savings deposits. A one-year CD does not meet the criteria in our definition of money; however, some economists might include them in a statistical definition of money for purposes of exploring the relationships among "money" and GNP, employment, and prices.

Other Producers of Money

In recent years regulatory changes have increased the moneyness of certain claims on other financial institutions to serve as close substitutes for demand deposits. Mutual savings banks and savings and loan associations as well as commercial banks in New England (Massachusetts, New Hampshire, Maine, Vermont, Rhode Island, and Connecticut) and New York offer interest-bearing savings accounts with the privilege of writing **negotiable orders of withdrawal (NOWs)**. Since a NOW looks like a check and, more important, functions like a check, customers in these states have the equivalent of interest-bearing demand deposit accounts.

Many credit unions recently have begun offering customers the ability to transfer funds from share accounts with a checklike instrument called a **share draft**. From the customer's point of view, this innovation, in effect, converts credit union savings shares into demand deposits.

One of the most interesting financial innovations in the 1970s was the **money market mutual fund**. Such funds consist primarily of CDs and short-term corporate and government securities. Shareholders usually receive yields much higher than those available on savings accounts in financial institutions. Since 1974, many funds have permitted shareholders to redeem shares simply by writing a check. This privilege effectively transforms fund shares into interest-bearing demand deposits. At the close of 1978, there were $11 billion in money market funds. The largest, Merrill Lynch's Ready Asset Fund, had $1.6 billion.

Deposits at **savings and loan associations (S&Ls)** also took on increased moneyness in the 1970s. S&Ls were granted authority to pay preauthorized bills for their depositors out of savings accounts and to make telephone transfers between a customer's S&L account and his or her bank account. A number of S&Ls also have established **remote service units** (RSUs), which are electronic teller machines that are "on line" with the S&Ls main computer and permit a customer to "tap" his or her savings account for cash in places like supermarkets and airports.

Measures of the Money Supply

At college football games, we sometimes see a student hold up a sign to the television camera which might read "Mom and Dad—Send Money! Love, Rick." If you think Rick has money problems, so does the Federal Reserve System, which has the task of measuring the money supply. As you can see from the last section, the financial scene in the 1970s has witnessed an expanding array of financial assets that either meet or come within an eyelash of meeting the criteria that we specified in our definition of money. Moreover, economists have done extensive research into the influence of changes in the money supply (measured in various ways) on GNP, employment, and prices. The realities of financial innovations of the 1970s and the findings of research caused the Fed to begin publishing several measures of the money supply. Definitions of the **monetary aggregates**, as they are sometimes called, are summarized in Table 1-1.

Table 1-1	
Measures of the Money Supply	
(January, 1979)	
M_1 = Currency and coin outside banks ($98 billion) plus commercial bank demand deposits ($262 billion).	$360 billion
M_1+ = M_1 plus savings deposits at commercial banks, NOW accounts at banks and thrift institutions, credit union share accounts, and demand deposits at mutual savings banks ($223 billion).	583 billion
M_2 = M_1 plus commercial bank time and savings deposits other than negotiable CDs in denominations of $100,000 or more ($515 billion).	875 billion
M_3 = M_2 plus deposits at mutual savings banks and S&L's and credit union shares ($630 billion).	1,505 billion
M_4 = M_2 plus negotiable CDs in denominations of $100,000 or more ($100 billion).	975 billion
M_5 = M_3 plus negotiable CDs in denominations of $100,000 or more.	1,605 billion

Source: Board of Governors of the Federal Reserve, *Federal Reserve Bulletin.*

Evolution of the Payments System

Now that we have seen some of the complexities involved in defining and measuring the money supply, it would be useful to trace briefly the evolution of the payments system.

Barter

A good way to gain insight into the contribution that the use of money makes toward a smoothly functioning economic system is to analyze the problems of an economy without money, that is, a **barter**

economy. Barter means to exchange goods and services that we have or produce for those that someone else has or produces.

There are a number of difficulties involved in a barter economy. The first one is the "too many prices problem." Imagine that you were on a Pacific island and that there were only five items to exchange: (1) bananas, (2) fish, (3) seashells, (4) fishnets, and (5) turtle eggs. How many different ratios (prices) exist among the items? Answer: 10.[1] These ratios would be in constant fluctuation as the supply and demand for each item changed. Suppose there were 100 items. Then the number of possible ratios would explode to 4,950. Can you imagine wandering around the marketplace trying to keep track of relative values? The point should be clear. There is an inordinate number of ratios or prices in a barter economy.

The next three problems of a barter economy involve the three great economic functions performed in every economy: (1) production, (2) distribution, and (3) consumption. Adam Smith, often called the father of economics, said in *The Wealth of Nations*, published in 1776, that specialization is the key to increasing production. In a barter economy, however, people tend to be **self-sufficient**, that is, they do everything for themselves. If the hut needs repairing, John Q. Native does it; if his wife wants fish for dinner tonight, he had better head for the beach with his net. But John does not become really proficient at any endeavor. He is a jack-of-all-trades and mediocre at all of them. On the other hand, if every person on the island selected one activity to specialize in, GNP would be larger than with a system of self-sufficiency. The point is that barter greatly constrains specialization, which is the key to increasing production and greater economic welfare.

The third problem in a barter economy involves **distribution**, the act of rewarding the factors of production. Suppose there are some rudimentary businesses on the island such as fishing with a fishing boat. The boat captain would have a difficult time paying the laborers at the end of the day. How many fish does he give each laborer? How does he differentiate for productivity? Does the most productive worker get an extra large fish or three extra small fish? Barter complicates the economic function of distribution.

The fourth problem involves **consumption**, the end of all eco-

---

1. The number of ratios existing in a barter economy is described by the following formula: $\frac{n^2 - n}{2}$, where n equals the number of items to be bartered.

nomic activity. Here we face the problem of **dual coincidence of wants**, an imposing-sounding term that simply means you must find someone who has what you want and wants what you have. Can you imagine the time wasted in searching for that special person? Out of frustration, many people may just quit and barter with someone who has a less acceptable item. Thus, barter severely restricts the range and freedom of consumption.

Designation of a Commodity as Money

From the problems outlined in a barter economy, you can understand why it was a happy day when someone got the idea to designate

Figure 1–3. Examples of primitive money

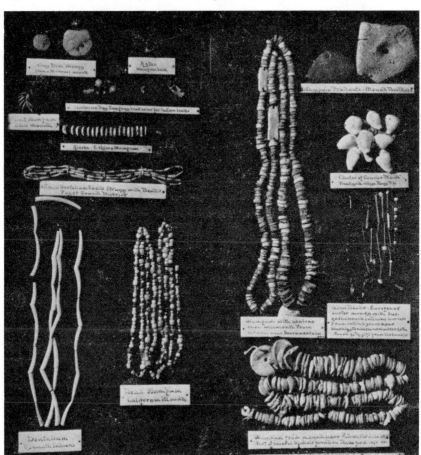

one of the items as a common denominator for all other items. In other words, suppose the value of all items was expressed in terms of seashells. Then people would have to remember only the number of seashells necessary to command a unit of the other items. For example, one bunch of bananas might equal 100 seashells. The natives on the island may not have known it at the time, but they had just instituted a crude monetary system with seashells as money. Look at the impact of this invention on the problems in a barter economy. Instead of 4,950 ratios in the 100-item economy, now there are only $n-1$, or 99. Now the natives can specialize in order to increase the level of GNP, forget the physical problems of distribution, and say goodbye to the problem of dual coincidence of wants.

Soon, however, the natives would discover new problems surrounding the use of a commodity as money. On the first day that seashells were designated as money, the native with insight would head for the beach with a basket to pick up seashells. He might even paddle over to the next island and gather seashells there. By now, you may have guessed what will happen when he returns to the marketplace; he will bid up all the exchange rates between seashells and the items that he wants, and the island would experience the world's first **inflation** (a rise in the general level of prices). Thus, the greatest problem with use of a commodity as money is **control of supply**. Jumping way ahead of ourselves, most economists believe that, in the long run, control of the money supply is the key to stable prices. Of course, the use of a commodity as money also would entail many practical problems with divisibility, uniformity, durability, portability, perishability, and storage.

Paper Money, Bookkeeping Credits, and Checks

The next improvements in the payments system stemmed from efforts to overcome the practical problems associated with the use of an uncontrolled commodity as money. Modern paper currency came into use in England during the seventeenth century. People there usually kept their gold and other valuables with the goldsmiths, who gave written receipts for the items deposited. The owners of the receipts found that they could exchange the receipts for goods and services. People accepted the receipts because they knew that the goldsmith would redeem the receipts with gold and other valuables.

Modern deposit banking and double-entry bookkeeping had their origins in Italy between 1200 and 1600. In the great banking houses of Florence, Venice, and Genoa, enterprising bankers discovered that they could make loans by simply adding credits to the accounts of their borrowers who also were depositors. They also learned that deposits could be transferred among accounts, and that not all depositors would descend on the bank at once to claim gold or silver.

Checks came into use in England during the last part of the eighteenth century. England's central bank, The Bank of England, became the sole issuer of currency in London, the financial center. The private banks, by necessity, became banks of deposit. Loans were made by creation of deposits, and checks became the instrument for transferring these deposits.

Electronic Funds Transfer (EFT)

Necessity is the mother of invention. As we have seen, throughout the evolution of the payments systems, problems cause people to look for solutions. And so it has become with checks. Checks were a very convenient way to transfer funds, until the banking system became inundated with mountains of checks and the handling costs spiraled. In 1977, the Fed processed 13.3 billion checks with a dollar amount of $5.5 trillion. This does not include checks outside the Fed, such as checks processed in and among banks themselves.

Early attempts to reduce check volume were instituted by the Fed through its **wire transfer system**, which links the Board of Governors, the Reserve banks and branches, the US Treasury, and more than 200 member banks. Components are linked by teletype lines to a central switch in Culpeper, Virginia. The **Culpeper Switch** permits the transfer of reserve balances from one member bank to another. These transfers may be for the accounts of the member banks or the customer. Money market banks in Chicago and New York have a similar communication system to the Fed, which enables them to transmit payments messages among themselves.

An important part of EFT are the **automated clearinghouses (ACHs),** which permit banks in cities where they are located to transmit debt and credit items among themselves by electronic impulse rather than by paper. The National Automated Clearing House Association was formed in 1974 as an independent corporation to develop the interregional exchange for paperless entries and to promote the ACH movement.

A number of other innovations have been introduced to reduce the mounting check volume. Many firms now meet their payroll by handing the bank one check and a computer printout or a reel of magnetic tape showing the individual amounts. Such **direct deposit systems** are in effect now for the social security and military retirement systems.

Automatic teller machines (ATMs) are another feature of EFT. These permit a customer to obtain cash by inserting a card in a machine and punching in his or her "secret code." ATMs reduce both paper and people costs. Another EFT innovation is **point-of-sale systems**, which allows a customer to pay for goods and services at the merchant location by having funds transferred from his or her demand deposit or credit card account to the merchant—either immediately or at the end of the month. Many observers believe that point-of-sale systems potentially could be the most significant innovation leading to reduced check volume.

EFT is another example of the use of technology to solve a problem. Undoubtedly, there are other innovations on the horizon. We probably will not achieve a "checkless society," but we will achieve a "less-

Figure 1-4 Data processing center at the Fed's Culpeper Switch (*Courtesy of the Federal Reserve Bank of Richmond*)

start driving it's early, very
 I can still do my banking at
rd Banking Center. What a
it is not to have to spend my
ak standing in line to make

**Vould you believe I'm
aving fun at my bank?**
 come in here to work the buttons on
his fantastic machine almost every
lay. I can check my balance, or
ransfer funds, or withdraw money.
And I love those little receipts you get
or each transaction. You know, once
ou get started, it's more fun than a
inball machine.

CITIBANK⊕
THE CITI

Figure 1-5   (Courtesy of Citibank, N.A.)

check" society. However, there are many unresolved issues with EFT. Many people are concerned with possible infringement on individual privacy because of possible unauthorized access to financial information. Also, from the regulatory point of view, there are questions involving competition between banks that can and cannot afford to participate in EFT systems. Does this mark the end of small banks? Many other questions remain; however, the great benefits to society from this application of technology to the fundamental problem of providing an efficient payments mechanism justifies the system and the effort to resolve these problems in an equitable manner.

Functions of Money

In this section we will examine five functions of money and answer this question: how well has money performed these functions in our country in the recent past, say, the 1970s?

Medium of Exchange

A primary function of money is as a **medium of exchange**. This means that money is the means by which we exchange the goods and services that we produce for the goods and services that others produce. This important function of money allows us to escape all the problems of barter enumerated earlier.

Money serves very well as a medium of exchange. Domestically, people seem ready and willing to accept money in exchange for goods and services. Of course, there is the problem of bad checks, but this problem stems from the dishonesty of the check writer and not the acceptability of demand deposits.

Unit of Account

Money serves as a **unit of account**, that is, the means by which we express relative economic values. We use money to keep score in the economic world just as the point is the unit of account in basketball. As a unit of account, money is the common denominator in the marketplace. Items on balance sheets are expressed in terms of money, not real quantities.

In the 1970s, as everyone knows, the United States experienced a rapid increase in the general level of prices. As measured by the **Consumer Price Index (CPI)**, between 1970 and 1978 prices increased 68 percent. Inflation has distorted money's ability to function effectively as a unit of account. For example, suppose that a lumber company's balance sheet showed a $1 million inventory in plywood in 1970 and the same total in 1980. We all would know that the company has a smaller pile of plywood in 1980. Money has served as an imperfect unit of accounting for economic values. There has been a slippage in the economy's yardstick.

Store of Wealth

Money is one of many **stores of wealth**, or, as Milton Friedman says, "temporary abodes of purchasing power." This function of money allows us to postpone the last half of the barter transaction. We can produce goods and services, receive money for them, then hold money until we are ready to purchase other goods and services. There are many other stores of wealth—land, stocks, bonds, mortgages, antique cars, diamonds, gold, Russian Imperial bonds issued before the Revolution. Money, however, represents perfect liquidity; it usually offers its holders instant command over other stores of wealth. On the other hand, money in the form of coin, currency, and demand deposits has an opportunity cost in terms of foregone interest. Inflation also reduces money's ability to command goods and services in the future. As the late Senator Everett Dirksen from Illinois used to say, "Inflation is the burglar in the bank account."

The inflation of the 70s has considerably lessened money's attractiveness as a store of wealth. Money has been superior to those assets, however, that did not appreciate in line with inflation. As a temporary abode for purchasing power, it is much better to hold money than hold a stock whose price gyrates all over the chart and which might be down when you need the money. In conclusion, money's performance as a store of wealth could be improved, but even in the face of eroding purchasing power, it has its virtues.

Standard of Deferred Payment

At one time or another all of us have borrowed money. That means that some person or financial institution has created for us **credit**, the obligation to repay money in the future. If you went down and bought a new, shiny red TRANS AM and signed a note with your banker, the note would state that you were to repay so many dollars, not a TRANS AM. The banker used money as a **standard of deferred payment**, a means of expressing a future financial obligation. After all, the banker knows that you probably will drive the car over salted roads next winter and get it nicked by careless people in parking lots.

How has money performed as a standard of deferred payment? Not very well in the 70s because of the same inflation that caused problems for functions two and three. When creditors use money to state future obligations and debtors repay in money that has less purchasing power, then real wealth is redistributed from creditors to debtors. These kinds of distortions are disruptive to the smooth functioning of financial markets in an economy that depends on credit to finance most of the private and public long-term investment projects.

Guarantor of Solvency

Somewhere between the Great Depression and the recession of 1973–1975, the word "solvency" disappeared from the working business vocabulary. Solvency means the ability to pay debts. During the 1973–1975 recession many businesses, primarily those related to real estate, became insolvent and declared bankruptcy. The lesson from this experience is that, if you have a debt listed on the right side of your balance sheet stated in dollars and coming due next week, the only way to guarantee your solvency is to match it with an equal amount of dollars on the left side. This balancing, of course, is irrefutable, and you might say that we are making much out of something minor. Full appreciation for this function of money may not be forthcoming until you enter the business world and experience the good feeling of being able to discharge your obligations on time as some of your less-able competitors fail because they did not.

How has money performed as a guarantor of solvency? Very well. Neither inflation nor deflation reduces money's effectiveness in this role. As long as the debt is stated in terms of dollars, then you can meet your contractual obligations by holding dollars. It does not matter that the real value of money rises or falls. Because the **face value**, or **nominal value**, of money remains constant, that is, the dollar unit is always one, money continues to serve well as a guarantor of solvency.

How to Find the Real Value of Money

We have learned that money's attractiveness as a unit of account, store of wealth, and standard of deferred payment has been reduced considerably in recent years because of inflation. These distortions make it imperative that you learn how to think about economic and financial transactions in real terms rather than nominal terms. This means that you must learn "to remove the veil of money" and look at the real economic quantities represented by money. The **real value of money** means the amount of goods and services that can be commanded in exchange. The best way to learn the concept is to do some problems.

"The Orange Inflation Problem"

Suppose that in year 1, you decide to spend $1 for some oranges, and oranges sell for 20¢ per pound. You could buy 5 pounds. Suppose that in year 2, you decide to spend $1 for oranges, but now oranges sell for 25¢ per pound. How many pounds could you buy? If you said 4 pounds, go to the head of the class. Now for an important conclusion. Between years 1 and 2, the price level of oranges rose 25 percent; however, the real value of money fell 20 percent. Therefore, you simply cannot take the percentage change in prices, change the sign, and call that the percentage in real value. However, for small changes in prices, this can be done because the difference diminishes.

We could have proven the decline in the real value of money without resorting to a grocer's scale. Suppose we use the concept of index numbers to construct an orange price index. In year 1, the base year, the orange price index would equal 100; in year 2 it would equal 125. We can find the value of money in year 2 in terms of year 1 purchasing power by **deflating**, that is, dividing the amount of money spent on oranges in year 2 by the price index in year 2, and multiplying by 100 (because the base is 100). Hence, the real value of money (orange purchasing power) in year 2 is

$$\frac{\$1}{125} \times 100 = \$.80$$

Thus, the real value of money has declined by 20 percent, the same answer that we found by a comparison of the weights of oranges in years 1 and 2. We can use the principles learned above to work some finance problems.

The Real Return on an Investment

Consider the following bond investment proposal:

Given:

1. Amount: $10,000
2. Coupon rate: 10 percent
3. Expected appreciation/depreciation: none
4. Holding period: 1 year
5. Expected marginal tax rate: 32 percent
6. Expected change in consumer price index: +6 percent

Find:

1. Expected gross return
2. Expected after-tax return
3. Expected real return

The **expected gross return** is equal to the interest earnings (coupon rate times purchase price) plus or minus the expected appreciation or depreciation in price. In the above example, the gross return is $1,000, or 10 percent.

The **expected after-tax return** is equal to the gross return less the **marginal tax rate**, which is the percentage of the last dollar's income that must be paid in federal and state income taxes. In the example, the after-tax return is $680.

The **expected real return** is equal to the after-tax return less the impact of inflation or deflation on both the after-tax return and principal. In the example, the real value of the original principal and after-tax return is

$$\frac{\$10,000 + 680}{106} \times 100 = \$10,075$$

Since the original investment was $10,000, this investment yields $75 or .75 percent. This means that at the end of a year, you could expect to command about three-fourths of 1 percent more goods and services than you could at the beginning of the year. Note that the effect of inflation was the same as that of the income tax; both took away purchasing power. Try reworking the problem under the assumption that the expected inflation rate will be 8 percent. Or assume that you held $10,000 in a noninterest-bearing investment but there was inflation of x percent.

The point of this exercise is to focus on the real payoff on an investment because those are the only terms that matter. If you considered only the gross yield or after-tax yield, then you would be a victim of the **money illusion**. That is, you would be looking only at nominal or face values and not at real values. If you thought that you would get rich with a gross return of 10 percent, then you are a victim. If you jump for joy if you get a salary adjustment of 6 percent while the inflation rate is 10 percent, then you are a victim. Granted 6 percent is superior to 5 percent, etc., but the point should be clear.

The Real Cost of a Debt

Let's look at the impact of inflation from the point of view of the debtor. Consider the following loan proposal:

Given:

1. Principal: $10,000
2. Interest rate: 10 percent
3. Maturity: 1 year
4. Expected marginal tax rate: 40 percent
5. Expected change in consumer price index: +7 percent

Find:

1. Expected gross cost
2. Expected after-tax cost
3. Expected real cost

The **expected gross cost** is $1,000, which is the interest rate times the principal.

The **expected after-tax cost** is equal to the expected cost less the reduction in income taxes because interest paid is deductible from gross income. In the example, you would deduct $1,000 in interest paid from gross income. Because you expected to pay taxes equal to 40 percent of that gross income, but now are relieved of that burden, you can offset the $400 benefit against the $1,000 gross interest cost to determine the after-tax cost of $600.

The **real cost of the debt** is equal to the after-tax cost less the impact of inflation or deflation on the after-tax interest cost and principal. Because of inflation the debtor expects to return to the creditor less command over goods and services than was received at the inception of the loan. In the example, the real value of the principal and interest is

$$\frac{\$10,000 + 600}{107} \times 100 = \$9,907$$

Since the original loan was $10,000, the real cost of the debt and the after-tax interest is $93 less than the amount borrowed. The debtor borrowed at a real interest rate of –.93 percent. There has been a transfer of real wealth from the creditor to the debtor. When many students see a negative real interest rate, they believe that some financial hocus-pocus has been pulled on them. The real victim was the creditor who did not insist on a high enough nominal rate to cover inflation and provide a positive real return on the loan.

To aid in understanding the concept of a negative real interest rate, consider this example. Suppose that man A lent man B 100 sheets of plywood for 1 year with the condition that B repay $100 worth of plywood. During the year the price of plywood rose from $1 to $2 per sheet. At the end of the year, man B hands man A 50 sheets of plywood. The use of money as a standard of deferred payment has led to the transfer of real wealth (50 sheets of plywood) from man A to man B. Plywood would have been superior to money as a standard of deferred payment. Man A's real return on the "investment" was –50 percent, while man B's real cost was –50 percent. Man A's balance still shows plywood inventory of $100, so money has been a poor unit of account. Moreover, balance sheet comparisons over time for man A are misleading.

Summary

Money is anything commonly used and generally accepted as a medium of exchange and unit of account. Besides these two functions, money also serves as a store of wealth, standard of deferred payment, and guarantor of solvency. Twelve Federal Reserve banks, the US Treasury, and commercial banks are the primary producers of money. However, in recent years, regulatory changes have made many of the claims of nonbank financial institutions equal or almost equal in "moneyness" to demand deposits. These changes have complicated the Fed's task of measuring the money supply and controlling it for purposes of stabilizing the economy. Inflation or deflation distorts money's functioning as a unit of account, store of wealth, and standard of deferred payment. An awareness of this will help us to understand the real return on an investment and the real cost of a debt, and to avoid becoming a victim of the money illusion.

Questions and Problems

1. Define money.
2. What institutions are the primary producers of money? What kinds of money does each produce? How does each form of money get into the hands of the public?
3. Why are checks not money?
4. Outline briefly the evolution of our payments system.

5. "Sometime in the next ten years, the United States will become a 'checkless' society." Do you agree? Explain.
6. List the advantages and disadvantages of EFT.
7. List and explain briefly the functions of money.
8. Make up and answer a "real value of money" problem.
9. Explain why the effects of inflation and an income tax are similar.

Suggestions for Additional Reading

Anderson, Paul S. "Currency in Use and Hoards." Federal Reserve Bank of Boston, *New England Economic Review* (March/April 1977), pp. 21–30.

Board of Governors of the Federal Reserve System. *Improving the Monetary Aggregates: Report of the Advisory Committee on Monetary Statistics.* Washington, D.C.: Board of the Federal Reserve System, June 1976.

Brunner, Karl, and Meltzer, Allan H. "The Uses of Money: Money in a Theory of an Exchange Economy." *American Economic Review* (December 1971), pp. 784–805.

Galbraith, John Kenneth. *Money: Whence It Came, Where It Went.* Boston: Houghton Mifflin Company, 1975.

Gambs, Carl M. "Money—A Changing Concept in a Changing World." Federal Reserve Bank of Kansas City, *Economic Review* (January 1977), pp. 3–12.

Niblack, William C. "Development of Electronic Funds Transfer Systems." Federal Reserve Bank of St. Louis, *Review* (September 1976), pp. 10–18.

2

The Basics of Deposit Creation and Destruction

In Chapter 1 you learned that commercial banks produce demand, time, and savings deposits, the sum of which comprises approximately 89 percent of M_2 and 94 percent of M_3. These two money supply measures generally are considered to be the most significant in terms of their effects on GNP, employment, and prices. Therefore, it is important to learn how banks produce deposits. The principles of deposit creation and destruction are to money and banking as blocking and tackling are to football—they are basic.

The main goals of this chapter are to (1) become familiar with some of the primary bank asset, liability, and capital accounts and how interbank transactions take place utilizing these accounts; (2) learn the basic principles of deposit creation and destruction for one bank and the banking system; and (3) analyze the bank lending misconception.

Let's Start A Bank

The Banker's T-Account

In the first accounting course, you learned that T-accounts are convenient devices to record debits and credits (pluses and minuses) to various accounts such as cash, land, and accounts receivable. You also learned that for every debit, there must be a credit; that is, we have a double-entry bookkeeping system. In banking we often need to illustrate the effects of certain transactions on a bank's financial condition. The device used to do this is a type of T-account. But on the left side we record changes in the various asset accounts and on the right side we post changes in the various liability and capital accounts. Bankers make two entries on their T-account—either a plus on each side, a minus on each side, or a plus and a minus on one side. If you remember that a balance sheet must balance, then you will not get one side "overloaded" with pluses or minuses.

Preopening and Opening Day Transactions

Starting a bank is a herculean task, but a very rewarding experience. Much hard work transpires before opening day. In this section we will use the creation of a bank as the vehicle to introduce the principal bank asset and liability accounts, illustrate how various transactions affect bank balance sheets, and set the stage for learning the principles of deposit creation.

Sell stock and open correspondent bank account. After receipt of approval for a charter from the Comptroller of the Currency in the case of a national bank or the appropriate state regulatory authority in the case of a state bank, one of the first tasks is to sell stock and place the proceeds in an account with another commercial bank, called a **correspondent bank**. Large banks in money centers such as New York, Chicago, and San Francisco, and banks in regional centers such as Minneapolis, Charlotte, or Dallas, create correspondent bank departments that provide a wide range of services in return for implicit compensation in the form of deposits or explicit payment in the form of fees. Suppose we sell 300,000 shares (par $5) at a price of $10 per share (that is, with a premium above par of $5) in a bank that we will name Republic National Bank (RNB). The par value indicates how much capital will be allocated to the **common stock account**. We decide to allocate two-thirds of the premium above par to the surplus account, while the remainder will be allocated to undivided profits. **Surplus** contains more or less permanent capital because permission must be received from the appropriate regulatory authority before making any change in this account. The **undivided profits** account is used to absorb organizational expenses and initial operating losses during the first year or two of business. Earnings before and after opening day will be credited to undivided profits. The stock sale is successful and the checks are bundled and sent to our correspondent bank, First National Bank (FNB), for collection. FNB, in turn, sends the checks to the Fed for collection from the drawee banks.

RNB		*FNB*	
Deposit at FNB +$3 mil.	Common stock (300,000 × $5) +$1.5 mil. Surplus +1.0 mil. Undivided profits +.5 mil.	Reserve at FR +$3 mil.	Deposit of RNB +$3 mil.

FR		*Banks, A,B,C, etc.*	
	Reserve of FNB +$3 mil. Reserve of Banks, A,B,C, etc. −$3 mil.	Reserve at FR −$3 mil.	Demand deposits of customers −$3 mil.

Note that the Fed credited FNB's **reserve account**, which is, in effect, a demand deposit account for banks with the Fed. A bank deposits checks drawn on other banks to its reserve account at the Fed. The Fed decreases each drawee bank's reserve account by the amount of the check and sends it to the drawee bank. The drawee bank then decreases the depositor's demand deposit account by the amount of the check and posts the corresponding decrease in its reserve balance at the Fed.

Purchase Federal Reserve Bank stock. Since RNB is a national bank, it must be a **member bank**, that is, a member of the Federal Reserve System. Therefore, RNB must purchase stock in the Federal Reserve Bank equal to 3 percent of its capital stock and surplus accounts. This amounts to $75,000, and the bank will receive a 6 percent dividend on this stock. RNB instructs FNB to remit $75,000 to the Fed.

RNB		FNB		FR	
FR bank stock +$75,000		Reserve at FR −$75,000	Deposit of RNB −$75,000		FR bank stock +$75,000
Deposit at FNB −$75,000					Reserve of FNB −$75,000

Purchase furniture and equipment.   RNB wishes to have an attractive home office and modern equipment. These items cost $225,000 and RNB pays with a check on its account with FNB. The furniture and equipment dealer deposits the check in Bank A, which sends it to the Fed for collection.

RNB		FNB		FR	
Deposit at FNB −$225,000		Reserve at FR −$225,000	Deposit of RNB −$225,000		Reserve of FNB −$225,000
F&E +$225,000					Reserve of Bank A +$225,000

Establish reserve at Fed.   As you learned above, reserve deposits at the Fed serve a number of purposes. RNB establishes its reserve balance at the Fed by instructing FNB to transfer $2 million from its Fed reserve balance to RNB's account with the Fed.

RNB		FNB		FR	
Reserve at FR +$2 mil.		Reserve at FR −$2 mil.	Deposit of RNB −$2 mil.		Reserve of RNB +$2 mil.
Deposit at FNB −$2 mil.					Reserve of FNB −$2 mil.

Note that all transfers were accomplished by bookkeeping entries. This is a surprise to students who have a preconception that most financial transactions are effected in currency.

Request coins and Federal Reserve notes from the Fed. One of the most important services that banks provide their customers is that of supplying coin and currency needs. The Fed ships coin and currency without charge to member banks. Coins are a liability of the Treasury, but are held as an asset by the Fed; Federal Reserve notes are a liability of the various FRBs and do not appear on the Fed's balance sheet until issued. RNB requests $50,000 in coin and $150,000 in Federal Reserve notes.

RNB		FR	
Cash-in-vault +$200,000		Coin −$50,000	Reserve of RNB −$200,000
Reserve at FR −$200,000			Federal Reserve notes outstanding +$150,000

Purchase Treasury bills from Fed. Prior to opening, a prospective member bank may invest only in T-bills. RNB purchases $1 million of 91-day Treasury bills from the Fed, which, as fiscal agent for the

Figure 2–1. Cash-in-vault (*Courtesy of NCNB*)

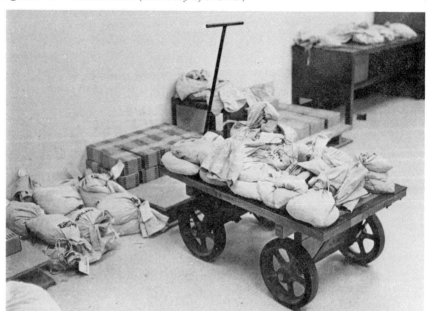

Treasury, auctions T-bills to investors every Monday. T-bills are sold on a discount from par, that is, the difference between the purchase price and par represents interest earned. The Fed simply debits RNB's reserve account for the purchase price of $980,000, and credits the Treasury's General Account at the Fed.

RNB		FR
T-bills +$980,000 Reserve at FR −$980,000		Reserve of RNB −$980,000 US Treasury General Account +$980,000

Pay organizational expenses. Organizational expenses consist of salaries and benefits of officers and staff, stationery and supplies, consultants' costs, filing fees, and so on. For simplicity, RNB will pay $100,000 of organizational expenses at once.

RNB		
Deposit at FNB −$100,000	Undivided profits	−$100,000

Treasury bills mature. At the end of ninety-one days, the T-bills mature, and RNB receives a $1 million credit in its Fed reserve account.

RNB[1]		FR
Reserve at FR +$1 mil. T-bills −$980,000	Undivided profits +$20,000	Reserve of RNB +$1 mil. US Treasury General Account −$1 mil.

1. In the "real world," banks accrue income and expenses on a daily basis. The $20,000 credit to individual profits would accrue over ninety-one days and not all at once.

Receive deposits. The time has come for the grand opening. A ribbon cutting ceremony, balloons, badges that say "The Republic For Which We Stand," and cakes and cookies all are part of the festivities. The primary objective of all of this is to take deposits (and, hence, reserves) away from our competitors. RNB has a good opening day; it receives $2 million in demand deposits, $1 million in savings deposits, and $1 million in time CDs. The checks transferring these funds are on local banks and are sent to the local Fed clearing center for collection and immediate credit to RNB's reserve account.

RNB		FR		Banks, A,B,C, etc.	
Reserve at FR +$4 mil.	Demand deposits +$2 mil. Savings deposits +$1 mil. Time CDs +$1 mil.	Reserve of RNB +$4 mil. Reserves of Banks A,B,C, etc. -$4 mil.	Reserve at FR -$4 mil.	Demand deposits -$4 mil.	

Figure 2-2. Ribbon-cutting ceremony at a new branch bank (*Courtesy of the National Bank of North America*)

Construct a balance sheet. RNB has had a whirlwind of activity. At the end of the day, RNB's cashier constructs a balance sheet so that on the next day, the bank's officers can determine the amount of loans and investments that may be made. To construct a balance sheet, you would set up a regular T-account for each RNB asset, liability, and capital account and post each entry. Take the net balance in each account and post to the balance sheet, which is shown below.

RNB Balance Sheet (end of opening day)			
Cash-in-vault	$ 200,000	Demand deposits	$2,000,000
Deposit of FNB	600,000	Savings deposits	1,000,000
Reserve at FR	5,820,000	Time CDs	1,000,000
FR bank stock	75,000	Common stock	1,500,000
F & E	225,000	Surplus	1,000,000
		Undivided profits	420,000
Total	$6,920,000	Total	$6,920,000

RNB is in fine shape. However, salaries, interest on time and savings deposits, and other expenses accrue daily, so it is time to put some earning assets on the books.

Deposit Creation at One Bank

Some Important Definitions

Before we determine RNB's lending ability and learn the principles of deposit expansion and contraction, we need to know the following definitions:

1. **Reserve requirement**—the Federal Reserve or state regulation relating to the holding of reserves; such a regulation specifies what assets count as legal reserves, the deposits and other liabilities that must be matched by legal reserves, and the applicable reserve ratios.

2. **Legal reserves**—those assets that may be counted for purposes of meeting the Federal Reserve or state reserve requirement.

3. **Reserve ratio**—that percentage of a bank's deposits or other liabilities that must be held in the form of legal reserves in order to meet the Federal Reserve or state reserve requirement.

4. **Required reserves**—that portion of a bank's legal reserves that must be held, given the bank's deposits and other liabilities and the applicable Federal Reserve or state reserve ratios.

5. **Excess reserves**—that portion of a bank's legal reserves in excess of its required reserves.

6. **Primary deposit**—a deposit made in a bank in the form of coin, currency, or checks drawn on other banks.

7. **Secondary deposit**—a deposit that may be created by a bank as it makes a loan or investment.

The Limit on Deposit Creation at One Bank

How much can RNB lend? At any moment in time, one bank's potential for new lending is limited to an amount equal to its excess reserves. This is called the **excess reserve rule**. To find a bank's excess reserves, use the following steps:

Step 1—determine the bank's total legal reserves. What assets count as legal reserves? For a member bank, cash-in-vault and balances at the Federal Reserve qualify. For a state nonmember bank, it depends on the applicable state requirement, but typically cash-in-vault and balances in correspondent banks meet the requirement. RNB is a member bank, so its legal reserves are calculated as follows:

Cash-in-vault	$ 200,000
Reserve at FR	5,820,000
Total legal reserves	$6,020,000

Step 2—calculate required reserves by multiplying the applicable reserve ratio times the appropriate deposit category. Assume that the Fed specifies the following reserve ratios: 10 percent for demand deposits, 5 percent for savings deposits, and 1 percent for time CDs. RNB's required reserves are calculated as follows:

Demand deposits	$2,000,000 × 10 = $200,000
Savings deposits	1,000,000 × .05 = 50,000
Time CDs	1,000,000 × .01 = 10,000
Total required reserves	$260,000

Step 3—calculate excess reserves. Excess reserves equal legal reserves minus required reserves. Therefore, excess reserves for RNB are

Legal reserves	$6,020,000
Required reserves	−260,000
Excess reserves	$5,760,000

As explained above, at any moment in time, excess reserves at one bank indicate the amount of new loans or investments that the bank can make. Thus, RNB could make new loans or investments up to $5,760,000. Why is RNB limited to this amount? What is the rationale for the excess reserve rule? It will be easier to answer these questions in a minute. Meanwhile, let's go ahead and illustrate the three primary ways that banks make loans and investments.

Three Ways to Make a Loan or Investment

1. Create deposits. Most bank loans and investments are made simply by crediting the demand deposit account of the borrower. That is, the bank creates deposits for the borrower at the same time that it creates an asset (the loan). Suppose that by this method on the first day RNB made a $5 million loan to borrower A. Here are the entries for the bank and the borrower:

RNB		A	
Loan to A +$5 mil.	Demand deposits of A +$5 mil.	Demand deposits +$5 mil.	Loan +$5 mil.

As a result of this entry, the US money supply (M_1 through M_5) increased by $5 million. Note that RNB did not lend other people's deposits; it created new deposits. Within a few days, RNB fully expects that A will write a check on the proceeds, the payee will deposit it in his bank, and that the check will clear against RNB through the Fed.

RNB			FR	
Reserve at FR −$5 mil.	Demand deposits of A −$5 mil.			Reserve of RNB −$5 mil.
				Reserve of other banks −$5 mil.

2. *Issue cashier's check.* When they receive a loan, some borrowers wish to receive a cashier's check payable to another party. A **cashier's check**, or **officer's check**, is an order on the bank to pay on demand and signed by a bank officer. The party receiving the check is more assured that the order will be paid than if he or she had received a nonofficial, personal check on the bank. Suppose that borrower B requests a loan for $750,000 to purchase some inventory and wishes to receive a cashier's check payable to his or her supplier. Here are the appropriate entries:

RNB			B	
Loan to B +$750,000	Cashier's checks outstanding +$750,000		Inventory +$750,000	Loan +$750,000

When the cashier's check clears through the Fed, here are the entries:

RNB			FR	
Reserve at FR −$750,000	Cashier's checks outstanding −$750,000			Reserve of RNB −$750,000
				Reserve of other banks +$750,000

Cashier's checks outstanding are classified as demand deposits; thus, RNB increased the money supply by $750,000 when it issued the check. When the payee of the cashier's check deposited it in another bank, he received a credit in his demand deposit account. Hence, the money supply remained $750,000 above its previous level.

3. *Issue currency.* Sometimes a borrower wishes to receive currency in the loan process. It is more risky to walk out of the bank with currency, but RNB strives to please its customers. Suppose that borrower C obtains a $10,000 loan and receives the proceeds in currency. Here are the entries:

RNB		C	
Loan to C +$10,000 Cash-in-vault −$10,000		Cash +$10,000	Loan +$10,000

Recall that cash-in-vault is not a part of the money supply. Thus, when RNB gives C $10,000 in currency, the money supply increases by a similar amount.

After these three loan transactions, here is RNB's balance sheet:

RNB			
Cash-in-vault	$ 190,000	Demand deposits	$2,000,000
Deposit at FNB	600,000	Savings deposits	1,000,000
Reserve at FR	70,000	Time CDs	1,000,000
FR bank stock	75,000	Common stock	1,500,000
F & E	225,000	Surplus	1,000,000
Loans	5,760,000	Undivided profits	420,000
	$6,920,000		$6,920,000

If we calculated RNB's excess reserves now, we would find them equal to zero—no excess reserves, no lending ability. The rationale for the excess reserve rule for one bank should be clear. One bank fully expects to lose reserves equal to the amount of the newly created deposits. The maximum amount that a single bank can lose and not be deficient in required reserves is an amount equal to its excess reserves. Now you know the basic principle for money creation for one bank.

Deposit Contraction at One Bank

Deposits are created by banks, but can deposits be destroyed? Yes, it happens every time a loan payment is made by check or an investment security is sold by the bank or repaid by its issuer. Suppose that borrower A is one of our original depositors and that she decides to make a $1 million payment on her loan. Borrower A walks into RNB and hands the note teller a check on RNB and payable to RNB for $1 million. Here are the entries:

RNB		A	
Loan to A $-\$1$ mil.	Demand deposits of A $-\$1$ mil.	Demand deposits at RNB $-\$1$ mil.	Loan $-\$1$ mil.

This transaction causes the US money supply to decline by $1 million. Money has been destroyed. RNB gave up its claim on A in exchange for A giving up her claim on RNB.

It also is important to note that the actual loan repayment did not create lending ability (excess reserves) equal to the amount of the repayment. RNB gained excess reserves equal only to the amount of the required reserves released (.10 × $1 million, or $100,000).

Deposit Expansion for the Banking System

An Example

It is time to change gears and learn the principles of deposit expansion for the banking system. The best approach to this important subject is to begin with an example.

Assume that there are a number of banks comprising a system of banks. To simplify the discussion, assume that none of the banks has any assets or liabilities, there are no time or savings deposits, and that a 10 percent reserve ratio applies to demand deposits. Assume also that the Fed wishes to expand reserves and, therefore, allows the banking system to expand the money supply. The Fed creates reserves for the banking system when it purchases securities in the open market. This process is called **open market operations**, and we will have much more to say about it later in the book. The Fed decides to purchase $1 million in securities from Merrill Lynch (ML), and the Fed hands ML a check for $1 million. ML deposits the check in Bank A, which deposits the check with the Fed for collection. Here are the entries:

FR		ML		Bank A	
Securities +$1 mil.	Reserve of Bank A +$1 mil.	Securities −$1 mil.		Reserve at FR +$1 mil.	Demand deposits of ML +$1 mil.
		Demand deposits at Bank A +$1 mil.			

When the Fed receives the check from Bank A, it simply credits $1 million to the reserve account of Bank A. The Fed creates reserves in the same manner that a bank creates money. This is the primary means that the Fed uses to allow the money supply to grow.

Bank A received a primary deposit and has excess reserves of $900,000. Following the excess reserve rule, it could create new loans and investments and demand deposits equal to that amount. Suppose that Mr. Able requests and receives a $900,000 loan from Bank A. He then writes a check for $900,000 to transfer the funds to Apex, Inc. Apex deposits the check in Bank B, which clears it through the Fed. Here are the entries for Bank A:

Bank A		
Receive deposits	Reserve at FR +$1 mil.	Demand deposits of ML +$1 mil.
Creates a new loan and money	Loan +$900,000	Demand deposits of Mr. Able +$900,000
New borrower writes check	Reserve at FR −$900,000	Demand deposits of Mr. Able −$900,000

Bank B received a primary deposit of $900,000 and has excess reserves of $810,000. Mr. Baker requests and receives a loan in this amount. He pays a firm that deposits the check in Bank C. Here are the entries for Bank B:

	Bank B	
Receive deposits	Reserve at FR +$900,000	Demand deposits of Apex, Inc. +$900,000
Creates a new loan and money	Loan +$810,000	Demand deposits of Mr. Baker +$810,000
New borrower writes check	Reserve at FR -$810,000	Demand deposits of Mr. Baker -$810,000

We could extend this example to the nth bank. Here is the summary T-account showing ultimate changes in the balance sheets for all banks in the system through Bank n.

	Changes for All Banks			
Reserves	Bank A	$ 100,000	Demand deposits A	$ 1,000,000
	B	90,000	B	900,000
	.	.		.
	.	.		.
	n			.
Total reserves		1,000,000		.
Loans and Investments	Bank A	900,000		.
	B	810,000		.
	.	.		.
	.	.		.
	n			.
Total loans and investments		9,000,000		.
				n
Total		$10,000,000	Total	$10,000,000

Counting the initial deposit in Bank A, the banking system has expanded deposits by ten times the initial increment to reserves. We are able to write in the sum of the right-hand column without adding individually banks A through n because of this line of reasoning. First, when the total change in deposits is realized, the $1 million in new legal reserves are absorbed as required reserves. That is, the $1 million is being fully utilized to support deposits. So at the point of full reserve utilization, we can write the following equation:

$$(1) \quad \Delta TDD_p \times r_d = \Delta TLR$$

Where ΔTDD_p is the change in potential demand deposits, r_d is the reserve ratio on demand deposits, and ΔTLR is the change in legal reserves. Dividing both sides by r_d, we find that

$$(2) \quad \Delta TDD_p = \frac{\Delta TLR}{r_d}$$

Then separating r_d, we obtain

$$(3) \quad \Delta TDD_p = \Delta TLR \times \frac{1}{r_d}$$

Substituting the numbers from the example, we find

$$(4) \quad \Delta TDD_p = \$1 \text{ mil.} \times \frac{1}{.10}$$

$$(5) \quad \Delta TDD_p = \$10 \text{ mil.}$$

The Principles

Let's slow down and set forth the principles of deposit expansion for the banking system. When the Fed increases reserves, it increases the banking system's deposit expansion potential. There are two determinants of the change in potential: (1) the change in reserves and (2) the reserve ratio. Because the reserve ratio is a fraction, a given change in reserves will support a multiple amount of deposits. In our example, $1 million in new reserves will support $10 million in new deposits. If the reserve ratio had been 100 percent, then the change in deposit potential would have equaled the change in reserves. Thus, *the change in deposit potential is a multiple of the change in reserves because we have a fractional reserve banking system.*

Will the Deposit Potential Be Reached?

In our example, deposits at Bank A,B, . . . n neatly totaled $10 million. However, there are four assumptions necessary for this condition to be realized.

First, *no bank must hold excess reserves*, that is, each must lend to its potential. Holding excess reserves short-circuits the potential because other banks in the system do not receive the maximum amount of primary deposits and reserves.

Second, *there must be active demand for money*. The public must be willing to borrow. The Fed controls the potential money supply, but the public determines the actual money supply.

Third, *there must be no external cash drain*. That is, no borrower must request his or her loan proceeds in currency. If this happens, reserves leave the banking system, and these funds cannot support deposits within the banking system. For example, for every $100 in currency withdrawn, potential deposits decline by $1,000.

Finally, *no borrower must convert loan proceeds received in the form of demand deposits into time or savings deposits*. If this occurs, reserves that were intended to support potential demand deposits now must be matched against time and savings deposits. However, for broader definitions of the money stock, such as M_2 and M_3, this assumption is irrelevant because time and savings deposits are included in these money measures.

The Banking Paradox

At this point, let's compare the principles of deposit expansion for one bank with those for the banking system. This is a good way to review. There is an apparent inconsistency between the principles of deposit expansion for one bank and those for the banking system. One bank can create new deposits in an amount equal to excess reserves; however, the banking system can expand deposits by a multiple of the excess reserves in the system. This statement is often called the **banking paradox**. Why is this statement an apparent inconsistency instead of a real inconsistency?

One bank limits its deposit expansion to an amount equal to excess reserves because it fully expects to lose reserves equal to the created deposits when the borrower transfers the funds. On the other hand, for the system, each bank has to match reserves only fractionally against newly received primary deposits. Each bank can expand deposits by an amount equal to excess reserves. The sum of the newly created deposits throughout the system will exceed the initial amount of excess reserves in the system. In other words, when the initial amount of excess reserves is spread among a system of banks, and when each bank has to hold reserves equal to only a fraction of any newly received deposits, the reserves can support a multiple amount of deposits. Thus, after adequate explanation, we see that there is only an apparent inconsistency between the principles of deposit expansion for one bank and those for the system.

Deposit Contraction for the Banking System

Just as the Fed is able to increase the banking system's deposit potential by a multiple of the increment to reserves, it also can reduce this potential by a multiple of the decrease in reserves. The Fed decreases the deposit potential by selling securities in the open market. Suppose that the Fed sold ML $1 million in securities with payments made by a check on Bank A. The Fed debits A's reserve account for $1 million and returns the check to A, where ML's demand deposit is reduced by $1 million. Here are the entries:

FR		ML		Bank A	
Securities	Reserve	Securities		Reserve	Demand
-$1 mil.	of Bank A	+$1 mil.		at FR	deposits of
	-$1 mil.			-$1 mil.	ML -$1 mil.
		Demand			
		deposits at			
		Bank A			
		-$1 mil.			

If Bank A had no excess reserves prior to the purchase, it now is deficient by $900,000, assuming a 10 percent reserve ratio. Bank A is not deficient by $1 million because $100,000 is "released" from required reserves by the $1 million deposit loss. Bank A could make up this deficiency by selling $900,000 in securities to the depositors of another bank or by reducing demand deposits by ten times $900,000 or $9 million. The latter is a poor choice because a bank does not keep its customers if it frequently calls up borrowers with demand notes and orders them down to the bank to pay. The first alternative is usually followed, but this puts Bank B in the hole by $810,000. Bank B then must unload securities equal to the reserve deficiency. The process continues until a total of $9 million in additional deposits has been destroyed throughout the banking system. Counting the $1 million decline at Bank A, deposits throughout the system must fall by $10 million.

We can prove this total with the formula learned earlier. The only difference is that the change in total legal reserves will be minus. Thus,

$$(1) \quad \Delta TDD_p = \Delta TLR \times \frac{1}{rd}$$

$$(2) \quad \Delta TDD_p = -\$1 \text{ mil.} \times \frac{1}{.10}$$

$$(3) \quad \Delta TDD_p = -\$10 \text{ mil.}$$

Deposit potential falls by a multiple of the decrement in reserves because of our fractional system. Prior to the Fed's action the $1 million in reserves supported $10 million in deposits because reserves must be matched only fractionally against deposits.

There is an important difference between deposit expansion and deposit contraction for the banking system. *Deposit expansion may take place, but deposit contraction must take place.* Only the profit motive compels banks to lend when there are excess reserves in the system; however, when there is a deficiency in required reserves in the system, deposits must decline or the deficient bank will be fined by the Fed.

Do Banks Accept Deposits and Lend Them to Qualified Borrowers?

It is time to analyze perhaps the greatest misconception about banks. To the question posed in the heading most people would answer "yes." People perceive of banks as barns; you can take out of them only what you put in, whether it is money or hay. People see other people lined up at the teller window depositing checks and currency, and they see other people shaking hands with a loan officer and walking away smiling as if they just had received a loan. However, there is no way that a bank legally can debit (decrease) one depositor's account for a given sum and then credit (increase) another depositor's account by the same amount. Neither can the bank debit one depositor's account and credit loans; the entry does not balance. As you have learned, what happens in the typical loan transaction is that the bank creates a new deposit at the same time that it creates a new asset—the loan; no depositor loses his or her claim on the bank.

Summary

Here are the basics of deposit creation. One bank can create new deposits in an amount equal to its excess reserves. However, a system of banks can create deposits in a multiple of the excess reserves that exist in the system. The single bank has a lower limit because it fears loss of the newly created deposits (a liability) and an equal amount of reserves (an asset). The amount of excess reserves is the maximum that it can lose and not be deficient in required reserves. On the other hand, banks in a system lose reserves only to each other, and when these reserves are spread among a large number of banks these funds can support a larger amount of deposits. This is because each bank has to hold reserves equal to only a fraction of its deposits. Just as the fractional reserve system allows a multiple expansion of deposits, it also forces a multiple contraction when reserves are removed from the system.

Postscript

Study and review the material in the chapter until you have mastered it. The principles discussed are fundamental to a good understanding of our money and banking system.

Questions and Problems

1. Illustrate for all banks concerned and by means of T-accounts the following transactions:
    (a) Bank A sells 200,000 shares of common stock at $15 per share (par $5) with the excess above par divided equally between surplus and undivided profits. Bank A deposits the checks from the sale of the stock with Bank B, which sends the items to the Fed for collection.

(b) Bank A transfers $1 million from Bank B to the Fed.
(c) Bank A requests from the Fed $100,000 in Federal Reserve notes and $50,000 in coin.

2. Distinguish between reserve requirement and reserve ratio.

3. Explain the excess reserve rule as it applies to deposit creation at one bank.

4. Illustrate by means of T-accounts the three ways that a bank may make a loan or investment.

5. Explain deposit contraction at one bank.

6. What is the banking paradox? Why is it an apparent inconsistency and not a real inconsistency?

7. "Banks accept deposits and lend them to qualified borrowers." Do you agree? Explain.

8. "For the banking system deposit expansion must take place, but deposit contraction may take place." Do you agree? Explain.

Suggestions for Additional Reading

Nichols, Dorothy M. *Modern Money Mechanics, A Workbook on Deposits, Currency, and Bank Reserves.* Federal Reserve Bank of Chicago, 1975.

3

Financial Intermediation in the Economy

Commercial banks are the predominant financial institution in our economy. Banks are a primary supplier of money and credit. However, nonbank financial institutions (NFIs) also are important suppliers of money (broadly defined) and credit. Banks and NFIs compete intensely for funds and for loans and investments. All financial institutions and consumers, businesses, and governments interact in the financial sector and the resulting flows of funds and interest rates have a tremendous impact on GNP, employment, and prices (the economic sector). The Fed, which has the primary task of influencing the levels of GNP, employment, and prices, has a predicament because the impact of its policies basically is on the banking system. The Fed, however, has a significant indirect impact on the NFI's ability to provide money and credit simply by its regulation of the banking system and its influence on interest rates.

If all of this sounds complicated, it is. Therefore, before we proceed to the study of the banking system and the role and impact of the Fed, it would be helpful to have an overview of financial intermediation in our economy. In this chapter we shall (1) examine the functions of financial markets and financial intermediaries in the circular flow of economic activity and (2) discuss the specific functions of the major financial intermediaries.

The Circular Flow of Economic Activity

Let us begin our quest to understand how financial intermediaries, including commercial banks, link with the economic system with the aid of a familiar economic model—the circular flow diagram. The principal advantage of using the circular flow diagram is that it depicts and relates in one diagram the major economic functions—production, distribution, and consumption. The circular flow diagram provides the "big picture" of an economy as it attempts to provide its citizens with goods and services. Usually, the circular flow diagram is introduced on the second or third day of class in the principles of economics course. After developing the model for a simple economy without financial markets and financial intermediaries, we will expand the traditional diagram by linking financial markets and financial intermediaries into the economic system.

Simple Economy

The term **simple economy** means an economy that performs no saving and undertakes no capital investment. In other words, people spend everything that they earn for consumer goods and services, and no provision is made for replacing or increasing the stock of capital. It is assumed also that there is no governmental sector and that only family units are consumers of goods and services. In reality, of course, businesses also are consumers. Finally, it is assumed that no pool of savings exists from prior periods.

As shown in Figure 3-1, the production of goods and services is performed by rudimentary business enterprises that acquire resources from the factor owners and produce goods and services. These resource owners provide land, labor, capital, and entrepreneurship to businesses in return for payments in the form of rent, wages, and interest. Wearing their second hat as consumers, factor owners, in turn, use their income to acquire goods and services from the businesses.

If all resources in the economy are employed fully, enough income is generated to enable consumers (factor owners) to acquire all the goods and services that their resources have helped to produce. The outer flow of income to the factor owners matches the flow of expenditures from consumers to pay for goods and services. Moreover, if several other assumptions were made, the **product market**

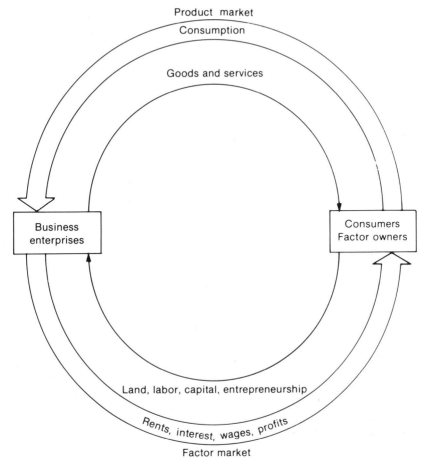

Figure 3-1. Circular Flow Diagram for a "Simple" Economy

would be in equilibrium with the **factor market;** that is, the top half of the diagram would be in equilibrium with the bottom half.

Advanced Economy

The circular flow diagram for the simple economy does not take into account several important aspects of the economy. First, some consumers may not wish to spend all of their income on goods and services; that is, they may wish to *save.* Second, other consumers may wish to acquire more goods and services than their current incomes allow them to purchase. Third, some businesses may wish to acquire additional capital. Fourth, governments may levy taxes and spend the funds for goods and services.

If some consumers decide not to spend all of their income, other things being equal, they short-circuit the smooth functioning of the economy. Businesses will take this as a signal to reduce production because they do not want inventories to pile up in their warehouses. Cutting back on production reduces the flow of payments to the factor owners, who, unfortunately as consumers, find that their efforts to save become difficult as income declines.

Although a surfeit of funds may exist in the hands of some consumers, there may exist simultaneously for other consumers and businesses a demand for those funds to finance the purchase of consumer durables and capital goods. If these demanders are able to acquire funds and to channel them back into the spending stream, then the level of economic activity will be sustained, and there will be no cyclical fluctuations or unemployment of human or nonhuman resources.

Figure 3–2 depicts the **advanced economy** and the interrelationships among the financial and economic sectors. Linked to the traditional circular flow diagram are the organized security markets and the major financial intermediaries. **Organized security markets** are places like the New York Stock Exchange where shares in America's businesses are bought and sold in a regulated environment. A **financial intermediary** is an institution that acquires funds by creating claims against itself in the form of deposits and shares and that, in turn, creates credit as it provides loanable funds for borrowers. Businesses and governments as well as consumers are considered as spenders and savers (lenders). On the other side, consumers and governments as well as businesses are considered as borrowers. Savers have two options: (1) they may place funds directly in the organized security markets in exchange for bonds, stocks, and other securities or (2) they may acquire deposits, shares, or other claims issued by financial intermediaries. Not shown is a third option, which involves saving in the form of currency, coin, and direct purchase of resalable assets.

Organized security markets and financial intermediaries serve as links between lenders and borrowers. In addition, there are links between the security markets and the financial intermediaries themselves. The latter may issue or buy securities in the security markets, thereby improving the efficiency of the process of providing funds to creditworthy users of funds.

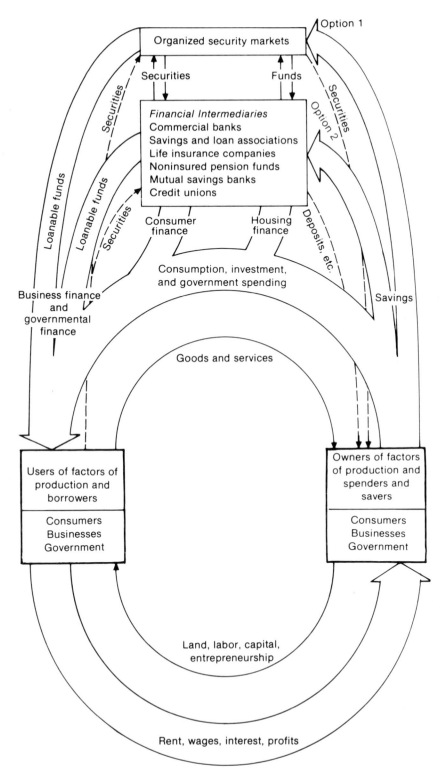

Figure 3-2. Circular Flow Diagram for an "Advanced" Economy

49

Although this representation of the financial linkages in an advanced economy abstracts from the complex interrelationships that exist in a financially sophisticated economy such as that of the United States, it does indicate the vital role that security markets and financial intermediaries play in facilitating aggregate supply and demand. Sometimes in emphasizing the need for the stabilizing influences of monetary policy, it is easy to forget that the private sector, through security markets and financial intermediaries, already has done much to assist the economy toward full employment by providing funds to borrowers who wish to purchase goods and services. In spite of the built-in stabilizing influence of security markets and financial intermediaries, adjustments through public policy are needed occasionally to smooth the flow of economic activity.

General Functions of Financial Intermediaries

Create Loanable Funds

All financial intermediaries have the ability to create credit and, therefore, augment the total supply of loanable funds. Ordinarily, when commercial banks create credit (acquire loans and investments), they expand their liabilities in the form of demand deposits. NFIs such as savings and loans and mutual savings banks (MSBs) also add to the supply of loanable funds when they create credit. Suppose that the public deposits checks for $1 million in an S&L, which in turn deposits them in its bank account. Afterwards, the S&L sets aside a 5 percent reserve, makes mortgage loans of $950,000, and hands the borrowers the loan proceeds in the form of checks on its bank account. Here are the entries:

Bank		S&L	
Public deposits −$1 mil.	Deposit in bank +$1 mil.	Deposits +$1 mil.
S&L deposit +$1 mil.			
S&L deposit −$950,000	Mortgage loans +$950,000		
Public deposits +$950,000	Bank deposit −$950,000		

Figure 3–3.   (Courtesy of the Federal Reserve Bank of New York)

There is no net change on the bank's balance sheet. But the public now holds $1 million more in financial claims (the S&L deposit), and the public is able to make additional purchases of $950,000 because the S&L made loans. The dollars that NFIs lend are just as spendable as those borrowed from a bank.

The growing importance of NFIs also has policy implications for the Fed as it seeks to stabilize economic activity. NFIs have the ability to expand the supply of loanable funds and, hence, possibly thwart the Fed's efforts. Because of this, a number of experts advocate broadening the Fed's control to NFIs.

The ability of financial intermediaries to create credit and expand the supply of loanable funds contributes greatly to the smooth functioning of the economy. Stated differently, they help to bridge the gap between production and consumption. The excess demand by creditworthy borrowers is translated into effective demand for goods and services by intermediaries who expand the supply of loanable funds to augment current income available for purchases.

Reduce Risk Exposure

One of the reasons that financial intermediaries have been successful in attracting funds is that they reduce the exposure to risk that savers ordinarily would have to face. Without intermediaries, savers would have to evaluate the **credit risk** (the chance of nonpayment at maturity) for each borrower to whom they have entrusted funds. This, of course, would take time and specialized knowledge. By employment of experts in credit analysis, through diversification, and through economies of scale, financial intermediaries reduce the risk exposure to the individual saver. The federal government has further reduced the risk exposure faced by savers through insurance funds for savers at commercial banks, S&Ls, MSBs, and credit unions.

Provide Liquidity

When savers place funds in intermediaries, they benefit from the law of large numbers. When intermediaries issue money claims to a large number of savers, it is possible to predict within fairly narrow limits the expected number of claims that will be cashed in over a period of time as well as the expected future inflow of funds. Acting independently, individual savers may participate in the everyday economic processes of production, distribution, and consumption with some degree of certainty that they can liquidate their claims on financial intermediaries without delay. This freedom is important because it is known that the level of investment and consumption spending is a function of the degree of liquidity of money claims on financial intermediaries. Part of the decline in investment and consumption during the Great Depression may be traced to the public's uncertainty regarding the liquidity of their financial assets and their subsequent demand to hold more money.

Thus the importance of financial intermediaries to the smooth functioning of the American economy should not be underestimated. Economic historians properly state that the rapid and large-scale development of financial intermediaries in this country was a necessary condition for our nation's meteoric economic rise during this century. Saving, borrowing, consumption, and investment have been encouraged and facilitated by our system of financial intermediaries. On the other hand, the economic development of Russia and the South American, African, and Asian countries has been retarded because of the relatively undeveloped financial intermediaries in these areas. Recognizing that financial intermediaries perform functions that are important to the economic and social well-being of all its citizens, the federal and state governments in the United States have chosen to encourage and protect these institutions through numerous statutes and regulations.

Specific Functions of Financial Intermediaries

The purpose of this section is to discuss briefly the specific functions performed by the major financial intermediaries.

Commercial Banks

At the end of 1978 commercial bank assets accounted for 49 percent of the total assets for all major financial intermediaries. As our most important intermediary, banks perform five primary functions: (1) hold deposits, (2) provide a payments mechanism, (3) create money and credit, (4) provide trust services, and (5) provide other services.

Deposits.   Deposits or claims on commercial banks are held for at least four reasons: (1) to carry out everyday transactions, (2) as a reserve against future contingencies, (3) to finance future purchases, or (4) because the deposit holder does not wish to hold savings in the form of equities, debt instruments, or claims on nonbank intermediaries in view of his or her expectations concerning business trends, interest-rate movements, and price trends. **Transactions balances** usually are held in the form of demand deposits, which, as their name implies, are claims on banks that must be met without delay. These working balances are held by their owner to carry out everyday business needs, such as buying goods and services and paying workers. Some demand deposits are held as **compensating balances**—that portion of loan proceeds the borrower agrees to keep on deposit as implicit compensation to the bank for the loan. The amount of working balances held in banks is primarily a function of the volume of transactions that must be effected within a short-run time horizon, the ease with which these balanceholders can acquire loans, the opportunity cost of holding noninterest-bearing funds, and the transactions cost of making transfers from interest-bearing deposits or securities to demand deposits.

Table 3-1

Total Assets of Major Financial Intermediaries, Selected Years, 1960-1978
(billions of dollars)

Year End	Insured Commercial Banks	Savings and Loan Associations	Life Insurance Companies	Noninsured Pension Funds	Mutual Savings Banks	Credit Unions	Total
1960	$ 255.7	$ 71.5	$119.6	$ 33.1	$ 40.6	$ 5.7	$ 526.2
1965	374.1	129.6	158.9	59.2	58.2	10.6	790.6
1970	572.7	176.2	207.3	97.0	79.0	18.0	1,150.2
1971	635.6	206.0	222.1	106.4	89.4	21.1	1,280.6
1972	732.8	243.1	239.7	117.5	100.6	24.8	1,458.2
1973	827.1	271.9	252.4	126.5	106.7	28.4	1,613.0
1974	906.3	295.5	263.3	133.7	109.6	31.9	1,740.3
1975	944.7	338.2	289.3	145.2	121.0	38.0	1,876.4
1976	1,011.1	392.0	320.6	160.4	134.7	44.9	2,063.7
1977	1,129.7	459.2	350.5	181.5	147.3	54.1	2,322.3
1978	1,268.5	523.6	389.0	187.3[a]	158.2	62.6	2,589.2

[a]As of June 30, 1978.

Source: Board of Governors of the Federal Reserve, *Federal Reserve Bulletin*; Securities and Exchange Commission, *Statistical Bulletin*, and unpublished data.

Figure 3-4. NCNB Tower in Charlotte, North Carolina

Bank balances also are held as a reserve against future contingencies. These **precautionary balances** may be held in the form of demand, time, or savings deposits. Precautionary balances may be held by individuals, for example, to meet possible future medical expenses or simply to provide for retirement. Businesses hold precautionary balances to meet fixed expenses if strikes by employees reduce output or if a recession occurs and sales turn downward or just as part of the firm's overall liquidity position.

Bank deposits may be held to finance future expenditures. Sometimes balances are accumulated by individuals to purchase a high-priced item or service, such as a piano or a trip to Europe. Businesses might accumulate balances to finance a small plant addition or to purchase another business. Balances held for this finance motive may be in demand, time, or savings accounts.

Finally, bank balances are held as an alternative to holding equities, debt instruments, or claims on other financial intermediaries. Income recipients must make two decisions: (1) what percentage of income to consume or save and (2) in what form to hold the amount that is saved. As shown in the circular flow diagram, funds not consumed (saved) may be placed in the securities markets in exchange for equities or debt instruments or they may be placed in financial intermediaries in exchange for deposits or other claims. The form in which to hold savings depends on the saver's expectations with respect to the business cycle, interest-rate movements, price trends, or other factors. For example, if interest rates are expected to rise, that is, if the prices of debt instruments are expected to fall, savers might prefer bank deposits to debt instruments. On the other hand, if the economy is about to recover from a recession, savers might shift from bank balances to equities in anticipation of a rebound in these issues. In theory, a saver should allocate funds among savings forms until the expected marginal return from each form is equal.

Regardless of why funds are held at banks, the accumulation of these deposits results in an increase in reserves, which gives an individual bank the ability to create money and credit equivalent to its excess reserves.

Payments mechanism.   In addition to serving as custodians of demand deposits, banks also perform the valuable function of transferring these balances among accounts. This is done by means of checks issued by depositholders. Banks provide a payments and collection system largely to attract deposits.

The amount spent for tellers, bookkeepers, computers, postage, checks, forms, and advertising in connection with the payments system is a large percentage (perhaps a third) of total bank costs. It is estimated that banks recoup only a fraction of this expense through service charges. To an extent, bank borrowers subsidize bank depositholders and checkwriters.

Money and credit.   A unique characteristic of a commercial bank is its ability to create money (demand deposits). When a commercial bank makes a loan or an investment, it creates liabilities against itself in the form of demand deposits as it creates the obligation to repay the money on a specific future date (credit). When a nonbank financial intermediary makes a loan or an investment, it creates credit in exactly the same way that a bank does, but, in the process of credit creation, the nonbank financial intermediary transfers to the borrower demand deposits that it has in its commercial bank account or currency that it has in its vault.

After a borrower receives the demand deposits created by the bank, he or she will use them to accomplish the purpose for which the loan was granted. If the borrower is a business, it might have received a loan to purchase newly produced capital equipment (investment), or to pay its employees (distribution), or to purchase office supplies (consumption). If the borrower is a consumer, he or she might use the proceeds to purchase an automobile or a boat (consumption). If the borrower is a state or local government, the proceeds might be used to finance the construction of a hospital (government spending). Use of these funds to purchase goods and services usually stimulates businesses to increase the utilization of labor resources in order to produce more goods and services. The act of production, of course, creates income in the hands of factor owners, who are also consumers. Because they have more income, consumers then are in a position to buy more goods and services.

Trust services. A trust, essentially, is a fiduciary relationship involving property. The sharp growth in income and wealth in this country has created a great need for the long-run safekeeping and management of vast amounts of property. Commercial banks, in order to attract and to retain large individual and corporate deposits, moved into the business of providing trust services and, therefore, are fulfilling an important need in the economy. As of December 31, 1977, banks were administering $935 billion in trust assets. Trust assets at several banks are greater than the bank's own assets.

The trust business may be divided into two segments: personal and corporate. Most banks with trust departments provide only personal trust services. Although the corporate trust business is growing, it still is concentrated primarily with banks located in large metropolitan areas. Personal trust services may include estate and trust planning, serving as executor and/or trustee under a will, serving as guardian of a minor or a person ruled incapable of managing his or her own financial affairs, providing investment counseling and management, providing tax counseling and tax return preparation, and serving as custodian of securities, which also may involve the collection of dividend and interest income.

In the area of corporate trust services, a bank may serve as trustee of pension and profit-sharing plans. Under such an agreement, the bank receives the funds from the corporation, invests them, collects the income, and pays out the benefits. Banks also may serve as the trustee for a bond issue. This involves, first, ensuring that the corporation as a bond issuer fulfills all its obligations to the bondholders. In effect, the bank represents the interests of the bondholders. Second, as trustee for the bond issue, the bank receives the necessary funds from the corporation to pay any interest and principal payments that are due.

Other corporate trust services involve stock transfer and registration. As stock-transfer agents, the bank will maintain stockholder records and handle stock transfers. As registrar, the bank seeks to ensure that the stock is not overissued. Most corporate stock certificates are, therefore, signed by both the stock-transfer agent and the registrar.

Finally, corporate trust departments have had active roles in many of the corporate mergers and takeover bids that occurred in recent years. A corporation interested in absorbing another company or, perhaps, only in taking a position in the stock, could place funds with a bank trust department that would take custody of any tendered stock and make payment to the tendering stockholders.

Other services. The list of other services provided by banks is extensive. Many services are given primarily to attract deposits. Some of these are provided free to customers; others are performed for a fee. Because of rising costs, many banks, with the aid of better functional cost data, recently have begun to evaluate the profit contribution (negative or positive) of all bank services.

A partial list of miscellaneous services provided by banks includes Christmas Clubs, traveler's checks, bill collection for customers, wire transfers of money, business and financial advice, credit cards, safe deposit boxes, lockboxes, and foreign exchange. Numerous banks have affiliates that perform travel agency functions, mortgage banking, factoring, and data processing, and that provide certain types of insurance, courier services, and equipment leasing.

Savings and Loan Associations

The S&L concept originated in 1831 when a group of citizens in Frankford, Pennsylvania, met to form a cooperative home-financing society. Their purpose was to accumulate savings from association members in order to allow other members to buy homes. Today, S&Ls, building and loan associations, cooperative banks, or homestead associations, as they sometimes are called, rank as the second most important financial intermediary in the country.

S&Ls operate under either a state or federal charter. Federally chartered S&Ls must belong to the Federal Home Loan Bank (FHLB) System and are required to have their savings accounts insured by the Federal Savings and Loan Insurance Corporation (FSLIC). At the close of 1978, there were 2,000 federally chartered S&Ls. On the same date, there were 2,723 state-chartered S&Ls, of which 2,053 were FSLIC insured. All other state-chartered S&Ls were insured by organizations established by the respective state legislatures or by private insurance companies.

Between 1960 and 1978 the number of S&Ls declined from 6,320 to 4,723 because of mergers. Many small associations found it difficult to compete with larger associations who offered a broader range of services and also benefited from economies of scale.

Between 1960 and 1978, S&L assets rose from $72 billion to $524 billion. S&Ls achieved this remarkable growth by an aggressive campaign for savings deposits. Traditionally, S&Ls offered only a basic passbook savings account, but in the late 1960s, they began to offer an assortment of savings accounts and CDs. As may be seen in Table 3-2, savings capital from all sources comprised 82.3 percent of the sources of S&L funds. Borrowed money comprised 8.2 percent of the total liabilities and net worth and represented mainly advances from the FHLB to member associations. The FHLB raises funds in the open market through the sale of securities and then lends them to associations who face legitimate credit demands that they cannot fulfill. On the asset side, S&Ls are required by law to invest primarily in mortgages, and at the close of 1978 these instruments comprised 82.7 percent of total assets. Cash and investment securities represented 8.6 percent of total assets.

Member associations are subject to short-term and overall **liquidity requirements** as specified by the FHLB Board. These requirements specify that saving deposits and borrowings repayable on demand or in one year or less must be matched by liquid assets. These assets may be in the form of cash, demand deposits, US government and federal agency securities with remaining terms to maturity of five years or less, commercial bank time deposits with remaining

Table 3-2

Assets, Liabilities, and Net Worth of Savings and Loan Associations, December 31, 1978 (billions of dollars)

Assets	Amount	Percent	Liabilities and Net Worth	Amount	Percent
Mortgages	$432.9	82.7%	Savings capital	$431.0	82.3%
Cash and investment securities	44.8	8.6	Borrowed money	43.0	8.2
			Loans in process	10.7	2.0
Other	45.9	8.8	Other	9.9	1.9
			Net Worth	29.0	5.5
Total	$523.6	100.0%	Total	$523.6	100.0%

Note: Details do not add due to rounding.

Source: Board of Governors of the Federal Reserve, *Federal Reserve Bulletin.*

terms to maturity of not more than one year, banker's acceptances with a remaining maturity of not more than nine months, and state and municipal securities with remaining maturities of not more than two years. Since 1972, the Board has required that a specified portion of the total liquidity be held in qualifying short-term investments. All of the investments cited above may be included in the short-term liquidity reserve except US government and agency issues with maturities longer than twelve months, commercial bank time deposits and banker's acceptances with maturities longer than six months, and all municipal securities. At the end of 1978, the short-term liquidity ratio was 3 percent, while the overall liquidity ratio was 7 percent. The Board is empowered by law to vary the overall liquidity ratio between 4 and 10 percent. Generally, it reduces the liquidity ratio when overall savings inflows decline and increases the ratio when inflows are more abundant.

In the 1970s, the FHLB Board encouraged greater competition between S&Ls and commercial banks by allowing federal S&Ls to offer new services. These include remote service units in super-markets and airports, preauthorized payments from a customer's savings account, telephone transfers, and NOW accounts in the Northeastern states. As pointed out in the last chapter, these innovations increase the moneyness of S&L deposits. Also, they complicate the Fed's economic stabilization function.

Life Insurance Companies

Like all financial intermediaries, life insurance companies receive funds in return for a promise to pay. The terms of this promise to pay, however, differ from that generally offered by other intermediaries. Life insurance companies promise to pay their policyholders under such conditions as death of the insured, surrender of the policy, or at the end of a specified period of time.

In the United States at the end of 1978, there were 1,789 life insurance companies with total life insurance in force of $2.8 trillion. As shown in Table 3–3, slightly over two-thirds of total assets were in corporate bonds and mortgages. Life insurance companies prefer these long-term, secure assets because of the long-term, certain

Figure 3–5. New York Life Insurance Company Building in New York City

nature of their obligations to policyholders. The bulk of life insurance company liabilities are **policy reserves**, which are policyholder claims on assets. Reserves are determined on an actuarial basis, taking into account future premium income, assumed interest earnings, operating expenses, and expected mortality experience. Remember, policy reserves are liabilities, not "funds set aside for our policyholders," as some insurance company ads state.

As financial intermediaries, life insurance companies slipped into third place, thanks to their slower rate of growth and the more rapid growth of S&Ls. Inflation has somewhat reduced the attractiveness of life insurance policies that have a cash value, that is, those that build up a savings fund over time. The expansion of public and private pension plans and the increasing burden of the social security tax have slightly dampened potential sales. However, because there is no substitute for a well-planned life insurance program, life insurance companies will continue to be a dominant factor in the financial markets.

Private Noninsured Pension Funds

Private noninsured pension funds are financial entities established mainly by corporations to provide retirement and deferred profit-sharing benefits to employees. The word "private" is used to distinguish these pension funds from those established by a governmental unit; the word "noninsured" denotes the fact that the funds are

Table 3-3

Assets of Life Insurance Companies, December 31, 1978
(billions of dollars)

Assets	Amount	Percent
Mortgages	$105.9	27.2%
Corporate bonds	161.9	41.6
Corporate stocks	35.4	9.1
Government securities	19.6	5.0
Policy loans	30.2	7.8
Real estate	11.8	3.0
Other	24.2	6.2
Total	$389.0	100.0%

Note: Details do not add due to rounding.

Source: Board of Governors of the Federal Reserve, *Federal Reserve Bulletin.*

not accumulated with insurance companies. Pension funds are financial intermediaries because they collect funds from corporations and sometimes their employees in return for a promise to pay an income to these employees when they retire. These contributions provide the basis for an expansion of loanable funds and the acquisition of earning assets. At mid-1978, assets of private noninsured pension plans totaled $187.3 billion, of which $93.9 billion were common stock, $50.0 billion were corporate and other bonds, and $2.6 billion were mortgages.

Mutual Savings Banks

The first **mutual savings bank (MSB)** was founded in Scotland in 1810 by the Reverend Mr. Henry Duncan. The idea quickly spread to this country with the founding in 1816 of the Provident Institution for Savings in the Town of Boston and The Philadelphia Savings Fund Society, both of which today are among the nation's largest MSBs.

As financial intermediaries, MSBs issue claims on themselves primarily in the form of time and savings deposits. However, recent creation of NOW accounts at MSBs in New England and legislation in most other states granting MSBs authority to offer traditional checking accounts have considerably expanded the deposit-gathering potential for these institutions. As may be seen in Table 3-4, the importance of these privileges is noticeable. Between 1972 and 1974, MSB assets grew by $9 million; however, over the next two years, assets climbed over $25 billion.

As shown in Table 3-4, at the end of 1978, 60.2 percent of MSB assets were in mortgages, with corporate securities (primarily bonds) a distant second at 25.2 percent of assets. Cash assets comprised only 2.3 percent of MSB assets. This is because MSBs are not subject to reserve requirements and because deposit turnover is very low. Nationwide, MSBs are not an important factor because they are confined primarily to the Northeast.

Credit Unions

A **credit union (CU)** is a cooperative self-help thrift and loan society composed of individuals bound together by some tie such as a common employer; membership in a labor union, a church, or a fraternal order; or residence in a well-defined geographic area. Mem-

Table 3–4

Assets, Liabilities, and Net Worth of Mutual Savings Banks, December 31, 1978 (billions of dollars)

	Amount	Percentage Distribution
Assets		
Mortgage loans	$ 95.2	60.2%
Other loans	7.2	4.6
Securities:		
U.S. government	5.0	3.2
State and local government	3.3	2.1
Corporate and other securities	39.8	25.2
Cash	3.7	2.3
Other	4.0	2.5
Total	$158.2	100.0%
Liabilities and Net Worth		
Deposits	142.6	90.1
Other	4.7	3.0
General reserve accounts	10.9	6.9
Total	$158.2	100.0%

Note: Details do not add due to rounding.

Source: Board of Governors of the Federal Reserve, *Federal Reserve Bulletin.*

bers purchase savings shares in the CU and receive dividends which average well above those paid by other thrift institutions. Only members enjoy the privilege of borrowing from a CU. Loans usually are for the payment of current expenses, the purchase of automobiles and other consumer durables, and for home repair and modernization, but some CUs have a limited number of real estate loans outstanding.

The first CU in the United States was formed in 1909. CUs, however, did not become significant factors in the financial markets until the 1960s. Between 1960 and 1978, CU assets rose from $5.7 billion to $62.6 billion. At the end of 1978, there were 21,935 CUs in operation.

CUs perform valuable services for their members. They provide a convenient place for members to save and borrow. Interest rates may not exceed 1 percent per month on the unpaid balance, which, on an annual basis, is less than that charged at most retail credit outlets, bank installment loan departments, and on bank charge cards. As intermediaries, CUs provide not only an above-average return on savings but also a below-average cost to consumers.

Recently, a number of CUs across the nation have begun to offer share drafts, which, in effect, convert savings share accounts into interest-bearing checking accounts. Given the large number of CUs in operation, their strategic location to the income source, and the CU growth momentum of the 1970s, CUs have the potential to become much more important on the financial scene in the years ahead.

Summary

Financial markets and financial intermediaries serve as a link between lenders and borrowers. Those economic units that wish to defer spending may do so by exchanging money for securities, deposits, shares, and other financial claims. Economic units that wish to spend in excess of current income may do so by offering financial claims against themselves in return for money. There are two primary options open to lenders and borrowers: (1) the organized security markets and (2) financial intermediaries. Financial intermediaries perform three general functions: (1) the creation of loanable funds for creditworthy borrowers and, for savers, (2) a reduction in risk exposure, and (3) increased liquidity.

Assets of the major financial intermediaries totaled $2.6 trillion at the end of 1978. Although commercial banks are the predominant financial intermediary, S&Ls and CUs have enjoyed higher growth rates since 1960. Since 1974, MSBs have had accelerated growth. In recent years, the advent of NOW accounts, share drafts, and several EFT innovations have made NFIs more competitive with banks. The increasing importance of NFIs complicates the Fed task of promoting economic stability and creates the need for Congress to review and possibly revamp the regulation of all financial intermediaries.

Questions and Problems

1. Explain why in a simple economy the product and factor markets tend to be in equilibrium.
2. What distinguishes an advanced economy from a simple economy?
3. Define financial intermediary.

4. List and explain briefly the general functions performed by financial intermediaries.

5. List and describe briefly the specific functions performed by commercial banks.

6. Compare the services offered by banks and S&Ls.

7. How does the nature of a life insurance company's promises to pay influence its investment strategy?

Suggestions for Additional Reading

Brockschmidt, Peggy. "Credit Union Growth in Perspective." Federal Reserve Bank of Kansas City, *Economic Review* (February 1977), pp. 3–13.

Chandler, Lester V. *The Monetary-Financial System.* New York: Harper & Row, Publishers, 1979.

Debs, Richard A. "Our Changing Financial System." Federal Reserve Bank of New York, *Monthly Review* (May 1976), pp. 119–123.

Dobson, Steven W. "Development of Capital Markets in the United States." Federal Reserve Bank of Dallas, *Business Review* (April 1976), pp. 1–11.

Gibson, Katharine. "The Early History of Initial Impact of NOW Accounts." Federal Reserve Bank of Boston, *New England Economic Review* (January/February 1975), pp. 17–26.

Krooss, Herman E., and Blyn, Martin R. *A History of Financial Intermediaries.* New York: Random House, 1971.

Lovati, Jean M. "The Growing Similarity Among Financial Institutions." Federal Reserve Bank of St. Louis, *Review* (October 1977), pp. 2–11.

Robinson, Roland I., and Wrightsman, Dwayne. *Financial Markets: The Accumulation and Allocation of Wealth.* New York: McGraw-Hill Book Company, 1974.

Stigum, Marcia. *The Money Market: Myth, Reality and Practice.* Homewood, Ill.: Dow Jones-Irwin, 1978.

2

Commercial Banking

4

Structure and Regulation of the Banking Industry

This is the first of three chapters dealing with commercial banking. This long chapter introduces you to the structure and regulation of the banking industry, while the next two chapters deal with the sources and uses of bank funds. After studying these chapters, you may be so interested in the subject that you sign up for a full course on commercial banking.

Specifically, in this chapter we shall (1) look at the complex classification of banks and regulatory interrelationships that characterize the banking structure, (2) note the trends in number of banks and branches, (3) discuss banking entry (chartering) and concentration, and (4) examine the important aspects of bank branching, bank mergers, and bank holding companies.

Who's Who in the Banking Structure

Some Important Definitions

Most people think that a bank is a bank is a bank. On the surface they are right until they examine our crazy-quilt banking regulatory framework. The best way to start sorting out who's who in the banking industry is to define the major classes of banks.

National bank—a bank chartered by the federal government, specifically, the Comptroller of the Currency.

State Bank—a bank chartered by a state government.

Member bank—a bank that is a member of the Federal Reserve System. All national banks are member banks. State banks have the option of becoming a member bank.

Nonmember bank—a bank that is not a member of the Federal Reserve System.

Insured bank—a bank whose depositors are insured by the Federal Deposit Insurance Corporation (FDIC). All member banks are insured banks.

Noninsured bank—a bank whose depositors are not insured by the FDIC.

National and State Banks

As shown in Table 4-1, at the end of 1978, fewer than one-third of all banks were national banks, but these institutions held 54.3 percent of all bank deposits. A national bank receives its charter from the Comptroller of the Currency in the Treasury Department in Washington. A state bank receives its charter from the appropriate state banking authority. Because the United States has two levels of government chartering banks, we are said to have a **dual banking system**. More will be said later in the chapter about chartering and the dual banking system. A bank chooses to have a national charter primarily because of the prestige involved. The public tends to perceive national banks as safer and stronger than state banks. This, of course, is not necessarily so. Former shareholders of Franklin National Bank and U.S. National Bank, both billion-dollar giants that failed, would make good rebuttal witnesses on this point. Nevertheless, national banking laws and regulations are more stringent than state banking laws and regulations. National banks are examined by the Comptroller; however, because they are member banks and insured banks, national banks also are subject to the Fed Board's and the FDIC's regulations. A **bank examination** checks a bank's compliance with banking laws and regulations. It is not a **bank audit**, which involves verification of assets and liabilities.

State banks are subject to state banking laws and regulations. If the state bank joins the Fed and becomes a state, member bank, then it also becomes subject to Fed Board and FDIC regulations. If the state

Table 4-1

Distribution of Banks and Bank Deposits by Regulatory Status,
December 31, 1978 (billions of dollars)

Bank Status	Number of Banks 14,819 Number	Percent of Total Banks %	Total Deposits $1,038.8 Amount	Percent of Total Deposits %
1. National banks	4,620	31.2	$ 563.8	54.3
State banks	10,199	68.8	475.0	45.7
2. Member banks	5,615	37.9	741.8	71.4
Nonmember banks	9,204	62.1	297.0	28.6
3. Insured banks	14,471	97.7	1,012.6	97.5
Noninsured banks	348	2.3	26.2	2.5

Source: FDIC, unpublished data.

bank opts only for FDIC insured status, then state and FDIC regulations apply.

The hierarchy of federal banking authorities is cumbersome and confusing. Regulations and the degree of enforcement vary from agency to agency. For many years, there have been proposals to reorganize the federal banking authorities into one agency. Costly duplication would be eliminated if a set of uniform laws and regulations applied to all banks. A consolidation of the federal banking agencies should improve the "equal treatment of equals" with respect to enforcement of banking laws and regulations.

A Member Bank: To Be or Not To Be

As shown in Table 4-1, at the close of 1978, member banks held 71.4 percent of total bank deposits. However, in 1967 member bank deposits accounted for 82.5 percent of total deposits. From these data, it appears that some banks do not like being a member of the Federal Reserve System. The problem of attrition has the Fed really worried. It affects the Fed's ability to control the money supply and, hence, influence economic activity. There are several proposals on the drawing board to make membership compulsory, but also, at the same time, to eliminate some of the disadvantages of membership.

Let's look at the advantages and disadvantages of Fed membership. The privileges of membership include (1) free clearing and collection of checks through the Fed, (2) currency and coin shipped free of charge, (3) the opportunity to obtain loans from the Fed, (4) a 6 percent dividend on Fed bank stock, and (5) participation in the election of six of the nine directors at the district Federal Reserve Bank.

On the other hand, member banks have several disadvantages vis-à-vis nonmember banks. First, the member bank reserve ratios are higher. Second, nonmember banks may count a wider range of assets as legal reserves. Nonmember banks typically may count correspondent balances as legal reserves. In some states, Treasury, agency, and municipal securities, CDs, and even uncollected deposits (cash-items-in-the-process-of-collection) count as legal reserves. Since correspondent balances and securities would be held anyway, and since uncollected deposits yield no income, it is obvious that member banks are at a definite disadvantage with respect to legal reserve composition. Indeed, this is the member bank's biggest complaint against Fed membership.

Robert E. Knight of the Federal Reserve Bank of Kansas City made a detailed study of the "net burden/benefit" of Fed membership.[1] For member banks, he calculated the benefit of clearing checks through the Fed and the burden of higher reserve ratios and a narrower range of legal reserves; for nonmember banks, he calculated the burden of holding correspondent balances and the benefit of having lower reserve ratios and a wider range of legal reserve assets. His conclusion was that Fed membership was a burden to member banks with deposits of less than $1 billion, but a benefit to member banks above that deposit mark.

The Fed Board's Proposal for Competitive Equality and Fed Membership

To encourage membership in the Federal Reserve and to promote competitive equality among member banks and other financial institutions, the Fed in mid-1978 proposed some important legislation to Congress.[2] The two components of the proposal are (1) the require-

1. Robert E. Knight, "Comparative Burdens of Federal Reserve Member and Nonmember Banks," Federal Reserve Bank of Kansas City, *Monthly Review* (March 1977), pp. 13–28.

2. Anne Marie Laporte, "Competitive Equality and Federal Reserve Membership—The Board of Governors' Proposal," Federal Reserve Bank of Chicago, *Economic Perspectives* (July/August 1978), pp. 8–13.

ment that all financial institutions hold reserves at the Fed against transaction accounts and (2) a comprehensive program providing for explicit pricing of Fed services and for reducing the cost of Fed membership. A **transaction account** is a "deposit or account on which the depositor or accountholder is allowed to make withdrawals by negotiable or transferable instrument or other similar items for the purpose of making payments to third persons or others." A key part of the Fed's proposal to Congress is the **Reserve Requirements Act**, which would make transaction accounts of more than $5 million at any federally insured commercial bank, MSB, S&L, and CU subject to reserve requirements established by the Fed Board. Reserve ratios would be established by the Fed Board within a range of 7 to 22 percent for demand deposits and from 3 to 12 percent on transaction accounts other than demand deposits. Required reserves of all depository institutions would be held in the form of vault cash and reserves at the Fed. Institutions that are not members of the Fed also would have the choice of keeping reserves in a member bank or in the FHLB, as long as the member bank or FHLB held the funds in the form of Federal Reserve balances. Funds passed through to the Fed would not be subject to reserve requirements or FDIC insurance assessment. Member banks would benefit by restructured and lower reserve requirements on demand deposits and by compensation for required reserve balances at the Fed. On the other hand, banks would begin paying for check processing, check transportation, and automated clearinghouse services.

Congress did not enact the Fed's proposal in 1978. But it is a good bet that Congress will pass the Fed's proposal or a very close version. In view of the member bank attrition problem and the growing competitive pressure from NFIs, the proposed legislation is needed and would benefit the public.

The Banking Structure in Transition

Changes in the Number of Banks

During the first two decades of the 1900s the number of banks in the United States increased almost 2.5 times, from 12,427 in 1900 to 30,456 in the peak year of 1921 (see Figure 4-1). This sharp rise in banking institutions stemmed largely from the "free banking" policies

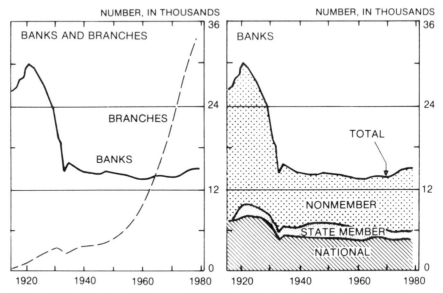

Figure 4-1.   Number of Commercial Banks in the United States, 1915–1977
Source: Board of Governors of the Federal Reserve, *Historical Chart Book.*

of both the Comptroller of the Currency and the various state chartering authorities. Virtually every group that applied for a bank charter received one. As a result of this "overchartering," the banking industry became replete with weak institutions that could not weather the impending economic storms.

Between 1921 and 1929, there was a net reduction of 5,486 banks. Most of these had capital of $25,000 or less and were located in agricultural communities which suffered from several adverse developments during the 1920s. First, following the end of World War I, prices for farm products declined sharply, which made it difficult for many farmers to repay loans. Second, land prices fell with farm prices, causing the collateral value of many mortgages held by banks to decline below the amount of debt they supported. Third, the migration of people toward the cities left many "country-store" banks with insufficient customers to operate profitably. Finally, the increased demand for banking services that could be provided only by large institutions led to the absorption of many banks.

The real "shake-out" in the banking industry occurred between 1930 and 1933. During this four-year period, 10,763 banks either failed or were merged with strong banks. The banking collapse during the early Depression years was the result of many factors, including (1) the Fed's failure to provide adequate liquidity for the banking system, (2) inadequate control by the banking regulatory authorities over the quality of bank credit extended, (3) a paucity of capable banking executives, and (4) too many undercapitalized banks.

To weed out weak banks and restore the public's confidence, President Roosevelt, by executive proclamation, declared a **Banking Holiday** on March 6, 1933, and closed all banks. Within ten days, most of the sound banks had reopened, and by June 30, 1933, there were 14,207 banks in operation.

As shown in Figure 4–1, the number of banks has declined slowly since 1933, except for a slight increase between 1963 and 1965. During the latter period, Comptroller of the Currency James J. Saxon encouraged the chartering of new banks, both national and state, in order to provide a stimulus to banking competition. At the close of 1978, there were 14,819 banks in operation.

Changes in the Number of Branches

A **unit bank** operates from only one location. A **branch bank** operates from two or more locations. The real impetus to branch banking in this country occurred in 1909, when California moved to permit statewide branch banking. Other states followed this precedent and relaxed their branching restrictions. The number of branches rose from less than 100 in 1910 to 150 in 1920, and 375 at the end of 1929. After the reorganization of the banking industry in 1933, the number of branches rose only slightly until the end of World War II. Between 1947 and 1978, the number of branches increased from 3,007 to 33,868.

Banking Entry: The Regulatory Framework

Origin and Evolution of the Dual Banking System

As we have seen, the United States has a dual banking system. Prior to 1863, and with the exception of the charters granted to the First and Second Banks of the United States in 1791 and 1816, only state legislatures had the right to charter banks. With the passage of the National Banking Acts of 1863 and 1864, provision was made for the granting of national bank charters through the office of the Comptroller of the Currency in the Treasury Department. Under the National Banking Acts, minimum capital and reserve requirements were established, and a number of restrictions were placed on lending activities. By specifying a set of statutory requirements for the chartering of national banks, the National Banking Acts also incorporated the principle of free banking, which had originated in Michigan in 1837 and in New York in 1838. **Free banking** meant that theoretically any group meeting the minimum requirements could receive a bank charter. In practice, however, the Comptroller exercised much discretionary authority in his decisions to approve or deny charter applications.

The concept of a dual banking system with its separate entry routes into banking was altered considerably with the permanent provision for federal deposit insurance through the FDIC in the Banking Act of 1935. This act requires that the Comptroller of Currency (for prospective national banks) and the Federal Reserve (for prospective state, member banks) certify to the FDIC that certain criteria have been evaluated in approving the charter. In addition, the FDIC must consider these criteria before insuring the deposits of a state, nonmember bank. Because of the attractiveness of federal deposit insurance, the FDIC acquired, in effect, a veto power over charters granted to state, nonmember banks.[3] Thus, the federal level of government has effective control over banking entry, even though states retain the right to issue charters.

Although the states no longer have effective control of state bank entry standards, two important aspects of the dual banking system remain. First, because a proposed bank-organizing group has the right to petition two different levels of government for a charter, there is a greater likelihood that the application will be reviewed and acted upon in a fair and nondiscriminatory manner. Second, new charter applicants still retain, under the concept of a dual banking system, the right to choose the supervisory framework under which they will operate. Therefore, although banking entry is effectively under federal control, the continued states' right to charter banks provides a system of checks and balances in our bank chartering arrangements.[4]

3. Some states stipulate that deposits must be insured by the FDIC before a charter can be issued.

4. For a good discussion of these and other aspects of our dual banking system, see William J. Brown, *The Dual Banking System in the United States* (Washington, D.C.: The American Bankers Association, 1968).

Federal Criteria for a New Bank

The considerations that the Banking Act of 1935 required to be evaluated before a proposed bank can receive a national charter, join the Federal Reserve System, or be issued deposit insurance are as follows:

1. The financial history and condition of the bank.
2. The adequacy of its capital structure.
3. Its future earnings prospects.
4. The general character of management.
5. The convenience and needs of the community to be served by the bank.
6. Whether or not its corporate powers are consistent with the purposes of this act.

The typical first step taken by a group that wishes to form a bank and satisfy these criteria is to have an economic feasibility study performed by a professor of finance or by a consulting firm. A determination of feasibility involves consideration of the adequacy of existing banking and financial facilities and services in the community, whether or not the economic and financial resources of the community are growing rapidly enough to support the entry of a new bank without causing any other bank or financial institution to become unprofitable or illiquid, and whether or not the proposed directors and management have the necessary experience and financial acumen to operate the bank profitably. Besides satisfying the organizers that a need exists and that the bank can be a profitable venture, the study should aim also to convince the bank chartering agencies and the FDIC that a need exists. Therefore, the study should be organized in such a way that it provides extensive information and answers to satisfy the federal criteria (and state criteria, if applicable) and the many detailed questions in the charter application.

Following submission of the feasibility study and the application for a charter and deposit insurance (if the bank is to be a state, non-member, insured bank), the appropriate regulatory authorities then conduct an intensive survey to determine if the proposed bank meets the criteria. The survey team talks with bankers and citizens in the community and makes an extensive background investigation of the financial affairs and business dealings of the proposed directors and management. In effect, the survey team subjects the proposed bank and its organizers to a "worthiness" test that attempts to ensure that the public interest will be served if the bank is allowed to open.[5]

Rationale for the Regulation of Banking Entry

Entry into the banking industry is regulated primarily because of the strategic place that banks occupy in our economic and financial system. As we noted in Chapter 3, banks hold deposits and provide the nation with an efficient payments transfer mechanism. When a bank fails, its depositors sometimes are denied use of their funds temporarily, and some accountholders eventually may even lose a portion of their uninsured deposits. Moreover, the general public's confidence in the banking system is shaken in various degrees by bank failures, which always seem to be well publicized.

The banking regulatory authorities probably could reduce the failure rate of existing banks, which, in recent years, has been less than ten banks a year, by declaring a moratorium on bank charters. This approach, however, would deny the public the benefits that accrue from the periodic entry into the market of another competitor. A new bank causes every other bank to reevaluate both the quality and the quantity of its services. Each bank is an alternative source of credit, and this is important, especially for small businesses. Usually, a new bank also offers some services or conveniences that are not otherwise being provided. In general, a newcomer increases the "vigor of competition."

The bulk of the initial deposits and capital for a new bank usually will come from the established banks and other financial institutions in the community. The task of the banking regulatory authorities is to weigh the positive benefits of the new bank against the possibility that existing banks and financial institutions will be placed in jeopardy. This is why it is very important to estimate carefully the future growth in financial resources in the community where the new bank is to locate. As we have seen, the economy and deposits in the community should

5. For a discussion of public control over banking entry, see David C. Motter, "Bank Formation and the Public Interest"; Sam Peltzman, "Bank Entry Regulation: Its Impact and Purpose"; and Donald Jacobs, "The Framework of Commercial Bank Regulation: An Appraisal," in The Administrator of National Banks, *Studies in Banking Competition and the Bank Structure* (Washington, D.C.: 1966), pp. 233–299, 337–351.

be growing fast enough to permit the new bank to enter without causing any other bank or financial institution to become unprofitable or illiquid.

Concentration in the Banking Industry

At the end of 1978, there were 14,819 commercial banks in the nation. This seems like a great many banks. We have noted that this total is a function of the liberal chartering policy prior to 1920 and the high number of failures in the Great Depression and the 1930s. However, it also is the result of a number of states prohibiting or limiting branch banking; unit banks have to be chartered in large numbers to provide the convenience that the public demands.[6] For example, at the end of 1978 banks in Florida, Texas, and Illinois comprised approximately 22 percent of the national total. In Florida branching is severely restricted, while in Texas and Illinois it is prohibited.

Analysis of Table 4–2 reveals two primary conclusions: (1) there is a large number of small banks and (2) the twenty-two largest banks

Table 4–2

Distribution of Insured Banks and Deposits by Size of Banks December 31, 1977

Asset Size	Number of Banks	Percent of Total Banks	Deposits (millions of dollars)	Percent of Total Deposits
Less than 5 million	1,376	9.3%	$ 3,832.5	0.4%
5–9.9 million	2,623	17.8	17,408.7	1.8
10–24.9 million	4,932	33.5	73,553.3	7.8
25–49.9 million	2,991	20.3	93,336.6	9.9
50–99.9 million	1,502	10.2	92,770.4	9.8
100–299.9 million	857	5.8	118,813.6	12.6
300–499.9 million	166	1.1	53,894.2	5.7
500–999.9 million	144	1.0	75,465.5	8.0
1–5 billion	129	0.9	186,210.5	19.7
5 billion or more	21	0.1	228,337.2	24.2

Source: FDIC, *Annual Report.* (Totals do not include foreign deposits.)

6. The pros and cons of branch banking are discussed in the next section.

account for a significant percentage of the total deposits in the industry. But, is either finding "bad" for the banking convenience and needs of the public?

With respect to the large number of small banks, a significant percentage are in states that limit or prohibit branch banking. Many small banks are inefficient, high-cost operations and enjoy a monopoly in one-bank towns. But, small banks are a part of Americana. Small banks financed a developing nation. Small banks offer a refreshing alternative to customers who do not wish to be just another number in a large, impersonal bank.

On the other hand, are the twenty-two heavyweights (shown in Table 4–3) going to absorb all the other banks and reap monopoly profits in many communities? Is banking bigness badness? The an-

Table 4–3
Deposits of the 22 Largest Banks, (billions of dollars) December 31, 1978

Bank	Head Office	Deposits
1. Bank of America NT & SA	San Francisco	$ 76.8
2. Citibank NA	New York	61.6
3. Chase Manhattan Bank NA	New York	49.5
4. Manufacturers Hanover Trust Co.	New York	32.1
5. Morgan Guaranty Trust Co.	New York	28.6
6. Chemical Bank	New York	24.9
7. Continental Illinois National Bank and Trust Co.	Chicago	20.9
8. Bankers Trust Co.	New York	18.4
9. First National Bank of Chicago	Chicago	17.5
10. Security Pacific National Bank	Los Angeles	17.0
11. Wells Fargo Bank NA	San Francisco	14.8
12. Marine Midland Bank	Buffalo	11.4
13. Crocker National Bank	San Francisco	11.2
14. United California Bank	Los Angeles	10.2
15. Irving Trust Co.	New York	9.5
16. Mellon Bank NA	Pittsburgh	8.5
17. First National Bank of Boston	Boston	7.6
18. National Bank of Detroit	Detroit	7.0
19. Bank of New York	New York	5.9
20. Republic National Bank	Dallas	5.3
21. First Pennsylvania Bank NA	Philadelphia	5.3
22. Seattle First National Bank	Seattle	5.2
		$449.2

Source: The American Banker. (Totals include foreign deposits.)

swer to the first question is "no." As we shall see later in this chapter, the banking regulatory authorities look at every merger to determine whether the financial benefits outweigh the anticompetitive effects. The dual banking system provides two avenues for charters and this improves the chances for approval for legitimate chartering proposals.

The answer to the second question is "not necessarily." Small banks have their place, but so do large banks. Large firms with large financing requirements need large banks. The economic development of unit banking states may have been retarded because of below-average bank size. But it is difficult to argue this now because political boundaries are not barriers to capital in modern times when national accounts banking officers roam the countryside looking for customers.

Thus far we have looked at banking concentration within a national framework. There is also the small customer, whose "world" is his or her hometown, and the vast majority of our communities are one-and-two-bank towns. That means that these markets are far from the perfectly competitive norm that yields services at the lowest cost. On the other hand, large firms usually have borrowing alternatives among all of the nation's giant banks. These customers benefit from a degree of competition more closely akin to purely competitive conditions. Thus, across the nation, banking concentration and competition vary from town to town and with the size of the customer.

Branch Banking

The question of branch banking versus unit banking probably ranks as the number one banking issue. At the center of the debate is the power of individual state legislatures to determine the extent to which both state and national banks may branch within state boundaries. As you might expect, the large banks want statewide branching, while the small banks want unit banking or limited branching to keep the large banks out of their area. Before we examine the branch banking-unit banking question, let's look at the federal and state regulation of branch banking.

Federal and State Regulation

The present federal regulatory framework for branch banking is contained in the Banking Act of 1933 and its subsequent amendments. The major provisions of this act are discussed below.

First, a state's branching limitations on its own state banks apply to national banks located within its boundaries. In other words, a national bank may only branch within a state to the extent that the state banks are permitted, and no state permits its banks to branch across state lines. For example, in Texas a national bank may not establish branches because state banks are not allowed to do so, but a national bank in California may establish branches in any part of that state. A summary of state banking statutes is in Table 4–4.

Second, regardless of state law, permission to branch must be received by national banks from the Comptroller of the Currency, by state, member banks from the Federal Reserve Board of Governors, and by state, nonmember, insured banks from the FDIC. Other than the relevant state limitations and certain minimum capital require-

---

Table 4–4
Summary of State Branch Banking Statutes
December 31, 1978

Statewide Branch Banking	Limited Branch Banking	Unit Banking
Alaska	Alabama	Colorado
Arizona	Arkansas	Illinois
California	Florida	Kansas
Connecticut	Georgia	Minnesota
Delaware	Indiana	Missouri
District of Columbia	Iowa	Montana
Hawaii	Kentucky	Nebraska
Idaho	Louisiana	North Dakota
Maine	Massachusetts	Oklahoma
Maryland	Michigan	Texas
Nevada	Mississippi	West Virginia
New Jersey	New Hampshire	Wyoming
New York	New Mexico	
North Carolina	Ohio	
Oregon	Pennsylvania	
Rhode Island	Tennessee	
South Carolina	Wisconsin	
South Dakota		
Utah		
Vermont		
Virginia		
Washington		

Source: Adapted from compilations of the Board of Governors of the Federal Reserve.

ments mentioned below, there are no specific criteria imposed by law on the Comptroller in considering a proposed national bank branch. In contrast, the Board of Governors and the FDIC must take into account the same factors as those required for deposit insurance certification.

Third, for out-of-town branches, national banks must have minimum aggregate capital equal to (1) that required to establish an equal number of separate national banks or (2) that required by state law to establish state bank branches, whichever is greater. No additional capital is required to establish in-town branches, if they are permitted.

Fourth, national and state member banks may establish seasonal agencies in resort areas for the receipt and payment of deposits without an additional capital requirement, but only if the area is without banking facilities, if at least countywide branching is permitted, and if the area is within the head-office county of the national bank concerned.

With respect to state regulation, as shown in Table 4-4, most states restrict branch banking. However, there is a trend underway toward statewide branching. In 1960, only sixteen states permitted statewide branching; sixteen states had limited branching; and eighteen states had unit banking. In 1978, twenty-one states had statewide branching, while seventeen states had limited branching and only twelve states had unit banking. By 1985, the movement toward more liberalized intrastate branching may be at full bloom.

Branch Banking vs. Unit Banking: Pros and Cons

Probably the first shot in this war was fired in the late eighteenth century by state bankers who objected to the location of branches of the First BUS in their communities. President Andrew Jackson, a champion of state banks, challenged and defeated the Second BUS and its branch system in the 1830s. In most of the states in which branching is limited or prohibited, liberalization of the branch banking laws is a perennial question. Let's examine the issues.

Competition.   An important question has been the impact of branching on banking competition. Competition, in this sense, refers to how banks react to the price and nonprice moves of their rivals. Generally, banks attempt to avoid price competition. They prefer, instead, to engage in nonprice activities that attempt to gain customers with elaborate advertising campaigns, catchy slogans, pretty tellers, friendly service, and so on. However, nonprice competition in banking is costly, and it involves a waste of resources if it does not result in a wider range of services or more efficient operations. Guttentag and Herman found "some limited and inconclusive evidence that nonprice competition is more intense under branch than under unit banking."[7]

Banks do tend to engage in price competition with nonbank intermediaries. Since 1966 banks have reacted quickly, within the limits permitted by Regulation Q, to interest-rate increases on savings deposits in those areas in which S&Ls are important competitors. Moreover, most banks respond to rate changes on consumer credit by the large finance companies and CUs. There is probably no significant difference between branch banking and unit banking structures as to the speed and intensity of the reaction to price changes on those services offered by nonbank intermediaries that are sufficiently close substitutes for those provided by banks.

The price of banking services.   It is virtually impossible to generalize about whether branch banking leads to higher or lower prices for banking services. There is some evidence that branching into nonmetropolitan areas may place some downward pressure on rates for small business loans and mortgage loans. On the other hand, rates on savings deposits and service charges tend to rise in a nonmetropolitan area following the entrance of another bank via merger.[8]

Operational efficiency.   One of the key issues in the debate is whether branch banks are more efficient to operate than unit banks. Proponents of branch banking frequently argue that branching enables banks to grow larger and to achieve economies of scale, that is, reductions in long-run average costs. There are two possible sources of these economies. First, banks should benefit greatly from labor specialization. Because banks provide such a wide range of services and employ so many highly skilled personnel to provide these services, operations must reach a comparatively large size before maximum proficiency is attained. Second, economies tend to accrue

7. Jack M. Guttentag and Edward S. Herman, "Banking Structure and Performance," New York University Graduate School of Business Administration, *The Bulletin,* 41–43 (February 1967), p. 17.
8. Guttentag and Herman, pp. 21–22.

as banks achieve greater diversification in their loan portfolio, which, in turn, should lead to fewer defaults.[9]

There is some evidence that there are economies of scale in banking.[10] These cost savings appear to be greatest for banks up to the $10 million level and then taper off in the intermediate range ($10–$200 million). Not much is known about economies of scale for banks larger than this.

On the other hand, it has been found that branch banks tend to have higher costs than unit banks in the same size category.[11] The conclusion is that "economies of scale in banking do exist, but they are relatively small and are actually less important than the diseconomies of branch structure."[12] However, branch systems in given size classes should be expected to have higher expense ratios because branch offices provide additional convenience, which tends to inflate costs.[13] On the basis of the studies cited in this section, it cannot be stated conclusively that branch banking promotes operational efficiency.

Allocational efficiency.   Another issue in the branch banking debate relates to allocational efficiency, that is, the extent to which loanable funds are made available to the highest and best use in the economy. Branch banks, through their offices, have a ready mechanism for the transfer of loanable funds to the most creditworthy borrowers within the bank's market area. Some branches in slow-growth areas might be principally receivers of deposits and have a loans-to-deposits ratio of 20 percent; branches in areas with a great demand for loans might have a loans-to-deposits ratio of 150 percent or more and hence primarily be users of funds. Branch banking systems tend to have a higher loans-to-assets ratio than unit banks, which would indicate that branch banks may have an edge over unit banks in promoting allocational efficiency. There seems to be no support for the criticism that is sometimes made that branch banks tend to lend a disproportionate amount of funds through their head-office city branches to the detriment of borrowers served by branches elsewhere in the system.

9. Lyle E. Gramley, *A Study of Scale Economies in Banking* (Kansas City: Federal Reserve Bank of Kansas City, 1962), pp. 4–5.
10. Guttentag and Herman, chap. 5.
11. Paul M. Horvitz, "Economies of Scale in Banking," in the Commission on Money and Credit, *Private Financial Institutions* (Englewood Cliffs, N.J.: Prentice-Hall, 1963), pp. 28–33.
12. Horvitz, p. 52.
13. Guttentag and Herman, p. 25.

Loans-to-deposits ratios at branches in these outlying areas frequently exceed those at branches in the head-office city.[14]

Another question under the heading of allocational efficiency is whether branch banks or unit banks provide a larger number of office facilities in their respective service areas. One study found that metropolitan areas with branch banking had considerably more offices than did areas with unit banking.[15]

Finally, with respect to the range of auxiliary services, such as trust services, payroll accounting, and foreign exchange, it has been found that large banks, which usually are branch banks, tend to offer a wider range of services than do smaller banks.[16]

Other issues. Several other issues in the branch banking debate deserve consideration. First, sometimes it is charged that branch banking personnel are more impersonal than unit banking employees. There is evidence that this may be true because frequently branch offices serve as training facilities for new employees who do not remain at an office long enough to establish a continuing relationship with customers. On the other hand, many branch banks make a great effort to staff their various offices with employees and officers recruited from the local area to be served who are familiar with the people and the economy of that community.

Another criticism frequently made of branch banks is that branch loan officers are so restricted by managerial rules and limitations that they can make only small loans and are not in a position to assist and advise large borrowers effectively. Again, there is an element of truth in this assertion because branch systems do tend to place low lending limits on branch officers, and large loan requests must be referred to senior management at the head office for approval. Delays at branches in approving loan requests may be one of the disadvantages of branch operations, but submission of the larger loan requests to a group of officers who may not know the borrowers personally would tend to benefit both the borrower and the bank, if loans of doubtful quality are weeded out by the application of uniform credit standards. Thus, a more objective appraisal of loan requests may be one of the virtues of branch banking.

14. Guttentag and Herman, pp. 26–27.
15. Guttentag and Herman, p. 28.
16. Guttentag and Herman, p. 29.

Finally, proponents of branch banking sometimes claim that branch banks are safer than unit banks. They point out that most of the bank failures in recent years have been unit banks. This is true, but it should be remembered that almost all banks have federal deposit insurance, and actual deposit losses have been insignificant in recent years.

Interstate Branching: The Next Big Issue?

Now that there is evidence that the statewide branch banking movement is gaining momentum, perhaps the next big issue will be interstate branching. Essentially, the same questions that were relevant in the intrastate branching debate, such as competition, pricing of banking services, and allocational efficiency, will be germane to interstate branching. Essentially, the same questions that are rele-it and the little banks that oppose it. The big banks, through their holding companies, already own finance company and mortgage servicing offices across the country. It would take very few hours for these banks to put up a sign that reads "XYZ branch bank" instead of "Friendly Fred's Finance Company." Interstate branching is not on the horizon yet. You can bet your last Federal Reserve note that small banks and regional banks, MSBs, S&Ls, and CUs will circle their wagons and shoot it out on this one (and probably win).

Bank Mergers

A **merger** occurs when one bank absorbs another bank and operates it under its own charter. From the acquiring bank's vantage point, the principal motives behind these mergers usually include the need (1) for additional loanable funds, (2) for capital and greater lending limits to one borrower (which, for national banks, are 10 percent of capital), (3) to follow shifts in population, (4) to benefit from economies of scale, (5) for loan diversification, and (6) for defensive expansion to keep up with or forestall competition. From the viewpoint of the acquired bank, primary motives for merger include (1) a failing or floundering condition, (2) a management succession problem, and (3) inducements to shareholders in the form of higher market values for their stock and higher dividend income.

Most of the benefits from bank mergers cited above accrue to the banks involved and not necessarily to the communities affected. However, there are several possible social benefits from bank mergers. First, the public benefits if it is spared the disruptive effects from a bank failure or the inefficiency of a floundering bank. Second, if a management succession problem could result in the loss of banking services to a community, then, obviously, the public stands to benefit from a merger. Third, mergers frequently result in an expansion in the range and quality of banking services in a community. For example, many small banks are not large enough to offer trust services, investment advisory services, and mortgage loans on a profitable basis. There is a good chance that a large bank could offer these and other services at the newly acquired bank with little or no expansion in staff or costs. Fourth, it is sometimes argued that mergers are needed to build bigger banks to provide larger lines of credit. A few big banks are needed in our banking system to meet the credit needs of large businesses, and mergers have helped many of our banking giants to attain their present size. However, capital is free to flow across state lines even though banks are not permitted to branch across state lines. Small banks very readily can get their correspondent banks to participate with them in loans to meet credit demands that are beyond their lending limits. There is a point when the benefits from permitting large banks to become bigger may not outweigh the loss of a small, but independent, source of bank credit.

Approval of bank mergers rests with the federal banking agency having primary regulatory authority over the surviving bank; to wit, the Comptroller for national banks, the Fed Board for state, member banks, and the FDIC for state, nonmember, insured banks. In addition, the Attorney General and the two agencies not directly involved must render an opinion regarding the probable effects of the merger on competition. The Bank Merger Act of 1960 spells out the following factors that must be considered in passing upon a merger application:

1. Financial history and condition of the banks involved.
2. Adequacy of the resulting bank's capital structure.
3. Future earnings prospects of the resulting bank.
4. General character of the resulting bank's management.
5. Convenience and needs of the community to be served.
6. Assurance that the resulting bank's corporate powers are consistent with the Bank Merger Act.
7. Evaluation of the probable effects of the merger on competition.

In 1963 in a test of the new act, the US Supreme Court held in the *Philadelphia* case that Sec. 7 of the Clayton Act applied to banking. In 1964, the high court held in the *Lexington* case that Sec. 1 of the Sherman Act applied to banking. Application of both antitrust acts to banking caused great uncertainty in the industry. To alleviate the problem, Congress passed the Bank Merger Act of 1966, which was a combination of the 1960 merger act and the antitrust law. The new act went a long way toward eliminating some of the uncertainty and confusion by requiring each of the banking agencies, the Attorney General, and the courts to consider the same factors when evaluating a proposed bank merger. Below is the pertinent provision in the new act:

1. The responsible agency shall not approve
    (A) any proposed merger which would result in a monopoly, or which would be in furtherance of any combination or conspiracy to monopolize the business of banking in any part of the United States, or
    (B) any other proposed merger transaction whose effect in any section of the country may be substantially to lessen competition, or tend to create a monopoly, or which in any other manner would be in restraint of trade, *unless it finds that the anticompetitive effects of the proposed transaction are clearly outweighed in the public interest by the probable effect of the transaction in meeting the convenience and needs of the community to be served.*

    In every case, the responsible agency shall take into consideration the financial and managerial resources of the existing and proposed institutions and the convenience and needs of the community to be served.

Sections (A) and (B) contain identical or nearly identical standards of illegality as specified in Secs. 1 and 2 of the Sherman Act and Sec. 7 of the Clayton Act. Aided by several high court decisions since 1966 that have clarified issues, regulatory guidelines for judging bank mergers seem fairly clear at this time.

Bank Holding Companies

Some Important Definitions

A **bank holding company** is any company that owns or controls the voting stock of one or more banks. There are **one-bank hold-**

ing companies, which own or control a single bank, and **multibank holding companies**, which own or control two or more separately incorporated banks. The operation of two or more banks under a holding company also is called **group banking**. Today, all bank holding companies are **registered bank holding companies** because they must register and file reports with the Fed Board of Governors.

The Bank Holding Company Movement

The bank holding company movement originated around the turn of the century. An early holding company was the present Northwest Bancorporation, which was organized in 1903 and which by 1908 held an interest in thirty-one banks.[17] In addition, the predecessors to Atlantic Bancorporation of Jacksonville and Washington Bancshares, Inc., of Spokane had their origins in the first decade of this century.[18]

The main thrust of the early bank holding movement, however, came in the period immediately preceding the Great Depression. Between 1925 and 1930, seven of the present top fifteen multibank holding companies were formed. Although the holding company movement occurred predominantly in the Midwest and Northwest, present-day giants were formed in the South, East, and West as well. By 1931, there were 97 bank holding companies, with 978 banks and 1,219 branches in the United States.[19]

There were several reasons for the great expansion of bank holding companies toward the close of the 1920s. First, following its success as a device to control large numbers of companies in other industries, the holding company seemed like an ideal means to reap the financial advantage of common ownership of several banks. Often, this advantage was the ready access to funds for the holding company's financial and nonfinancial affiliates.[20] Second, holding companies offered a means to have multiple-office banking systems in areas where branching was restricted. Third, holding companies provided a means

---

17. Charles S. Popple, *Development of Two Bank Groups in the Central Northwest* (Cambridge, Mass.: Harvard University Press, 1944), p. 68.
18. W. Ralph Lamb, *Group Banking* (New Brunswick, N.J.: Rutgers University Press, 1961), p. 82.
19. C.E. Cagle, "Branch, Chain, and Group Banking," in *Banking Studies* (Washington, D.C.: Board of Governors of the Federal Reserve System, 1941), pp. 134, 136.
20. As defined in the Banking Act of 1933, a bank **affiliate** is an organization owned or controlled by a bank or its stockholders or its executive officers serving as directors.

to expand across state lines. In fact, the founders of Transamerica Corporation, in 1928, envisioned eventually controlling banks across the nation through six regional holding companies.[21]

During the Great Depression, many holding companies and their affiliated banks were dissolved. However, none of the banks affiliated with the leading multibank holding companies in the Northwest and Far West were suspended.[22] Close supervision and counsel and contributions of funds to prevent impairment of capital were the principal means used to keep individual banks from failing. By 1936, there were only 52 holding companies, with 479 banks, 847 branches, and $6.8 billion in deposits.

After World War II, there was a postwar resurgence of holding company expansion. A large part of this growth occurred between 1954 and mid-1956 as many holding companies moved swiftly to expand out of fear that restrictive Congressional legislation dealing with bank holding companies was forthcoming. A second impetus to deposit growth in group systems was the rebuilding of Transamerica Corporations' bank stock portfolio after its divestment of Bank of America.[23]

Registered Bank Holding Companies

Multibank holding companies.   Congress moved to limit the activities of bank holding companies through passage of the Bank Holding Company Act of 1956. This act required all bank holding companies owning or controlling 25 percent of more of the voting shares of each of two or more banks, or controlling in any manner the election of a majority of the directors of each of two or more banks, to register with, and be regulated by, the Board of Governors. Companies owning or controlling only one bank were exempt from these requirements. At the end of 1956, there were 53 multibank companies holding 428 banks, 783 branches, and $14.8 billion in deposits registered with the Board of Governors (Table 4-5). From this point until 1965, the percentage of total deposits held by multibank holding companies

21. Palmer T. Hogenson, *The Economies of Group Banking* (Washington, D.C.: Public Affairs Press, 1955), p. 4.
22. Marcus Nadler and Jules I. Bogen, *The Bank Holding Company* (New York: Graduate School of Business Administration, New York University, 1959), p. 11.
23. Gerald C. Fischer, "Market Extension by Bank Holding Companies: History, Economic Implications, and Current Issues," *Proceedings of a Conference on Bank Structure and Competition* (Chicago: Federal Reserve Bank of Chicago, 1969), pp. 45-46.

Table 4-5

*Registered Bank Holding Companies,
Selected Years, 1956–1977*

Year Ending	Number of Companies	Banking Offices		Total Deposits (billions of dollars)	Total Deposits Percentage of All Bank Deposits
		Banks	Branches		
1956	53	428	783	$ 14.8	7.5%
1960	47	426	1,037	18.3	8.0
1962	49	442	1,215	21.2	8.1
1965	53	468	1,486	27.6	8.3
1966	65	561	1,802	41.1	11.6
1967	74	603	2,085	49.8	12.6
1968	80	629	2,262	57.6	13.2
1969	97	723	2,674	62.6	14.3
1970	121	895	3,260	78.1	15.5
1971	1,567	2,420	10,832	297.1	55.3
1972	1,607	2,720	13,441	379.4	61.5
1973	1,677	3,097	15,374	446.6	65.4
1974	1,752	3,462	17,131	509.7	68.1
1975	1,821	3,674	18,382	527.5	67.1
1976	1,802	3,791	19,199	553.6	66.1
1977	1,913	3,903	21,223	814.3	72.0

Note: Holding companies listed for the 1956–1970 period are multibank holding companies as defined in the Bank Holding Company Act of 1956, as amended. Data for 1971 and subsequent years include companies that had reported to the board under the Bank Holding Company Act Amendments of 1970 and, therefore, include multibank and one-bank holding companies. Data for 1977 include foreign offices.

Source: Board of Governors of the Federal Reserve, *Banking and Monetary Statistics, 1941–1970;* and *Annual Statistical Digest, 1971–1975 and 1973–1977.*

increased only slightly. However, between 1966 and 1970, the number of multibank holding companies more than doubled, and the percentage of total deposits held increased from 11.6 to 15.5 percent. Concern over possible future restrictions on holding company activities was the primary motivating factor behind many of the holding company formations during this period.

Since 1970 the number of multibank holding companies has risen sharply. By the end of 1977, there were 306 multibank holding companies controlling 2,301 banks with 10,982 branches. Banks in these multibank holding companies held deposits of $410.8 billion, or 36.3 percent of the total in the nation.

One-bank holding companies.   Encouraged, in part, by the loophole in the Bank Holding Company Act of 1956, the growth of one-bank holding companies was phenomenal, especially after 1965. As shown in Table 4–6, between the end of 1965 and the end of 1968, the number of one-bank holding companies increased from 550 to 783, and the share of total deposits held by these companies rose from 4.5 to 24.9 percent. By the end of 1970, there were 1,318 one-bank holding companies, with 39.7 percent of total deposits controlled by these companies. As a result of the December 31, 1970, amendments to the Bank Holding Company Act, one-bank holding companies were required to register with the Board of Governors. As may be seen in Table 4–6, the number of one-bank holding companies stabilized after the requirement to register was instituted. One-bank holding companies continued to be formed, but a number of previously formed one-bank holding companies acquired stock in other banks, thereby converting to multibank holding companies. By the end of 1977, there were 1,607 one-bank holding companies, with 10,241 branches. One-bank holding company banks held deposits of $403.5 billion, or 35.7 percent of the total in the nation.

Table 4–6

One-Bank Holding Companies, Selected Years, 1955–1977

Year Ending	Number of One-Bank Holding Companies	Holding Company Deposits (billions of dollars)	Percentage of All Bank Deposits
1955	117	$ 11.6	1.7%
1965	550	15.1	4.5
1968	783	108.2	24.9
1970	1,318	191.0	39.7
1973	1,282	207.4	30.4
1974	1,340	222.4	29.7
1975	1,419	230.0	29.2
1976	1,504	267.1	31.9
1977	1,607	403.5	35.7

Note: Data for 1977 include foreign offices.

Source: U.S. Congress, House Committee on Banking and Currency, *The Growth of Unregistered Bank Holding Companies—Problems and Prospects,* Committee Print, 91st Congress, 1st session, 1969, p. 5; *Federal Reserve Bulletin;* Board of Governors of the Federal Reserve, *Annual Statistical Digest, 1971–1975 and 1973–1977.*

Federal Regulation

Federal regulation of bank holding companies is spelled out primarily in the Bank Holding Company Act of 1956 and its amendments. The 1956 act required all bank holding companies to register with the Board of Governors. A bank holding company was defined as a corporation, business trust, association, or similar organization owning or controlling 25 percent or more of the voting shares of each of *two or more banks*, or controlling in any manner the election of a majority of the directors of each of two or more banks, or acting as trustee for shareholders or members who control 25 percent or more of the voting share of each of two or more banks. Approval from the Board of Governors must be received before a bank holding company could acquire over 5 percent of the voting stock of any bank, or before two bank holding companies could merge. In reviewing holding company applications for the above, the Board had to consider five factors:

1. The financial history and condition of the company or companies and banks concerned.
2. Their earnings prospects.
3. The character of their management.
4. The convenience, needs, and welfare of the communities and areas concerned.
5. Whether or not the effect of the acquisition or merger or consolidation would be to expand the size or extent of the bank holding system beyond the limits consistent with adequate and sound banking, the public interest, and the preservation of competition in the field of banking.

With respect to nonbanking businesses, the 1956 act stipulated that registered holding companies could own shares of any company if all its activities were of a financial, fiduciary, or an insurance nature, provided the Fed Board determined such activities *to be so closely related to the business of banking as to be a proper incident thereto* (italics added).

In 1966 amendments were added to the original act so that antitrust considerations must be taken into account by the Fed Board as a condition of approval for any holding company acquisition.

On December 31, 1970, President Nixon signed into law amendments that changed the definition of a bank holding company to include those that control one bank. The 1970 act further provided that the Fed Board, in its determination of whether a nonbanking activity is "closely related to banking or managing or controlling banks" must consider "whether the activities can be reasonably expected to produce benefits to the public, such as greater convenience, increased competition, or gains in efficiency, that outweigh possible adverse effects, such as underconcentration of resources, decreased or unfair competition, conflicts of interest, or unsound banking practices."

Nonbanking Activities

With the new guidelines for nonbanking set forth in law, bank holding companies began in early 1971 a mad rush to enter nonbanking fields "closely related to banking." Table 4–7 contains a listing of the status of bank holding company nonbanking activities. Every major bank holding company now has major nonbanking activities. For example, BankAmerica Corporation has sixteen nonbanking subsidiaries, including FinanceAmerica, a major consumer and commercial lending company with 382 offices throughout the United States and Canada; BA Mortgage and International Realty Corporation, with eleven offices around the country; and BA Cheque Corporation, which sells "World Money" Travelers Cheques at 30,000 outlets in more than 150 countries and territories. Obtain an annual report from a bank holding company and look at the extensive array of nonbanking activities.

What are the reasons that bank holding companies want to be in closely related nonbanking businesses? As bank earnings came under profit pressure from many sources, banks began to look for lucrative and diversified sources of revenue to offset rising costs. A finance company, a data processing company, a mortgage company, and/or a factoring company looked like made-to-order companions under the holding company umbrella. The prospect of economies of operation also was enticing, as in the areas of purchasing, personnel administration, advertising and public relations, and audit and examination, to name a few. Moreover, holding companies offered additional opportunities to raise funds in the money and capital markets for use in banking and nonbanking activities. For example, bank holding com-

Figure 4-2. BankAmerica Corporation's nonbank subsidiaries

panies may issue **commercial paper** (short-term promissory notes) to raise funds, whereas banks may not issue this form of debt.

Concluding observations. The bank holding company movement or revolution has created "financial department stores" around the country. The list of financial services is extensive. However, it must be pointed out that in the 1973–1975 recession and in the ensuing fallout, practically every bank holding company with a mortgage subsidiary and a finance company subsidiary sustained heavy loan losses. Bankers learned the hard way that nonbanking activities were a drag on holding company earnings. As Paul Nadler of Rutgers University has said many times, "bankers learned from the experience that it was not so bad to be just in the banking business."

Table 4–7

Status of Bank Holding Company Nonbanking Activities

Activities approved by the Board	*Activities denied by the Board*
1. Dealer in banker's acceptances	1. Equity funding (combined sale of mutual funds & insurance)
2. Mortgage banking	
3. Finance companies	2. Underwriting general life insurance
a. consumer	3. Real estate brokerage
b. sales	4. Land development
c. commercial	5. Real estate syndication
4. Credit card insurance	6. General management consulting
5. Factoring company	7. Property management
6. Industrial banking	8. Nonfull-payout leasing
7. Servicing loans	9. Commodity trading
8. Trust company	10. Issuance and sale of short-term debt obligations ("thrift notes")
9. Investment advising	
10. General economic information	11. Travel agency
11. Portfolio investment advice	12. Savings and loan associations
12. Full payout leasing	
a. personal property	
b. real property	
13. Community welfare investments	
14. Bookkeeping & data processing services	
15. Insurance agent or broker—credit extensions	*Activities pending before the Board*
	1. Armored car services
16. Underwriting credit life & credit accident & health insurance	2. Underwriting mortgage guarantee insurance
17. Courier service	3. Underwriting & dealing in U.S. Government and certain municipal securities
18. Management consulting to non-affiliate banks	
19. Issuance of travelers' checks	4. Underwriting the deductible part of bankers' blanket bond insurance (withdrawn)
20. Bullion broker	
21. Land escrow services	
22. Issuing money orders and variable denominated payment instruments	5. Management consulting to non-affiliated depository type financial institutions
23. U.S. savings bonds	

Source: Adapted from Dale S. Drum, "Nonbanking Activities of Bank Holding Companies," in Federal Reserve Bank of Chicago, *Economic Perspectives* (March/April 1977), p. 14.

Summary

The United States has a dual banking system because two levels of government—federal and state—charter banks. Banks that have federal charters are national banks that must be members of the Federal Reserve System and must have FDIC insurance. State banks may be members of the Fed; if so, they must be insured. A state, nonmember bank may or may not opt for FDIC insurance. The federal government has effective control over banking entry because of the inducement of FDIC insurance.

Banking concentration is high, with 9 percent of the banks holding 70 percent of the bank deposits. As more states swing toward permitting some form of branch banking, concentration ratios on a national and state level will continue to rise.

Virtually all bank merger applications must be approved by one of the three federal banking authorities. The biggest development in merger regulation within the last fifteen years has been the application of the antitrust laws.

The bank holding company movement has been the most important development in banking in modern times. As of the end of 1977, 72 percent of all bank deposits are controlled by bank holding companies. The list of approved nonbanking activities for bank holding companies is extensive. The typical large bank holding company has a finance company, a mortgage company, and a computer service company.

Questions and Problems

1. Define (a) national bank, (b) state bank, (c) member bank, and (d) insured bank.
2. What are the merits of having a dual banking system?
3. List and explain briefly the advantages and disadvantages of Fed membership.
4. Outline and describe briefly the Fed Board's proposal to encourage competitive equality and Fed membership.
5. List the federal criteria for the approval of a new bank.
6. Explain the rationale for the regulation of banking entry.
7. Discuss the pros and cons of the branch banking vs. unit banking issue.

8. In your opinion, what would be the pros and cons of interstate banking?
9. Outline the federal criteria for approval of a bank merger.
10. What is the rationale behind the one-bank holding company movement?

Suggestions for Additional Reading

Benston, George J. *Federal Reserve Membership: Consequences, Costs, Benefits and Alternatives.* Chicago: Association of Reserve City Bankers, 1978.

Board of Governors of the Federal Reserve System. *The Federal Reserve System, Purposes and Functions.* Washington, D.C.: Board of Governors of the Federal Reserve System, 1974.

Brown, William J. *The Dual Banking System in the United States.* Washington, D.C.: The American Bankers Association, 1968.

Drum, Dale S. "Nonbanking Activities of Bank Holding Companies." Federal Reserve Bank of Chicago, *Economic Perspectives* (March/April 1977), pp. 12–21.

———. "MBHC's: Evidence After Two Decades of Regulation." Federal Reserve Bank of Chicago, *Business Conditions* (December 1976), pp. 3–15.

Gallick, Edward C. "Bank Profitability and Bank Size." Federal Reserve Bank of Kansas City, *Monthly Review* (January 1976), pp. 11–16.

Gilbert, R. Alton. "Utilization of Federal Reserve Bank Services by Member Banks: Implications for the Costs and Benefits of Membership." Federal Reserve Bank of St. Louis, *Review* (August 1977), pp. 2–15.

Heggestad, Arnold A., and Mingo, John J. "Price, Nonprices, and Concentration in Commercial Banking." *Journal of Money, Credit, and Banking* (February 1976), pp. 107–117.

Kaminow, Ira. "The Case Against Uniform Reserves: A Loss of Perspective." Federal Reserve Bank of Philadelphia, *Business Review* (June 1974), pp. 16–21.

Knight, Robert E. "Comparative Burdens of Federal Reserve Member and Nonmember Banks." Federal Reserve Bank of Kansas City, *Economic Review* (March 1977), pp. 13–28.

Laporte, Anne Marie. "Competitive Equality and Federal Reserve Membership—The Board of Governors' Proposal." Federal Reserve Bank of Chicago, *Economic Perspectives* (July/August 1978), pp. 8–13.

Nadler, Paul S. *Commercial Banking in the Economy.* New York: Random House, 1979.

Rose, Sanford. "Bank Regulation: The Reforms We *Really* Need." *Fortune* (December 1977), pp. 123–134.

Salley, Charles D. "Banking Markets and Future Entry." Federal Reserve Bank of Atlanta, *Economic Review* (March 1975), pp. 30–35.

Scott, John Troy. "Public Policy Toward Competition in Banking." Federal Reserve Bank of Boston, *New England Economic Review* (July/August 1977), pp. 44–50.

Watson, Ronald D.; Leonard, Donald A.; and Behravesh, Nariman. *The Decision to Withdraw: A Study of Why Banks Leave the Federal Reserve System.* Research Paper No. 30. Philadelphia: Federal Reserve Bank of Philadelphia, 1977.

Sources of Bank Funds: Deposits, Capital, and Other Liabilities

In this chapter we focus on the liabilities side of a bank's balance sheet. Liabilities are the sources of bank funds. When a bank creates liabilities against itself, it simultaneously acquires assets (usually reserves), which increases the bank's ability to make loans or purchase securities. In recent years bankers have learned that bank profits depend just as much on liability management as they do on asset management.

The primary aims of this chapter are to (1) examine the nature and ownership of demand, time, and savings deposits, which are the principal bank liabilities, (2) discuss the forms and functions of bank capital, and (3) describe the major bank nondeposit liabilities, and (4) take a look at the FDIC and some of its activities.

The Bank Balance Sheet

Before we turn our attention to the liabilities side, let's take a quick look at the entire bank balance sheet. A condensed balance sheet for all insured commercial banks at the end of 1978 is shown in Table 5-1. As may be seen, deposits comprise 79 percent of all sources of funds. For the time being, do not worry about the nature of the other liabilities; just note that, individually, they are rather minor sources of funds.

Table 5-1

Assets and Liabilities of Insured Commercial Banks,
December 31, 1978 (billions of dollars)

	Amount	Percent of Total
Assets		
Cash and due from banks	$ 178	14%
Securities	278	22
Federal funds sold and securities purchased under agreements to resell	49	4
Loans, net	680	54
Fixed assets	20	2
Other assets	64	5
Total	$1,269	100%
Liabilities and Capital		
Demand deposits	$ 399	31%
Time and savings deposits	614	48
Federal funds purchased and securities sold under agreements to repurchase	91	7
Capital notes and debentures	6	1
Equity capital	87	7
Other liabilities	72	6
Total	$1,269	100%

Note: Details may not add due to rounding.

Source: FDIC, unpublished data.

On the assets side, loans are the major use of funds, making up 54 percent of the total. Securities, which are just another form of loans, comprise 22 percent of assets. Cash assets, mainly cash-in-vault, balances at the Fed, correspondent balances, and cash-items-in process-of-collection (checks) comprise only 14 percent of total uses of funds. Again, at this time do not worry about the other asset items.

Demand Deposits

Nature and Uses

Demand deposits are bookkeeping credits that a bank agrees to redeem without prior notice. Demand deposits are transferred from owner to owner by means of check. As seen in Table 5–1, at the end of

1978 there were $399 billion in demand deposits at insured banks. This total reflects the decisions of all bank deposit holders as to what percentage of all bank deposits (demand, time, and savings) and currency and coin they wish to hold in demand form. Demand deposits are the money form used to effect the vast majority of all financial and economic transactions. Demand deposits are created in the lending and investing process, when customers exchange currency and coin for demand deposits, or when a customer wishes to exchange time and savings deposits for demand deposits.

Ownership

There are four main groups of demand deposit holders: (1) businesses and persons, (2) governments, (3) domestic commercial and mutual savings banks, and (4) foreign governments and banks.

Business and personal deposits. Individuals, partnerships, and corporations (IPC) held about three-fourths of all demand deposits at the end of September, 1978 (Table 5–2). This was virtually identical to the percentage held in 1965. Moreover, recent Fed surveys have shown that businesses hold slightly more than half of all IPC demand deposits, while consumers hold about one-third of the total. Financial businesses such as finance companies, life insurance companies, and CUs account for slightly less than 10 percent of the total. Knowledge of the ownership composition of demand deposits is important for those studying the demand for money and to bank marketing officers who have responsibility for planning funds acquisition programs.

Also classified as business and personal deposits are certified and officer's checks, cashier's checks, letters of credit, and traveler's checks, all of which accounted for 3.9 percent of demand deposits. A **certified check** is a regular check drawn by a customer on his or her bank, which in turn, stamps it "certified" or "guaranteed." An **officer's check** or **cashier's check** is an order on the bank to pay on demand drawn by a bank officer. A **letter of credit** authorizes specified individuals to draw drafts on the bank payable on demand. A **traveler's check** is an engraved instrument that gives the holder the right to demand money at any time. Banks charge their customers a small fee for selling them any of these instruments. Of course, banks immediately deduct the amount of any of these obligations issued from the customer's account.

Table 5-2

Ownership of Demand Deposits in All Insured Commercial Banks,
December 31, 1965, and September 30, 1978 (millions of dollars)

Types of Deposits	December 31, 1965	% of Total	September 30, 1978	% of Total
Business and Personal Deposits				
Individuals, partner-ships and corporations	$139,078	75.7%	$279,651	75.8%
Certified and officer's checks, letters of credit, traveler's checks, etc.	5,932	3.2	14,253	3.9
Government Deposits				
US Government	5,524	3.0	7,942	2.2
States and subdivisions	14,242	7.7	17,122	4.6
Domestic Interbank Deposits				
US commercial banks	15,779	8.6	39,596	10.7
US mutual savings banks	860	0.5	1,282	0.3
Foreign Government and Bank Deposits, etc.				
Foreign governments, central banks, etc.	893	0.5	1,805	0.5
Foreign banks	1,529	0.8	7,379	2.0
Total demand deposits	$183,837	100.0%	$369,030	100.0%

Source: FDIC, *Annual Report* and Board of Governors of the Federal Reserve, *Federal Reserve Bulletin.*

Government deposits. The US government deposits represent funds held in **Treasury Tax and Loan (TT&L)** accounts. Virtually every bank in the country has qualified to have a TT&L account. Businesses may make their monthly or quarterly tax payments to a bank for credit to the TT&L account. Banks also may pay for Treasury securities by crediting the TT&L account. The Treasury makes daily and weekly "calls" on TT&L accounts to transfer funds to the Treasury's general account at a Federal Reserve bank. Calls are effected at the Fed simply by debiting the reserve account of the remitting bank and crediting the Treasury's general account. On September 30, 1978, TT&L deposits accounted for only 2.2 percent of all demand deposits.

On the other hand, states and their subdivisions held over two times more demand deposits than the Treasury. Of course, there are many state and local governmental units across the nation. Also, these governmental units tend to receive funds less frequently than the Treasury. Moreover, these governmental units do not have the ability to smooth their cash holdings with weekly sales of T-bills. Therefore, for these reasons, state and local government balances should be higher, and at the end of September, 1978, were the third most important source of demand deposits.

Domestic interbank deposits. The balances that commercial banks keep with each other comprise the second largest category of demand deposits. These interbank, or correspondent, balances represent implicit compensation for services performed, the main one of which is check collection. Other significant services performed include loan participations, currency and coin shipments, credit information, portfolio planning, and international banking. If Congress passes the Fed's membership proposal, look for correspondent balances to slip. Even without this reform, more and more correspondent banking services are coming under fee arrangements.

Foreign governments and banks. Foreign government demand deposits are relatively unimportant. However, note that between December, 1965, and September, 1978, foreign banks increased their demand deposits in US banks almost fivefold. Much of this increase represents reciprocal deposits. Whatever the reasons, this increase is indicative of the growth in foreign involvement with our economy and financial sector.

Time and Savings Deposits

Types and Uses

There are three kinds of time deposits: (1) savings deposits, (2) time deposits, open account, and (3) time certificates of deposit (CD).

Savings deposits. There is a long, technical definition of **savings deposits**, but essentially there are deposits evidenced by a passbook and held by individuals and nonprofit organizations. Profit-seeking businesses also may hold such deposits not to exceed $150,000. The bulk of these funds is held by individuals, and banks do not require a written notice of redemption. Most savings deposit holders consider these funds as "temporary abodes for purchasing power" that pay interest. Since November 1, 1978, banks have had the authority to transfer deposits from a customer's savings deposit to his or her demand accounts to cover checks as they are presented for payment. Under these **automatic transfer accounts**, a customer has a zero balance in his or her demand deposit and all funds are held in a savings account for which interest is earned until they are transferred to the demand account. Most plans have a small charge for each transfer, but the charge is waived if the customer keeps a minimum balance, such as $2,000. Automatic transfer accounts, in effect, convert a bank demand deposit account into a NOW account.

Time deposits, open account.   A **time deposit, open account (TDOA)** is a deposit, other than a CD, with a fixed maturity and a written contract which specifies that the depositor may not withdraw the funds prior to maturity without losing 90 days' interest and having all interest for the remainder revert to the rate payable on savings deposits. The 90-day, 6-month, and 1-year bank passbook plans that you see advertised extensively are TDOAs. Because of the longer maturity, interest rates are higher than on savings deposits. The "open account" part means that you may add to the account any time, but each individual deposit has its own maturity.

Profit-seeking businesses are not limited in the amount of funds that can be held in a TDOA. TDOA holders usually have a longer-run objective than do savings deposit holders. TDOA balances are held to meet "rainy day" needs, to finance specific consumption, such as a vacation or college tuition payments, or in lieu of stocks and bonds whose value is uncertain.

Time certificate of deposit.   A **time certificate of deposit (CD)** is a deposit evidenced by a negotiable or nonnegotiable instrument— on its face the certificate provides that the amount of each deposit is payable (1) on a certain date, specified on the certificate, but not less than 30 days after date of deposit; or (2) at the expiration of a specific period, again not less than 30 days after the date of the instrument; or (3) upon written notice to be given not less than 30 days before the date of repayment. In February, 1961, metropolitan New York banks began to promote negotiable CDs as a "creative response" to the efforts of corporate cash managers to pare demand balances to a minimum, and the banks' own need for funds to meet anticipated loan demand. At the end of 1960, negotiable CDs totaled slightly over $1 billion. At the end of 1977, there were $74 billion outstanding at the large banks that report their weekly balance sheet totals to the Fed. By January 31, 1979, this total had reached over $96 billion as the large banks had to bid aggressively for funds.

Negotiable CDs are denominated in amounts ranging from $100,000 to $10 million, with a $1 million face value as a standard trading unit. The principal holders of these large CDs are large corporations, state and local governments, foreign governments, central banks, official institutions, and wealthy individuals. The main advantage of CDs over T-bills is that the maturity date can be tailored to fit the special needs of the purchaser. Negotiable CDs are highly liquid because several securities dealers across the country offer a secondary market in these instruments.

Nonnegotiable CDs also have been developed extensively since the mid-1960s. These instruments are denominated in amounts ranging from $500 to $100,000, with $5,000 and $10,000 as typical face values. The principal purchasers of nonnegotiable CDs are individuals, small-to-medium-sized businesses, and state and local governments.

Commercial banks were authorized to offer **money market certificates (MMCs)** effective June 1, 1978. MMCs are a type of

Figure 5-1. A $500,000 CD

nonnegotiable CD with the maximum interest equal to the average discount rate at which 6-month T-bills were awarded in the most recent auction. Savings and loans and MSBs may offer MMCs at a rate of one-fourth percent higher than commercial banks if the 6-month T-bill rate is above 9 percent. The discount is the amount below par ($1,000). Thus, a T-bill with 182 days (six months) to maturity selling at a 7 percent discount could be purchased at a dollar discount of $353.89 per $10,000, or a price of $9,646.11. By permitting MMCs, the federal regulatory authorities wished to prevent **financial disintermediation**, the public's withdrawal of funds from financial institutions. This tends to occur especially during periods when rates on money market securities rise above rates payable at financial institutions. Financial disintermediation, of course, limits the institutions' ability to meet the credit needs of its customers. Initial public acceptance of MMCs appears to be great.

Ownership

Business and personal deposits. Between December, 1965, and September, 1978, business and personal deposits as a percentage of all bank time and savings deposits declined from 88.2 percent to 76.4 percent (Table 5–3). There was a significant shift in the composition of the total from savings to the "other IPC" category composed of TDOAs and CDs. The primary reason for this was the higher yields payable on TDOAs and CDs.

Government deposits. US government time and savings deposits are relatively unimportant. With unlimited borrowing potential, the Treasury has no need for precautionary balances. It adjusts its cash position basically through its weekly auction of T-bills. On the other hand, state and local governments are important holders of time and savings deposits, especially CDs. Local governments depend on revenue sources such as the property tax, which is collected once a year but more or less spent uniformly over the year. Hence, these governments have a need for interest-bearing deposits.

Domestic interbank deposits. Periodically, a small bank might buy a CD from another bank, usually its correspondent. It is a good short-term investment for a new bank until its loan portfolio is built up. However, on September 30, 1978, banks accounted for $8 billion, or 1.3 percent of all time and savings deposits.

Table 5-3

Ownership of Time and Savings Deposits
in All Insured Commercial Banks,
December 31, 1965, and September 30, 1978 (billions of dollars)

Ownership Classes of Deposits	December 31, 1965	% of Total	September 30, 1978	% of Total
Business and Personal Deposits				
Savings deposits	$ 92,555	62.7%	$218,947	37.0%
Deposits accumulated for payments of loans	1,078	0.7	79	a
Other IPC time deposits	36,562	24.8	292,120	49.4
Government Deposits				
US government	281	0.2	946	0.2
States and political sub-divisions	12,170	8.2	63,385	10.7
Domestic Interbank Deposits				
US commercial banks	510	0.3	7,961	1.3
US mutual savings banks	162	0.1	399	0.1
Foreign Government and Bank Deposits, etc.				
Foreign governments, central banks, etc.	4,086	2.8	6,672	1.1
Foreign banks	271	0.2	1,381	0.2
Total time deposits	$147,676	100.0%	$591,890	100.0%

aLess than 0.1 percent.

Note: Details may not add due to rounding.

Source: FDIC, *Annual Report* and Board of Governors of the Federal Reserve, *Federal Reserve Bulletin.*

Foreign governments and banks. On September 30, 1978, foreign governments, central banks, and official institutions held $6.7 billion in US bank time and savings deposits. This was only 1.1 percent of the total. These foreign holders hold these funds as official international reserves and in anticipation of buying Treasury bills and other debt

Table 5-4

Maximum Interest Rates on Commercial Time and Savings Deposits (percent per annum)

	In Effect March 31, 1979		Previous Maximum	
	Percent	Effective Date	Percent	Effective Date
Savings	5	7/1/73	4-1/2	1/21/70
Negotiable orders of withdrawal (NOW) accounts[a]	5	1/1/74	(f)	—
Money market time deposits of less than $100,000[b]	(e)	(e)	(e)	(e)
Other Time				
30–89 days:				
multiple-maturity	5	7/1/73	4-1/2	1/21/70
single-maturity			5	9/26/66
90 days to 1 year:				
multiple-maturity	5-1/2	7/1/73	5	7/20/66
single-maturity				9/26/66
1 to 2 years	6	7/1/73	5-1/2	1/21/70
2 to 2-1/2 years			5-3/4	1/21/70
2-1/2 to 4 years	6-1/2	7/1/73	5-3/4	1/21/70
4 to 6 years[c]	7-1/4	11/1/73	(e)	—
6 to 8 years[c]	7-1/2	12/23/74	7-1/4	11/1/73
8 years or more[c]	7-3/4	6/1/78	(g)	—
Issued to governmental units (all maturities)	8	6/1/78	7-3/4	12/23/74
Individual retirement accounts and Keogh H.R. 10 plans[d]	8	6/1/78	7-3/4	7/6/77

[a]For authorized states only, Federally insured commercial banks, savings and loans associations, cooperative banks, and mutual savings banks were first permitted to offer negotiable orders of withdrawal (NOW) accounts on Jan. 1, 1974. Authorization to issue NOW accounts was extended to similar institutions throughout New England on Feb. 27, 1976.

[b]Must have a maturity of exactly 26 weeks and a minimum denomination of $10,000, and must be nonnegotiable.

[c]$1,000 minimum except for deposits representing funds contributed to an Individual Retirement Account (IRA) or a Keogh (H.R. 10) Plan established pursuant to the Internal Revenue Code. The $1,000 minimum requirement was removed for such accounts in December, 1975, and November, 1976, respectively.

[d]Three-year minimum maturity.

[e]Commercial banks, savings and loan associations, and mutual savings banks were authorized to offer money market time deposits effective June 1, 1978. The ceiling rate for commercial banks is the discount rate on most recently issued six-month U.S. Treasury bills. The ceiling rate for savings and

issues. Foreign bank holdings of time and savings deposits are relatively unimportant.

Interest Paid

Congress first enacted legislation to regulate interest payments on bank deposits in the Banking Act of 1933. This act prohibited interest payments on demand deposits and required the Fed Board to limit interest paid on member bank time and savings deposits. The Fed Board's ceilings on time and savings deposits are set forth in its Regulation Q. Since 1936, the FDIC has set identical maximum rates for nonmember, insured banks. Table 5-4 contains the Regulation Q ceilings in effect on March 31, 1979. The Reg. Q ceilings have generated considerable debate in the industry and among the banking regulatory and academic economists. The principal argument for interest rate ceilings is that they prevent competitive rate increases among banks, thus reducing the need for banks to reach out for lower-quality but high-yielding assets. Also, it is alleged that interest-rate wars among banks lead to lower earnings, which limits the growth of bank capital.

On the other hand, interest rate ceilings limit a bank's ability to compete for funds when market rates rise above the ceilings. As mentioned earlier, this leads to disruptive financial disintermediation. Also, as a form of price fixing, the Reg. Q ceilings lead to a misallocation of financial resources toward those borrowers who look for funds primarily in the organized securities markets and not financial intermediaries.

In 1973, the Fed suspended the interest ceiling on CDs of $100,000 or more in order to enable banks to bid for funds and retard financial

---

loan associations and mutual savings banks is ¼ per cent higher than the rate for commercial banks when the six-month bill rate is 8-3/4 per cent or less. Thrift institutions may pay a maximum 9 per cent when the six-month bill rate is between 8-3/4 and 9 per cent. When the six-month bill rate is 9 per cent or more, the 1/4 point interest differential is removed.

[f]No separate account category.

[g]Between July 1, 1973, and October 31, 1973, there was no ceiling for certificates maturing in four years or more with minimum denominations of $1,000; however, the amount of such certificates that an institution could issue was limited to 5 per cent of its total time and savings deposits. Sales in excess of that amount, as well as certificates of less than $1,000 were limited to 6½ per cent ceiling on time deposits maturing in 2½ years or more.

Source: Board of Governors of the Federal Reserve, *Federal Reserve Bulletin.*

disintermediation. According to most economists, this was a step in the right direction. There have been numerous proposals to phase out the Reg. Q ceilings, and it seems certain that it is in the cards within the not-too-distant future.

The Changing Deposit Mix

As we have seen, during the last decade total time and savings deposits increased sharply in relation to demand deposits. Time and savings deposits rose from 44.6 percent of total deposits in December, 1965, to 61.6 percent of the total in September, 1978. The causes and implications of this shift in the deposit mix are explored in this section.

Causes

The principal cause of the shift toward time and savings deposits is the rising level of interest rates paid by banks. From 1936 to 1957, the maximum rate payable on bank savings deposits was 2.5 percent. From 1957 to 1962, the ceiling was 3 percent. During the Great Depression, banks were flush with funds, and the demand for credit was weak. From 1942 until 1951, the Fed pegged interest rates at low levels to create low financing costs for World War II debt and to prevent holders of the debt from possible losses if security prices began to decline. With the famous **Fed-Treasury Accord** of March, 1951, the Fed no longer had to peg interest rates. Since that time, except for periods associated with recessions, the secular trend in interest rates has been upward.

Another cause of the shift in deposit mix is the improved cash management of corporate treasurers. Rising interest rates increased the opportunity cost of holding demand deposits. Some of these cash management techniques were improved billing and bookkeeping systems brought about by the use of computers; lockbox arrangements whereby banks in different parts of the country served as depositories for locally due bills; and the wire transfer of funds whereby balances due in other parts of the country could be transferred immediately, without the delay normally accompanying check transfers. All of these techniques enabled corporate treasurers to reduce their cash balances and prompted the development of CDs.

Individuals also began to economize on demand deposits through the use of credit cards. These devices permitted individuals to shift funds into time and savings deposits.

Implications

A time-honored principle of finance is to match short-term liabilities with short-term assets and long-term liabilities with long term assets. Historically, most commercial bank liabilities were of a very short-run nature; that is, they were payable on demand. This is why banks, until recent years, primarily made only short-term loans. The large-scale shift in deposits from demand to time and savings deposits has had obvious implications for asset management. For example, with the lengthening of the deposit structure, banks have used this opportunity to make more term loans to business.[1] Whereas before, businesses looked to banks primarily for seasonal financing, they now consider banks a primary source of loans with maturities up to ten years and, in some cases, longer. Banks also have used the longer-term nature of their liabilities as a rationale for stepping up their mortgage-lending activities.

The shifting deposit mix also has had important implications for investment management. During the last decade, banks have added sharply to their holdings of municipal securities. Moreover, investment strategy with respect to Treasury securities has changed. Many banks now reach out and purchase higher-yielding Treasury notes and bonds, if investment analysis warrants the move. It should be pointed out, however, that banks have *had* to look for longer-term loans and investments in order to cover the higher interest rates on time deposits. The extension of the maturity of the asset portfolio has been partly out of necessity. As a result of the shifting deposit mix, banks now are more effective competitors with life insurance companies and other suppliers of long-term funds.

The FDIC and Deposit Insurance

Origin and Purpose

As a result of the wave of bank failures prior to and during the Great Depression, Congress provided, temporarily, for national deposit insurance in the Banking Act of 1933. A permanent plan of deposit insurance through the FDIC was put in operation on January 1, 1934. The initial amount of insurance provided was $2,500, but this coverage

1. *Term loans* are those with an original maturity of one year or longer.

was raised to $5,000 in mid-1934. Subsequently, the insurance maximum was increased to $10,000 in 1950, $15,000 in 1966, $20,000 in 1969, and $40,000 in 1974 ($100,000 for time and savings deposits of governmental units).

Contrary to popular belief, the FDIC insures depositors, not deposits. The purpose of deposit insurance is to indemnify depositors up to the maximum coverage, if a bank has to suspend its operations. Presently, a husband and wife can maintain separate accounts, and also a joint account in one bank and have deposit insurance on the three separate accounts totaling $120,000. This couple could maintain three separate accounts in any number of insured banks and receive similar coverage in each institution.

Monetary economist, Milton Friedman, has stated that "the most important monetary event after 1933 was the establishment of Federal insurance of bank deposits."[2] Because of the existence of the FDIC, depositors believe that their money is safe and secure. Actually, however, only 65.9 percent of the total bank deposits at the end of 1977 were covered by the $40,000 of insurance coverage, and the amount of the insurance fund ($8 billion) constituted only 1.15 percent

Figure 5-2. Depositors are insured for up to $40,000 by the FDIC

2. Milton Friedman, *A Program for Monetary Stability* (New York: Fordham University Press, 1959), p. 20.

of these insured deposits. The contribution of the FDIC is, therefore, largely psychological. Be that as it may, the existence of the FDIC reduces greatly the chance of massive bank runs like those that occurred in the Great Depression.

The cost of FDIC insurance coverage is nominal. The statutory annual premium is one-twelfth of 1 percent of total assessable deposits of each insured bank. Because deposit losses have been relatively small, the FDIC now credits each bank's current assessment with 66 2/3 percent of net assessment income (gross assessment income less administrative and operating expenses and net additions to reserve to provide for insurance losses). This credit reduced the net assessment rate to 1/26 of 1 percent in 1978.

FDIC Deposit-Insurance Activities

As the deposit-insurance agency, the FDIC, by law, has an active program of loss prevention. That is, it attempts to minimize deposit losses through its supervisory and examination functions. The FDIC, or the other regulatory agencies, conducts a regular examination of each insured bank. If, through ordinary supervision, examination, and consultation, the FDIC is unsuccessful in getting a bank to correct an unsafe or unsound banking practice or a violation of law or regulation, then it may initiate proceedings to terminate the bank's insured status. Before that happens, however, the bank is given a specified period of time in which to correct the irregularity.

In the case of an actual bank failure, the FDIC may either (1) pay off the depositors and attempt to liquidate the assets or (2) have a solvent bank assume all the liabilities and sound assets. The FDIC prefers the second method because it results in continued banking services at the existing locations, and it tends to minimize the FDIC's total payout since another bank exists to collect the loans outstanding. Between 1934 and 1978 the FDIC dealt with 548 bank failures, of which 304 were classified as payoff cases and 244 were assumption cases.

Bank Capital

Forms

Common stock, surplus, and undivided profits. The capital accounts at most banks consist of common stock (usually termed "capital stock"), surplus, and undivided profits. The sum in the **common stock account** is equal to the number of common shares outstanding times the par value of the stock. The **surplus account** reflects the sale of common stock at a premium over the par value. The **undivided profits** account is similar to the earned surplus account of nonbank businesses. As undivided profits accrue, funds may be shifted from this account to the surplus account.

Preferred stock. **Preferred stock** is a form of equity capital whereby the holder has a claim on earnings, dividends, and assets (in the event of liquidation) superior to that of common stockholders. Because many banks in financial difficulty during the Great Depression issued preferred stock to the Reconstruction Finance Corporation as a means of raising needed capital, a stigma was placed upon this form of bank equity capital. The issuance of preferred stock by banks was taken as a sign of weakness. In the late 1960s, however, a number of banks issued preferred stock (convertible and nonconvertible) in connection with mergers with other banks. A peak of $107.3 million was reached in 1970. Since then the amount of preferred

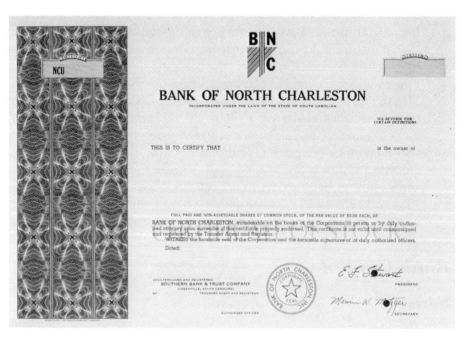

Figure 5-3. A bank stock certificate

stock outstanding has declined markedly, primarily because of exchanges of convertible preferred for common shares.

The principal advantage of preferred stock over alternative means of raising bank capital is that the former has no maturity and carries no voting privilege. On the other hand, dividends paid by the bank on preferred stock are nondeductible for income tax purposes, which makes the cost of capital from this source very high. Moreover, investors are not attracted to preferred stock since its appreciation potential is limited.

Capital notes and debentures. **Capital notes and debentures** are long-term obligations to repay money in the future. They carry fixed interest rates, and their claim for payments is subordinated to that of depositors and other creditors. Capital notes and debentures essentially are alike, differing only in their form, security, and issuing procedures. Banks can thank Comptroller of the Currency James J. Saxon for his ruling in late 1962 permitting national banks to issue convertible and nonconvertible debentures. Since this ruling, state banking authorities have given the green light for state banks to issue these instruments.

Capital notes and debentures may contribute in several ways to improved capital adequacy. First, because their claim is subordinated to that of depositors and other creditors, these instruments increase the issuing bank's ability to absorb losses. Second, capital notes and debentures have a fixed interest rate; hence, there is a possible positive leverage effect on equity capital if bank earnings increase.

Reserves for contingencies and other capital reserves. Also included in bank capital are **reserves for contingencies and other capital reserves**, which merely are funds set aside from undivided profits. An example of a contingency reserve is a reserve established because of a pending lawsuit. Funds tabbed for retirement of preferred stock are an example of a capital reserve.

Functions of Bank Capital

A primary function of bank capital is to demonstrate to the public and to the bank regulatory authorities a bank's ability to absorb unanticipated losses.[3] When a loan goes into default, the bank must

3. For a discussion of this function of bank capital, see Roland I. Robinson and Richard H. Pettway, *Policies for Optimum Bank Capital* (Chicago: Association of Reserve City Bankers, 1967), chap. 3.

remove the loan from the asset side and make a debit entry in the reserve account. If losses are large enough to eliminate the reserve for possible loan losses and undivided profits, the bank is in danger of becoming insolvent; that is, its claims on assets exceed its assets. Further losses would wipe out "permanent capital" in the form of surplus and common stock. Thus, larger capital accounts show the world that the bank could absorb larger losses, thereby affording greater protection to uninsured depositor funds.

A bank expects to have some losses in its loan portfolio. This is why it has a reserve for possible loan losses. But the unanticipated losses by their very nature cannot be planned for. The source of these losses might be a natural disaster, inept public policy, managerial lapses, or a very deep recession.

As a protective cushion, bank capital has a certain psychological value. If depositors and borrowers are convinced that a bank has adequate capital to weather economic storms, the former are less likely to initiate a bank run, and the latter may be more inclined to repay their obligations on time.

Bank capital also is a source of operating funds. When a bank sells common stock or capital notes and debentures it gains cash assets and the ability to acquire other assets.

A third function of bank capital is to measure shareholder claims on assets. At the end of 1978, shareholders had claim to only 7 percent of all insured bank assets.

Finally, an overlooked function of bank capital is to facilitate shareholder pressure toward managerial efficiency.[4] Unlike all CUs and MSBs, and some S&Ls and life insurance companies, all banks have shareholders. Because these investor-owners have a vested interest in banks becoming more profitable, perhaps of all classes of financial intermediaries, banks are under the greatest pressure to operate more efficiently.

Nondeposit Liabilities

The Concept of Liability Management

Traditionally, banks more or less have accepted their deposits and other liabilities as given and have concentrated on the management of

---

4. George R. Morrison and Richard T. Selden, *Time Deposit Growth and the Employment of Bank Funds* (Chicago: Association of Reserve City Bankers, 1965), p. 66.

assets in order to achieve certain objectives in terms of liquidity, safety, and income. In tight money periods, such as 1973–74, banks are faced simultaneously with a short supply of loanable funds and huge demands for credit, primarily from corporate borrowers. This dilemma forces the banks that want to accommodate the credit needs of many of their old and established customers to bid aggressively for deposits and to develop new sources of loanable funds. Beginning with the tight money period of 1966, the emphasis in bank management seemed to shift from asset management to **liability management**, which is simply the location and acquisition of adequate funds from sources with the lowest possible cost. In addition to the traditional sources of deposits and capital, many banks, in practicing liability management, acquire the funds to meet their customers' needs through various nondeposit liabilities including (1) federal funds purchased, (2) Eurodollar borrowings, (3) borrowing from Federal Reserve banks, (4) banker's acceptances outstanding, (5) commercial paper sold by a bank holding company, (6) loans sold outright or through participation repurchase agreements, and (7) sale-and-leaseback arrangements.

Liabilities

Federal funds purchased.   **Federal funds** are excess reserves that banks lend to each other, usually overnight. Prior to 1966, most banks that purchased federal funds were attempting to meet temporary reserve deficiencies. Perhaps the first sign that banks were practicing liability management was when a number of banks began to use the federal funds market as a continuing source of loanable funds. The primary sources of federal funds were banks located outside of the money market cities of New York, Chicago, and Boston. In 1974, during the peak of the tight money period, the bid price on federal funds reached 13 percent.

Eurodollar borrowings.   **Eurodollars** are dollar-denominated deposits held in banks located outside the United States. These deposits may be in foreign commercial banks or in the foreign branches of US commercial banks. The Eurodollar market centers in London, but other cities in Western Europe, Japan, and the Bahamas are included also. Eurodollars may be owned by US or foreign citizens, businesses, or governments. Eurodollars have two basic characterics: (1) they are short-term obligations to pay dollars and (2) they are liabilities of banking offices located outside the United States. These deposits may originate in several ways. First, foreign or US citizens may simply transfer dollars from a US bank to a foreign bank or to a branch of a US bank. Second, foreigners may receive checks drawn on US banks and deposit the funds in dollar accounts in their banks. Or, third,

NCNB
Confirmation and Advice
ORIGINAL

North Carolina National Bank
Funds Management Group
One NCNB Plaza
Charlotte, N.C. 28255

Bond Sales 704/374-5441
Money Market Sales 704/374-8751
Bond Operations 704/374-5230
Money Market Operations 704/374-5156

See Reverse Side For Additional Terms
Please Retain This Copy For Your Records

WE CONFIRM THE FOLLOWING PURCHASE FROM YOU 08/01/79 | Trade Date 08/01/79 | Reference No. 033917

Par Value	Rate	Maturity Date	Price	Yield	Basis	Settlement Date
10,000,000.00	9.5	08/02/1979	100.000		9.50	08/01/79

FEDERAL FUNDS
PRINCIPAL 10,000,000.00

Security Number	Salesman	Customer No.	Account No.
98 FFP033917	SOS	999995	900080179

99-9999999
ANY BANK
MAIN STREET
ANYWHERE, U S A 99999

Net Amount 10,000,000.00
Payment and Delivery Instructions
WE CHARGE CHECKING ACCOUNT

Figure 5-4a. Confirmation of Federal Funds Purchased

NCNB
Confirmation and Advice
ORIGINAL

North Carolina National Bank
Funds Management Group
One NCNB Plaza
Charlotte, N.C. 28255

Bond Sales 704/374-5441
Money Market Sales 704/374-8751
Bond Operations 704/374-5230
Money Market Operations 704/374-5156

See Reverse Side For Additional Terms
Please Retain This Copy For Your Records

WE CONFIRM THE FOLLOWING MATURITY 08/01/79 | Trade Date 08/01/79 | Reference No. 033917

Par Value	Rate	Maturity Date	Price	Yield	Basis	Settlement Date
10,000,000.00	9.5	08/02/1979	100.000		9.50	08/02/79

FEDERAL FUNDS
PRINCIPAL 10,000,000.00

INTEREST AMOUNT 2,638.89

Security Number	Salesman	Customer No.	Account No.
98 FFP033917	SOS	999995	900080179

99-9999999
ANY BANK
MAIN STREET
ANYWHERE, U S A 99999

Net Amount 10,002,638.89
Payment and Delivery Instructions
WE CREDIT CHECKING ACCOUNT

Figure 5-4b. Confirmation of Federal Funds Returned

foreign central banks and official institutions may place large dollar deposits in local banks in order to stabilize money market conditions. The maturity of Eurodollar deposits ranges from call to over one year, but the majority mature in three months or less.

US banks first began to borrow significant amounts of Eurodollars in 1966 when a sharp outflow of CDs occurred. As with federal funds, banks turned what ordinarily is a temporary source of liquidity into a source of long-term funds to meet loan demands. Between mid-1966 and mid-1969, Eurodollars obtained by US banks solely from their foreign branches increased from $2 billion to over $14 billion. Besides borrowing Eurodollars directly, US banks also sold loans and other assets to their branches and encouraged their customers to borrow directly from these branches or from foreign banks. At the end of 1978, the large weekly reporting banks had slightly more than $10.1 billion in Eurodollars borrowed from their foreign branches.

There are several reasons for the sharp growth in Eurodollar borrowings. First, Eurodollar deposits are not subject to Reg. Q ceilings. Second, these deposits are not subject to the FDIC insurance assessment or, until the summer of 1969, reserve requirements. The interest rate on three-month Eurodollar deposits climbed to over 13 percent during the tight money years of 1969 and 1974.

Borrowings from Federal Reserve Banks. Banks that are members of the Federal Reserve System enjoy the privilege of borrowing from their Federal Reserve bank. These banks get either direct advances secured by US Government obligations or discount loans to obtain funds to meet deposit withdrawals or the legitimate credit demands of their customers.

Acceptances. A **banker's acceptance** is a draft (written order) drawn by an individual or firm upon a bank ordering the bank to pay a sum of money on a specified date in the future. When the bank "accepts" the paper drawn by a customer, the bank guarantees to redeem the paper at maturity. Because of this guarantee, the paper is more marketable. In return for this service, the bank receives a small fee and a promise from the customer to provide the bank with funds to redeem the paper at maturity. The bank's books now show an asset (customer's liability on acceptances outstanding) and a liability (acceptance executed for customers). Banker's acceptances arise out of transactions involving the export or import of goods. Acceptances arising from these transactions are "eligible" to serve as collateral for loans at the Federal Reserve. Acceptances used for other types of loans are termed "ineligible" to serve as collateral at the discount window.[5] During 1969 and 1970, banks began to create more ineligible acceptances as a way to meet their customers' credit needs.

Commercial paper.   A bank may not sell commercial paper, but its holding company may. Proceeds from the sale of commercial paper by a bank holding company may be used to purchase loans from the bank's portfolio. The bank then has funds to make new loans. Bank-related affiliates, such as a finance or mortgage company, also may issue commercial paper to finance their activities. Effective September 17, 1970, the Fed Board of Governors placed a reserve requirement on bank-related commercial paper. At the close of February, 1979, there was over $16 billion in bank-related commercial paper outstanding.

Loans sold outright or participation repurchase agreements.   Another technique to acquire loanable funds is to sell loans outright or participation in pools of loans under repurchase agreements to other banks, corporate customers, and individuals.[6] Although it is an established practice to sell loans or to execute repurchase agreements with other banks, the new aspect of these transactions introduced in 1969 was to sell loans or participations to nonbank customers at rates and maturities not subject to Reg. Q. In 1969 the Fed Board moved to place repurchase agreements with the nonbank public under reserve requirements and Reg. Q. At the end of February, 1979, large weekly reporting banks had over $3.5 billion in loans sold outright.

Sale-and-leaseback arrangements.   Another technique to acquire loanable funds is for a bank to sell its bank buildings or equipment to a bank subsidiary or to an outside investor, who, in turn, would lease it to the bank. If the bank realizes more than the depreciated book value for the assets, this excess is credited directly to the common equity account.

---

5. Ineligible acceptances are often called "working capital acceptances" or "finance bills."

6. Under **repurchase agreements**, banks sell loans or securities under an agreement to repurchase them at a later date. These agreements usually have a maturity of two months to one year. Under such agreements loans or securities would be offered to holders at interest rates competitive with other money market rates. When a repurchase agreement is executed, the bank increases a liability account, "Loans Sold Under Repurchase Agreement," and it receives a corresponding increase in a cash or reserve account.

Summary

Deposits are the primary source of bank funds accounting for 79 percent of the total. Equity and debt capital represent 7 and 1 percent, respectively. Fed funds purchased and securities sold under purchase agreements account for 7 percent of total sources, while other liabilities supply 6 percent.

Within the deposit structure, the big story is the shift in funds from demand to time deposits caused by rising interest rates and improved corporate cash management techniques. This shift permits banks to reach for longer-term loans and investments.

Bank capital's basic function is to convince the public and regulatory authorities that the bank can absorb unanticipated losses. Whether it will or not is known for sure only after the fact. But the more, the better.

Nondeposit liabilities such as federal funds purchased, Eurodollar borrowings, and commercial paper sold by a bank holding company or an affiliated company are coming on strong as sources of funds. In 1969, the Fed moved to place reserve requirements on Eurodollar borrowing, but it has not imposed the Reg. Q ceiling on interest rates payable on these liabilities.

Questions and Problems

1. Define demand deposits.
2. Aside from the fact that they earn a small fee, why do banks like to sell traveler's checks?
3. Why do banks hold demand deposits with each other?
4. Why does virtually every bank seek to have a TT&L account?
5. Explain the nature of (a) savings deposits, (b) time deposits, open account, and (c) time certificates of deposit.
6. Why do states and political subdivisions hold a majority of their deposits in interest-bearing form?
7. Discuss the arguments for and against the Reg. Q ceilings.
8. Explain the causes and implications of the changing deposit mix.
9. How does the FDIC handle a bank failure?
10. List and explain briefly the functions of bank capital.
11. Explain the nature of the liability management concept for banks.

Suggestions for Additional Reading

Beebe, Jack. "A Perspective on Liability Management and Bank Risk." Federal Reserve Bank of San Francisco, *Economic Review* (Winter 1977), pp. 12–25.

Boehne, Edward G. "Coming: A New Phase for Regulation Q." Federal Reserve Bank of Philadelphia, *Business Review* (November/December 1978), pp. 3–11.

Higgins, Bryan. "Interest Payments on Demand Deposits: Historical Evolution and the Current Controversy." Federal Reserve Bank of Kansas City, *Economic Review* (July/August 1977), pp. 3–11.

Kasriel, Paul L. "New Six-Month Market Certificates—Explanations and Implications." Federal Reserve Bank of Chicago, *Economic Perspectives* (July/August 1978), pp. 3–7.

Morrison, George R., and Selden, Richard T. *Time Deposit Growth and the Employment of Bank Funds.* Chicago: Association of Reserve City Bankers, 1965.

Summers, Bruce J. "Bank Capital Adequacy: Perspectives and Prospects." Federal Reserve Bank of Richmond, *Economic Review* (July/August 1977), pp. 3–8.

Taggart, Robert A., Jr. "Regulatory Influences on Bank Capital." Federal Reserve Bank of Boston, *New England Economic Review* (September/October 1977), pp. 37–46.

Valerius, Jean L. "Liabilities That Banks Manage." Federal Reserve Bank of Chicago, *Business Conditions* (June 1975), pp. 3–9.

Watson, Ronald D. "Insuring Some Progress in the Bank Capital Hassle." Federal Reserve Bank of Philadelphia, *Business Review* (July/August 1974), pp. 3–18.

Wood, Oliver G., Jr. *Commercial Banking.* New York: D. Van Nostrand, 1978.

———, and Porter, Robert J. *Analysis of Bank Financial Statements.* New York: Van Nostrand Reinhold, 1979.

6

Uses of Bank Funds: Cash Assets, Investments, Loans, and Other Assets

In Chapter 5, we looked at the sources of bank funds—the liabilities side of the balance sheet. In this chapter, we will examine the uses of bank funds—the assets side of the balance sheet. Specifically, we shall (1) outline the banker's dilemma: liquidity versus profitability, (2) discuss the nature and importance of bank liquidity, (3) examine the nature and distribution of the major classes of bank assets, such as cash, federal funds sold and securities purchased under resale agreements, investments, loans, and other assets, (4) analyze the sources and uses of bank income, and (5) investigate bank profitability.

The Banker's Dilemma: Liquidity versus Profitability

When a bank makes an entry on the liabilities side of its balance sheet, it records a claim on assets or, in other words, a promise to pay money in the future. Most of those promises stipulate that payment will be made at the end of a certain period of time, as in the case of TDOAs and CDs. Banks, however, promise to redeem demand deposit liabilities on demand. Banks could prepare for the contingency that holders of demand deposits, currently due time deposits, and other liabilities might all request their funds at the same time by holding cash assets equal to 100 percent of these claims. Because cash assets yield a zero return, however, banks would have to charge demand depositors prohibitively high service fees in order to earn a sufficient income to pay expenses and a fair return on shareholders' capital. Obviously, this course of action would be implausible because other financial intermediaries offer alternative means for storing and transferring funds.

At the other extreme, in an effort to maximize income, banks could acquire only high-yielding, long-term assets and hope that the daily inflow of new funds would be greater than, or equal to, the daily requests for deposit redemption and loans. It is highly unlikely, of course, that the inflows and outflows of funds will always balance. Obviously, the best strategy for banks to follow lies somewhere between the two extremes of holding all cash or all relatively illiquid assets.

Banks strive to find the optimal balance between liquidity and profitability in the management of their assets and liabilities. In the ordering of priorities, however, meeting deposit and other liability claims clearly stands ahead of earning a profit. If depositors and other liability holders do not have confidence that banks can honor their promises, they simply will refuse to place funds in banks. The acquisition of deposits and other funds, of course, is a necessary condition for the expansion of loans and investments beyond the amount permitted by the use of capital only. Maintaining adequate liquidity is perhaps the most important constraint upon bank management's primary objective—maximizing profits.

Bank Liquidity

An **individual bank's liquidity** is its ability to meet deposit withdrawals, maturing liabilities, and legitimate loan requests without delay. A bank is considered "liquid" if it holds cash assets (cash-in-vault, balances at the Fed, or correspondent balances) equal to its expected liquidity demands. If it holds less than this amount of cash assets, it must have other assets (primarily federal funds sold and short-term securities) that can be exchanged for cash assets without delay and without undue loss of market value, or have the ability to acquire cash assets through creation of various liability management techniques described in the last chapter.

In estimating liquidity requirements, banks must analyze carefully the seasonal movements in deposits and credit demands. These **seasonal or short-term liquidity requirements** depend primarily on the market served by the bank. For example, banks in agricultural communities experience a deposit runoff in the spring, when supplies are purchased, and a deposit buildup in the fall, when crops are sold. **Cyclical or long-term liquidity requirements**, which stem from cyclical movements in the level of economic activity, are the most difficult to forecast. Cyclical liquidity needs are the greatest near the end of a business cycle when firms become hard-pressed for cash and also turn to their banks for loans to purchase supplies ahead of anticipated price increases, to make the quarterly income tax payment, or for many other needs. On the other hand, during recessions and periods of slow growth, cyclical liquidity demands are low primarily because corporate liquidity tends to improve, therefore lessening credit demands. Although forecasting short- and long-term liquidity needs is one of the toughest tasks in bank management, the chance of a nationwide liquidity panic like that experienced in the Great Depression virtually has been eliminated. A more enlightened Fed, the creation of the FDIC, more stringent bank examinations to improve asset quality, and the exit of thousands of undercapitalized banks are some of the reasons for increased public confidence in the banking system and the lessened chance of bank runs.

Cash Assets

There are four types of cash assets: (1) cash-in-vault, (2) cash-items-in-process-of-collection, (3) balances at the Fed, and (4) correspondent balances.

Cash-in-Vault

Banks hold cash-in-vault as an accommodation to their customers. Although the great majority of payments today are effected with checks and credit cards, currency and coin are needed for vending machines and small, day-to-day transactions. Banks replenish vault cash by requesting it from the Fed or correspondent banks. Because currency and coin are nonearning assets and a target of bank robbers and burglars, banks try not to have excess cash balances. Since 1960, vault cash has served as a legal reserve for member banks. The distribution of cash and other assets at insured banks on September 30, 1978, is shown in Table 6-1.

Cash-Items-in-Process-of-Collection

Each day, a bank receives deposits of checks and currency and coin. The checks deposited frequently are not payable at the bank where deposited but must be sent to the bank on which they are drawn for payment. These checks sent for payment are referred to as "cash items."

Checks drawn on other banks in the city where deposited ordinarily present no problem since they usually are collected through the local clearinghouse the same day they are deposited.[1] Checks drawn on out-of-town banks may be sent directly to the drawee bank or, more typically, to the Fed or correspondent bank for collection. Cash items sent to the Fed are credited to the individual bank's reserve account based on a predetermined schedule established by the Fed. Some cash items are credited immediately, but others are deferred from one to two days. Cash items sent to a correspondent bank for collection also usually are credited to the transmitting bank's account, based on the time it takes for the correspondent bank to receive credit, although some correspondent arrangements stipulate that an immediate credit will be granted to the remitting bank's account.

Since cash-items-in-process-of-collection represent a nonearning asset, banks attempt to use every means possible to speed their collection. Although cash items are subtracted from gross deposits for purposes of reserve computation, banks would prefer to have these items count as deposits and also have the corresponding credit in their reserve account.

Balances at Federal Reserve Banks

The Federal Reserve Act specifies that member banks must keep balances at a Federal Reserve bank or branch. Nonmember banks

1. It is a common practice for banks in a community to form a clearinghouse for the collection and payment of checks and other cash items originating locally. At a designated time, representatives of all banks in the area meet to exchange these items. Those banks with net clearing obligations usually pay by check on the Fed or correspondent bank.

Table 6-1

Distribution of Assets at Insured Commercial Banks
(September 30, 1978)

Asset Account	Amount (millions of dollars)	% of Total
Cash Assets		
Currency and coin	$ 12,135	%
Reserves with Federal Reserve banks	28,043	
Balances with domestic banks	45,752	
Balances with foreign banks	3,295	
Cash-items-in-process-of-collection	69,156	
Total	158,380	13.2
Federal Funds Sold and Securities *Purchased Under Resale Agreements*	41,258	3.4
Investments		
US Treasury	95,068	
Other US Government agencies	40,078	
States and political subdivisions	121,260	
Other securities	5,792	
Total	262,199	21.9
Loans		
Commercial and industrial	213,123	
Real estate	203,386	
Consumer		
Installment	131,571	
Single payment	30,027	
To . . . financial institutions	37,072	
To . . . security brokers and dealers	11,042	
To . . . farmers	28,054	
All other loans	21,640	
Total loans, gross	675,915	
less unearned income on loans	-17,019	
less reserves for loan losses	- 7,431	
Total loans, net	651,465	54.4
Fixed Assets	22,448	1.9
Other Assets	62,745	5.2
Total Assets	1,198,495	100.0

Source: Board of Governors of the Federal Reserve, *Federal Reserve Bulletin.*

have the privilege of maintaining a balance at the Fed for purposes of clearing checks. Banks use their reserve account much like an individual uses its demand deposit account. They may write checks on it, make deposits to it, and permit the Fed to debit the account in order to remit funds due other banks or the Treasury. The Fed also may make member banks loans by crediting funds to their reserve accounts. In recent years member banks have tended to hold approximately 25–30 percent of their total cash assets in the form of balances at Federal Reserve banks.

Balances in Correspondent Banks

Balances in correspondent banks represent an implicit payment for services performed. Large money market and regional banks are the principal institutions that solicit balances from other banks. Typically, small banks in the hinterland maintain accounts in several regional banks and an account in the closest national money center, such as New York, Chicago, or San Francisco. Large regional banks would tend to carry balances in most of the other regional centers within their geographic quadrant of the country and in all of the national money centers.[2] The most important service performed by correspondent banks is check clearing. The size of the correspondent balances held will depend largely on the volume of checks remitted for collection and the nature and frequency of other services performed, such as investment counseling, securities trading, and loan participations. During recent years, correspondent balances have come under closer scrutiny by all banks involved. The high opportunity cost of holding excess balances has caused most banks to trim to a minimum the balances held with their city correspondents. As a result, it is believed that most correspondent accounts are only marginally profitable to the holder. On September 30, 1978, demand interbank balances represented 28.9 percent of the total cash assets held by insured banks.

Federal Funds Sold and Securities Purchased Under Resale Agreements

In recent years banks have stepped up their activity in **federal funds**, which, as we saw in Chapter 5, are excess reserves that banks

---

2. Current correspondent relationships for banks are listed in *Polk's World Bank Directory* (Nashville, Tenn.: R.L. Polk and Co.).

lend to each other usually on an overnight basis.[3] For the lending bank, fed funds sold are a profitable, short-term use of funds. The rate earned is called the **federal funds rate**. In 1974, during the peak of the tight money period, as we noted, the bid price on fed funds reached 13 percent, and there have been isolated instances of banks receiving up to 21 percent on fed funds. For the purchasing bank, funds purchased represent an easy way to replenish temporarily deficient reserve balances. Large regional and money market banks, however, tend to stay in a net fed funds purchased position. Typically, these banks purchase large amounts of fed funds from small and medium-sized banks then sell part of the funds to other banks. Because regional and money market banks purchase more fed funds than they sell, they are financing some long-term assets such as loans with short-term obligations.

Securities purchased under resale agreements (repos) take place when a bank enters into an agreement with a securities dealer to purchase a given amount of obligations and to resell them to the dealer at a specified time and price. With this technique, the bank is guaranteed a fixed return, and the dealer acquires funds to make adjustments in his or her inventory or for other purposes. The importance of fed funds sold and repos is shown by their comprising 3.4 percent of total bank assets as of September 30, 1978.

Bank Investments

Objectives of the Investment Portfolio

Supplementary income. Banks usually have residual funds that may be invested in Treasury, agency, and state and local government obligations to provide supplementary income, except during the last phases of an economic expansion, when most banks have more loan requests than they can fulfill. Although funds allocated for investments tend to be residual in nature, the performance of the investment portfolio often is the difference between average and above-average profitability.

A bank's investments are limited by law to debt obligations. These securities yield income in the form of (1) interest and (2) capital gains,

---

3. The word "federal" stems from the fact that the funds are transferred on the books of the Fed. However, in recent years, the term "federal funds" has evolved to include excess reserves that are sold and transferred among commercial banks on the books of banks.

Figure 6-1. A bank trading room (*Courtesy of NCNB*)

which represent an appreciation of market price over the purchase price.[4] Debt obligations yield interest income from the date of purchase. Capital gains accrue either when the general level of market interest rates falls or when a security (other than a Treasury bill) approaches maturity and its price increases as some investors are willing to accept a lower yield in return for the more liquid asset. On the other hand, the level of market interest rates may rise, thus causing banks to have securities with losses in their portfolio. Some banks ignore these losses and hold their investments primarily for the interest income. Other banks, in addition to trying to earn a satisfactory interest income on their portfolio, seek to avoid such losses and attempt to realize capital gains by buying securities if there is an expectation of a fall in the market interest rate, or even by selling securities short if there is an expectation of a rise in money market rates.[5]

4. Treasury bills are purchased at a discount from par. The difference between the purchase price and the sale price of par, if held to maturity, is treated as ordinary interest income.

5. **Selling short** involves borrowing securities (usually from a dealer) and selling them with the intention of buying them back later at a lower price, whereupon the securities are then returned to the lender.

Supplementary liquidity.   The second objective of portfolio management is to provide supplementary liquidity. Although a liquidity manager attempts to forecast the bank's expected liquidity requirements over the next twelve months and the bank may hold secondary reserves equal to some percentage of these requirements, there always is the possibility that deposits will not grow as rapidly as planned or that loan demand will exceed the forecast. Moreover, something unforeseen, such as a hurricane, tornado, drought, or plant closing, might occur in the area, thus causing deposits to decline and loan repayments to be delayed. Obviously, such contingencies could play havoc with the best-laid liquidity plans. A bank confronted with abnormal liquidity demands may be forced to sell securities from its investment portfolio to supplement funds raised from the sale of secondary reserves and borrowing.

Bank Eligible Investments

There are three principal categories of bank investments: (1) US Treasury obligations, (2) US government agency obligations, and (3) obligations of states and political subdivisions.

US Treasury obligations.   There are three primary types of Treasury debt: (1) Treasury bills, (2) Treasury notes, and (3) Treasury bonds. There are four series of **Treasury bills:** (1) 3-month bills and (2) 6-month bills, which normally are auctioned every Monday for payment and delivery the following Thursday; (3) 12-month bills, which usually are sold at monthly auctions about one week before the end of each month; and (4) tax-anticipation bills (TABs), which are issued irregularly and have maturities that are one week after corporate tax-payment dates or may be redeemed for cash on the maturity date. Bills are issued at a discount; thus, the difference between the purchase price and the par value represents the interest earned.

Treasury notes are coupon issues that pay interest semiannually and have initial maturities ranging from one to ten years. **Treasury bonds** are coupon issues that pay interest semiannually and have initial maturities in excess of five years.

Safety of principal and interest is the most distinguishing characteristic of Treasury obligations. Investors know that the federal government never has repudiated or defaulted on its debt and that it can raise large sums to meet future interest payments through its vast powers of taxation.

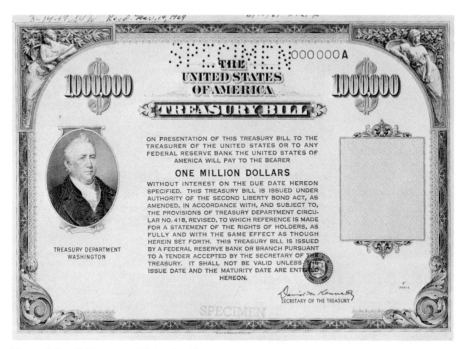

Figure 6–2. A Treasury bill for $1,000,000

Treasury obligations are readily marketable because thirty-five Federal Reserve-recognized primary government securities dealers, including the large money market banks, stand ready "to make a market" in this debt. Moreover, the market for Treasuries generally has the desirable characteristics of **breadth**, that is, there are many buyers and sellers in the market daily, and **depth**, that is, any significant price movements in either direction will attract sufficient buying or selling interest to keep the market relatively stable. Because of this breadth and depth, the maximum spread between the bid and asked prices typically is only one-eighth of a point (1 point = $10) on one to three-year maturities and one-fourth of a point on longer-term securities.[6]

On September 30, 1978, insured banks held $95 billion in Treasury obligations. This included short-term debt that can be converted quickly into cash and longer-term holdings that are considered part of the "permanent" investment portfolio.

6. The **bid price** is the highest price at which a security can be sold; the **asked price** is the lowest price at which the security can be purchased.

US Government agency obligations. In the financial markets, **agencies** are the obligations òf government-sponsored enterprises, federal agencies, and certain international institutions. **Government-sponsored enterprises** issuing securities include (1) the Bank for Cooperatives, (2) Federal Home Loan Banks, (3) Federal Intermediate Credit Banks, (4) Federal Land Banks, (5) the Federal National Mortgage Association (Fanny Mae),[7] (6) the Federal Home Loan Mortgage Corporation, (7) the Student Loan Marketing Association, and (8) the United States Postal Service. **Federal agencies** with outstanding obligations include (1) the Federal Housing Administration, (2) the Government National Mortgage Association (Ginnie Mae), (3) the District of Columbia Armory Board, (4) the Export-Import Bank of the United States, (5) the Farmers Home Administration, (6) the General Services Administration, (7) the Maritime Administration, (8) the Small Business Administration, (9) the Tennessee Valley Authority, (10) the Washington Metropolitan Area Transit Authority, and (11) the Department of Housing and Urban Development. International institutions that issue bank-eligible debt include (1) the International Bank for Reconstruction and Development (World Bank), (2) the Inter-American Development Bank, and (3) the Asian Development Bank.[8] Between 1965 and 1978 the outstanding obligations of government-sponsored enterprises and federal agencies increased from $8.9 to $132 billion.

Special mention should be made of the Federal Financing Bank (FFB), an instrumentality of the US Treasury established in May, 1974, to consolidate the financing of a variety of federal agencies and other borrowers whose obligations are guaranteed by the federal government. The FFB's objectives are to reduce the cost of borrowing and to smooth the flow of funds to governmental agencies. The FFB is authorized to borrow from the US Treasury and to borrow from the public by the issuance of obligations of the US government similar to Treasury obligations. To date, with the exception of one issue of eight-month bills, the FFB has financed itself by borrowing

---

7. The Bank for Cooperatives and the Federal Intermediate Credit Banks in December, 1968, and the Federal National Mortgage Association in December, 1968, converted to private ownership.

8. An excellent, concise description of each of these agencies is contained in the First Boston Corporation, *Handbook of Securities of the United States Government and Federal Agencies and Related Money Market Instruments,* 28th ed. (Boston: The First Boston Corporation, 1978).

from the US Treasury. Since its inception, the FFB has financed a number of agencies through loans and purchases of obligations.

Although agencies are not direct obligations of the Treasury, they do, in one way or another, involve federal sponsorship or guarantees. Thus agencies are considered virtually safe from default. Given the nature of the private enterprises that the government has kept from failing, it is difficult to imagine that it would permit one of its agencies to default. Agencies have initial maturities ranging from thirty days to over twenty years; however, the bulk of these obligations mature within five years, making them very attractive to banks.

Because agencies theoretically involve some slight credit risk and are not quite as marketable, they usually yield slightly more than Treasuries of comparable maturity. Interest income on agencies is subject to regular federal income taxes; however, with the exception of Fannie Mae and Ginnie Mae obligations issued since August 2, 1954, agencies are exempt from state and local income or property taxes.

On September 30, 1978, insured banks held over $40 billion in agency debt. As with Treasuries, short-term agencies are held primarily for liquidity purposes, while longer-term obligations are more or less permanent holdings.

Municipals. The term "municipals" encompasses all securities issued by states and their political subdivisions. Between 1965 and 1977, total state and local debt outstanding increased from $100 to $240 billion. Funds raised by the sale of these obligations are used to finance a myriad of capital projects, such as schools, roads, and hospitals, demanded by a growing and more affluent society.

There are two general types of municipal securities: (1) general obligation bonds (GOs) and (2) revenue bonds. GOs are backed by the taxing power and full faith and credit of the issuing governmental unit. **Revenue bonds** ordinarily are issued by public authorities, such as the Port of New York Authority, to erect public facilities, such as bridges, airports, and tunnels. The sources of funds to pay principal and interest generally depend on the nature of the project financed. Typical revenue sources include user charges on utilities, tolls, commissions, fees, special taxes, and rental payments.

Banks usually invest only in the four top grades of municipals as rated by Moody's or Standard and Poor's. Only the largest and most creditworthy municipals enjoy a national market. The great attraction of municipals is that their interest income is exempt from federal income taxes. In addition, most states exempt bonds issued within the state from property taxation and its own income taxes.

Between the end of 1965 and September 30, 1978, bank investment in municipals increased from $38 to $121 billion. Greater emphasis on municipals stems from the growth in time and savings deposits and attractive after-tax yields. Banks also use municipals to meet the collateral requirement for fiduciary, trust, and public funds. This is the requirement that banks pledge securities against these deposits for all amounts above that covered by the FDIC.

Bank Loans

General Considerations

After acquisition of adequate fixed assets and making provisions for required reserves and adequate liquidity, banks attempt to satisfy the legitimate loan demands in the communities or specialized credit markets that they serve. Excess funds are placed in Treasuries, agencies, or municipals. Loans rank ahead of investments in the allocation of assets because they generally have a higher yield, are an important determinant of deposit acquisition, and stimulate local economic development, which enhances the future growth of deposits and loans at the bank.

The size and composition of loan demand at an individual bank is determined by a number of factors. First, the location of the bank determines to a large extent who the borrowers will be. Large money market banks in New York deal with the corporate giants headquartered there. Similarly, regional banks in North Carolina have an above-average amount of loans to textile and furniture manufacturers. National economic conditions also are an important determinant of total loan demand. The demand for credit is related to the business cycle, but with a two-to-four-month lag. That is, loan demand peaks two to four months after the peak in the business cycle and picks up two to four months after the trough. Commercial loan demand, in particular, is responsive to changes in economic conditions.

Local economic conditions sometimes deviate from the national trend and, hence, affect both the quantity and composition of loan demand. For example, economic growth in the Sunbelt states generally has been faster than the national average. On the other hand, when the aerospace industry is in the doldrums, economic growth in the Pacific Northwest is slow and unemployment high.

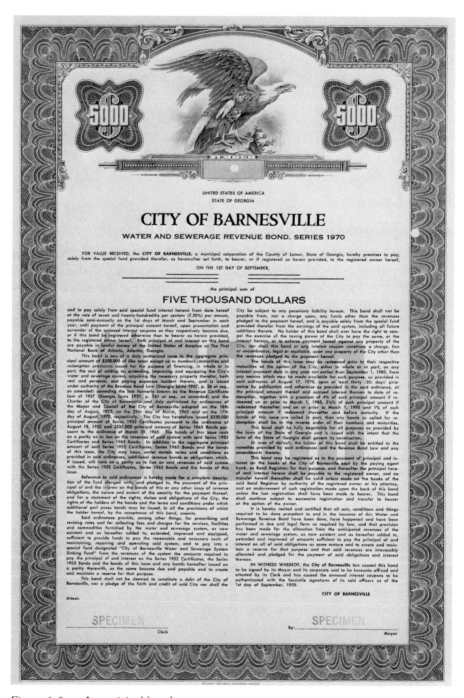

Figure 6-3a.   A municipal bond

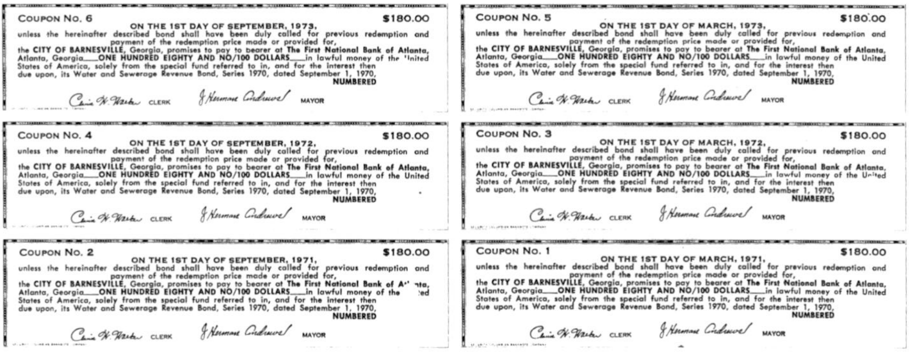
COUPON No. 6 $180.00
ON THE 1ST DAY OF SEPTEMBER, 1973,
unless the hereinafter described bond shall have been duly called for previous redemption and payment of the redemption price made or provided for,
the **CITY OF BARNESVILLE**, Georgia, promises to pay to bearer at **The First National Bank of Atlanta**, Atlanta, Georgia___**ONE HUNDRED EIGHTY AND NO/100 DOLLARS**___in lawful money of the United States of America, solely from the special fund referred to in, and for the interest then due upon, its Water and Sewerage Revenue Bond, Series 1970, dated September 1, 1970,
NUMBERED
CLERK MAYOR

COUPON No. 5 $180.00
ON THE 1ST DAY OF MARCH, 1973,
unless the hereinafter described bond shall have been duly called for previous redemption and payment of the redemption price made or provided for,
the **CITY OF BARNESVILLE**, Georgia, promises to pay to bearer at **The First National Bank of Atlanta**, Atlanta, Georgia___**ONE HUNDRED EIGHTY AND NO/100 DOLLARS**___in lawful money of the United States of America, solely from the special fund referred to in, and for the interest then due upon, its Water and Sewerage Revenue Bond, Series 1970, dated September 1, 1970,
NUMBERED
CLERK MAYOR

COUPON No. 4 $180.00
ON THE 1ST DAY OF SEPTEMBER, 1972,
unless the hereinafter described bond shall have been duly called for previous redemption and payment of the redemption price made or provided for,
the **CITY OF BARNESVILLE**, Georgia, promises to pay to bearer at **The First National Bank of Atlanta**, Atlanta, Georgia___**ONE HUNDRED EIGHTY AND NO/100 DOLLARS**___in lawful money of the United States of America, solely from the special fund referred to in, and for the interest then due upon, its Water and Sewerage Revenue Bond, Series 1970, dated September 1, 1970,
NUMBERED
CLERK MAYOR

COUPON No. 3 $180.00
ON THE 1ST DAY OF MARCH, 1972,
unless the hereinafter described bond shall have been duly called for previous redemption and payment of the redemption price made or provided for,
the **CITY OF BARNESVILLE**, Georgia, promises to pay to bearer at **The First National Bank of Atlanta**, Atlanta, Georgia___**ONE HUNDRED EIGHTY AND NO/100 DOLLARS**___in lawful money of the United States of America, solely from the special fund referred to in, and for the interest then due upon, its Water and Sewerage Revenue Bond, Series 1970, dated September 1, 1970,
NUMBERED
CLERK MAYOR

COUPON No. 2 $180.00
ON THE 1ST DAY OF SEPTEMBER, 1971,
unless the hereinafter described bond shall have been duly called for previous redemption and payment of the redemption price made or provided for,
the **CITY OF BARNESVILLE**, Georgia, promises to pay to bearer at **The First National Bank of Atlanta**, Atlanta, Georgia___**ONE HUNDRED EIGHTY AND NO/100 DOLLARS**___in lawful money of the United States of America, solely from the special fund referred to in, and for the interest then due upon, its Water and Sewerage Revenue Bond, Series 1970, dated September 1, 1970,
NUMBERED
CLERK MAYOR

COUPON No. 1 $180.00
ON THE 1ST DAY OF MARCH, 1971,
unless the hereinafter described bond shall have been duly called for previous redemption and payment of the redemption price made or provided for,
the **CITY OF BARNESVILLE**, Georgia, promises to pay to bearer at **The First National Bank of Atlanta**, Atlanta, Georgia___**ONE HUNDRED EIGHTY AND NO/100 DOLLARS**___in lawful money of the United States of America, solely from the special fund referred to in, and for the interest then due upon, its Water and Sewerage Revenue Bond, Series 1970, dated September 1, 1970,
NUMBERED
CLERK MAYOR

Figure 6–3b. Redemption coupons for a municipal bond

The direction of monetary and fiscal policy affects the demand for loans and the willingness of bankers to lend. If credit conditions are expected to tighten, corporate treasurers will attempt to borrow ahead of the time when credit availability may be lessened. Finally, in the age of multinational corporations and worldwide lending, general international economic conditions and those in specific countries have an important impact on loan demand.

Types of Bank Loans

Commercial and industrial. Commercial and industrial loans, that is, loans to businesses, comprised one-third of total bank loans on September 30, 1978. These loans may be classified either as **short-term loans**, those with an initial maturity of less than one year, or **term loans**, those with initial maturity of more than one year. At large weekly reporting banks, short-term loans comprised about half of outstanding commercial and industrial loans.

Prior to the Great Depression, bankers were proponents of the **commercial loan** or **productive credit theory** of bank lending.[9] This theory held that a bank should make only short-term, self-liquidating loans. By "short-term" bankers meant a period only long enough to allow, for example, a borrowing manufacturer to produce and sell his product, a retailer to buy and sell an inventory of goods, or a farmer to plant, harvest, and sell his crops. The term "self-liquidat-

9. In England, the counterpart of this theory was called the **real-bills doctrine**. A real bill simply is a promissory note or evidence of indebtedness that results from the production, movement, or distribution of real goods.

ing" meant that the loan itself generated the means for repayment. That is, with the loan proceeds, the borrower had the financial means to produce or acquire goods which, when sold, provided the funds to repay the loan. Bankers also believed that they should make only short-term, self-liquidating commercial loans in order to have a dependable source of liquidity. Because virtually all deposits were demand liabilities, bankers felt that they had to match short-term assets with these short-term obligations. Thus, the commercial loan theory was a theory of bank lending and a theory of bank liquidity. Since the notion of holding a separate category of readily marketable assets to meet liquidity needs did not originate until the 1930s, when the supply of short-term, high-quality securities (T-bills) became more readily available, the early bankers were correct to keep loan maturities short. Today, most bank loan officers will tell you that they always prefer lending short to lending long.

Why do businesses need short-term loans? Essentially, when the inflow of funds from cash sales and collection of receivables is not large enough to cover outlays for such items as inventory, operating expenses, debt payments, income taxes, and dividends without dipping into the minimum cash balance that the firm wishes to maintain, short-term loans are needed. These short-term or seasonal credit requirements are shown in the firm's **cash budget**, which summarizes expected inflows and outflows of cash usually on a month-to-month basis for the next twelve to twenty-four months. During those months when cash needs exceed cash inflow, the business requires short-term financing. On the other hand, when the firm has excess cash, these funds may be invested in money market instruments such as CDs, T-bills, commercial paper, or banker's acceptances.

Unsecured short-term loans to firms with superior credit ratings usually are called **working capital loans**. Loan proceeds are co-mingled with other funds and used for a variety of purposes. If the firm does not enjoy a superior credit rating, it probably will have to borrow on a secured basis for its working capital needs. If accounts receivable or inventory is used as security, the loan is called an **accounts receivable loan** or an **inventory loan**, as the case may be, even though the funds are co-mingled and used for many purposes.

Consumer.   Consumer loans encompass all loans to individuals to finance the purchase of goods and services. Over the last fifty years, consumer loans have provided an important stimulus to economic activity by helping to bridge the gap between production and consumption. Consumer credit has permitted and encouraged people to buy "big ticket" items, such as automobiles and consumer durables, and to pay for them later in convenient monthly installments out of earned income.

As shown in Table 6–1, on September 30, loans to individuals, both installment and single-payment, totaled over $162 billion and ranked as the second largest loan category. Bankers have not always been so enthusiastic about consumer lending. Prior to the Great Depression, bankers felt that consumer loans did not fall within the commercial loan theory of bank lending; consumer loans were "unproductive" and "undignified." These bankers failed to realize that by financing consumer expenditures, consumer loans would lead indirectly to greater production. Today, banks are the largest source of consumer credit.

Consumer loans are classified as installment or single payment. Automobile loans make up about 45 percent of bank consumer installment debt. Other major types of the debt include mobile home loans, home improvement loans, and credit card and bank check credit loans. Bank credit card loans have grown by leaps and bounds in recent years. Under this arrangement, a consumer purchases an item with his or her credit card. The merchant discounts the sales slip with the bank. The bank credits the merchant less the discount, which usually ranges from 1 to 4 percent and creates a loan for the purchaser. If the purchaser repays the loan within twenty-five days, there is no charge. If he or she pays after twenty-five days, the monthly interest charge typically ranges from $1-1\frac{1}{2}$ percent, depending on the state.

Single-payment consumer loans are for a variety of purposes. Single-payment credit is used to pay for consumer goods, personal taxes, life insurance premiums, and a myriad of other items.

Real estate loans. Although it is well known that commercial banks are the primary source of short-term credit, many people are unaware that these institutions allocate a significant portion of their funds for real estate loans. On September 30, 1978, real estate loans comprised 31 percent of outstanding bank loans. Residential loans made up 58 percent of all real estate loans; loans secured by commercial, industrial, and other nonfarm property comprised 26 percent of the total; while construction and land development accounted for 13 percent of total real estate loans.

After extolling the virtues of short-term lending, the obvious question is why are banks so heavily into real estate lending? The basic reasons that bankers offer are, first, the growth in time and savings deposits encouraged banks to match these long-term sources of funds with long-term assets, such as mortgage loans, term loans, and municipals. Second, mortgage loans offer a moderately good yield. In 1978 yields on new home loans averaged nearly 10 percent, and rates on bank loans to finance commercial and industrial property ranged from 10–15 percent. Another rationale for making real estate loans is that it offers banks the opportunity to obtain deposits and sell other services.

A word of warning is called for. The real estate loan portfolio of banks and their mortgage subsidiaries was the chief source of loan losses during the 1973–1975 recession and subsequent years. Several bank failures are attributed primarily to managerial ineptness in the real estate lending area. Bankers should not forget that most of their sources of funds are short-term, and this by itself is enough to dictate that the great majority of their assets must be short-term. If they feel that some real estate loans are necessary, then they must ensure that qualified loan officers make them and only after a clear evaluation of the risks.

Loans to financial institutions. This loan category includes those made to other domestic banks, banks in foreign countries, finance companies, S&Ls, life insurance companies, MSBs, real estate investment trusts (REITs), and mortgage companies. On September 30, 1978, loans to these institutions represented 6 percent of total bank loans. Loans to finance companies, life insurance companies, and other nonbank and nondepository institutions accounted for 44 percent of this loan classification.

Loans to farmers. Bank loans to farmers totaled $28 billion on September 30, 1978. Banks still are important sources of farm credit in spite of the many federal and specialized sources of farm credit. At many small rural banks, farm loans are the largest class of loans outstanding.

Other Assets

Within the "other assets" category are "fixed assets," which include buildings, furniture, and real estate. On September 30, 1978, banks had $22 billion invested in fixed assets. This represented less than 2 percent of total assets. Also included in other assets is $7 billion in **direct lease financing**, which involves the leasing of equipment such as airplanes, ships, and all types of equipment. Instead of lending the money to the customer to buy the equipment, the bank buys the equipment and leases it to the customer, who pays monthly or quarterly installments to the bank.

Bank Profitability

Table 6-2 contains the income statement for insured commercial banks in 1978. The principal source of bank income is the interest, fees, and similar charges levied against all assets classified as loans and discounts. In 1978 loan income accounted for two-thirds of total bank income. Income on US Treasury, agency, and municipal obligations comprised 11.2 percent of total income.

On the expense side, interest on CDs of $100,000 or more, deposits in foreign offices, and other deposits absorbed 44.2 percent of operating income. In 1965, these expenses took only 30 percent of operating income. "People costs" in the form of salaries and employee benefits absorbed 16.5 percent of operating income.

There are three primary measures of bank income: (1) income before income taxes and securities gains or losses, (2) income before securities gains or losses, and (3) net income. Income before income taxes and securities gains and losses divided by operating income yields the bank **gross profit margin**, which was 13.3 percent for the industry in 1978. Net income divided by operating income yields the bank **net profit margin**, which was 9.5 percent during the same year. In 1978, banks earned after taxes 12.3 percent on equity capital and 0.72 percent on assets. Many experts are worried that these yields are not high enough to attract needed capital to the banking industry in the years ahead.

Summary

The banker's dilemma involves the relative proportions of zero- and low-yielding liquid assets and high-yielding, less liquid assets that banks should hold. Bankers have an obligation to the claimholders who entrusted funds to them and to the shareholders who seek an adequate return. Bankers have no choice; they must satisfy both classes of constituents. Banks are able to hold a minimum amount of

Table 6-2

Income of Insured Commercial Banks in the United States, 1978

Income Item	Amount (millions of dollars)	Percent of Operating Income
Operating Income		
Interest and fees on loans	$ 76,090	67.1%
Interest on balances with banks	6,712	5.9
Income on federal funds sold and repos	3,677	3.2
Interest on US Treasury securities	4,720	4.2
Interest on agencies	1,878	1.7
Interest on municipals	6,032	5.3
Interest on other bonds, notes, and debentures	864	0.8
Dividends on stock	108	0.1
Income from direct lease financing	860	0.8
Income from fiduciary activities	2,135	1.9
Service charges on deposit accounts	2,045	1.6
Other service charges, commissions, and fees	2,930	2.6
Other income	5,398	4.8
Total Operating Income	113,449	100.0
Operating Expenses		
Salaries and employee benefits	18,728	16.5
Interest on CDs of $100,000 or more	11,722	10.3
Interest on deposits in foreign offices	14,558	12.8
Interest on other deposits	23,891	21.1
Expense of federal funds purchased and repos	7,250	6.4
Interest on other borrowed money	1,348	1.2
Interest on subordinated notes and debentures	448	0.4
Net occupancy expense	2,752	2.4
Furniture and equipment	1,815	1.6
Provision for possible loan losses	3,521	3.1
Other expenses	12,346	10.9
Total Operating Expenses	98,379	86.7
(A) Income before income taxes and securities gains or losses	15,069	13.3
Applicable income taxes	-4,156	3.7
(B) Income before securities gains or losses	10,913	9.6
Security gains or losses, net of taxes	-217	0.2
Extraordinary items, net of taxes	45	a
(C) Net Income	10,744	9.5

[a]Less than 0.1 percent.

Note: Details may not add due to rounding.

Source: FDIC, unpublished data.

liquid assets because the prospect of wholesale bank runs and liquidity panics was virtually eliminated with the creation of the FDIC. At the end of September 1978 banks held only 13.2 percent of their assets in cash form.

After adequate provision for liquidity, loans represent the most productive use of funds. On September 30, 1978 loans made up 54.4 percent of bank assets. Of this total, commercial loans and consumer loans comprised approximately one-third and one-fourth, respectively.

Residual funds are placed in municipals because of the tax-free income and Treasuries and agencies because of the safety aspect.

Contrary to popular opinion, banking is not a high-profit industry. In 1978, banks earned only 12.3 on equity capital and 0.72 on assets. During that year interest on deposits took 44.2 percent of operating income, while salaries and employee benefits equaled 16.5 percent of operating income. Banking profitability must be increased in order to attract needed capital in the years ahead.

Questions and Problems

1. Explain the banker's dilemma.
2. Distinguish between seasonal and cyclical liquidity requirements.
3. Why are the chances of a Great Depression type liquidity crisis not likely now?
4. Why should banks collect cash items as quickly as possible?
5. Discuss the objectives of a bank's investment portfolio.
6. List and explain briefly the general considerations affecting a bank's loan portfolio.
7. Explain the commercial loan theory of bank lending.
8. Distinguish between a bank's gross profit margin and its net profit margin.

Suggestions for Additional Reading

American Bankers Association. *The Role of Investments in Bank Asset Management.* Washington, D.C.: The American Bankers Association, 1974.

Banks, Lois. "The Market for Agency Securities." Federal Reserve Bank of New York, *Quarterly Review* (Spring 1978), pp. 7–21.

Baughn, William H., and Walker, Charls E., eds. *The Bankers' Handbook.* Homewood, Ill.: Dow Jones-Irwin, 1978.

Hayes, Douglas A. *Bank Lending Policies: Domestic and International,* 2nd ed. Ann Arbor, Mich.: Bureau of Business Research, University of Michigan, 1977.

Johnson, Rodney. "A Fresh Look at the Municipal Bond Market." Federal Reserve Bank of Philadelphia, *Business Review* (July/August 1976), pp. 11-22.

Laporte, Anne Marie. "ABC's of Figuring Interest." Federal Reserve Bank of Chicago, *Business Conditions* (September 1973), pp. 3-11.

McCurdy, Christopher J. "The Dealer Market for United States Government Securities." Federal Reserve Bank of New York, *Quarterly Review* (Winter 1977-1978), pp. 35-47.

McDonough, William R. "Large Banks Employ Flexible Maturity Structures." Federal Reserve Bank of Dallas, *Review* (February 1975), pp. 10-14.

Merris, Randall C. "Prime Rate Update." Federal Reserve Bank of Chicago, *Economic Perspectives* (May/June 1978), pp. 14-16.

Schweitzer, Stewart A. "Bank Loan Losses: A Fresh Perspective." Federal Reserve Bank of Philadelphia, *Business Review* (September 1975), pp. 18-29.

3

Central
Banking

7

Structure and Operation of the Federal Reserve System

This is the first of three chapters dealing with central banking. A **central bank** is a governmental institution charged with the responsibility for management of the money supply and regulation of the commercial banking system in order to achieve national economic goals such as full employment, stable prices, and satisfactory economic growth. Our central bank was established in 1913 and is called the Federal Reserve System or simply "The Fed" for short. The next two chapters describe "The Framework for Monetary Control" and "Instruments of Monetary Control."

In this chapter we shall (1) look at the problems that led to establishment of the Fed; (2) examine the structure of the Fed including the Board of Governors, the Federal Open Market Committee, Federal Reserve banks, and the Federal Advisory Council; (3) analyze the Fed's service, supervisory, and regulatory functions; and (4) discuss the issue of the Fed's independence from the executive branch of government.

Problems Leading to the Fed's Creation

In 1980, the Fed will be *only* sixty-seven years old. Some readers may think that anything over thirty is old, but the fact remains that the

149

Fed is a relatively young central bank when compared with the age of others around the world. The Bank of Sweden dates to 1656. The Bank of England, which was a model for some of the important features of the Fed, was created in 1694, while the Bank of France started in 1800.

George Washington took office in 1789. Why did the US wait 124 years before it got a central bank? Actually, the First BUS from 1791 to 1811 and the Second BUS from 1816 to 1836, in part, acted like central banks because some of their activities influenced the ability of the state banks to expand money and credit. For example, if the BUS wished for the state banks to expand credit, it expanded loans; this tended to increase the reserves of state banks, thereby enabling them to expand loans. If the BUS wished to restrain the state banks, it presented state bank notes to the state banks for redemption in specie (gold). This drained reserves from the state banks and reduced their money and credit-creating ability.

From the closing of the Second BUS in 1836 until the Civil War, populist ideas prevailed; there was no political support for a central bank. However, the practice of each bank issuing its own notes created chaos. In the everyday course of commerce, people had to shuffle through the bank notes and see if the bank listed on each note was still in business. Counterfeit notes were ubiquitous. However, Congress, through passage of the National Currency Act of 1863 and the National Banking Act of 1863, laid the groundwork for a uniform currency through the chartering of national banks by the Comptroller of the Currency. National banks had to pledge Treasury securities with the Comptroller in order to obtain uniform national bank notes to issue to the public in the lending process. To eliminate the state bank notes in circulation, Congress levied its famous "10 percent annual death tax" on any bank issuing state bank notes. Can you imagine the interest rates that state banks would have had to charge in order to pay the 10 percent tax, expenses, and earn a profit? As might be predicted, the 10 percent death tax provided the *coup de grâce* to state bank notes, and the nation began to enjoy the benefits of a uniform currency.

The provisions of the National Banking Acts encouraged banks to keep their reserves with banks in larger cities such as New York and Chicago. "City banks" benefited from these deposits because they gave them the resources to expand loans and investments. "Country banks" could draw on these funds to meet the credit needs of their customers, primarily farmers. During ordinary times, city banks were liquid enough to meet the country banks' withdrawal demands, which usually came in the spring as farmers borrowed to finance production. However, if credit demands were high and city banks were heavily involved in meeting the demands of their own customers, the city banks had extreme difficulty redeeming the claims of the country banks. The stress and strain created by the situation produced what were called "money panics," which is just another name for a liquidity crisis or a "credit crunch" like that experienced in 1966, 1970, and 1974. We had money panics in 1866, 1873, 1884, 1893, and 1907. Following the Panic of 1907, Congress decided it was time to do something, so it created the National Monetary Commission, whose task was to make a thorough study of our entire banking and monetary situation. The commission conducted lengthy hearings and a large number of special studies. Finally, in 1912, even before the commission had finished its work, a bill was introduced in Congress to establish a central bank. After much debate and a lot of compromise, Congress passed the Federal Reserve Act, and President Woodrow Wilson signed it into law on December 23, 1913.

Figure 7-1. Federal Reserve building in Washington, D.C.

Structure of the Federal Reserve System

Our central bank is not one building in one location. The Federal Reserve System consists of (1) the Board of Governors, (2) the Federal Open Market Committee, (3) the twelve Federal Reserve banks and their branches, and (4) the Federal Advisory Council. The interrelationship among these elements is shown in Figure 7–2.

Board of Governors

At the top of our central banking structure is the Board of Governors in Washington. The Board consists of seven members, who are appointed by the President of the United States and confirmed by the Senate. Members are appointed for fourteen-year terms, and terms are arranged so that one expires every two years. This is to preclude presidents from stacking the Board primarily with people of their political and economic philosophy. Members may not be reappointed, but if a member is appointed to fill the remaining term of a previous member, he then may be appointed to a full fourteen-year term. The president names the chairman and vice-chairman from among the Board members for four-year terms, and they may be redesignated.

The Board's primary function involves the formulation of monetary policy. It also has broad supervisory and regulatory responsibilities over the activities of commercial banks and the operations of the Federal Reserve banks. Here is a list of the Board's ten most important functions:

1. Overall supervision of the Federal Reserve banks.
2. Sit on the Federal Open Market Committee.
3. Set reserve requirements.
4. Approve changes in the discount rate.
5. Set margin requirements.
6. Set maximum interest rates that banks can pay on time and savings deposits.
7. Regulate bank mergers where the surviving bank is a state member bank.
8. Regulate bank holding company activities.

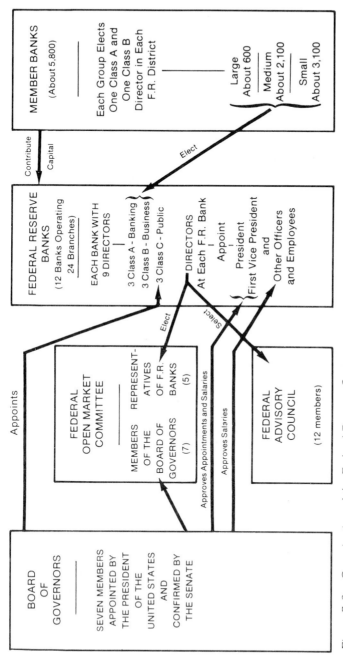

Figure 7–2. Organization of the Federal Reserve System

Source: Board of Governors of the Federal Reserve, *The Federal Reserve System: Purposes and Functions* (Washington, D.C., 1974).

9.   Supervise member bank international operations.

10.   Administer consumer protection legislation.

We will have more to say about these functions in this and later chapters.

Federal Open Market Committee

The Federal Open Market Committee (FOMC) determines policy with respect to **open market operations**, which is the buying and selling of securities by the Fed for its own account. Open market operations are the most powerful technique of monetary control because it affects commercial bank reserve positions, which are a primary determinant of the banking system's ability to create money and credit.

The FOMC is composed of the seven members of the Fed Board, the president of the Federal Reserve Bank of New York, and one Reserve bank president chosen annually from each of the following groups of Reserve banks:

1.   Boston, Philadelphia, and Richmond
2.   Cleveland and Chicago
3.   Atlanta, Dallas, and St. Louis
4.   Minneapolis, Kansas City, and San Francisco

The president of the New York Fed is a permanent member of the committee because open market operations are conducted out of that bank. By tradition, the FOMC has elected the chairman of the Fed Board as its chairman and the president of the New York Fed as vice-chairman. The committee meets in the Board's office in Washington every four to five weeks. We will have more to say in the next chapter about open market operations as a policy instrument.

Federal Reserve Banks

The Federal Reserve System's operations are conducted from twelve Federal Reserve banks located throughout the country. In addition, these banks have twenty-five branches and a number of facilities primarily to assist in clearing checks. The boundaries of the twelve Federal Reserve districts and locations of the various banks and branches are shown in Figure 7–3.

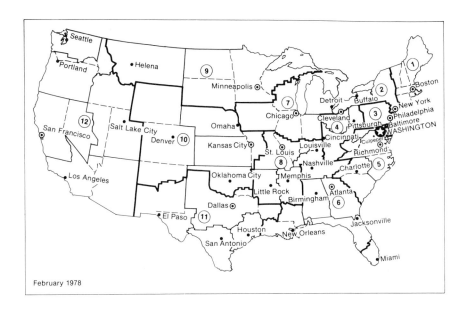

February 1978

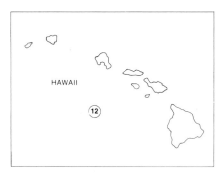 

LEGEND

▬ Boundaries of Federal Reserve Districts	⊙	Federal Reserve Bank Cities
─ Boundaries of Federal Reserve Branch Territories	•	Federal Reserve Branch Cities
★ Board of Governors of the Federal Reserve System	·	Federal Reserve Bank Facility

Figure 7-3.   Boundaries of the Federal Reserve districts and their branch territories

Source: Board of Governors of the Federal Reserve, *Federal Reserve Bulletin.*

At this point it is appropriate to ask, Why do we have the regional system of Reserve banks? There are both political and economic reasons for it. First, as hinted earlier, there was a great deal of controversy surrounding the creation of the central bank. Fearing Eastern control of the Fed, many senators from the West and South were skeptical of the new bank. To obtain the necessary support for passage of the Federal Reserve Act, senators in the outlying areas were promised that a Reserve bank would be placed "in their area." A second rationale for the regional system stemmed from the economic diversity of the various sections of the country. The North was industrial; the South was agricultural, while the West was developing rapidly. Accordingly, the character of the banks in each region differed. Therefore, it was reasonable to expect that a Reserve bank in various regions would be closely attuned to special problems indigenous to the region. Moreover, a dispersion of Reserve banks would facilitate check clearing. Today, it is generally agreed that the regional Federal Reserve bank concept has served us well.

Each Reserve bank has nine directors; they are divided into three classes of three directors each. Class A directors represent the banking industry; Class B directors come from agriculture, commerce, and industry. Class A and B directors are elected by the member banks in the district. The Fed Board appoints Class C directors, and it designates one of the three as chairman and another as deputy chairman of the bank's board. No Class B or C director may be an officer, director, or employee of a bank; in addition, Class C directors are prohibited from being shareholders of a bank. The term of office of all directors is three years. Large banks do not dominate the director election process because member banks are grouped into large, medium, and small banks with each group electing one A and one B director.

Reserve bank directors perform several functions including overall supervision of their bank's operation. They set or affirm the discount rate on short-term collateral loans to member banks and on any loans that may be extended to nonmember institutions. Also, the directors appoint and recommend the salaries of the bank's president and first vice-president. All director actions are subject to the Fed Board's approval.

The Reserve banks earn income primarily from the interest on the Fed's holdings of securities. A secondary source is the income received from discounts and advances made to member banks. Uses of the earnings include payment of expenses (including an assessment by the Fed Board to defray its expenses), the statutory 6 percent dividend on Federal Reserve bank stock, and any additions to the Fed's surplus. The remainder is returned to the Treasury and called "interest on Federal Reserve notes outstanding." Since 1914 more than 80 percent of the Fed's earnings have been returned to the Treasury.

Federal Advisory Council

The Federal Advisory Council consists of one prominent banker from each district. The Council meets quarterly in Washington and confers and advises with the Fed Board on economic and banking matters.

Service Functions of the Fed

Provide Currency

The Fed performs a vital service by accommodating the currency needs of the public. As we have seen, Federal Reserve notes represent

Figure 7–4. Meeting of the Board of Governors of the Federal Reserve Board in April, 1979 (*Courtesy of the Federal Reserve Board*)

about 90 percent of all currency in circulation. In addition, the Treasury issues coins to the Reserve banks, which, in turn, issue them to requesting banks. Mutilated and worn currency is returned to the Reserve banks for destruction. In 1977, exclusive of the currency itself, it cost the Fed $183 million to provide the currency function. This was 27 percent of the total Fed expenses. The importance of providing currency should not be underestimated. The Fed has overall responsibility for control of the total money supply. However, the public determines the composition of the money supply to be held, and the Fed stands ready to accommodate this demand either by issuing more currency or by accepting excess currency from the public. The use of currency and coin is a cumbersome and dangerous way of effecting payments. But if the public wants to use currency and hold currency as a store of value, it is the Fed's job to see that an adequate supply is available. If the public has confidence that it can exchange deposits for currency, this tends to quell any innate fears about money and banks in general.

Collection of Checks

One of the mandates of the Federal Reserve Act was that the new central bank establish a national system for check clearing. Prior to this time, it frequently took two weeks or longer for a check to clear. Today, a bank that clears a check through the Fed receives credit for it within two days. In 1977 the Reserve banks processed 13 billion checks, with a total value of $43 trillion. During that year it cost $247 million, or 36 percent of all Fed expenses, to provide check-clearing services for the banking system and public. Between 1974 and 1977 the volume of checks cleared through the Fed increased 23 percent, but the number of employees involved with the service declined from 7,500 to 6,500, which indicates that the Fed has been successful in substituting labor-saving capital equipment for labor in the labor-intensive function of check clearing.

How are checks cleared? After a check is written, there are three possible routes that it can take back to the bank on which it was drawn. First, it could be deposited or cashed at the same bank on which it was drawn. If deposited, the bank credits the account of the depositor and debits the account of the writer. If cashed, the bank gives out coins and currency and debits the account of the writer. At the end of the month, the bank sends him or her the canceled check and a statement.

The second possibility is that the check will be presented to another bank in the same town. In this case, the receiving bank credits the depositor's account or counts out cash; then the bank usually takes the check to the local **clearinghouse**, the meeting place, such as a bank or local Fed clearing center, where area banks meet to exchange checks drawn on each other. A bank that has more checks drawn on it than it brings for collection pays the net difference by a transfer from its reserve balance on the books of the Fed or a check on another commercial bank.

The third possible disposition of the check is that it will be deposited in a different bank in a different city. In this situation the receiving bank could (1) present it directly to the drawee bank, (2) send it to a correspondent bank, or (3) send it to the Reserve bank or branch. We know what happens in situation (1). In situation (2), typically, a correspondent bank receiving the check would credit the deposit account of the sending bank and send the check to the Reserve bank or branch for credit to the correspondent's reserve account. The Fed then would reduce the drawee bank's reserve account and send the check to the drawee bank, which, in turn, reduces the writer's demand deposit.

In situation (3), if the check is sent directly to the Reserve bank or branch, the Fed simply increases the reserve balance of the sending bank, reduces the reserve balance of the drawee bank, and forwards the check to the drawee bank. If the drawee bank is in another Federal Reserve district, the local Reserve bank receiving the check still credits the reserve account of the sending bank, but the local Reserve bank then airmails the check to the Reserve bank nearest the sending bank. This Reserve bank reduces the reserve account of the drawee bank and forwards the check to the drawee bank. This Reserve bank owes the sending Reserve bank for the check. If this claim is not fully offset by counterclaims, the net balance is settled by a bookkeeping entry in the **Interdistrict Settlement Fund** maintained by the Board of Governors in Washington. Each Reserve bank maintains a credit balance in the fund; at the end of each day, any net balance due a Reserve bank is added to the account and any net amount owed to another Reserve bank is deducted from the account.

Over the years, the Fed's check-clearing service has allowed our payments system to function effectively and, thereby, facilitate economic growth and development. Without an efficient check-clearing system, the US could not have achieved a GNP of $2.5 trillion. An efficient check-clearing and payments system frees human resources to concentrate on innovative and more essential pursuits that expand the GNP.

Wire Transfers

The Reserve banks and their branches have a system of interconnected computers that permits banks and customers anywhere in the country to "wire" funds to other banks in the country. The word "wire" stems from the wire telegraphic system that existed prior to the early 1970s. Suppose that a firm in New York owed $500,000 to a firm in Dallas due today. The New York firm hands, say, Morgan Guaranty a check for that amount. Morgan then wires the funds to the Dallas Fed and requests that it transfer the funds to the Dallas firm by way of, say, Republic National Bank in Dallas. The New York Fed deducts the funds from Morgan's reserve balance, while the Dallas Fed adds the amount to Republic's reserve balance. The New York Fed settles with the Dallas Fed through the Interdistrict Settlement Fund. The New York firm benefits because it discharged its obligation on time, while the Dallas firm gains through instant use of the money. The Fed encourages the use of wire transfers because they reduce paperwork, labor, and postage costs.

In addition to money, the Fed also uses its computer facilities to transfer marketable Treasury and certain agency securities and make interest payments on this debt. As these obligations are in bearer form, there is considerable risk in physical transfer. The Fed and the Treasury have worked out a system by which ownership in the above securities is recorded on the Fed's books and transfers are made through the computer network. Suppose that Union Bank in Los Angeles wishes to sell $5 million of Treasury notes to First National Bank in Boston. The Los Angeles Fed branch retires the notes on its books, credits Union Bank's reserve account, and wires the Boston Fed to issue a like amount of Treasury notes with the same coupon rate and maturity to First National Bank. The Boston Fed reduces First National's reserve balance and settles the reserve transfer through the Interdistrict Settlement Fund.

Fiscal Agent for the Government

The Fed also serves as the fiscal agent for the Treasury and various federal agencies. Under the fiscal agency function, the Fed holds the Treasury's checking account, receives applications from the public for securities being offered, allots the obligations among the bidders, delivers the securities, collects payment from the buyers, redeems securities, transfers securities through its computer network, pays interest coupons when presented, and, as discussed earlier, automatically credits interest on that debt held on its books. The Treasury reimburses the Fed for most of these services. In 1977, the Fed's gross cost of performing the fiscal agency function was $73 million, or 11 percent of its total expenses. The Fed had 2,000 employees involved with the fiscal agency function.

Supervisory and Regulatory Functions

In earlier chapters we have touched on the Fed's supervisory and regulatory functions, and we will have more to say about them later. However, in this chapter dealing specifically with the Fed, it would be useful to list and describe briefly the Fed's major supervisory and regulatory roles.

Bank Supervision

The Fed has statutory authority to supervise and examine member banks. However, through agreement, the Comptroller of the Currency has primary responsibility for supervision and examination of national banks, which comprise 82 percent of all member banks. The Comptroller keeps the Fed informed of the condition of these banks. This leaves the Fed with primary supervision over 995 state member banks. The Board of Governors delegates certain supervisory and regulatory functions to the district Reserve banks. Two major functions include examinations and approval of branch applications.

Merger and Holding Company Responsibilities

As explained in Chapter 4, the Board of Governors has responsibility for approval of bank mergers where the surviving bank is a state member bank. The Board also must render an opinion on the competitive factor in all other bank mergers not within its jurisdiction.

The Board has responsibility under the Bank Holding Company Act of 1956 for regulation of bank holding companies and their nonbanking activities. As stated earlier, the bank holding company movement has been the most important banking development in modern times. Nearly three-fourths of all bank deposits are held by banking subsidiaries of holding companies. Moreover, holding companies have branched into many nonbanking pursuits. The Fed Board has responsibility for the determination of which nonbanking activities are permissible and for the approval of each holding company's request to engage in these activities. Needless to say, in the 1970s, the rush to form holding companies and move into nonbanking activities has kept the Board staff busy.

International Banking Responsibilities

The Fed Board has three statutory responsibilities in the supervision and regulation of the international operations of member banks. These relate to (1) issuing licenses for foreign branches and regulating the scope of these activities, (2) chartering and regulation of **Edge Act corporations**, which are the international subsidiaries of member banks, and (3) authorizing overseas investments by banks, Edge Act corporations, and bank holding companies, and regulating activities of foreign subsidiaries.

In recent years, the foreign activities of member banks have expanded dramatically. At the end of 1977, member banks had 738 branches in 84 foreign countries and overseas areas. In addition, there were 116 Edge Act corporations in operation. More than one-third of the deposits of the twenty largest banks were held in foreign offices. Foreign operations contribute over half of the profit of several bank holding companies. With this degree of overseas involvement, the Fed Board has a great regulatory and supervisory responsibility to protect banking assets, and hence, depositors in these institutions.

Consumer Protection

The Consumer Credit Protection Act, which passed in 1968, has been the basis for more than a dozen laws and amendments designed by Congress to help the consumer. Below is a list of the principal consumer credit laws:

Act	Enacted
Truth in Lending	1968
Fair Credit Billing	1974
Equal Credit Opportunity	1974
Amendments to Truth in Lending	1974
Real Estate Settlement Procedures	1974
Federal Trade Commission Improvement	1975
Home Mortgage Disclosure	1976
Consumer Leasing	1976
Amendments to Equal Credit Opportunity	1976
Community Reinvestment	1977

It would take the rest of this book to enumerate these laws and all the "thou shalts" and "thou shalt nots." Essentially, these laws are designed to assist the consumer to understand the nature and cost of credit; to understand the bills received; to settle billing disputes promptly; to shield consumers from discrimination when they apply for credit; to protect them from shoddy goods and services purchased with a credit card; to help them through large and complicated transactions such as home buying and leasing of personal property; and to ensure that the credit needs of the entire community, including low- and moderate-income neighborhoods, are met and are consistent with the safe and sound operation of the lending institutions.

In most cases, Congress has directed the Fed Board to write the regulation; however, enforcement rests with a dozen federal agencies, including the Board, which enforces consumer protection laws only with respect to state member banks.

Federal Reserve Independence

In recent years the issue of Fed independence has surfaced again and offers a serious challenge to the central bank's ability to perform its mission. In this section we will examine the meaning of the term and the pros and cons of independence.

Meaning and Manner of Fed Independence or Insulation

By the "Fed's independence," we mean that it is insulated from political control and special interest groups. The word "independence" has been overused by the press, some members of Congress, and others. "Insulated" is a more accurate description of the situation. Independence implies a freedom from accountability and a lack of responsiveness to changing national priorities. But neither one of these can be substantiated by the facts. We will have more to say on this in a moment.

The Fed is insulated in several ways from direct political control by the executive branch, transitory political pressures from Congress, and special interest groups. First, Board members serve fourteen-year terms and staggered appointments to keep members from being dependent on, or allied to, the current administration or political party. Members may be removed only for "cause." Second, the Fed finances its activities with earnings from its assets and, therefore, is not subject to the usual budgetary process. This is intended to assure that Congress will not try to use "the power of the purse" in order to induce Fed officials to pursue policies they otherwise might consider poorly suited to the nation's needs. Third, the Fed's expenditures are not subject to the audit and criticism of the General Accounting Office, Congress's "watchdog" agency.

Rationale for Independence

When the Fed was established, it was Congressional intent that the central bank be insulated from political control and special interest groups. According to Arthur Burns, former chairman of the Board of Governors, "the reason for this insulation is a very practical one, namely, recognition by the Congress that governments throughout history have had a tendency to engage in activities that outstrip the taxes they are willing or able to collect. That tendency has generally led to currency depreciation, achieved by strategems ranging from clipping of gold or silver coins in earlier times to excessive printing of paper money or to coercing central banks to expand credit unduly in more modern times."[1]

In most countries, the central bank is a part of the executive branch of government. Monetary policy is carried out according to the wishes and whims of the head of state. In our country, by insulating the central bank from direct political control of the executive branch and

1. Arthur F. Burns, "The Importance of an Independent Central Bank," *Federal Reserve Bulletin* (September 1977), p. 779.

Congress, we tend to force some element of fiscal discipline. That is, spending not matched by taxes must be financed by Treasury debt issues that must compete for funds with private issues in the financial markets. The Treasury, under authority from the head of state, cannot finance its deficits simply by having the central bank purchase the debt directly.[2] Admittedly, in recent years Congress has shown a willingness to run persistent deficits with interest on the federal debt now accounting for more than 10 percent of the budget. However, it is conceivable that these deficits could have been higher if the Treasury had "carte blanche" at the Fed.

Criticism of the Fed's Independence

Criticism of the Fed's independence comes primarily from several vocal members of Congress, some academic economists, and, from time to time those that have occupied the White House. Essentially, critics in Congress and the executive branch are frustrated because they cannot instruct the central bank on what to do. They contend that the Fed is unaccountable and unresponsive to changing national priorities. Those government officials and academic economists that believe **fiscal policy** (the use of the government's taxing and spending powers) has an active role to play in economic policy are frustrated because monetary policy sometimes negates fiscal action. They would like better coordination of fiscal and monetary policy. Also, some critics philosophically just do not like the aloofness and conservative air of the Fed and its officials. Moreover, to these critics, the Fed represents an anomoly during times when there is a tendency to "democratize" all decision-making processes in our society.

Some of the criticism of the Fed's independence is unfounded. With respect to accountability, the Fed is accountable to Congress for all of its actions, including monetary policy, regulatory responsibilities, and for services to banks and the public. It renders an annual report to Congress, and its governors and staff testify very frequently before Congressional committees. With respect to the criticism that the Fed is "unresponsive to changing national priorities," this is just not so. The Fed does not like recessions or inflation. The Fed's policies are "fair game" for everyone who thinks he or she knows something about how to operate the central bank. This includes Congress; professional

2. By law, the US Treasury can sell only $5 billion in debt directly to the Fed.

economists; financial, business, and community leaders; the press; and ordinary citizens. Professor Edward J. Kane of The Ohio State University has pointed out that other federal agencies in Washington lobby intensely with the Fed for their "constituents"—the Labor Department for the unemployed, the USDA for farmers, HUD for the cities, HEW for its many beneficiaries, and so on. Also, there is lively debate concerning Fed policies within the Fed Board, its staff, and the staff of the individual Reserve banks. It is a tossup as to who has the most Monday morning quarterbacks: The Washington Redskins or the Fed! At least the 'skins just have to play sixteen games a year!

Summary

The Fed was born out of the need for monetary stability and to prevent money panics. Our central bank is composed of four major elements: (1) the Board of Governors, (2) the FOMC, (3) the twelve Reserve banks and their branches, and (4) the Federal Advisory Council. The Board of Governors has overall supervisory authority over the entire central bank. In the area of monetary policy, the Board sits on the FOMC, sets reserve requirements, and approves changes in the discount rate. The FOMC sets policy for open market operations, which are the most important tool for effecting monetary policy.

The Fed performs vital service functions. It is the source of currency, operates a national system of check collection, and acts as fiscal agent for the Treasury.

The Fed's supervisory and regulatory functions primarily involve member banks and, in particular, state member banks. The Fed approves mergers where the surviving bank is a state member bank and has total jurisdiction over bank holding companies and their nonbanking activities. In recent years, the Fed has taken on added responsibilities in the area of consumer protection.

The question of the Fed's independence is a live and vital issue. Proponents of independence point to the need to maintain a strong central bank insulated from political control. Congressional critics and others in government who oppose the concept basically are frustrated because they cannot instruct the Fed on what to do. Those that prefer the active use of fiscal policy are frustrated because they believe that monetary policy frequently negates the effects of fiscal actions.

Questions and Problems

1. Describe the problems that pointed to the need to establish a central bank in this country in 1913.
2. List the Fed Board's ten most important functions.
3. List and describe briefly the service functions performed by the Federal Reserve banks.
4. Define independent central bank.
5. Discuss the issue of the Fed's independence.

Suggestions for Additional Reading

Burns, Arthur F. "The Importance of an Independent Central Bank." *Federal Reserve Bulletin* (September 1977), pp. 777–781.

———. "Maintaining the Soundness of Our Banking System." Federal Reserve Bank of New York, *Monthly Review* (November 1974), pp. 263–267.

Eastburn, David P. "The Fed in a Political World." Federal Reserve Bank of Philadelphia, *Business Review* (October 1975), pp. 3–9.

Federal Reserve Bank of Minneapolis. "Perspectives on Federal Reserve Independence: A Changing Structure for Changing Times." *Annual Report.* Minneapolis: Federal Reserve Bank of Minneapolis, 1976.

Hoskins, W. Lee. "Should the Fed Sell Its Services?" Federal Reserve Bank of Philadelphia, *Business Review* (January 1975), pp. 11–17.

8

The Framework
for Monetary Control

In the last chapter we explored the Federal Reserve System's structure and service, supervisory, and regulatory functions. These functions are important, but control of the money supply is the Fed's number one task. Recall from earlier in the book that the Fed controls the money supply through its influence on the quantity of legal reserves and its absolute control of reserve ratios. As a first approximation this is basically true; but as you might have suspected, and to use a favorite expression, "there is a little more to it than that." The main task in this chapter is "to learn a little more" on the subject.

The specific goals in this chapter are (1) to examine the major asset, liability, and capital items on the FED's balance sheet, (2) to learn the nature and function of the bank reserve equation, and (3) to discuss the monetary base-multiplier approach to monetary control.

Federal Reserve Assets

As we have learned, member bank reserves are liabilities of the Reserve banks. Changes in any other Fed asset, liability, or capital account change reserves dollar for dollar. Before learning how this takes place, it is necessary to understand the nature of each Reserve bank account.

Gold Certificates

Table 8–1 contains the consolidated balance sheet of the Reserve banks on March 28, 1979. The first asset is gold certificate credits. In earlier days, actual gold certificates were issued. Today, gold certificates are bookkeeping credits. The Treasury issues gold certificate credits to the Reserve banks to replenish the Treasury's account after gold is purchased. Below is the T-account illustrating a Treasury gold purchase and the subsequent issuance of gold certificate credits.

Treasury		FR		Commercial Bank	
Gold +$100			Reserve deposit +$100	Reserve at FR +$100	Demand Deposits +$100
USTGA −$100			USTGA −$100		
USTGA +$100	Gold certificates +$100	Gold certificates +$100	USTGA +$100		

Table 8-1
Consolidated Statement of Condition of Federal Reserve Banks, March 28, 1979 (millions of dollars)

Assets		Liabilities and Capital	
Gold certificates	$ 11,481	Federal Reserve notes	$100,896
Special drawing rights (SDRs)	1,300	Member bank deposits	29,063
Coin	380	U S Treasury deposits (USTGA)	3,178
Loans to member banks	1,495	Foreign and other deposits	932
U S government and agency		Deferred availability cash items	6,019
securities	112,169	Other liabilities	1,902
Cash-items-in-process-of-collection	11,529	Capital paid in	1,110
Bank premises and other assets	6,509	Surplus	1,078
		Other capital accounts	685
Total	144,863	Total	144,863

Source: Board of Governors of the Federal Reserve, *Federal Reserve Bulletin.*

Suppose that the Treasury purchased $100 of gold from a mining company. It would pay for the gold with a check on the US Treasury General Account (USTGA) at the Fed. The miner deposits the check in his bank, and the bank clears the check through the Fed. To replenish its account, the Treasury issues gold certificates to the Fed, which picks them up as assets and credits the USTGA.

Formerly, the Fed had to hold gold certificates equal to a minimum of 25 percent of outstanding Federal Reserve notes and deposit liabilities. As the gold supply declined and gold certificates were retired, the anticipated difficulty in meeting this statutory requirement caused Congress to abolish the gold certificate requirement for Fed deposit liabilities in 1965 and for notes outstanding in 1968. Below is the T-account illustrating the sale of gold and the subsequent retirement of gold certificates.

Treasury			FR		Commercial Bank	
Gold			Reserve	Reserve	Demand	
−$100			deposit	at FR	deposits	
			−$100	−$100	−$100	
USTGA			USTGA			
+$100			+$100			
USTGA	Gold	Gold	USTGA			
−$100	certificates	certificates	−$100			
	−$100	−$100				

Suppose that the Treasury sells $100 of gold to a domestic company, which pays for it with a check on its bank. The Treasury deposits the check at the Fed, which reduces the reserve account of the bank, and returns the check to the bank. The Treasury then retires an equivalent amount of gold certificates.

Although the 25 percent minimum gold certificate requirement has been abolished, the Fed still pledges its gold certificate credits as "collateral" for Federal Reserve notes issued. Realistically, gold certificate credits are no longer important in the big scheme of things. What is important is that Treasury gold sales and purchases lead to a decrease and increase, respectively, in member bank reserves. Note that the impetus for these sales and purchases lies with the Treasury, not the Fed. Thus, Treasury gold actions eventually lead to multiple contractions and increases in the money supply. The Fed, which has primary responsibility for controlling the money supply, must take the effects of these gold sales and purchases into account. We will have more to say about this later in the chapter as we study the bank reserve equation.

One more aspect about gold is that, by law, the Treasury's physical gold is carried on the books at $42.22 per ounce. From 1934 to 1972, the statutory gold price was $35 per ounce. In 1972, as the free market price of gold began to take off into the stratosphere, Congress decided to increase the value to $38 per ounce. A year later, it was raised to $42.22 per ounce, where it stands today. When these increases occurred, the value of the certificate credits at the Fed increased, and the Treasury got a small windfall gain in its general account.

Special Drawing Rights (SDRs)

Special Drawing Rights (SDRs), or "paper gold," as they are sometimes called, are created by the International Monetary Fund (IMF) as part of an effort to increase international reserves. When the Treasury takes down SDRs from the IMF, it issues them to the New York Federal Reserve Bank, which, in turn, credits a special Treasury checking account. The Treasury then can write checks on this account. When the checks clear through the Fed, member bank reserves increase.

Coin

Coin is Treasury coin and a small amount of US notes, silver certificates, and other Treasury currency. The Fed issues these coins to member banks to accommodate public demand.

When the Treasury issues coins to the Fed, it indirectly leads to an increase in member bank reserves. Here is the T-account to illustrate this:

Treasury		FR		Commercial Bank	
USTGA +$100	Coin +$100	Coin +$100	USTGA +$100		
USTGA −$100			USTGA −$100	Reserve at FR +$100	Demand deposits +$100
Pencils +$100			Reserve deposit +$100		

Suppose that the Treasury issues $100 of coins to the Reserve Bank. The Fed credits the USTGA and picks up the coins as an asset. The Treasury then could write a check on its general account to buy some pencils. When the check clears, member bank reserves increase. The transaction is rather difficult to understand because the increase in reserves is one step removed from the actual increase in coins.

Loans

The Fed is the ultimate source of liquidity to the banking system. Through its ability to lend to member banks, the Fed can create reserves for individual banks and the banking system. The rate charged for loans from the Fed is called the **discount rate**. Loans are classified either as discounts or advances. **Discounts** are made when a member bank presents customers' short-term commercial, industrial, agricultural, or other business paper for rediscounting. Because these obligations probably were discounted first by the member bank when the loan was made, rediscounting just means that the debt was discounted again, this time by the member bank. **Advances** are loans made on the borrowing bank's promissory note and are secured, usually by Treasury or agency obligations. Because of greater flexibility, advances comprise the vast bulk of all Fed loans.

The Fed also makes seasonal and emergency loans to member banks. Since 1973, member banks may obtain a **seasonal loan** if they demonstrate a seasonal need for funds and lack access to national money markets. These banks may borrow for up to ninety days and renew if seasonal needs exceed original expectations. **Emergency loans** may be made for extended periods of time to banks with exceptional circumstances such as sustained deposit drains, impaired access to money market funds, or poor loan repayment performance. Banks in areas that suffer national disasters probably would have need for an emergency loan.

On the top of page 173 is the T-account to illustrate the Fed making an advance and the bank repaying it. To make a loan to a member bank, the Fed creates an asset (the loan) and creates reserves for the bank. Loan repayment is very simple; the bank just requests the Fed to reduce their reserve balance and mark the loan "paid."

	FR		Commercial Bank	
Bank obtains loan from Fed	Loan +$1 mil.	Reserve deposit +$1 mil.	Reserve at FR +$1 mil.	Loan from FR +$1 mil.
Bank repays loan at Fed	Loan -$1 mil.	Reserve deposit -$1 mil.	Reserve at FR -$1 mil.	Loan from FR -$1 mil.

Securities

The Fed purchases Treasury and agency securities in the process of conducting open market operations. As may be seen in Table 8-1, these obligations comprise 77 percent of all Reserve Bank assets. It is through open market operations that the Fed has its primary influence on member bank reserves and, hence, the money supply. Below is the T-account illustrating the Fed's purchases of securities from a dealer. We looked at this in Chapter 2, but a review will do no harm.

FR		Security Dealer		Commercial Bank	
Securities +$1 mil.	Reserve deposit +$1 mil.	Securities -$1 mil.		Reserve at FR +$1 mil.	Demand deposits +$1 mil.
		Demand deposits +$1 mil.			

Suppose that the Fed purchases $1 million of securities from a government securities dealer. The Fed gives the dealer a check, and the dealer promptly deposits it in his bank. The bank clears it through the Fed, which pays the check by crediting the reserve account of the sending bank. Because of its ability to create reserves in the process of making loans and purchasing securities, the Fed is the ultimate source of liquidity for the banking system. These reserves are the foundation for a multiple expansion of the money supply.

When the Fed sells securities, there is an equal and opposite effect on the money supply. Here is the T-account illustration:

FR		Security Dealer		Commercial Bank	
Securities −$1 mil.	Reserve deposit −$1 mil.	Demand deposits +$1 mil. Securities −$1 mil.		Reserve at FR −$1 mil.	Demand deposits −$1 mil.

Suppose that the Fed sells $1 million of Treasury securities to a dealer, who pays for them with a check on a commercial bank. The Fed takes the check, reduces the drawee bank's reserve deposit, and returns it to the drawee bank, which, in turn, reduces the dealer's demand deposit. Unless it had excess reserves, the drawee bank now is deficient in required reserves and must sell securities or buy Fed funds to make up the deficiency. As explained in Chapter 2, the necessity to maintain reserve positions forces the banking system to reduce deposits by a multiple of the amount of reserves destroyed.

Cash-Items-in-Process-of-Collection

Cash-items-in-process-of-collection are checks deposited by commercial banks with the Federal Reserve banks but, as of the date of the statement of condition, have not been deducted from the drawee bank's reserve balance. Cash items are the Fed's second largest asset. On the liability side is a counterpart account, **deferred availability cash items**, which are checks that have not been added to the reserve account of the sending bank. The difference between cash-items-in-process-of-collection and deferred availability cash items is called **float**. Understanding float and its impact on bank reserves is a little difficult, so let's look at the T-accounts.

Suppose that Bank A receives a $1,000 check on Bank B from a customer. Bank A credits the customer's demand deposit account, increases an asset account called cash-items-in-process-of-collection, and forwards the check to its Reserve bank for collection. When the Reserve bank receives the check, it increases by $1,000 both cash-items-in-process-of-collection (an asset) and deferred availability cash items (a liability). It is the Fed's policy to credit deferred availability cash items to the sending bank's reserve account in two days or less. Checks on local or nearby banks are paid immediately or within one day. Checks from more distant banks are credited on the second day.

FR		
Checks are deposited	Cash-items-in-process-of-collection +$1000	Deferred availability cash items +$1000
Two days later		Deferred availability cash items −$1000 Reserve at Bank A +$1000
Four days later	Cash-items-in-process-of-collection −$1000	Reserve at Bank B −$1000

Commercial Bank A		
Checks are deposited	Cash-items-in-process-of-collection +$1000	Demand deposits +$1000
Two days later	Cash-items-in-process-of-collection −$1000 Reserve at FR +$1000	
Four days later		

Commercial Bank B		
Checks are deposited		
Two days later		
Four days later	Reserve at FR −$1000	Demand deposits −$1000

Back to our example, after two days the Reserve bank reduces deferred availability cash items and increases the reserve balance of Bank A. At this point, Bank B's reserve balance has not been reduced.

After two more days, the Reserve bank reduces the reserve balance of Bank B.

Let's analyze what happens in the above example with respect to reserves for the banking system. At the end of two days, reserves increased in the banking system. This increase in reserves for checks not yet collected is called **float**. Float is measured by the difference between cash-items-in-process-of-collection and deferred availability cash items on the Fed's books. Thus, on the March 28, 1979, Fed balance sheet, float for the banking system totaled $5,510,000,000. In the banking system, float exists primarily because the Reserve banks cannot physically move the checks to each other for collection as quickly as they agree to credit the sending bank. The speed of collection is affected by transportation schedules, weather's impact on these schedules, computer breakdowns, and the sheer volume of checks. Check volume increases after paydays and at the end of the month. Check volume also increases around holidays, such as Easter, Fourth of July, and Christmas. In sum, the Fed's policy to grant credit for checks prior to the time that it collects these checks creates instability in the quantity of bank reserves, and, hence, in the money supply. In effect, this practice makes the Fed's other task as manager of the money supply rather difficult. To smooth the effects of these fluctuations in float on reserves, the Fed periodically sells and buys securities to reduce or augment reserves for the system, as the situation requires. Purchases and sales of securities for these purposes, and to counter other undesirable changes in the sources and uses of reserves, are known as **defensive open market operations**.

Bank Premises and Other Assets

Bank premises are the Reserve bank buildings, branches, and clearing facilities around the country. Accrued interest, primarily on the Fed's holdings of Treasury and agency securities, and holdings of foreign currencies comprise the bulk of the "other asset" account.

Federal Reserve Liabilities

Federal Reserve Notes Outstanding

Federal Reserve notes outstanding include those held by the public, in the vaults of banks, and held by the Treasury. On March 28, 1979, they comprised over 70 percent of all Fed liabilities. This account does not include unissued Federal Reserve notes in the Reserve Bank vaults. The Fed issues Federal Reserve notes to accommodate public demand for them. However, it is very important to understand that when the public wishes to hold more Federal Reserve notes, member bank reserves decline. On the liability side of the Reserve Bank's balance sheet, Federal Reserve notes outstanding increase and reserve deposits decline. If the commercial bank that receives these notes then turns around and issues them to customers, then the net effect of an increase in Federal Reserve notes outstanding is a multiple contraction in the total money supply because reserves decline.

Member Bank Reserves

Member bank reserves are simply the demand balances in reserve accounts of member banks and represent the Fed's second largest liability. Banks use these accounts in the same way that you would use your demand deposit account. Banks deposit checks to them, write checks on them, wire funds from them, and exchange reserve balances for Federal Reserve notes and coin.

US Treasury Deposits

Treasury deposits at the Reserve banks are held in the USTGA. Funds are transferred to this account from TT&L accounts at commercial banks. Funds build up in TT&L accounts from the deposit of taxes and the sale of securities to banks and the public. Below is the T-account to illustrate the transfer of $1 million in funds from a TT&L account to the USTGA account at a Reserve bank.

FR		Commercial Bank	
USTGA +$1 mil.	Reserve at FR		TT&L deposit −$1 mil.
Reserve deposit −$1 mil.		−$1 mil.	

The Fed increases the USTGA account and reduces the bank's reserve balance. The bank records the decrease in the TT&L account and the decrease in reserve deposits at the Reserve bank. The decline in reserves caused by the Treasury's movement of funds to the Fed leads to a multiple decline in the money supply. To offset this decline, the Fed must purchase securities in an amount equal to the Treasury's transfer from the TT&L account.

On the other hand, when the Treasury writes checks on its account at the Reserve Bank, member bank reserves increase.

Treasury		*FR*		*Commercial Bank*	
USTGA −$100		USTGA −$100	Reserve at FR +$100	Demand deposits +$100	
Pencils +$100		Reserve deposit +$100			

Suppose that the Treasury purchases $100 worth of pencils. The pencil supply company deposits the check in its bank, which promptly sends it to the Reserve Bank for collection. The Reserve Bank reduces the USTGA and increases the sending bank's reserve deposit. This transaction has the same effect on member bank reserves as the Fed's open market purchase of securities. The increase in reserves lays the foundation for a multiple expansion in the money supply. If the Fed does not wish for the Treasury's actions to have this effect, it must sell securities in an equal amount to offset the anticipated money supply increase.

Foreign and Other Deposits

Foreign central banks, the IMF, the United Nations, the International Bank for Reconstruction and Development (World Bank), and certain other foreign and domestic official institutions keep demand balances with the Reserve banks. These funds are transferred to the Fed from commercial banks. This is accomplished on the Fed's books by a reduction in member bank reserves and an increase in foreign deposits. In absolute amount, foreign deposits are not large; however, increases and reductions in these accounts have the same effect on member bank reserves as do Treasury actions in its general account.

Other Liabilities

"Other liabilities" include dividends payable to member banks and accrued between payment dates (the last business day of June and December), sundry items payable, and accrued expenses.

Capital Paid-In

Capital paid-in represents the par value of the Federal Reserve Bank stock purchased by member banks. This is equal to 3 percent of the member bank's common stock and surplus. When a new bank joins the Federal Reserve System or a member bank increases its common stock through sale to the public or stock dividends, they must purchase additional stock. Payment for this stock is effected on the Fed's books by a reduction in the member's reserve balance and an increase in capital paid-in. On the other hand, retirement of stock has opposite signs. In the aggregate, such transactions are small and can be offset by open market operations.

Bank Reserve Equation

Derivation of Concept

In the above discussion of the major Fed accounts, it was pointed out how changes in Fed asset and liability accounts affect member bank reserves on the Fed's books. A very important conclusion is that *the Fed does not have absolute control over member bank reserves on its own books;* but it does have relative control through its ability to conduct defensive open market operations. Because of the need to control reserves in order to control the money supply, the Fed has developed a framework for taking into account the impact of these "other" influences and its own upon member bank reserves on the Reserve banks' books. It is called the **bank reserve equation**. In order to understand this concept, let's go back to the Fed's balance sheet.

A balance sheet is an equation:

(1) Assets = Liabilities + Capital

The Fed's balance sheet may be written as follows:

(2) *FR* Assets = Liabilities + FM Capital +
$$+ \text{Member Bank Reserves}$$

Solving for member bank reserves, we have:

(3) Member Bank Reserves (MBR_{FR}) (on the FR's books)
$$= FR \text{ Assets} - FR \text{ Liabilities} - FR \text{ Capital}$$

From this equation, we see that member bank reserves increase if FR assets increase or if either FR liabilities or FR capital decrease. Federal Reserve assets (such as securities) are sources of reserves or factors supplying reserves; FR liabilities (such as the USTGA) and capital are competing uses of reserves or factors absorbing reserves.

Equation (3) is correct, but it omits two Treasury monetary accounts that affect member bank reserves: (1) Treasury coin and currency outstanding, which is a source of reserves, and (2) Treasury holdings of coin and currency in its own vault, which is a use of reserves. In addition, it is more accurate to substitute the Treasury's gold stock for gold certificate credits outstanding as a source of reserves, and to substitute currency in circulation for Federal Reserve notes outstanding as a use of reserves. The two Treasury monetary accounts and the two substitutions will be explained in the next two sections. At this point, our principal objective is to show that by combining the Treasury's monetary accounts with the Fed monetary accounts and making two adjustments, we derive the bank reserve equation, the framework for bringing together all the influences on member bank reserves on the Fed's books.

We know that Fed and Treasury asset accounts are sources of reserves and Fed and Treasury liability accounts are uses of reserves. So we can write the consolidated bank reserve equation as follows:

(4) MBR_{FR} = Sources of Reserves – Competing Uses of Reserves

Or, in different words:

(5) MBR_{FR} = Factors Supplying Reserves (FSR)
$$- \text{ Factors Absorbing Reserves } (FAR)$$

Below is the detailed bank reserve equation:

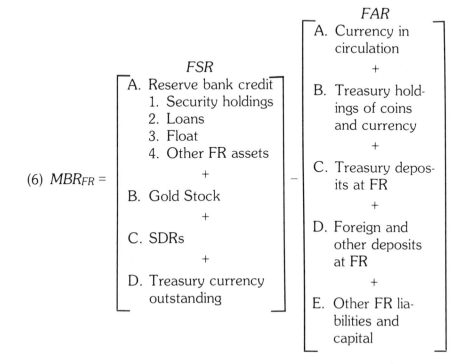

$$(6)\ MBR_{FR} = \begin{bmatrix} FSR \\ \text{A. Reserve bank credit} \\ \quad \text{1. Security holdings} \\ \quad \text{2. Loans} \\ \quad \text{3. Float} \\ \quad \text{4. Other FR assets} \\ + \\ \text{B. Gold Stock} \\ + \\ \text{C. SDRs} \\ + \\ \text{D. Treasury currency} \\ \quad \text{outstanding} \end{bmatrix} - \begin{bmatrix} FAR \\ \text{A. Currency in} \\ \quad \text{circulation} \\ + \\ \text{B. Treasury hold-} \\ \quad \text{ings of coins} \\ \quad \text{and currency} \\ + \\ \text{C. Treasury depos-} \\ \quad \text{its at FR} \\ + \\ \text{D. Foreign and} \\ \quad \text{other deposits} \\ \quad \text{at FR} \\ + \\ \text{E. Other FR lia-} \\ \quad \text{bilities and} \\ \quad \text{capital} \end{bmatrix}$$

Factors Supplying Reserves

Table 8–2 contains the bank reserve equation for March 28, 1979. Federal Reserve credit accounts for 83 percent of the total sources of reserves. When the Fed purchases securities or acceptances, makes loans to member banks, permits float to increase, or adds to other FR assets, member bank reserves increase. The Fed increases an asset account and simultaneously increases member bank reserves, a liability.

Earlier in the chapter you learned that when the Treasury purchases gold, it leads to an increase in member bank reserves. Sometimes in the past, the quantity of gold certificates issued by the Treasury has been slightly less than the dollar value of the Treasury's gold stock. Therefore, the gold stock usually is more accurate than gold certificates as a measure of the Treasury's influence on bank reserves through its gold purchase and sale activities. Recently, however, gold certificates outstanding have equaled the value of the

Table 8-2
Bank Reserve Equation, March 28, 1979
(millions of dollars)

Sources (Factors supplying reserve funds)	
A. Reserve bank credit	
1. Security holdings	$112,169
2. Loans	1,495
3. Float	5,510
4. Other FR assets	6,509
Subtotal	125,683
B. Gold stock	11,481
C. SDRs	1,300
D. Treasury currency outstanding	12,085
Total sources	150,549
minus	
Uses (Factors absorbing reserve funds)	
A. Currency in circulation	112,228
B. Treasury holdings of coin and currency	374
C. Treasury deposits at FR	3,178
D. Foreign and other deposits at FR	271
E. Other FR liabilities and capital	5,436
Total uses	121,487
equals	
MBR_{FR}	29,062
+ Cash-in-vault[a]	9,753
Total member bank reserves	38,815

[a]Estimated.

Source: Board of Governors of the Federal Reserve, *Federal Reserve Bulletin.*

gold stock, so either measure is accurate. The Treasury's present policy is not to purchase gold because the world price is well above the statutory price. Instead, the Treasury has been auctioning off small amounts of gold. These changes in the gold stock have a very small effect on member bank reserves. SDRs change infrequently, so that this item is not a significant source of instability in reserves.

Treasury currency outstanding is the second largest source of reserves. This item increases over time as the public demands more coins. As explained earlier, increases in Treasury currency leads to an increase in the Treasury's general account and, as these funds are disbursed, member bank reserves increase. All sources of reserves totaled $150,549,000,000 on March 28, 1979.

Factors Absorbing Reserves

As shown in Table 8–2, a total of $121,487,000,000 was absorbed into competing uses. When factors absorbing reserves increase, member bank reserves decline. Conversely, when factors absorbing reserves decline, member bank reserves increase. Currency in circulation is the largest use of reserves; it absorbed 75 percent of the total supplied on March 28, 1979. **Currency in circulation** consists of Federal Reserve notes and Treasury coin held outside the vaults of the Treasury and Federal Reserve. It is more accurate to substitute the broader "currency in circulation" concept because the issuance of coins has the same effect on member bank reserves as the issuance of Federal Reserve notes.

Increases in **Treasury holdings of coin and currency** in its vault and **Treasury deposits** affect member bank reserves in the same manner. When the Treasury moves coins into its vault from a commercial bank or makes a call on TT&L accounts in order to add to its account at the Fed, these transactions lead to a decrease in bank reserves. Treasury cash holdings are not a significant source of instability, but from time to time fluctuations in the Treasury's deposits at the Reserve banks has been a source of instability.

Increases in **foreign deposits** at the Fed and increases in other Fed liabilities and capital absorb reserves. Conversely, decreases in these accounts supply reserves.

On March 28, 1979, after factors absorbing reserves are subtracted from factors supplying reserves, there were $29,062,000,000 in member bank reserves on the Fed's books.

Add Cash-in-Vault

The bank reserve equation yields an incomplete statement of total legal reserves because it omits cash-in-vault. Currency in circulation consists of Federal Reserve notes and Treasury currency and coin outstanding. Currency in circulation also may be classified as (1) that held in bank vaults and (2) that held by the public. That portion held in bank vaults must be added to reserves on the Fed's books to compute total member bank reserves. As shown in Table 8–2, cash-in-vault totaled $9,753,000,000 on March 28, 1979, thus making total member bank reserves $38,815,000,000.

Changes Over Time in Major Factors Supplying and Absorbing Bank Reserves

Figure 8–1 shows changes in several major sources and uses of bank reserves over time. As may be seen, currency in circulation has increased steadily since 1960. If no other action had been taken, this increase would have caused a drastic reduction in reserves and a greater drop in the money supply. Note, however, that Reserve Bank credit increased at a slightly faster pace to negate the effects of the increase in currency in circulation, the decline in the gold stock, and to accomplish growth in the money supply.

Use of the Bank Reserve Equation to Compute Changes in Reserves

The bank reserve equation is a picture of the sources and uses of reserves at one point in time. The Fed, however, is more interested in changes in the equation between two points in time. Suppose during one week, the following items in the equation changed:

Reserve	Changes (millions of dollars)
Loans	– 4
Float	+ 6
Gold stock	– 1
Treasury currency outstanding	+ 2
Currency in circulation	+10
Treasury deposits at FR	– 3

What would be the change in member bank reserves at the Fed? There are two ways to compute the answer.

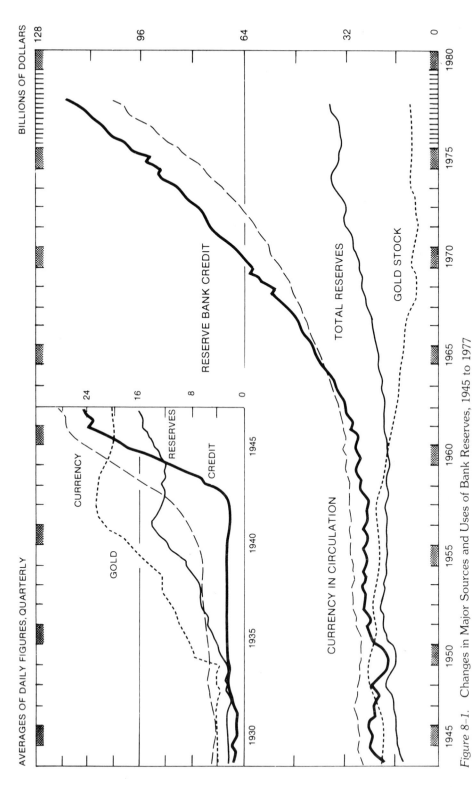

Figure 8-1. Changes in Major Sources and Uses of Bank Reserves, 1945 to 1977

Source: Board of Governors of the Federal Reserve, *Historical Chartbook.*

185

Method A.   Add *FSR* and *FAR* and find the net difference as shown below:

Method A:

	FSR	FAR
	-4	+10
	+6	- 3
	-1	
	+2	
Net	+3	+ 7

Using the bank reserve equation and placing Δs in front of the items to denote "changes in," we have:

(1) $\Delta MBR_{FR} = \Delta FSR - \Delta FAR$
(2) $\Delta MBR_{FR} = +3 - (+7)$
(3) $\Delta MBR_{FR} = -4$

Member bank reserves decreased by -4 because *FAR* increased by +7, while *FSR* only increased by +3.

Method B.   Another way to compute the answer is to make two columns and record factors under the "+" column if they increased reserves and under the "–" column if they decreased reserves, regardless of which side of the equation they are on. For example, loans changed by -4; thus this item, which normally increases reserves, is recorded under the minus column. Currency in circulation changed by +10; since this factor normally reduces reserves, it also is recorded under the "–" column. Computation under method B is shown below.

Method B:

Factors Affecting Reserves

	+	–
	6	4
	2	1
	3	10
Total	11	15

Thus,

$$(1)\ \Delta MBR_{FR} = \Delta FSR - \Delta FAR$$
$$(2)\ \Delta MBR_{FR} = +11 - (+15)$$
$$(3)\ \Delta MBR_{FR} = -4$$

In methods A and B, the effects of change in cash-in-vault may be added to changes in reserves on the Fed's books to find changes in total member bank reserves. Ordinarily, these changes are small.

How the Fed Uses the Bank Reserve Equation to Determine the Quantity of Securities to Purchase or Sell

The Fed determines what quantity of reserves will produce the money supply needed to achieve the Fed's goals. Suppose the Fed determines that reserves should decrease by $4 million during the week. Since reserves declined by this amount, the Fed need not buy or sell any securities. On the other hand, suppose the Fed determined that member bank reserves should increase by $5 million. Analysis of changes in the bank reserve equation during the week indicates that the Fed should purchase $9 million of securities. Proof of this is shown below:

(1) Desired ΔMBR_{FR} = ΔNon-FR Controlled Factors + ΔSecurities

Rewriting (1), we have:

(2) ΔSecurities = Desired ΔMBR_{FR} - ΔNon-FR Controlled Factors

Substituting, we have:

$$(3)\ \Delta\text{Securities} = +5 - (-4)$$
$$(4)\ \Delta\text{Securities} = +9$$

The Monetary Base-Multiplier Approach to Monetary Control

In the last section, we learned how the amount of member bank reserves depends on all the factors in the bank reserve equation. We studied the determinants of member bank reserves because they are a primary determinant, along with the reserve ratio, of the money supply. Recall from Chapter 2 that we derived the following money supply determination equation:

$$TDD_p = TLR \cdot \frac{1}{r_d}$$

where

TDD_p = potential demand deposits
TLR = total legal reserves
r_d = reserve ratio on demand deposits

This simple framework was useful at the time, but depended on many simplifying assumptions. For example, it does not take into account currency drains, shifts between demand and time deposits, distribution of deposits between member and nonmember banks, the portion of total deposits held by governments, and the different reserve ratios that apply to various types of deposits. In this section, we shall discuss a money supply determination framework that more closely approximates "the institutional realities of the U.S. banking system."[1] This framework is one in which M_1 can be expressed as the product of the monetary base (B) times a multiplier (m).[2]

$$M_1 = mB$$

It is a very simple framework and is very similar to our earlier money supply equation. Thus, if B is $150 billion and m equals 2.5, then M_1 equals $375 billion. Let's discuss the monetary base and the multiplier.

Monetary Base

The **monetary base** simply is the amount of member bank reserves on the Fed's books plus currency in circulation. Thus, in the bank reserve equation, if we move currency in circulation down to the bottom of the chart and add it to member bank reserves on the Fed's books, the total will equal the monetary base. Many economists believe that the monetary base is a superior reserve aggregate to manage because it includes reserves in all bank vaults and because increases in reserves caused by open market purchases are more closely correlated with the monetary base than with reserves on the

1. Jerry L. Jordan, "Elements of Money Supply Determination," Federal Reserve Bank of St. Louis, *Review* (October 1969), p. 11. Much of this section is derived from this excellent article.

2. This framework also may be applied to M_2 or any other money supply measure.

books of the Fed. We do not have to worry about adding in cash-in-vault or the effects of currency drains out of the banking system because this broader monetary base concept encompasses these drains. Figure 8–2 depicts the monetary base for the period November, 1977, to mid-January, 1979.

Multiplier

We also need a broader multiplier concept.[3] Our simple multiplier assumes that only demand deposits exist in the system. For example,

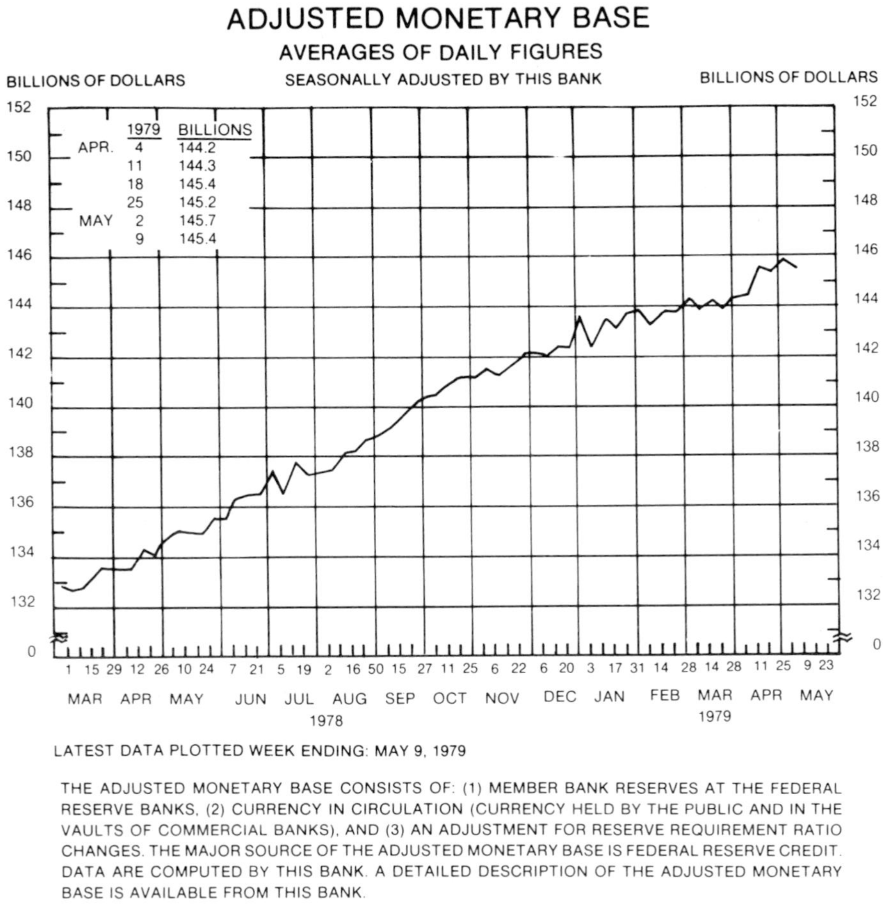
ADJUSTED MONETARY BASE
AVERAGES OF DAILY FIGURES
SEASONALLY ADJUSTED BY THIS BANK
BILLIONS OF DOLLARS
BILLIONS OF DOLLARS
1979 BILLIONS
APR. 4 144.2
11 144.3
18 145.4
25 145.2
MAY 2 145.7
9 145.4
152 150 148 146 144 142 140 138 136 134 132 0
1 15 29 12 26 10 24 7 21 5 19 2 16 50 15 27 11 25 6 22 6 20 3 17 31 14 28 14 28 11 25 9 23
MAR APR MAY JUN JUL AUG SEP OCT NOV DEC JAN FEB MAR APR MAY
1978
1979
LATEST DATA PLOTTED WEEK ENDING: MAY 9, 1979
THE ADJUSTED MONETARY BASE CONSISTS OF: (1) MEMBER BANK RESERVES AT THE FEDERAL RESERVE BANKS, (2) CURRENCY IN CIRCULATION (CURRENCY HELD BY THE PUBLIC AND IN THE VAULTS OF COMMERCIAL BANKS), AND (3) AN ADJUSTMENT FOR RESERVE REQUIREMENT RATIO CHANGES. THE MAJOR SOURCE OF THE ADJUSTED MONETARY BASE IS FEDERAL RESERVE CREDIT. DATA ARE COMPUTED BY THIS BANK. A DETAILED DESCRIPTION OF THE ADJUSTED MONETARY BASE IS AVAILABLE FROM THIS BANK.

Figure 8–2. The Monetary Base, March 1978–May 1979
Source: Federal Reserve Bank of St. Louis, *U.S. Financial Data.*

3. Much of this theory of the expanded multiplier concept was developed by Jordan, pp. 12–19.

if B equals $150 billion and r equals 10 percent, then M equals $1,500 billion.

$$(1) \quad M_1 = \frac{B}{r}$$

$$(2) \quad M_1 = \frac{\$150 \text{ billion}}{.10}$$

$$(3) \quad M_1 = \$1,500 \text{ billion}$$

Let's bring other influences into the multiplier concept.

The "r-ratio."   A more complete multiplier concept must take into account that our banking system has member and nonmember banks, and different reserve ratios on different types of deposits. For the banking system, the total amount of reserves can be expressed as a proportion (r) of total bank deposits:

$$R = r(D + T + G)$$

where

$$D = \text{private demand deposits}$$
$$T = \text{private time deposits}$$
$$G = \text{TT\&L deposits}$$

Rewriting,

$$r = \frac{R}{(D + T + G)}$$

Thus, the "r-ratio" is computed by dividing total reserves by total deposits.

The "k-ratio."   The public wishes to hold currency in some ratio to demand deposits, say $.30 for every $1.00 in demand deposits. To the extent that the public wishes to hold currency, the deposit-creating ability of the banking system is less. Currency (C) can be expressed as a proportion (k) of demand deposits (D). Thus,

$$C = kD$$

or

$$k = \frac{C}{D}$$

This ratio depends on the age distribution of the population, income levels, the utilization of credit cards and vending machines, and public preference for currency.

The "t-ratio." Some portion of legal reserves must be used to support time deposits. To the extent that the public wishes to hold time deposits, reserves are unavailable to support demand deposits. Since reserve ratios on time deposits are lower than on demand deposits, a given amount of reserves can support a larger amount of time deposits. Time deposits (T) can be expressed as a proportion (t) of demand deposits (D). Thus,

$$T = tD$$

or

$$t = \frac{T}{D}$$

The t-ratio depends on bank interest rate levels, income levels, public propensity to save, and competition from other thrift institutions.

The "g-ratio." Banks must hold reserves against government deposits just as they do against private deposits. To the extent that reserves are used to support government deposits, they cannot be used to support private deposits. Government deposits (G) can be expressed as a proportion (g) of private demand deposits (D). Thus,

$$G = gD$$

or

$$g = \frac{G}{D}$$

The "g-ratio" depends basically on Treasury policy with respect to how much of its funds will be kept in TT&L accounts relative to the USTGA at the Fed.

Now let's bring all of these ratios into the multiplier concept. First, a few definitions:

(1) $M_1 = D + C$
(2) $B = R + C$
(3) $R = r(D + T + G)$
(4) $C = kD$
(5) $T = tD$
(6) $G = gD$

By substituting (3) and (4) in (2) we obtain:

$$(7)\ B = r(D + T + G) + kD$$

This expresses the monetary base solely in terms of the various types of deposits. Substituting (5) and (6) in (7) we get:

$$(8)\ B = r(D + tD + gD) + kD$$

This expresses the base solely in terms of private demand deposits to reduce the number of variables. Simplifying, we write (8) as

$$(9)\ B = [r(1 + t + g) + k] \cdot D$$

With manipulation we obtain:

$$(10)\ D = \frac{1}{r(1 + t + g) + k} \cdot B$$

Since we want to find D plus C, we use (4) and (10) to define C in terms of the base:

$$(11)\ C = \frac{k}{r(1 + t + g) + k} \cdot B$$

Substituting (10) and (11) in (1) gives

$$(12)\ M_1 = \frac{1 + k}{r(1 + t + g) + k} \cdot B$$

Hence, the multiplier is:

$$m = \frac{1 + k}{r(1 + t + g) + k}$$

Let's use our new knowledge to determine M_1. Assume the following monetary base and parameters of the multiplier:

$$B = \$150 \text{ billion}$$
$$t = 1.5$$
$$g = .04$$
$$k = .3$$
$$r = .1$$

Since $M_1 = \dfrac{1 + k}{r(1 + t + g) + k} \cdot B$, we can solve to find $M = \$352$ billion.

The multiplier contains all the influences on the money supply not embodied in the monetary base. As shown in Figure 8–3, the multiplier was relatively stable at approximately 2.6 for the March to September, 1978, period. Then it began to drift down slightly until, by late spring, 1979, it appeared to have settled at the 2.5 mark. If the multiplier is stable around 2.5, then the Fed can be relatively certain that every \$1 billion change in the monetary base will lead to a \$2.5 billion change in M_1. In practice, the Fed attempts to predict changes in the multiplier just as with the monetary base. The "t-ratio" has been trending upward since the early 1960s as time deposits have grown more rapidly relative to demand deposits. The "k-ratio" also has been rising as people have demanded more currency relative to demand deposits. The "r-ratio" is drifting downward, in part because of the shift in the number of banks from member bank to nonmember bank status, where reserve ratios are lower. Another reason for the decline is the rapid growth in time deposits which have lower reserve ratio applications. The "g-ratio" fluctuates within a narrow range. These "wiggles" are caused by the Treasury's discretion about what percentage of its funds to hold in TT&L accounts as opposed to the USTGA.

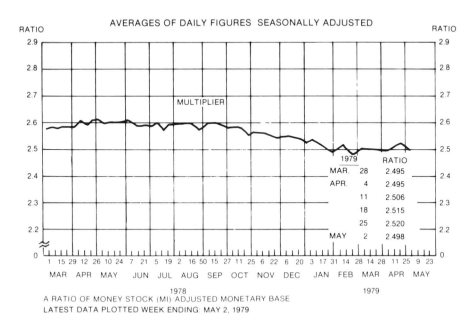

Figure 8-3   The Multiplier, March 1978–May 1979

Source: Federal Reserve Bank of St. Louis, *U.S. Financial Data.*

Summary

It is important to learn the nature of each major asset and liability account on the Fed's balance sheet. When the Fed acquires assets, member bank reserves increase; when a Fed liability (other than reserve deposits) increases, member bank reserves decrease. Securities acquired through open market operations comprise 77 percent of Fed assets. Federal Reserve notes outstanding comprise 70 percent of Fed liabilities and are issued in response to the public's demand for currency.

The bank reserve equation is the framework for bringing together all the factors supplying and absorbing bank reserves. Of all the factors in the equation, the Fed has absolute control only over securities. It is through its power to buy and sell securities that the Fed offsets undesirable fluctuations in these other factors and provides for growth in the money supply.

The monetary base-multiplier approach to monetary control is more realistic than the simple, introductory framework in Chapter 2. In this approach, $M_1 = mB$, where M_1 equals the narrow money supply, m = the multiplier, and B equals the monetary base. The multiplier is influenced by the reserve (r), currency (k), time deposit (t), and government deposit (g) ratios. The monetary base is defined as member bank reserves plus currency in circulation and is more closely correlated to Fed actions than to member bank reserves alone. Because the multiplier is rather stable, near the 2.5 level, the Fed is relatively certain that a $1 billion addition to the monetary base will lead to approximately a $2.5 billion increase in M_1.

Questions and Problems

1. Name the Fed's two largest assets and two largest liabilities.
2. Distinguish between discounts and advances as types of Fed loans.
3. Illustrate by means of T-accounts the following transactions for all banks and dealers concerned:
   (a) The Fed purchases securities from a dealer.
   (b) The Fed sells securities to a dealer.
4. Show by means of T-accounts for all banks concerned how float increases and decreases.

5.   Explain the bank reserve equation concept.

6.   Why does the Fed not have absolute control over member bank reserves on its books?

7.   Why does the bank reserve equation provide an incomplete determination of total legal reserves?

8.   Why is currency in circulation an absorbing item in the bank reserve equation?

9.   How does the Fed use the bank reserve equation in carrying out its primary function?

10.   Define (a) monetary base and (b) multiplier.

Suggestions for Additional Reading

Balbach, Anatol B., and Burger, Albert E. "Derivation of the Monetary Base." Federal Reserve Bank of St. Louis, *Review* (November 1976), pp. 2–8.

Burger, Albert E. "The Relationship Between Monetary Base and Money: How Close?" Federal Reserve Bank of St. Louis, *Review* (October 1975), pp. 3–8.

———. *The Money Supply Process.* Belmont, Calif.: Wadsworth Publishing Company, 1971.

———. "Explanation of the Growth of the Money Stock: 1974 to Early 1975." Federal Reserve Bank of St. Louis, *Review* (September 1975), pp. 5–10.

———., and Rasche, Robert H. "Revision of the Monetary Base." Federal Reserve Bank of St. Louis, *Review* (July 1977), pp. 13–28.

Cox, William N., III. "Controlling Money with Bank Reserves." Federal Reserve Bank of Atlanta, *Economic Review* (April 1973), pp. 55–59.

Jordan, Jerry L. "Elements of Money Stock Determination." Federal Reserve Bank of St. Louis, *Review* (October 1969), pp. 12–19.

Nichols, Dorothy M. *Modern Money Mechanisms: A Workbook on Deposits, Currency and Bank Reserves.* Chicago: Federal Reserve Bank of Chicago, 1975.

Rea, John D. "Behavior of the Monetary Aggregates and the Implications for Monetary Policy." Federal Reserve Bank of Kansas City, *Monthly Review* (September/October 1974), pp. 3–10.

Rutner, Jack L. "A Time Series Analysis of the Control of Money." Federal Reserve Bank of Kansas City, *Monthly Review* (January 1975), pp. 3–9.

———. "The Federal Reserve's Impact on Several Reserve Aggregates." Federal Reserve Bank of Kansas City, *Economic Review* (May 1977), pp. 14–22.

9

The Techniques
of Monetary Control

In the last chapter, we outlined the framework for monetary control. The money supply, M_1, was shown to be a product of the multiplier times the monetary base:

$$M_1 = mB$$

To change M_1 the Fed can pull the "m string" or the "B string." In this chapter we shall explain how the Fed changes m and B and uses other instruments to influence selectively the demand and supply for money and credit. Specifically, we shall (1) classify the tools of money and credit control; (2) discuss the Fed's three general tools of monetary control: open market operations, changes in reserve ratios, and changes in the discount rate; and (3) examine the selective tools of monetary control: margin requirements, the Regulation Q ceilings, World War II consumer and real estate credit controls, and moral suasion.

Classification of Techniques

Before we embark upon a discussion of individual techniques of monetary control, it would facilitate matters if we classify them along common lines.

197

Tools of Monetary Control	*Variables Influenced*
1. Quantitative or General Tools	
A. Open market operations	B (directly)
B. Changes in discount rate	B (indirectly)
C. Changes in reserve ratios	m
2. Qualitative or Selective Tools	
A. Margin requirements	demand for credit
B. Regulation Q ceilings	distribution of supply of credit
C. Consumer and real estate credit controls	demand for credit
D. Moral suasion	borrowing at the Fed (hence, B); the supply and demand for credit

Quantitative or general tools influence the quantity or supply of money and credit. These instruments are called "general tools" because they influence the overall supply of money and credit but do not influence directly the amount available to, or demanded by, specific sectors of the economy. As shown above, each of the quantitative tools affect either m or B in the framework for monetary control discussed in the last chapter.

Figure 9–1. (Courtesy of the Federal Reserve Bank of New York)

Qualitative or selective tools affect specific demands for credit. This group of tools includes **margin requirements**, the minimum down payment required to purchase securities on credit; **Regulation Q ceilings**, which set the maximum interest rates that banks can pay on time and savings deposits; and **consumer and real estate credit controls**, which, during periods of national emergency, specify the down payments and maturities on consumer and real estate loans. Figure 9–2 depicts the Federal Reserve System's relation to the instruments of monetary control. Moral suasion is the Fed's periodic efforts through speeches, press releases, and directives to influence member bank borrowing, bankers' willingness to lend, and the demand for credit.

The Fed prefers quantitative to qualitative tools because they do not involve direct interference in the allocation of money and credit. In other words, the Fed prefers to set the size of the pie instead of the size of the slices. In our economic system, private decisions generally are considered superior to public decisions.

Open Market Operations

Background

Open market operations represent the most important technique of monetary control. This is the only tool that directly affects the monetary base. The original Federal Reserve Act authorized the Reserve banks to hold securities. However, in the early days, the Fed purchased securities to receive the income to pay its expenses. It was not until 1923 that the Fed Board discovered that the purchase and sale of securities affected the flow of money and credit, and in that year an Open Market Committee of five presidents of Federal Reserve banks was formed to coordinate open market operations. The FOMC as we know it today was created by the Banking Acts of 1933 and 1935.

Formulation of Open Market Policy

As we learned in Chapter 7 the FOMC consists of seven members of the Fed Board, the President of the New York Federal Reserve Bank, and four other Reserve banks. The committee plus the seven nonvoting presidents meet in Washington about every four weeks to formulate open market policy. Prior to the meeting, each Reserve

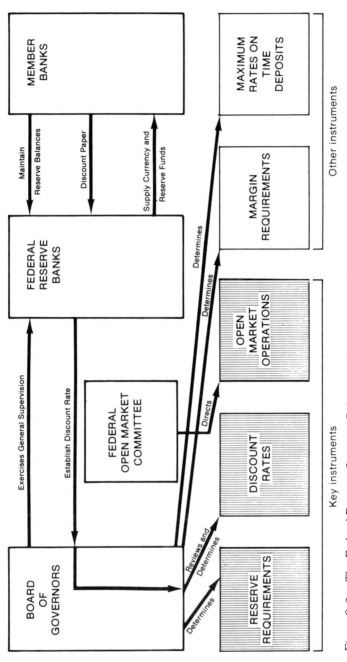

Figure 9-2. The Federal Reserve System—Relation to Instruments of Credit Policy

Source: Board of Governors of the Federal Reserve, *The Federal Reserve System, Purposes and Functions,* p. 50.

Figure 9-3. Federal Open Market Committee (*Courtesy of the Federal Reserve Board*)

bank president is briefed by his staff on local, national, and international economic and financial conditions. The Fed Board staff also prepares for distribution detailed econometric forecasts of GNP, employment, prices, and interest rates based on assumed rates of growth in various measures of the money supply. Also prior to the meeting, each committee member receives from the staff written reports on domestic and international economic and financial developments. In addition, each member analyzes drafts of alternative **policy directives** which might be used as guidelines for open market operations until the next meeting. These policy directives contain alternative annual rates of growth in the monetary aggregates and targets for the federal funds rate believed consistent with the committee's economic objectives.

When the Board and the twelve presidents assemble in Washington, they hear reports on domestic open market operations, developments in the financial markets, and the Fed's foreign exchange operations from (1) the manager of the System's Open Market Account, an executive vice-president at the New York Fed and (2) the deputy manager for domestic operations and the deputy manager for foreign operations, both senior vice-presidents at the New York Fed.

Next the Board staff presents oral reports on recent domestic and international economic and financial developments. Once a quarter, senior staff members present detailed economic and financial projections for the next twelve months. Then each of the nineteen principals presents his economic and financial conditions, the proposed alternative policy directives, and views on the manner in which open market operations should be carried out until the next meeting. Finally, the chairman of the FOMC, who traditionally has been the Chairman of the Board of Governors, summarizes the discussion, sets forth the concensus of the group, and puts before the meeting for final discussion and vote a policy directive that will provide the System's account manager with guidelines for conducting operations until the next meeting. Included in the directive are target ranges for growth in M_1 and M_2 for the current two-month period and an initial target for the federal funds rate between meetings. A vote is taken and recorded, and any dissenters have the reasons for the negative vote included in the record. Each quarter the FOMC votes on ranges of growth in M_1, M_2, and M_3 for the next four quarters following the last quarter. The manager takes this directive back to the New York Fed and uses it as his basic guideline for conducting operations until the next meeting.

Figure 9-4. Federal Reserve Bank of New York

Domestic Policy Directive

The first few paragraphs in the domestic policy directive contain a summary of economic and financial conditions. Then there are one or two paragraphs setting forth the FOMC's general policy with respect to the monetary and financial conditions necessary to achieve its objectives in the area of price stability, growth, unemployment, and international economic conditions. Included in these paragraphs is a discussion of the targets for the monetary aggregates and the federal funds rate. The final paragraph sets forth operating instructions to guide the Account Manager until the next FOMC meeting. Included are specific instructions with respect to the federal funds rate, monetary aggregates, and reserve and money market conditions. Below is the policy directive for the FOMC meeting held on February 6, 1979[1]:

> The information reviewed at this meeting suggests that in the fourth quarter of 1978 growth in real output of goods and services picked up sharply from the reduced rate in the third quarter. In December, as in the preceding two months, the dollar value of total retail sales expanded substantially, and industrial production and nonfarm payroll employment rose considerably further. Employment continued to grow in January, and the unemployment rate, at 5.8 percent, was virtually the same as in the final months of 1978. Over recent months, broad measures of prices and the index of average hourly earnings have continued to rise rapidly.
>
> The trade-weighted value of the dollar against major foreign currencies has tended upward since the turn of the year, returning to about its level in mid-December prior to the OPEC announcement of increased oil prices. The U.S. trade deficit in the fourth quarter of 1978 was at about the same rate as in the second and third quarters.
>
> M-1 increased little in December and appears to have declined in January, in part because of the continuing effects of the introduction of the automatic transfer service (ATS) on November 1, and M-2 and M-3 grew at relatively slow rates. With market interest rates relatively high, inflows to banks of the interest-bearing deposits included in M-2 slowed sharply, and inflows of deposits to nonbank thrift institutions slackened further. Over the year from the fourth quarter of 1977 to the fourth quarter of 1978, M-1, M-2, and M-3 grew about $7\frac{1}{4}$, $8\frac{1}{2}$, and $9\frac{1}{2}$ percent, respectively. Most market interest rates have declined on balance in recent weeks.

1. Board of Governors of the Federal Reserve, *Federal Reserve Bulletin*, April 1979.

Taking account of past and prospective developments in employment, unemployment, production, investment, real income, productivity, international trade and payments, and prices, it is the policy of the Federal Open Market Committee to foster monetary and financial conditions that will resist inflationary pressures while encouraging moderate economic expansion and contributing to a sustainable pattern of international transactions. The Committee agreed that these objectives would be furthered by growth of M-1, M-2, and M-3 from the fourth quarter of 1978 to the fourth quarter of 1979 within ranges of 1½ to 4½ percent, 5 to 8 percent, and 6 to 9 percent, respectively. The associated range for bank credit is 7½ to 10½ percent. These ranges will be reconsidered in July or at any time as conditions warrant.

In the short run, the Committee seeks to achieve bank reserve and money market conditions that are broadly consistent with the longer-run ranges for monetary aggregates cited above, while giving due regard to the program for supporting the foreign exchange value of the dollar and to developing conditions in domestic financial markets. In the period before the next regular meeting, System open market operations are to be directed at maintaining the weekly average federal funds rate at about the current level, provided that over the February–March period the annual rates of growth of M-1 and M-2, given approximately equal weight, appear to be within ranges of 3 to 7 percent and 5 to 9 percent, respectively. If growth of M-1 and M-2 for the two-month period appears to be outside the indicated limits, the Manager will promptly notify the Chairman, who will then consult with the Committee to determine whether the situation calls for supplementary instructions.

> Votes for this action: Messrs. Miller, Volcker, Baughman, Eastburn, Partee, Mrs. Teeters, Messrs. Wallich, Willes, and Mayo. Vote against this action: Mr. Coldwell. Absent: Mr. Winn. (Mr. Mayo voted as alternate for Mr. Winn.)

Mr. Coldwell dissented from this action because he preferred to direct open market operations early in the coming period toward a slight firming in money market conditions. He felt that the greatest danger currently was an intensification of inflationary pressures and that the longer-range prospects for inflation were unacceptable.

Executing Open Market Policy

Returning to the New York Fed with the directive, the Account Manager proceeds to execute open market policy through the purchase and sale of securities. This is carried out at the trading desk in the securities department of the New York Fed. The actual purchase and sale of securities is a relatively simple matter compared with the detailed work that must be done leading up to the decision to buy or sell. Every day, the staff provides information and projections on changes in bank reserve positions and the factors in the bank reserve equation not under Fed control, such as float, currency in circulation, and the Treasury's movement of funds into and out of the USTGA. On a rotating basis, representatives from several dealer firms meet daily with Fed officials to discuss developments in the financial markets. Early each day, traders around the Fed's desk are in touch with dealers trying to get a "feel" of the market. Shortly after 10:15 each day, Treasury and Fed officials hold a conference call on the outlook for changes in the USTGA. A daily conference call to review financial conditions is placed among the New York staff, the Board staff in Washington, and to a Reserve bank president on the FOMC. With all this information in hand, the Account Manager is ready to make an initial decision regarding open market operations for the day.

The trading desk uses three basic types of transactions in its conduct of open market operations: (1) outright purchases and sales, (2) matched sale-purchase transactions, and (3) repurchase agreements. **Outright purchases and sales** are transactions which increase or reduce securities holdings without any commitment to resell or repurchase. Outright purchases and sales are conducted with one or more of the thirty-five primary dealers[2] in US government securities. As shown in Table 9-1, outright purchases exceeded outright sales by a wide margin in 1977 and 1978. This is because each year the Fed had to increase its securities holdings to offset the rise in currency outstanding and other factors in the bank reserve equation, and to increase reserves to support growth in the money supply. Most outright purchases and sales take place in Treasury bills because it is the most active sector of the securities market; therefore, open market operations here tend not to be disruptive. The market for longer-term issues is thinner; hence Fed activity here tends to be destabilizing.

Matched sale-purchase transactions involve the Account Manager entering into a contract to sell for immediate delivery securities to a dealer and a matching contract to repurchase the

---

2. To qualify as a primary dealer, a firm must be adequately capitalized, submit daily reports on its positions and transactions, and provide periodic certified financial statements.

Table 9-1

Transactions of the System Open Market Account, 1977 and 1978
(millions of dollars)

	1977	1978
U.S. Government Securities		
Outright transactions		
Treasury bills:		
Gross purchases	13,738	16,628
Gross sales	7,241	13,725
Redemptions	2,136	2,033
Others within one year:		
Gross purchases	3,017	1,184
Gross sales	0	0
Exchange, or maturity shift	4,499	−5,170
Redemptions	2,500	0
One to 5 years:		
Gross purchases	2,833	4,188
Gross sales	0	0
Exchange, or maturity shift	−6,649	− 178
Five to 10 years:		
Gross purchases	753	1,526
Gross sales	0	0
Exchange, or maturity shift	584	2,803
Over 10 years:		
Gross purchases	553	1,063
Gross sales	0	0
Exchange, or maturity shift	1,565	2,545
All maturities:		
Gross purchases	20,898	24,591
Gross sales	7,241	13,725
Redemptions	4,636	2,033
Matched sale-purchase transactions		
Gross sales	425,214	511,126
Gross purchases	423,841	510,854
Repurchase agreements		
Gross purchases	178,683	151,618
Gross sales	180,535	152,436
Net change in U.S. Government securities	5,798	7,743
Federal Agency Obligations		
Outright transactions		
Gross purchases	1,433	301
Gross sales	0	173
Redemptions	223	235

> **Table 9-1 (cont.)**
> Transactions of the System Open Market Account, 1977 and 1978
> (millions of dollars)

	1977	1978
Repurchase agreements		
Gross purchases	13,811	40,567
Gross sales	13,638	40,885
Net change in federal agency obligations	1,383	– 426
Bankers Acceptances		
Outright transactions, net	– 196	0
Repurchase agreements, net	159	– 366
Net change in bankers acceptances	– 37	– 366
Total net change in		
System Open Market Account	7,143	6,951

Source: Board of Governors of the Federal Reserve, *Federal Reserve Bulletin.*

securities. Matched sale-purchase transactions permit the Account Manager to absorb reserves from the banking system on a temporary basis. Later, when the repurchase is consummated, reserves flow into the system. As shown in Table 9-1, matched sale-purchase transactions totaled over $510 billion in 1978.

Repurchase agreements (Rps) are arrangements whereby the Account Manager purchases securities from dealers who agree to repurchase them by a specified date. Rps are used to inject reserves in the system on a temporary basis and are dated to terminate in from one to fifteen business days, with the majority maturing in less than seven days.

Open Market Operations—An Evaluation

The technique of open market operations has several important advantages over other means of monetary control. First, it is the only technique that changes directly the monetary base. A change in the discount rate involves a change only in the price of borrowing reserves at the Fed, and this may or may not lead to a change in reserves. Second, open market operations is the only technique that permits the Fed to make "fine tuning" adjustments to the money supply. That is, the Fed can increase or decrease the monetary base by small amounts, which lays the foundation for small changes in the money supply. Third, utilizing open market operations provides the Account Manager with timing flexibility in changing the monetary base and the money supply. In the morning, he might temporarily inject reserves into the system with an Rp; then, if conditions change in the afternoon, he might execute a matched sale-repurchase agreement. Professor Milton Friedman, winner of the Nobel Prize in Economics, has pointed out many times that open market operations is the only tool needed to control the money supply.

Changes in the Discount Rate

Background

Changes in the discount rate was the only technique of monetary control embodied in the original Federal Reserve Act in 1913. Discounting was seen as a way to provide liquidity to the banking system and thereby eliminate future money panics. Banks faced with deposit runs or legitimate loan requests could rediscount customer notes with the Fed. The theory was that by lowering or raising the discount rate, the Fed could encourage or discourage member bank borrowing. Because the Bank of England had controlled the flow of money and credit in this manner for many years, the framers of the Federal Reserve Act felt changes in the discount rate was an essential power to grant to the new central bank. Also, their faith in the sufficiency of discounting was grounded on their belief in Say's Law and the commercial loan theory of bank lending.[3] **Say's Law**, named after the eighteenth-century economist J.B. Say, was the prevailing macroeconomic theory of the time and held that economic activity tended toward the full employment level. If this were true, then there would be no need for countercyclical changes in the money supply. As discussed earlier, the commercial loan theory of bank lending holds that banks should make only short-term, self-liquidating loans. If banks adhered to this theory, then money and credit would expand with the "needs of trade." The original Federal Reserve Act encouraged banks to follow the commercial loan theory by specifying that only short-term commercial and agricultural loans were **eligible**

3. Say's Law is discussed further in Chapter 10.

collateral for loans from the central bank. Discounting these loans was supposed to accommodate seasonal needs for credit and provide elasticity to the money supply. Indeed, during the 1920s, reserves supplied through discounting never fell below 37 percent of member bank reserves.

Administration of the Discount Window

Rules governing Reserve Bank lending are set forth in the Fed's Regulation A. As pointed out in the last chapter, there are two basic types of loans: discounts and advances. Loans to member banks may be classified according to purpose: (1) short-term adjustment credit, (2) seasonal credit, and (3) emergency credit. Ordinarily, the great majority of all Fed loans represents **short-term adjustment credit**, whose primary purpose is "in meeting temporary requirements for funds or to cushion more persistent outflows of funds pending an orderly adjustment of the bank's assets and liabilities." Each Reserve bank develops guidelines for providing adjustment credit. For example, according to guidelines at the Dallas Fed Discount Window, a bank that borrows under adjustment credit is not expected to be indebted for more than to six to eight continuous reserve periods (Thursday to Wednesday) or eight to ten of the previous thirteen reserve periods.[4]

To qualify for **seasonal credit**, a member bank must have a recurring seasonal need for funds and lack reasonably reliable access to the national money market. Seasonal credit was instituted in 1973 principally to assist small banks in rural and tourist areas, and is limited to the amount by which the member bank's seasonal needs exceed 5 percent of its average total deposits in the preceding year. In 1976, the seasonal privilege was liberalized to extend to banks which have net sales of Federal funds if such sales represent the bank's normal operating pattern. With computer analysis, Reserve banks are able to identify banks that qualify for seasonal credit. After these banks are identified and notified, they must arrange with the Reserve Bank for the seasonal credit. The Dallas Fed has determined that member banks borrowing under the seasonal privilege have the following characteristics: (1) are in cities with 6,000 to 15,000 in population; (2) have deposits ranging from $10 million to $30 million; (3) have

4. Leon W. Cowan, "Seasonal Borrowing Privilege Liberalized," Federal Reserve Bank of Dallas, *Business Review* (November 1976), p. 10.

borrowed for a duration of four to six months; (4) have had borrowings ranging from 80 to 150 percent of required reserves, but frequently reach two and one-half to three times required reserves on a daily average basis; and (5) typically have agricultural loans that comprise 30 to 60 percent total loans outstanding.[5]

Emergency credit is available to assist member banks in unusual or emergency circumstances such as may result from national, regional, or local difficulties or from exceptional circumstances involving only a particular member bank. A good example of emergency credit occurred in 1970 when the Penn-Central Railroad defaulted on its commercial paper. This caused buyers to shy away from commercial paper as an investment and forced many companies to turn to banks to obtain short-term funds. A number of banks involved were allowed to obtain emergency credit from the discount window. Thus, the Fed was able to fulfill its role as the **lender of last resort** and ultimate source of liquidity to the economy.

Another example of emergency credit occurred in 1974 when the Franklin National Bank ran into serious financial difficulties. The Fed extended emergency credit to the beleaguered bank totaling $1.8 billion—the largest loan ever made by the Fed. In this case, the Fed was truly the lender of last resort.

Since its early days, the Fed has stressed two principles governing discounting. First, discounting is a privilege, not a right. The Fed does not have to lend to a member bank. However, the seasonal borrowing privilege is almost a right and does represent a significant step by the Fed to be more accommodative through the discount window. Second, the Fed has classified several borrowing purposes as inappropriate. These include continuous borrowing and borrowing to obtain a tax advantage, to profit from rate differentials, and to finance the speculation in securities, real estate, or commodities. Because of the general "thou shalt not" nature of Fed regulations and attitude regarding borrowing, most member banks have a pronounced "reluctance to borrow." However, in recent years, the discount rate typically has been below the Federal funds rate and the rate on negotiable CDs. During times of monetary restraint, this condition has led larger numbers of banks to the discount window and with increasing frequency.

5. Cowan, pp. 10–11.

Figure 9–5. (Courtesy of the Federal Reserve Bank of New York)

Changes in the Discount Rate

As pointed out earlier, when the Fed was created, the conventional wisdom was that increases in the discount rate discouraged borrowing, while decreases had the opposite effect. However, in modern times, the level of borrowing tends to rise during periods when the discount rate is increasing and vice versa (Table 9–2). How is this contradictory effect explained? During periods in which the discount rate is increasing, the Fed usually is not providing reserves at a rate that the banking system might prefer. A number of banks that cannot meet all of the legitimate loan demands of their customers turn to the Fed for loans, and the Fed tends to be accommodative. Higher discount rates are not a deterrent to borrowing because the rate that banks can earn on the funds usually has risen more than proportionately to any changes in the discount rate. On the other hand, during periods when there is slow credit demand and the Fed might be encouraging credit expansion through open market purchases, reductions in the discount rate will not induce banks to borrow from the Fed. This situation is similar to your local K-Mart running a "blue-light special," but you already have all of the item that you want. In sum, the direct relationship between the amount of Fed lending and the discount rate is another illustration of why "correlation does not

Table 9-2
Discount Rate (End of Month) and
Member Bank Borrowing (Monthly Averages), 1974–1979
(millions of dollars)

	1974		1975	
	Discount Rate	Borrowings	Discount Rate	Borrowings
Jan.	7-1/2	1,044	7-1/4	390
Feb.	—	1,186	6-3/4	147
Mar.	—	1,352	6-1/4	106
Apr.	8	1,714	—	110
May	—	2,580	6	60
June	—	3,000	—	271
July	—	3,308	—	261
Aug.	—	3,351	—	211
Sept.	—	3,287	—	396
Oct.	—	1,793	—	191
Nov.	—	1,285	—	61
Dec.	7-3/4	703	—	127

	1976		1977	
	Discount Rate	Borrowings	Discount Rate	Borrowings
Jan.	5-1/2	79	—	61
Feb.	—	76	—	79
Mar.	—	58	—	110
Apr.	—	44	—	73
May	—	121	—	200
June	—	120	—	262
July	—	123	—	336
Aug.	—	104	5-3/4	1,071
Sept.	—	75	—	634
Oct.	—	66	6	1,319
Nov.	5-1/4	84	—	840
Dec.	—	62	—	558

	1978		1979	
	Discount Rate	Borrowings	Discount Rate	Borrowings
Jan.	6-1/2	481	9-1/2	994
Feb.	—	405	—	973
Mar.	—	344	—	999
Apr.	—	539	—	897
May	7	1,227	—	1,777
June	—	1,111	—	1,396
July	7-1/4	1,286	10	1,179
Aug.	7-3/4	1,147		
Sept.	8	1,068		
Oct.	8-1/2	1,261		
Nov.	9-1/2	722		
Dec.	—	874		

Source: Board of Governors of the Federal Reserve, *Federal Reserve Bulletin.*

prove causation." The stance of open market policy and the demand for credit are largely responsible for the direct correlation between member bank borrowing and changes in the discount rate.

It must be pointed out, however, that raising the discount rate does deter some borrowing. Some banks just do not wish to pay the higher rate for funds. Without the increase, banks certainly would have wished to borrow more.

Another question regarding discount rate policy is whether changes in the discount rate lead or lag changes in the federal funds rate and the T-bill rate, the two key money market rates. Keep in mind that the discount rate is an administered rate, while these other two rates are market-determined rates set by supply and demand. As a general rule, changes in the discount rate lag these other rates. Close analysis of Figure 9-6 should reveal this. Thus, the Fed generally is playing "catch-up ball" by trying to keep the discount rate in line with these other rates. From time to time, when the Fed lags a bit in moving the rate upward, large money market banks will borrow from the Fed and obtain what they are not supposed to realize—a profit. The Fed usually moves quickly to bring the rate in line and sometimes admonishes the banks for borrowing.

Finally, some economists and bankers feel that the primary function of changes in the discount rate is to signal changes in monetary policy. Increases signal tight money, while decreases indicate easy money. To some bankers, increases in the discount have a psychological effect that causes them to become more reluctant to lend. Conversely, decreases have a similar bullish effect. However, there are strong reasons to believe that changes in the discount rate might have a perverse effect. For example, if borrowers believe that increases signal tight money, they may rush down to their bank and attempt to obtain funds before the crunch hits. Also, caution should be used in interpreting increases as tangible evidence of tight money. The absolute level of the rate does not indicate tightness or looseness; what is significant is the relationship of the discount rate to other money market rates.

Changes in the Discount Rate—An Evaluation

Most economists agree that changes in the discount rate are a rather ineffective technique of monetary control. The impetus to borrow lies with member banks; therefore, the Fed cannot accurately

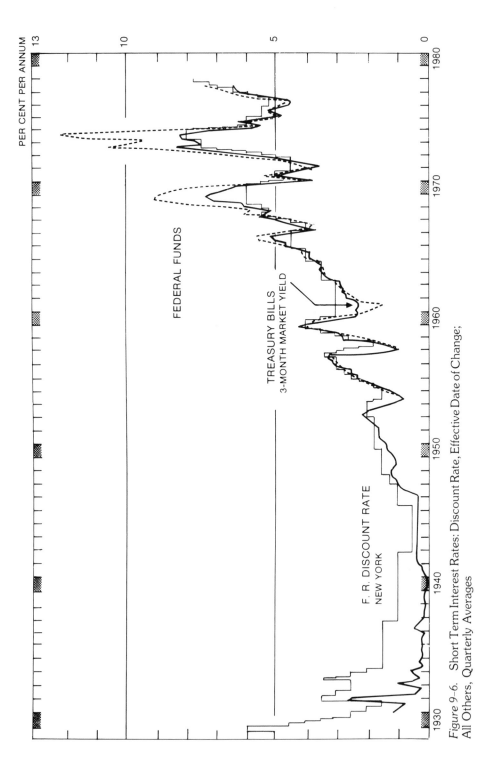

Figure 9–6. Short Term Interest Rates: Discount Rate, Effective Date of Change; All Others, Quarterly Averages

Source: Board of Governors of the Federal Reserve, *Historical Chart Book.*

forecast future changes in reserves. With respect to its role as a signal of the direction of monetary policy, this is true at times, but not always. Besides, the "announcement effect" of a change in the discount rate may trigger a perverse reaction in the marketplace. Even if the primary role of a change in the discount rate is a signal, we have better means available to indicate the direction of monetary policy—for example, a press release by the Fed. Then there should be no doubt about the Fed's intentions.

Changes in Reserve Ratios

Nature and Purpose of Legal Reserve Requirements

Since the early 1800s, several states have required banks to hold cash reserves such as gold coins against their deposit liabilities. Because a bank's ability to expand its loans through the issuance of more notes was limited by the amount of its legal reserves, these early reserve requirements served to limit somewhat the expansion of money and credit.

At some point in our banking history, it became popular to view cash requirements as a liquidity requirement that guaranteed that depositors could withdraw or transfer their deposits. The fallacy in this view is that required cash reserves are only a fraction of deposit liabilities; hence, depositors are protected only partially by legal reserve requirements. To illustrate, if the reserve ratio were 10 percent for demand deposits, then for each $100 in demand deposit withdrawals, only $10 would be released from required reserves. Thus, in a sense, required reserves are the most illiquid asset that banks hold.

The modern view of reserve requirements is that they are a fulcrum for monetary control. That is, they are the policy instrument that enables the Fed to manage the money supply by influencing the reserve base through open market operations. Because banks are required to hold specific assets in ratios to deposits and nondeposit liabilities, variation of the reserve base by open market operations permits the money supply to expand by a multiple of the change in the reserve base. Of course, we must recognize that released required reserves do cover a fraction of any deposit withdrawal; however, this is of secondary importance.

The Fed's Reserve Requirements and Ratios

An important banking reform effected by the Federal Reserve Act was the requirement that member banks hold all of their reserves at the Reserve banks. Member banks were prohibited from holding reserves in correspondent banks, a practice that contributed to the severity of the post-Civil War money panics. From the early days of the Fed until 1933, the reserve ratios were a fixed percentage of deposits. In 1933, an amendment to the Federal Reserve Act authorized change of reserve ratios under emergency conditions. In 1935, other amendments permitted the Fed to vary reserve ratios as a technique of monetary control and stipulated that authority to change reserve ratios rested exclusively with the Board of Governors. As shown in Table 9–3, under its new authority, the Board in 1936 and 1937 doubled reserve ratios on net demand deposits from 13 to 26 percent at central reserve city banks (New York and Chicago); from 10 to 20 percent at reserve city banks (any other city with a reserve bank or branch); and from 7 to 14 percent at country banks (all banks not in central reserve cities or reserve cities). Reserve ratios on time deposits for all classes of banks were raised from 3 to 6 percent. The purpose of the sharp increase in reserve ratios was to absorb the large amount of excess reserves that had built up in the banking system because of gold inflows. The Fed feared that the excess reserves, which had hit $7 billion, might fuel inflation. The increase in reserve ratios eliminated the excess reserves, but it also was largely responsible for the 1937–1938 recession and for halting the economic recovery that was underway.

As may be seen in Table 9–3, reserve ratios have drifted downward since their peak in 1948–1949. There have been a number of technical changes and adjustments in Fed reserve requirements and reserve ratios, most of which are detailed in Table 9–3. Since World War II the most important changes in reserve requirements include (1) legislation in 1959 permitting vault cash to count as legal reserves (this has been in effect for all banks since 1960); (2) in 1969 the imposition of reserve requirements on nondeposit sources of funds such as Eurodollar borrowings and commercial paper sold by bank holding companies; and (3) the shift in 1972 to graduated reserve ratios on net demand deposits.

Changes in Reserve Ratios as a Technique of Monetary Control

Over the last three decades the Fed has used changes in reserve ratios rather infrequently. Reserve ratios were increased during the Korean and Vietnam wars and several other times as part of general contracyclical measures. On more occasions, reserve ratios have been reduced to bolster a sagging economy. But, all in all, the Fed is reluctant to use changes in reserve ratios as a tool of monetary control. This is especially true for increases because they have such a large contractionary effect on required and excess reserves. A half-point increase across the board in reserve ratios increases required reserves by about $1 billion. Unless accompanied by open market purchases, the effect on the banking system and the economy is traumatic. Such an abrupt change causes many banks to have to sell securities at a loss, and it places undue burden on those firms looking to their bank for needed working capital. The Fed can achieve the same end with open market sales and with less disruption in the banking system and the economy.

Changes in Reserve Ratios—An Evaluation

Making changes in reserve ratios has one clear advantage over other techniques of monetary control: this is the best tool to use if large quantities of excess reserves must be absorbed or if the banking system needs instant liquidity across the board as in a national emergency.

On the other hand, changes in reserve ratios are very unwieldy; they cannot be used to fine tune the money supply. Second, increases in reserve ratios to effect tight money discriminate against member banks vis-à-vis nonmember banks, and this exacerbates the problem of attrition from the ranks of Fed members. Member banks are called upon to bear the brunt of tight money by a reduction in earning assets and, hence, in income. Finally, changes in reserve ratios may have the same perverse announcement effect as do changes in the discount rate.

Table 9-3
Member Bank Reserve Ratios, 1917-1979
(Percent of deposits)

Through July 13, 1966

Effective date	Net demand deposits			Time deposit (all classes of banks)
	Central reserve city banks	Reserve city banks	Country banks	
1917—June 21	13	10	7	3
1936—Aug. 16	19½	15	10½	4½
1937—Mar. 1	22¾	17½	12¼	5¼
May 1	26	20	14	6
1938—Apr. 16	22¾	17½	12	5
1941—Nov. 1	26	20	14	6
1942—Aug. 20	24	....	....	....
Sept. 14	22	....	....	....
Oct. 3	20	....	....	....
1948—Feb. 27	22	....	....	....
June 11	24	....	....	....
Sept. 24, 16	26	22	16	7½
1949—May 5, 1	24	21	15	7
June 30, July 1	....	20	14	6
Aug. 1	....	....	13	....
Aug. 11, 16	23½	19½	12	5
Aug. 18	23	19	....	....
Aug. 25	22½	18½	....	....
Sept. 1	22	18	....	....
1951—Jan. 11, 16	23	19	13	6
Jan. 25, Feb. 1	24	20	14	....
1953—July 9, 1	22	19	13	....
1954—June 24, 16	21	....	....	5
July 29, Aug. 1	20	18	12	....
1958—Feb. 27, Mar. 1	19½	17½	11½	....
Mar. 20, Apr. 1	19	17	11	....
Apr. 17	18½	....	....	....
Apr. 24	18	16½	....	....
1960—Sept. 1	17½	....	....	....
Nov. 24	....	....	12	....
Dec. 1	16½	....	....	....
1962—July 28	....	....	....	....
Oct. 25, Nov. 1	....	....	....	4

Table 9-3 (cont.)
Member Bank Reserve Ratios, 1917–1979
(Percent of deposits)

July 14, 1966, through Nov. 8, 1972 (deposit intervals are in millions of dollars)

Effective date	Net demand deposits — Reserve city banks 0-5	Over 5	Net demand deposits — Country banks 0-5	Over 5	Time deposits (all classes of banks) — Savings	Other time 0-5	Over 5
1966—July 14, 21	16½		12		4	4	5
Sept. 8, 15	.....	.....	.....	.....	.....	.....	6
1967—Mar. 2	.....	.....	.....	.....	3½	3½	.....
Mar. 16	.....	.....	.....	.....	3	3	.....
1968—Jan. 11, 18	16½	17	12	12½	.....	.....	.....
1969—Apr. 17	17	17½	12½	13	.....	.....	.....
1970—Oct. 1	.....	.....	.....	.....	.....	.....	5

Beginning Nov. 9, 1972 (deposit intervals are in millions of dollars)

Effective date	Net demand deposits 0-2	2-10	10-100	100-400	Over 400	Savings	Other time: 0-5 maturing in — 30-179 days	180 days to 4 yrs.	4 yrs. or more	Over 5, maturing in — 30-179 days	180 days to 4 yrs.	4 yrs. or more
1972—Nov. 9	8	10	12	16½	17½	3	3			5		
Nov. 16	...	....	....	13	....							
1973—July 19	...	10½	12½	13½	18							
1974—Dec. 12	...	....	....	....	17½					6	3	
1975—Feb. 13	7½	10	12	13	16½							
Oct. 30	...	....	....	....	....	....		3	1		3	1
1976—Jan. 8	...	....	....	....	....	3		2½			2½	
Dec. 30	7	9½	11¾	12¾	16¼	....						
In effect Feb. 28, 1979	7	9½	11¾	12¾	16¼	3	3	2½	1	6	2½	1

Legal limits—Feb. 28, 1979:	Minimum	Maximum
Net demand deposits:		
Reserve city banks	10	22
Other banks	7	14
Time deposits	3	10

Source: Board of Governors of the Federal Reserve, *Annual Report* and *Federal Reserve Bulletin.*

Selective Credit Controls

Margin Requirements

In the 1920s, the stock market boomed, thanks to easy credit available at banks and private lenders. Most loans carried interest rates between 12 and 18 percent, but borrowers were insensitive to the high cost of funds because the general level of stock prices doubled between 1925 and 1927 and doubled again between 1927 and 1929. In most cases, banks and private lenders had "in-house" margin requirements of approximately 10 percent. For example, in 1925 if you had bought 10,000 shares of a $10 stock, your margin requirement would have been $10,000. If the price per share doubled to $20, then your gross profit would have been $100,000 on an investment of $10,000. Your interest cost to borrow $90,000 at 15 percent for two years would have been $27,000, leaving you with a profit before taxes (which were very minimal) of $73,000 on an investment of $10,000. This would be a 730 percent gain over a two-year period. From this illustration, it should be clear why people were enthusiastic about buying stocks on credit.

Profits such as these sound fine until the implications are examined with respect to the economy as a whole. Some economists feel that easy credit was behind the rise in stock prices, and a rising stock market encouraged businesses to raise additional funds through new stock issues. Furthermore, they claim that these funds financed a surge in capital spending that could not be sustained into the 1930s. Also, the unrealistic expectations of continued profits in the stock market may have led to "conspicuous consumption" that could not be sustained. We all have heard stories from the roaring twenties of spending for lavish parties, air-conditioned doghouses, and the like.

After the stock market crash in October, 1929, and the further collapse to 1933, Congress held extensive hearings on the stock market and the possible causes of its crash. Based on its findings, Congress passed comprehensive legislation to regulate the securities industry and credit flowing into it. In the Securities Exchange Act of 1934, Congress designated the Fed Board of Governors to establish margin requirements for purchasing or carrying securities. Based on this act and its amendments, the Board imposed margin requirements on credit provided by brokers and dealers (Regulation T), banks (Regulation U), and other lenders (Regulation G). To prevent borrowers from obtaining foreign credit in excess of what might be supplied in this country and to improve overall compliance generally, all US persons must comply with Regulation X.

Margin requirements apply to corporate stocks and convertible bonds listed on national exchanges and on designated over-the-counter stocks. As may be seen in Table 9–4, margin requirements on margin stocks have been as low as 40 percent and as high as 100 percent. At the present time, margin requirements seem to have settled in at the 50 percent level.

There is a contrary school of thought regarding the need for control

Table 9–4

Margin Requirements, 1937–1979

(Percent of market value)

Period		On margin stocks			On convertible bonds			On short sales
Beginning date	Ending date	T	U	G	T	U	G	(T)
1937—Nov. 1	1945—Feb. 4	40						50
1945—Feb. 5	July 4	50						50
July 5	1946—Jan. 20	75						75
1946—Jan. 21	1947—Jan. 31	100						100
1947—Feb. 1	1949—Mar. 29	75						75
1949—Mar. 30	1951—Jan. 16	50						50
1951—Jan. 17	1953—Feb. 19	75						75
1953—Feb. 20	1955—Jan. 3	50						50
1955—Jan. 4	Apr. 22	60						60
Apr. 23	1958—Jan. 15	70						70
1958—Jan. 16	Aug. 4	50						50
Aug. 5	Oct. 15	70						70
Oct. 16	1960—July 27	90						90
1960—July 28	1962—July 9	70						70
1962—July 10	1963—Nov. 5	50						50
1963—Nov. 6	1968—Mar. 10	70						70
1968—Mar. 11	June 7	70			50			70
June 8	1970—May 3	80			60			80
1970—May 6	1971—Dec. 3	65			50			65
1971—Dec. 6	1972—Nov. 22	55			50			55
1972—Nov. 24	1974—Jan. 2	65			50			65
Effective Jan. 3, 1974		50			50			50

Note: For credit extended under Regulations T (brokers and dealers), U (banks), and G (other than brokers, dealers, or banks)

Source: Board of Governors of Federal Reserve, *Annual Report.*

over securities credit. Professor Milton Friedman has argued forcefully that margin requirements are an impediment to the free flow of funds and to the competitive market system.[6] In other words, it amounts to twisting the "invisible hand" that Adam Smith said was supposed to guide decision making and maximize overall economic welfare. Additional credit channeled into securities might facilitate capital spending which would modernize our productive capacity, and make our goods more competitive in world markets. Also, it would stimulate economic growth to absorb new entrants into the labor force. If you are concerned about banks making too many risky securities loans, this and the quality of all bank credit can be regulated directly through periodic bank examinations. What do you think? Should the government impose margin requirements?

The Regulation Q Ceilings

Coming out of Congressional hearings of the bank failures associated with the Great Depression was the allegation that many banks failed because they became embroiled in interest rate wars in competing for deposits and, thus, had to reach for more risky, higher-yielding loans and investments to cover the interest expenses. Reacting to this hypothesis, Congress included in the Banking Act of 1933 a provision that prohibited member banks from paying interest on demand deposits and gave the Fed the power to set ceilings on interest rates on time and savings deposits. In the Banking Act of 1935, the FDIC received similar authority over nonmember, insured banks. The Fed's rules regarding interest rate ceilings are embodied in Regulation Q. Table 9-5 chronicles the Reg. Q ceilings since 1933.

Initially, the Reg. Q ceilings were viewed as a way to keep bank costs down, not as a selective tool of credit control. Ceilings remained constant from 1936 to 1956; however, as banks began to compete with S&Ls for time and savings deposits, the ceilings were adjusted upward. In 1966, however, the demand for credit rose sharply and, together with the Fed's tight money policy, produced the first of three "money crunches" that the nation was to experience over the next eight years. As rates on money market instruments, such as T-bills and commercial paper, rose above the Reg. Q ceilings, savers began

6. Milton Friedman, *A Program for Monetary Stability* (New York: Fordham University Press, 1959), pp. 26–27.

to withdraw funds from banks, S&Ls, and MSBs and place them directly in the higher yielding securities.[7] This process was termed **financial disintermediation**. The inability to compete effectively for time and savings deposits meant that banks had to reduce those types of loans that they matched with longer-term sources of funds, namely, term loans, real estate loans, and municipals. For S&Ls, disintermediation meant a reduction in home mortgage lending. The same pattern developed in 1969, 1970, and 1974, but with greater intensity.

The use of the Reg. Q ceilings in this manner discriminated against small businesses that were unable to shift to other sources of funds, against any business dependent on bank credit, against state and local government capital spending because the bank market for municipals dried up, and against home buyers. On the other side of the balance sheet, Reg. Q ceilings discriminated against small savers who could not benefit from investments in higher yielding, money market debt. The Reg. Q ceilings represented price fixing that favored the large saver. All in all, most economists and Fed policymakers were not pleased with the disruption in the financial markets and the uneven incidence caused by the use of the Reg. Q ceilings as a tool of credit control.

In response to such criticism and in response to the failure of Penn-Central, the Fed, on June 24, 1970, suspended the ceilings on CDs of $100,000 or more and with maturities of 30–89 days. Penn-Central defaulted on its commercial paper; this caused lenders to shy away from all commercial paper and forced many firms using this short-term source of funds to turn to banks for loans. The suspension of interest rate ceilings on these CDs enabled banks to compete for deposits to meet this legitimate surge in loan demand. Following this suspension, money market rates abated, but in 1973 once again pushed above the ceilings. On May 16, 1973, the Fed suspended the ceilings on all longer-term $100,000 CDs. Today, there still is no ceiling on the rate that banks may pay on these obligations. Presently, there is a good deal of sentiment among economists and public interest groups to eliminate the Reg. Q ceilings; in the near future it seems fairly certain that this will be accomplished.

---

7. In 1966 Congress empowered the various regulatory agencies to extend interest ceilings to S&Ls and MSBs.

Table 9-5
Maximum Interest Rates Payable on Time and Savings Deposits, 1933–1979
(Percent per annum)

Nov. 1, 1933—July 19, 1966

Type of deposit	Effective date							
	Nov. 1, 1933	Feb. 1, 1935	Jan. 1, 1936	Jan. 1, 1957	Jan. 1, 1962	July 17, 1963	Nov. 24, 1964	Dec. 6, 1965
Savings deposits:								
12 months or more }	3	2½	2½	3	{4 / 3½}	{4 / 3½}	4	4
Less than 12 months }								
Postal savings deposits:								
12 months or more }	3	2½	2½	3	{4 / 3½}	{4 / 3½}	4	4
Less than 12 months }								
Other time deposits:								
12 months or more }	3	2½	2½	3	{4 / 3½}	4	4½ }	
6–12 months }								
90 days to 6 months	3	2½	2	2½	2½ }			5½
Less than 90 days... (30–89 days)	3	2½	1	1	1	1	4 }	

July 20, 1966—June 30, 1973

Type of deposit	Effective date			
	July 20, 1966	Sept. 26, 1966	Apr. 19, 1968	Jan. 21, 1970
Savings deposits	4	4	4	4½
Other time deposits:				
Multiple maturity:[1]				
30–89 days	4	4	4	4½
90 days to 1 year }				{5
1–2 years }	5	5	5	{5½
2 years or more }				{5¾
Single-maturity:				
Less than $100,000:				
30 days to 1 year }				{5
1–2 years }	5½	5	5	{5½
2 years or more }				{5¾
$100,000 or more:				
30–59 }			5	(2)
60–89 days }			5¾	(2)
90–179 }	5½	5½	6	(2)
180 days to 1 year }			} 6¼	(2)
1 year or more... }				(2)

Table 9-5 (cont.)

Maximum Interest Rates Payable on Time and Savings Deposits, 1933–1979
(Percent per annum)

Beginning July 1, 1973

	Effective date				
Type of deposit	July 1, 1973	Nov. 1, 1973	Nov. 27, 1974	Dec. 23, 1974	July 6, 1977
Savings deposits	5	5	5	5	5
Other time deposits (multiple- and single-maturity).[1]					
Less than $100,000:					
30–89 days	5	5	5	5	5
90 days to 1 year	5½	5½	5½	5½	5½
1–2½ years	6	6	6	6	6
2½ years or more	6½	6½	6½	6½	6½
Minimum denomination of $1,000:					
4–6 years .... }	(3)	7¼	7¼	{ 7¼	7¼
6 years or more .... }				{ 7½	7½
Governmental units	(4)	(4)	7½	7¾	7¾
Individual retirement accounts and Keogh (H.R. 10) plans[5]	......	......	......	......	7¾
$100,000 or more	(2)	(2)	(2)	(2)	(2)

[1]Multiple-maturity time deposits include deposits that are automatically renewable at maturity without action by the depositor and deposits that are payable after written notice of withdrawal.

[2]Maximum rates on all single-maturity time deposits in denominations of $100,000 or more have been suspended. Rates that were effective Jan. 21, 1970, and the dates when they were suspended are:

30–59 days	6¼ percent }	June 24, 1970
60–89 days	6½ percent }	
90–179 days	6¾ percent }	
180 days to 1 year	7 percent }	May 16, 1973
1 year or more	7½ percent }	

Rates on multiple-maturity time deposits in denominations of $100,000 or more were suspended July 16, 1973, when the distinction between single- and multiple-maturity deposits was eliminated.

[3]Between July 1 and Oct. 31, 1973, there was no ceiling for certificates maturing in 4 years or more with minimum denominations of $1,000. The amount of such certificates that a bank could issue was limited to 5 per cent of its total time and savings deposits. Sales in excess of that amount were subject to the 6½ per cent ceiling that applies to time deposits maturing in 2½ years or more.

Effective Nov. 1, 1973, a ceiling rate of 7¼ percent was imposed on certificates maturing in 4 years or more with minimum denominations of $1,000. There is no limitation on the amount of these certificates that banks may issue.

[4]Prior to Nov. 27, 1974, no distinction was made between the time deposits of governmental units and of other holders, insofar as Regulation Q ceilings on rates payable were concerned. Effective Nov. 27, 1974, governmental units were permitted to hold savings deposits and could receive interest rates on time deposits with denominations under $100,000 irrespective of maturity, as high as the maximum rate permitted on such deposits at any Federally insured depositary institution.

[5]Three-year minimum maturity.

Source: Board of Governors of Federal Reserve, Annual Report and Federal Reserve Bulletin.

Consumer Credit and Real Estate Credit Controls

During World War II and after, and during the Korean War, Congress empowered the Fed to set minimum down payments and maximum maturities on consumer installment credit to finance purchases of consumer durables. During the Korean War, this power was extended to include setting maximum maturities and maximum loan-to-value ratios on mortgage financed housing. The general argument in favor of direct controls such as these is that purchasers of these terms are insensitive to increases in the cost of credit brought about by use of general monetary tools. Therefore, credit extensions for these items must be regulated directly. Whereas most economists agree that consumer and real estate credit controls are necessary during times of national emergency, they do not favor their general use because this involves direct interference with the free market process.

Moral Suasion

Moral suasion is the use of speeches, press releases, and directives by members of the Fed Board to influence member bank borrowing, bankers' willingness to lend, and the demand for credit. Journalists sometimes refer to moral suasion as "jaw-boning" or "open-mouth operations." An example or moral suasion was in 1966 when Fed officials warned banks that if they did not stop liquidation of their holdings of municipal securities in order to obtain funds to meet business loan demand, they might not be able to borrow at the Fed if they got in a liquidity bind. Another example occurred in 1973 when banks with over $100 million in deposits were urged under the threat of tougher examinations to slow down their extension of lines of credit to businesses in order to reduce potential inflationary pressures. The general consensus of economists is that moral suasion is a useful supplementary tool, but is not a substitute for the quantitative tools.

Summary

The Fed's three primary techniques of monetary control are open market operations, changes in reserve ratios, and changes in the discount rate. Open market operations are the buying and selling of securities by the Fed to influence the reserve base. This technique is superior to all others because it is the only tool that directly influences the reserve base, can be used to fine tune the money supply, and provides the Fed with flexibility in timing changes in the reserve base and money supply.

Increases in the discount rate usually are associated with increases in borrowing and vice versa. This contradictory effect is caused by open market sales forcing banks to the discount window at the same time that the discount rate is increasing, and, on the other side of the coin, by open market purchases eliminating the need to borrow when the discount rate is reduced. Some experts believe that the primary role of changes in the discount rate is to signal changes in the direction of monetary policy. However, analysis of changes in bank reserves and other monetary indicators is superior to this crude device.

Changes in reserve ratios change the multiplier. As a technique of monetary control, changes in reserve ratios can bring about large and swift changes in the distribution of required and excess reserves. However, this tool is unwieldy and cannot be used to make fine-tuning adjustments in the money supply. Also, it discriminates against member banks vis-à-vis nonmembers.

Margin requirements specify the minimum down payment to buy securities on credit. Some economists feel that margin requirements are an unnecessary interference in the market mechanism.

During periods of rising rates the Reg. Q ceilings on interest rates that banks may pay on time and savings deposits have led to financial disintermediation. Most economists favor their repeal because they lead to disruptive shifts in the flow of funds in the financial markets during tight money periods and because they discriminate against small savers, small businesses, state and local governments, and home buyers during tight money periods.

Questions and Problems

1. List the tools of monetary control and the primary variables that they affect.
2. List and describe briefly the three basic types of Fed open market transactions.
3. Evaluate open market operations as a technique of monetary control.
4. "Member bank borrowing at the discount window usually increases when the discount rate is lowered." Do you agree? Explain.

5. Evaluate changes in the discount rate as a technique of monetary control.

6. Explain the old and new view of the purpose of legal reserve requirements.

7. Evaluate changes in reserve ratios as a technique of monetary control.

Suggestions for Additional Reading

Burke, William. "Primer on Reserve Requirements." Federal Reserve Bank of San Francisco, *Economic Review* (Winter 1974), pp. 18–31.

Friedman, Milton. *A Program for Monetary Stability.* New York: Fordham University Press, 1960.

———. "Controls on Interest Rates Paid by Banks." *Journal of Money, Credit, and Banking* (February 1970), pp. 15–32.

Humphrey, Thomas M. "The Classical Concept of the Lender of Last Resort." Federal Reserve Bank of Richmond, *Economic Review* (January/February 1975), pp. 2–9.

Kaminow, Ira, and James M. O'Brien, "Selective Credit Policies: Should Their Role Be Expanded?" Federal Reserve Bank of Philadelphia, *Business Review* (November 1975), pp. 3–22.

Knight, Robert E. "Reserve Requirements Part I: Comparative Reserve Requirements at Member and Nonmember Banks." Federal Reserve Bank of Kansas City, *Monthly Review* (April 1974), pp. 3–20.

———. "Reserve Requirements Part II: An Analysis of the Case for Uniform Reserve Requirements." Federal Reserve Bank of Kansas City, *Monthly Review* (May 1974), pp. 3–15.

4

Monetary and Income Theory

10

Classical Theories

Part 4 deals with **monetary theory**, a branch of macroeconomics that seeks to discover and explain how the demand and supply of money influence prices, interest rates, income, and employment. Monetary theory is the basis for **monetary policy**, which is the actual management of the money supply to achieve our national economic goals such as low levels of unemployment, price stability, adequate economic growth, and an improvement in our international merchandise trade balance.

The word "theory" frightens some students. The primary purpose of any theory is *to explain*. We have theories about *every* facet and phenomenon in life. There are theories about how to play defense in basketball, how to play a flute, and how to sew on a button. There are theories regarding history, psychology, mathematics, and economics. The second purpose of theory is *to predict*. For example, if we have a theory that an increase in the money supply leads to a decrease in interest rates, then the next time the money supply increases, we would predict that interest rates will fall. The third purpose of theory is to enable us *to control* the effects that emanate from a set of circumstances or causes. For example, some basketball coaches have a theory that a zone defense is the best way to play a team that has a speed advantage. They theorize that this defense makes it difficult for the opposing guards to drive for easy baskets. If their team can play a good, active zone, then the other team will score less, and their team's chances of winning the game are enhanced. The ultimate objective of monetary theory is to control the money supply in such a manner that the economic welfare of our citizens is maximized.

In this chapter, we will study several classical theories about income, interest rates, and money. It is very important to understand these older theories because they provide needed background to understand modern theories, and what's more, all are still true under certain assumptions. Specifically, in this chapter we shall (1) discuss Say's Law, the classical explanation of income, (2) examine the classical theory of interest, and (3) analyze the classical quantity theory of money.

The Classical Theory of Income and Interest

Say's Law

Prior to the Great Depression, economics was concerned primarily with microeconomics, the study of individual product price determination under various market conditions and the study of income distribution to the agents of production—land, labor, capital, and entrepreneurship. Between 1776 and the 1930s, most economists were uninterested in macroeconomics because they believed that Say's Law adequately explained the level of economic activity and employment. **Say's Law**, named after the French economist J.B. Say (1767–1832), is simply that "supply creates its own demand." This statement leaves many students cold the first time they hear it. A better statement is "the act of production generates exactly enough income to purchase all the goods and services produced." Thus, if Say's Law is true, there should never be a deficiency in aggregate demand; all the goods and services produced are taken off the market.

What is the rationale for Say's Law? Several factors are important. First, economists observed that human wants are insatiable. Second, in relation to those wants, resources are scarce. Third, people produce in order to consume. Therefore, all of the wages, rents, interests, and profits received will be spent to purchase all of the goods and services produced. There is no reason to delay spending in a world of insatiable wants. Under these conditions, the economy would tend toward the full employment level. Now perhaps you can

Figure 10-1. J.B. Say (1779-1832)

understand the attitude of most of the classical economists: why study real GNP if it's always at the full employment level?

At this point, you might ask how did the classical economists explain oversupply situations in the market for products and people? No problem. They acknowledged temporary gluts in both areas, but assumed that flexibility of prices and wages would take care of the situations. Next, some of you might be wondering how did they account for the possibility that some people might wish to save? This brings us to the classical theory of interest.

The Classical Theory of Interest

According to the classical economists, those who did not wish to consume may provide savings to investors in return for interest—the reward for not consuming. **Interest** is a payment for the use of savings. If these funds are channeled back into the spending stream, GNP will remain at the full employment level.

As shown in Figure 10-2, the savings supply schedule (S) is

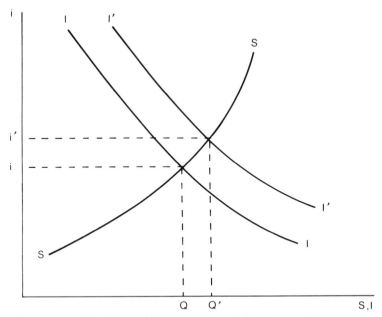

Figure 10–2   The Classical Determination of the Interest Rate

positively sloped, indicating that it will take higher interest rates to induce more saving. Most people prefer goods now to goods later; therefore, in order to overcome the **time preference** for goods now, the reward must be raised for foregoing increasing amounts of current consumption.

On the demand side, the demand schedule for savings to invest in capital projects (*I*) is negatively sloped, indicating that investors wish to employ more savings only if the rate of interest is lower. The quantity of savings that investors wish to borrow depends basically on the return on capital. Suppose you could buy a machine for $1,000 that will add $140 annually to the firm's net income over the useful life of the machine for ten years. What rate of interest would you be willing to pay to obtain savings to buy this machine? Those of you who have had a business finance course will recognize that we have slipped in a capital budgeting problem. What you have to do is calculate what rate of discount will make the sum of the present values of ten annual payments equal $1,000. If you tinker around, you will determine that a rate of about 6-5/8 percent will do the trick. This rate is known as the **marginal efficiency of investment (MEI)**. If the MEI exceeds the rate of interest you have to pay for funds by enough or more than enough to cover the risk, then you would borrow.

To construct a demand schedule for savings, we would have to tally at one moment in time all the individual amounts demanded by all investors at every interest rate. If we could do this, we would find a relatively small amount of funds demanded at high rates of interest because there are relatively few investments that yield high enough returns to justify paying such rates and cover risk. On the other hand, as we move down the scale there are larger and larger numbers of projects that have lower yields.

What amount of savings and what interest rate will clear the market? The answers to both of these questions are determined at the intersection of or equilibrium point for the supply and demand schedules for savings. The term **equilibrium** means "no net tendency to move." As shown Figure 10-2, the equilibrium interest rate is (i), while the equilibrium quantity of savings is (Q). At rates above the equilibrium rate, the quantity supplied exceeds the quantity demanded; thus, these rates will not clear the market. Similarly, at rates below the equilibrium rate, the quantity demanded exceeds the quantity supplied; hence, these rates are not equilibrium rates either. Only at the equilibrium rate is the total saving supplied equal to total demanded.

Suppose that businesses become more optimistic and wish to undertake more investment. This causes the demand schedule to shift to the right, and, as shown in Figure 10-2, the new equilibrium interest rate increases to i'. The total amount of savings and investment increases to Q', and the economy remains at full employment. In summary, it is through the interaction of the forces of demand and supply for savings that the market is cleared, and the volume of savings is recycled to appear as spending for goods and services.

What about the functions of money? Did changes in the money supply affect GNP, interest rates, employment, and prices? With respect to the first question, the classicals emphasized money's role as a medium of exchange and as a unit of account. Money was not viewed as an asset to hold for long periods of time. To the classicals, money was just a medium for people to exchange the value of what they produced for what others produced in order to satisfy insatiable wants. Money was considered a *veil* that hid the underlying exchange relations. The level of GNP was determined only by the quantity and quality of the **real factors**, such as land, labor, capital, and entrepreneurship. Changes in the quantity of money did not affect the level of GNP or employment. Neither did changes in the money supply affect the interest rate, which was determined by the supply and demand for savings. Changes in the money supply influenced only prices, as we shall explain in the next section.

The Classical Quantity Theory of Money

Evolution

The remainder of this chapter deals with the classical quantity theory of money, perhaps the oldest and best-known, but most controversial theory in economics. In its early, crude formulation, the **quantity theory of money** asserts that there is a direct and proportionate relationship between changes in the money supply and the general level of prices. The crude quantity theory may be expressed as $P = kM$, where P is a general index of prices, k stands for constant proportionality, and M equals the money supply. In this framework if the quantity of money doubled, the general level of prices would double. If the quantity of money increased 20 percent, the general level of prices would increase 20 percent, and so on.

The origins of the quantity theory go way back. Jean Bodin, a French economist writing in 1568 and generally regarded as the first exponent of the "crude" quantity theory of money as defined above, held that the influx of gold and silver was the chief cause of the rise in French prices. David Hume in his essay "Of Money" in 1752 had the earliest and best exposition of the quantity theory. These and other writers in the eighteenth and nineteenth centuries all linked changes in prices to changes in money, however it was defined.

The crude quantity theory was and is a useful starting point in the analysis of inflation. The general consensus among economists today is that it offers a reasonably good explanation of the inflation in Europe caused by bringing in gold and silver from the New World. Moreover, it explains periods of hyperinflation, such as that experienced in Germany between 1920 and 1923, when prices rose over one trillion percent as currency was printed by the carload. Finally, most economists agree with the basic thrust of the theory—that inflation occurring over a long period of time has as its root cause an expansion of the money supply. Nevertheless, we must point out that a precise one-for-one relationship between money and prices in the crude quantity theory depends on two key assumptions: (1) that the **velocity** or turnover of the money supply remains constant and (2) that the volume of goods and services to be purchased remains constant. The classical economists adhered to both assumptions because they felt that velocity tended to change very slowly over time and that the volume of goods and services was fixed at the full employment level because of Say's Law.

During the late nineteenth and early twentieth centuries the quantity theory was reformulated by Irving Fisher, a Yale economist and statistician, and by Alfred Marshall, A.C. Pigou, D.H. Robertson, and other economists at Cambridge University in England. Modern quantity theorists assert that the Fisher transactions and the Cambridge cash balances formulations are theories of the demand for money, not theories of price or income. The Fisher and Cambridge approaches were forerunners of all modern theories of the demand for money and provided the intellectual inspiration for **monetarism**, the school of thought which stresses that the demand for money is a stable function of many variables and that the money supply is the most important determinant of interest rates, income, employment, and prices.

Fisher's Transactions Approach

The starting point in Fisher's approach to the quantity theory of money is his famous equation of exchange. Fisher observed that every payment made for a product, a person's labor, the use of land, the use of capital, etc., may be viewed as the product of price times quantity. Thus, if we summed all the transactions during a year, then total expenditures would equal PT, where P is an average price and T is the aggregate amount of transaction units. On the other hand, expenditures made during a year may be viewed as the product of the average quantity of money (M) times the turnover (V). Therefore, Fisher's equation of exchange in "transactions form" is

$$MV = PT$$

Total expenditures equal total expenditures, a proposition that nobody will question. The equation of exchange is an accounting identity or, as economists say, a tautology—a statement that is true under all conditions but does not explain anything. It is important to understand that the equation of exchange is not the quantity theory of

Figure 10-3. Irving Fisher (1867–1947)

money. As we shall see, it is a framework for use in explaining the quantity theory of money.

The volume of transactions is a very cumbersome component in the equation. It includes payments for products, for intermediate transactions such as those that take place as goods are shuffled along the channels of production and distribution to the final purchaser, for agents of production, and in connection with financial transactions. With the development of national and social accounting concepts, economists substituted national income (y) for T in the equation of exchange. It is more relevant to economic welfare and can be estimated more precisely. In its "income form," the equation of exchange becomes

$$MV = Py$$

In this equation, P is considered passive and the resultant of changes in the other factors. M includes both currency and deposits. In Fisher's day banks could pay interest on demand deposits; therefore, Fisher really had a broad definition of M. T and y are determined by all the real factors such as the quantity and quality of the agents of production and technology. Additionally, T depends on the degree of vertical integration, which determines the number of intermediate transactions. T, of course, includes all financial transactions.

In essence, V is determined by every factor that affects the amount of money that people want to hold. Fisher, however, preferred to look at the other side of the coin, to wit, he discussed all the factors that affected how fast people paid money out. That is, he looked at money in motion, not at rest. Fisher cited the payment habits of people, the frequency of payment, and the pattern of receipts and disbursements as important determinants of velocity. Fisher also felt that interest rates and prices could affect the velocity of money. He felt that during periods of rising interest rates and rising prices, people would economize on their holdings of money. Therefore, the turnover of money supply would increase.

Fisher's tautological equation of exchange may be used to explain the quantity theory of money. If we assume that the velocity of money is relatively stable because payment habits change very slowly and if we assume that y is fixed at the full employment level because of Say's Law, then changes in the price level will be proportionate to changes in the money supply. To illustrate, suppose that in year 1, we have $M = \$250$ billion, $V = 4$, $P =$ a general price index equal to 100, and $y = \$1$ trillion. Thus,

$$P = \frac{M\bar{V}}{\bar{y}}$$

where "bar signs" denote constants. Substituting, we have

$$P = \frac{(\$250)(\bar{4})}{\$1 \text{ trillion}}$$

$$P = 100 \text{ (index)}$$

Suppose that in year 2, the average quantity of money doubles. Substituting in the original equation, we have

$$P = \frac{(\$500)(\overline{4})}{\$1 \text{ trillion}}$$

$$P = 200 \text{ (index)}$$

The Fisher equation also provides a convenient framework to illustrate what would happen if V or y changed. For drill, suppose that V increased by 25 percent, from 4 to 5, while M and y remained constant. As shown below, the price level would rise proportionately as "money moved faster to chase the same amount of goods."

$$P = \frac{(\$250)(5)}{\$1 \text{ trillion}}$$

$$P = 125 \text{ (index)}$$

Suppose that y fell by 20 percent, with M and V remaining constant. As shown below, the price level would rise proportionately as "the amount of money chased fewer goods."

$$P = \frac{(\$250)(\overline{4})}{800}$$

$$P = 125 \text{ (index)}$$

The Cambridge Cash Balances Approach

Alfred Marshall at Cambridge University was largely responsible for the development of supply and demand analysis to determine the price or value of individual products. Thus, it is not surprising to find that he and other economists there applied supply and demand analysis to the determination of the value of money.

The cash balances approach focused on the rationale for holding money. Like Fisher, the Cambridge economists felt that money's primary function was as a medium of exchange. However, the Cambridge economists analyzed why people held money to effect transactions. They reasoned that people have a demand to hold money equal to some fraction (k) of their annual expenditures (T).

Hence, the demand for money equals kT. Letting M stand for the average money supply and P represent an index of prices for these items, the transactions version of the cash balances equation of exchange is

$$M = kTP$$

This equation is also an accounting identity whereby the money available to be held equals the value of the purchasing power that people wish to hold. This equation proves nothing, but it provided the cash balances theorists with a framework to use supply and demand analysis to explain the general level of prices, that is, the value of money.

As with the Fisher equation, y may be substituted for T in the cash balances equation. The volume of annual expenditures is determined primarily by income, and this quantity is much more easily estimated. Now we are ready to state the quantity theory of money using the supply-demand framework of the cash balances equation.

Solving the equation for P, we have

$$P = \frac{M}{ky}$$

The numerator is the supply of money, while the denominator is the demand for money. The cash balances theorists also believed in Say's Law and the notion that the proportion of income that people wish to hold changed very little over time. Hence, if the demand for money is relatively stable, increases in the supply of money will have to work themselves out through higher prices.

To illustrate, suppose that the supply and demand for money are in equilibrium. The public wishes to hold command over one-fourth of their annual expenditures of $1 trillion, and the supply of money available to be held is $250 billion. Hence,

$$P = \frac{\$250 \text{ billion}}{\frac{1}{4}(\$1 \text{ trillion})}$$

$$P = 100 \text{ (index)}$$

Now suppose that the supply of money available to be held rose to $300 billion. In days gone by, this might have been caused by an inflow of gold or silver or by the government printing money and spending it for goods and services. In modern times it could occur if the Fed expanded reserves, and the banking system, in turn, created new deposits in a multiple of the change in reserves. At any rate, the public finds themselves with more money than they wish to hold. They will attempt to get rid of the money by spending it. Since the economy is at full employment, the only variable left to change is the price level. There is more money chasing the same quantity of goods. Solving for P, we have

$$P = \frac{\$300 \text{ billion}}{\frac{1}{4}(\$1 \text{ trillion})}$$

$$P = 120 \text{ (index)}$$

By using the supply and demand framework of the cash balances approach we have demonstrated the classical quantity theory of money: other things being equal, an increase in the money supply leads to a proportionate increase in prices.

For exercise, we can demonstrate other possibilities within the cash balances framework. Suppose that a combination of new technology and increases in investment spending causes income to rise to $1.2 trillion. If M and k remain constant, prices will fall by one-sixth. Hence, we have

$$P = \frac{\$250 \text{ billion}}{\frac{1}{4}(\$1.2 \text{ trillion})}$$

$$P = 83.3 \text{ (index)}$$

This set of circumstances should suggest to you the possible beneficial effects of technology and increased investment on the general level of prices in the current U. S. economic environment.

The cash balances framework also may be used to show what happens if the demand for money increases in the same ratio as an increase in the money supply. Thus, if M increases by 20 percent, and the demand for money increases by 20 percent (either k increases by 20 percent to 30 percent, or y increases by 20 percent, to $1.2 trillion, or a combination equaling a 20 percent increase in the demand for money), then P will remain unchanged. For example, if k increases to 30 percent, then

$$P = \frac{\$300 \text{ billion}}{.3 \ (\$1 \text{ trillion})}$$

$$P = 100 \ (\text{index})$$

Relationship of the Fisher V to the Cambridge k

The Fisher V and the Cambridge k are reciprocal. Hence, whatever determines V also determines k. In the income form of the Fisher equation

$$V = \frac{Py}{M}$$

In the Cambridge equation

$$k = \frac{M}{Py}$$

Hence,

$$V = \frac{1}{k} \qquad \text{and}$$

$$k = \frac{1}{V}$$

If people wish to hold money equal to one-fourth of total income, then $V = 4$. The total money supply of $250 billion has to turn over four times to purchase $1 trillion of goods and services. Viewed from the other direction, if the money supply turned over four times, then the people must have held one-fourth of their total income in the form of money balances.

Differences in Emphasis Between the Fisher and Cambridge Approaches

The Fisher approach emphasized money in motion effecting transactions, while the Cambridge approach emphasized money at rest held as cash balances. Both approaches acknowledged money's great function as a medium of exchange, but the Cambridge approach stressed money's usefulness as a temporary abode for purchasing power. Fisher discussed at length all the institutional factors that determine the speed and pattern of payments. This was valuable. If you read Fisher's *Purchasing Power of Money* you will be amazed at the minute detail with which he describes the factors that influence the velocity of money. On the other hand, the Cambridge approach laid the foundation for modern theories of the demand for money, which are discussed in Chapter 12. The Cambridge approach focused on what determines how much money people want to hold, and held that it was the interaction of the demand for money with the supply for money that determined the price level. Also, the Cambridge approach must be credited with spawning John Maynard Keynes' liquidity preference theory (read "demand for money theory") in 1936, and this theory occupied center stage for at least the next twenty years.

Summary

This chapter dealt with the three cornerstones of classical monetary and income theory: Say's Law, the classical theory of interest, and the classical quantity theory of money. First, Say's Law holds that the act of production generates exactly enough income to purchase all the goods and services produced. Because of a strong belief in Say's Law, economics concentrated on microeconomics from Adam Smith's time to the 1930s. Crucial assumptions underlying Say's Law are flexibility in wages, prices, and interest rates. The classical theory of interest holds that interest rates are determined by the supply and demand for savings. Underlying the supply schedule is the notion that interest is a payment to overcome time preference. Underlying the demand schedule is the concept of marginal efficiency of investment.

Finally, the classical quantity theory of money holds that other things being equal, there is a proportionate relationship between changes in the money supply and prices. The Fisher transactions approach and the Cambridge cash balances approach may be employed to explain the theory. At the heart of each approach is the equation of exchange, an accounting identity. The Fisher approach emphasizes the factors affecting the velocity of money, while the cash balances approach stresses why people hold money. Both approaches, especially the cash balances theory, inspired further work on the demand for money.

Questions and Problems

1. Define (a) monetary theory and (b) monetary policy.
2. Explain the primary purposes of any theory.
3. Define and explain the rationale for Say's Law.
4. Explain the classical theory of interest.
5. Explain the crude quantity theory of money.
6. Explain (a) the Fisher transactions approach and (b) the Cambridge cash balances approach to the quantity theory of money.
7. Show the relationship between the Fisher V and the Cambridge k.

Suggestions for Additional Reading

Dean, Edwin, ed. *The Controversy Over the Quantity Theory of Money*. Boston: D.C. Heath & Company, 1965.

Fisher, Irving. *The Purchasing Power of Money*. New York: The Macmillan Company, 1911.

Humphrey, Thomas M. "The Quantity Theory of Money: Its Historical Evolution and Role in Policy Debates." Federal Reserve Bank of Richmond, *Economic Review* (May/June 1974), pp. 2–19.

Keynes, John M. *A Treatise on Money*. New York: Harcourt, Brace and World, 1930.

Robertson, Dennis H. *Money*, 4th ed. New York: Harcourt, Brace and World, 1948.

11

Keynesian Income and Monetary Theory

In Chapter 10, we discussed the classical theories of income, interest, and money. These theories were considered so sacrosanct that most economists devoted their energies to the study of individual price determination and income distribution within the boundaries set by Say's Law. It took the Great Depression and the massive unemployment in the early 1930s to jolt the economics profession into reconsidering the classical explanations. The man who led the economics profession to rethink the classical theories and construct new ones was the great British economist John Maynard Keynes (1886–1946).

Because much of your first principles course in economics involved Keynesian economics or the study of GNP determination, our study of these principles is condensed to one chapter. It will not hurt you to review these concepts because they rank easily as one of the ten most important bodies of knowledge that you will learn in college.

In this chapter we shall (1) examine Keynes' criticism of classical theories, (2) review the $C + I + G + F$ method of aggregate demand determination, (3) explain the multiplier concept, (4) analyze Keynes' liquidity preference theory of interest, and (5) use $IS - LM$ curve analysis to integrate the monetary and real sectors.

246

Keynes and the Classical Theories

In October, 1929, the US stock market crash signaled the beginning of a decade of worldwide depression. Between 1929 and 1933, GNP in the United States fell by 50 percent, and unemployment in 1933 hit 25 percent of the labor force. This sorry state of affairs did not jive with Say's Law. Real world facts were inconsistent with the prevailing theory.

John Maynard Keynes was a remarkable person. He was a brilliant teacher and author, ran a large insurance company, advised the British Treasury, and helped govern the Bank of England. Keynes applied economic theory to the marketplace and made a fortune for himself and King's College, Cambridge. Keynes published many books. The two-volume *A Treatise on Money*, published in 1930, was an exposition in the quantity theory tradition. However, the economic facts of life in the 1930s led Keynes to rethink the classical theories and to publish in 1936 *The General Theory of Employment, Interest, and Money*. This book outlined a new theory of income determination that is the foundation of modern macroeconomics. Because of its influence on economic policymaking throughout the world, *The General Theory* ranks as one of the most influential books ever published.

Whereas Say's Law postulated that the economy would tend toward the full employment level, Keynes held that the equilibrium level of national income may be at less than the full employment level. He challenged the classical assumptions of flexible wages and prices by pointing to the real world experience of sticky wages and prices and uncleared markets for labor or products.

With respect to the interest rate bringing savings and investment into equilibrium, Keynes held that interest was the reward for not holding money, and not the reward for saving. Keynes argued that savings and investment were done by two different groups in the economy and the *planned* amount by each may not be equal even though *after-the-fact*, saving and investment must be equal. In place of the classical theory of interest, Keynes advanced his liquidity preference theory of interest, in which the interest rate was determined by the demand and supply for money. It was through his liquidity preference theory that Keynes integrated monetary and income theory.

With respect to the quantity theory as an explanation of prices, Keynes held that it was still true, but only at the full employment level,

Figure 11-1. John M. Keynes (1883–1946)

which was a special case. With his liquidity preference theory, Keynes opened up the possibility that changes in the money supply might influence output as well as prices.

It is important to understand that Keynes' theories were short-run oriented, whereas the classical theories focused on the long run. For example, in the long run, Say's Law is true. However, in the short run, aggregate demand may be insufficient to push the economy to the full employment level. Moreover, in the long run, the interest rate level depends largely on the supply and demand for savings. Finally, under the strict assumptions of the quantity theory, few economists would argue that there is not a proportionate relationship between money and prices.

In a nutshell, Keynes changed the orientation of economics from micro to macro, its focus from long-run to short-run, and its emphasis from aggregate supply to aggregate demand. In place of the laissez-faire approach, Keynes' theory provided a rationale for active government participation in the stabilization of aggregate demand. Let's turn now to the major components of aggregate demand.

Components of Aggregate Demand

You should remember from your first economics course the four components of GNP in symbol form: $C + I + G + F$. In this section, we will review the nature and principal determinants of each.

Consumption (C)

Consumption (C) includes primarily personal expenditures for food, clothing, automobiles, other consumer durables, and services. As shown in Table 11-1, C accounted for 64 percent of GNP in 1978. There were two major points in Keynes' theory of consumption: (1) that C was primarily determined by income (Y) and (2) that the public's marginal propensity to consume out of income was less than

Table 11-1

Income and Expenditures in the United States, 1978
(billions of dollars)

Types of Expenditures		Sources of Income	
Personal consumption expenditures (C)	$1,339.7	Compensation for employees	$1,301.2
		Proprietor's income	112.9
Gross private domestic investment (I)	344.5	Rental income	23.4
		Net interest	106.1
Government purchases of goods and services (G)	434.2	Corporate profits	160.0
		National Income	$1,703.6
Net exports of goods and services (F)	–11.8		
GNP	2,106.6		
less: Capital consumption allowances	216.9		
Indirect business taxes, etc.	117.9		
Business transfer payments	10.7		
Statistical discrepancy	.9		
plus: Subsidies less current surplus of government enterprises	3.7		
National income	$1,703.6		

Source: Economic Report of the President, January, 1979.

unity. From this last statement Keynes formulated his **law of consumption**: "On the whole and on the average, as income increases, consumption will increase, but by a lesser amount."

The relationship between consumption and income, or the consumption function, $C = f(Y)$, is shown in Figure 11–2(a). The 45° line is a reference line showing all points where total expenditures $(E) = (C + I + G + F)$ on the vertical axis equal total income (Y) on the horizontal axis. The consumption function (C) reflects the volume of consumption that will be forthcoming at each level of income. The slope of the C function, $\Delta C/\Delta Y$, is the **marginal propensity to consume (MPC)**. The difference between the consumption function and the 45° line is the saving function (S), shown in Figure 11–2(b).

While Keynes held that current income was the primary determinant of consumption, other economists have found that wealth, the distribution of income, size of population, interest rates and credit terms, taxes and transfer payments, and the general level of prices influence consumption. In addition, Professor Friedman's research has determined that consumption is primarily a function of **permanent income**, which is defined as expected income from wealth over a lifetime.

Investment (I)

Investment (**I**) is the purchase of newly produced capital equipment, nonresidential and residential structures, and the net change in business inventories. *I* does not include financial investment, which is the purchase of stocks, bonds, and other financial instruments. As shown in Table 11–1, *I* accounted for 16.4 percent of GNP in 1978. *I* is the most volatile element in GNP and, according to many economists, is largely responsible for cyclical movements in GNP.

A businessman purchases a capital good because he anticipates that it will contribute directly to the firm's net income. Virtually all capital goods have some positive effect on net income, so profit-seeking businesspeople rank prospective investments based on their time-discounted expected net rate of interest return, called the **marginal efficiency of investment (MEI)**. Technically, MEI is the rate of discount which will make the discounted present value of the future net returns equal to the cost of the capital good. MEI is similar to the internal rate of return concept that you studied in the business finance course.

(a) The Propensity to Consume

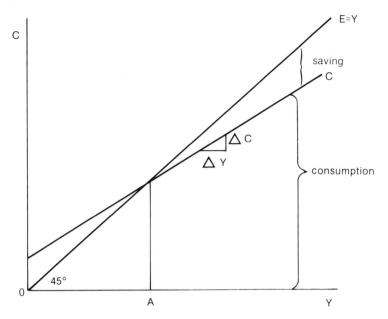

(b) The Propensity to Save

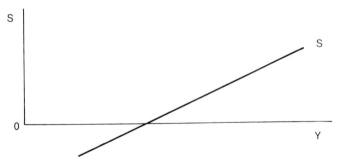

Figure 11-2 The Propensity to Consume and the Propensity to Save

To calculate MEI, first estimate the net annual return for the life of the machine. The net annual return is equal to gross annual return from sales of goods manufactured by the machine or the annual expense savings created minus any variable costs associated with the machine such as grease and tools minus income taxes on the additional net income generated. Second, estimate the salvage value of the machine at the end of its productive life. Finally, calculate what rate of discount will make the sum of the present values of the net annual returns and the salvage value equal to the cost of the machine. It is necessary to discount all future values because $1 payable at points in the future is not worth as much as $1 available at the present. Since the cost of the machine is in present value terms, it is necessary to reduce future returns to its present value equivalent in order to compare equals with equals.

After MEIs are calculated for all investment projects under consideration, they are arrayed from highest to lowest on a schedule called a **capital budget**. On this list, projects will be those undertaken up to the point where the MEI is equal to the interest cost to finance the project. If, at one moment in time, we could tally the MEIs on all investment projects in the economy, we would obtain an investment demand schedule like that shown in Figure 11-3. This schedule is drawn concave to the origin because MEIs tend to decrease at an increasing rate. This reflects the effects of increasing risks to firms undertaking higher levels of investment and the fact that the cost of producing capital goods increases at an increasing rate.

Slightly over half of all investment in 1978 consisted of the purchase of nonresidential and residential structures, with producers' durable

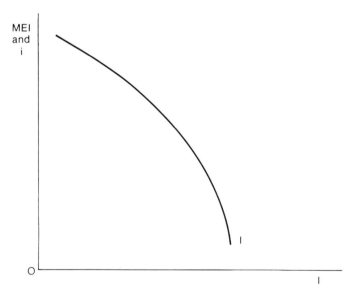

Figure 11-3 Investment Demand Schedule

equipment accounting for the bulk of the remainder. Nonresidential structural investment includes purchase of commercial and industrial buildings, while residential investment involves the purchase of homes and apartments. MEIs are calculated for business structures and apartments just as they are for producers' durable equipment. Residential investment, however, depends on a multiplicity of factors including population trends, age distribution of the population, number of family formations, government subsidy programs, and the cost and availability of credit.

Government Expenditures (G)

Government spending (G) consists of the amount spent by all levels of government for the purchase of goods and services. G does not include transfer payments because such outlays are not for the production of goods and services. In 1978, G accounted for 20.6 percent of GNP; federal government purchases represented 35.5 percent of this total, while state and local government purchases made up the balance.

All federal and most state and local government expenditures are autonomous and, therefore, not a function of the interest rate or credit conditions. However, state and local government capital expenditures are very dependent on the cost and availability of credit. In the Keynesian system, governmental expenditures may be used to close the gap between the equilibrium level of income based on private expenditures and the full employment level of income if it is higher.

Net Exports (F)

Net exports (F) equals the net difference between exports and imports of goods and services. However, in 1977 and 1978, imports exceeded exports; therefore, net exports was a negative number in GNP. C, I, and G include the value of imports to the extent that they are equal to exports. However, if exports are less than imports, the negative balance in the F component measures the extent that current domestic income does not appear to purchase domestic goods.

Determination of Equilibrium Level of Income

Equilibrium in the Keynesian income-expenditure approach exists when planned $I = S$. As shown in Table 11–1, we may calculate income on GNP by summing either the types of expenditures on current production or the sources of income on current production. Omitting G, the total expenditures equation is

$$Y = C + I$$

On the other hand, income recipients have two choices: to consume or to save. Hence, the total income equation is

$$Y = C + S$$

In equilibrium, expenditures must equal income, or the level of income must rise or fall. Hence, in equilibrium

$$C + I = C + S$$

Canceling the Cs, the equilibrium condition is

$$I = S$$

Graphical determination of the equilibrium using the "Keynesian cross diagram" is shown in Figure 11–4. For illustrative purposes, I is assumed constant at all levels of income and is added to C. The equilibrium level of income (Y_e) is found at the intersection of the $C + I$ line with the reference line. Income levels above this point cannot be sustained because $C + I$ spending is less than income. Income levels below this point cannot be sustained because $C + I$ spending is more than income. Hence, at Y_e, income = expenditures and $I = S$.

The Multiplier

The equilibrium level of income depends on (1) the characteristics of the consumption function and (2) the level of I. Changes in the level of income can be traced to shifts in C or changes in I. To determine how much a change in C or I will change Y, the new values of C or I must be added to the diagram.

Suppose that Congress enacts a tax cut to stimulate business investment. As shown in Figure 11–5, the investment line shifts from I to I' and the equilibrium level of income shifts from Y_e to Y'_e. Note

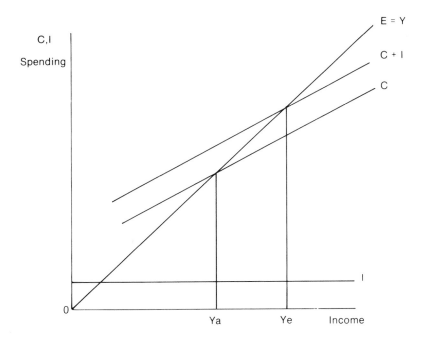

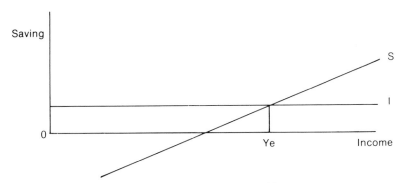

Figure 11-4 Determination of the Level of National Income

that the change from Y_e to Y'_e was much larger than the change from I to I'. This is because of the multiplier concept. The **investment multiplier** (M_I) is defined as the relationship between changes in Y and changes in I. M_I indicates the amount by which we must multiply I to obtain Y. Hence, $M_I \cdot \Delta I = \Delta Y$. Or,

$$M_I = \frac{\Delta Y}{\Delta I}$$

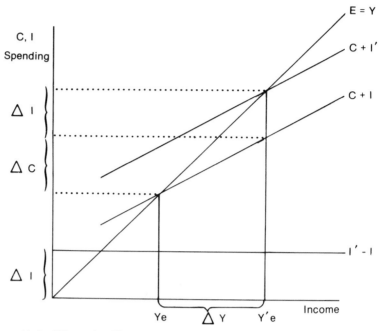

Figure 11-5 Effect of a Change in Investment Spending on the Equilibrium Level of Income

The composition of the change in income may be written as

$$\Delta Y = \Delta I + \Delta C$$

or

$$\Delta I = \Delta Y - \Delta C$$

Substituting, we have

$$M_I = \frac{\Delta Y}{\Delta Y - \Delta C}$$

Dividing through by ΔY yields

$$M_I = \frac{1}{1 - \dfrac{\Delta C}{\Delta Y}}$$

$MPC = \Delta C/CY$, so

$$M_I = \frac{1}{1 - MPC}$$

Thus, if MPC equals two-thirds, then a \$1 billion change in I will produce a \$3 billion increase in Y.

It is important to know that the multiplier concept also applies to changes in C, G, or F. Hence, changes in the determinants of any of these variables could set off spending increases that raise income by a multiple of the change. For example, suppose that in Figure 11-5, the equilibrium level of income Y'_e is not the full employment level of income. Congress might enact spending bills to increase income to the full employment level. G values may be added to the $C + I'$ line just like we added ΔI to the old $C + I$ line.

It should be noted that the multiplier also works in a negative direction. Decreases in any element of aggregate demand set off a multiple decrease in income. For example, a \$1 billion decline in G will produce a \$3 billion decrease in income.

The Liquidity Preference Theory of Interest

Introduction

Keynes rejected the classical theory that S and I will be equated by the interest rate. To Keynes, saving was determined largely by income which depended primarily on investment. Hence, the close connection between saving and investment ruled out these two forces as independent determinants of the interest rate.

Keynes viewed the interest rate as a monetary phenomenon determined by the supply and demand for money. To Keynes, income earners faced two great decisions: (1) to consume or save and (2) what form to hold savings—money or bonds. Money had no risk associated with it and yielded no interest. Bonds had two kinds of risk: (1) the **risk of default** at maturity and (2) the **money risk**—the risk that market yields may rise (bond prices fall), thereby causing bondholders to lose principal if the bonds had to be sold before maturity. Thus, the interest rate was the reward for not holding money.

The Demand for Money

Keynes took the Cambridge cash balances approach which focused on the demand for money and reformulated it as a theory of the demand for money. The Cambridge economists emphasized primarily the demand for money to use as a medium of exchange. However, Keynes identified three motives underlying the demand for money: (1) transactions, (2) precautionary, and (3) speculative.

Transactions motive. First, Keynes borrowed the transactions motive from the Cambridge cash balances approach. The **transactions motive** exists because people's income and payments are imperfectly synchronized. Transactions balances are used to purchase all sorts of goods and services between paydays. Keynes reasoned, as did the Cambridge economists, that the transactions motive depended mainly on the aggregate amount of payments, which was roughly proportional to income.

Precautionary motive. The **precautionary motive** underlies the demand for money to meet unexpected declines in income or increases in payments. Precautionary balances are "rainy day" money. Like transactions balances, precautionary balances are a function of the volume of payments and, hence, income. Additionally, the demand for precautionary balances depends on the subjective factor of uncertainty and to some limited extent on the interest rate, which measures the cost of holding such balances. The demand for transactions balances and that portion of precautionary balances that depends on income are combined into the L_1 function, shown in Figure 11-6. The Keynes L_1 function is shown to be a direct function

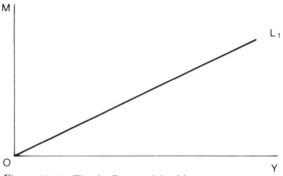

Figure 11-6   The L_1 Demand for Money

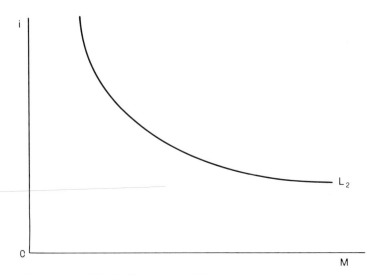

Figure 11-7 The L_2 Demand for Money

of income. The L_1 function is sometimes known as the demand for **active balances**.

Speculative motive. The **speculative motive** to hold money exists because people do not wish to hold bonds and bear the default and money risks. The word "speculative" is a misnomer in this instance because there is nothing speculative about holding money. It has a certain interest yield of zero, and its face value will not change because of changes in market interest rates. However, bondholders face both the default and money risks. You might wonder why Keynes considered only bonds as an alternative to money. What about equities and real assets? Actually, Keynes used bonds as a proxy for all asset alternatives to money and whose value fluctuates with changes in market rates of interest. In Chapter 12, we will consider a wider range of alternatives to money in several modern theories of the demand for money.

As shown in Figure 11-7, the speculative demand for **idle balances**, or the L_2 function, varies inversely with interest rates. There are three reasons for this relationship. First, at high rates of interest the opportunity cost of holding money is high; therefore, it is to be expected that people will want to hold small amounts of speculative balances. Conversely, at low rates of interest, the opportunity cost of holding money is small so people are willing to hold more money. Second, the money risk associated with holding bonds is lowest at high rates of interest and is highest at low rates of interest. People tend to have a concept of what is a "normal" rate of interest. When market rates are above this rate, the public perceives that rates are more likely to fall toward this level than rise further. Of course, if rates fall, bond prices will rise, and capital gains will be realized. Because the chance of a decrease in rates tends to outweigh the chance of an increase, people will opt for more bonds and hold less money. Finally, a "wealth effect" reinforces the demand for more money at low rates. When bond prices are higher, bondholders feel wealthier and will want to hold a percentage of this increase in wealth in the form of money.

Interest Rate Determination

The public's demand for money (L) consists of L_1, a positive function of income, and L_2, which varies inversely with the interest rate. As shown in Figure 11-8, the L_1 function is perfectly inelastic with respect to interest rates. L_2 values at all interest rate levels are added horizontally to L_1 to form the L schedule. The M curve is the

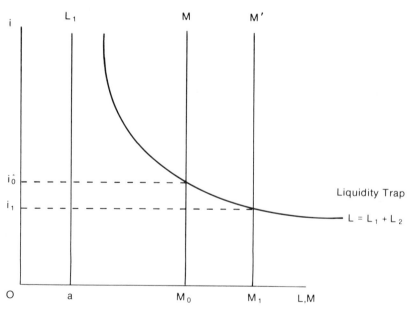

Figure 11-8   Determination of the Rate of Interest in the Keynesian System

supply of money schedule as determined by the Fed and is perfectly inelastic with respect to interest rates. The equilibrium interest rate (i_o) is determined at the intersection of the L and M curves. Rates above i_o will not hold because the quantity of money supplied is greater than the quantity demanded. Rates below i_o will not hold because the quantity demanded exceeds the quantity supplied. At i_o, the public wishes to hold Oa in active balances and aM_o in idle balances. Also at i_o, the demand and supply for bonds must be equilibrium. If this was not true, there would not be equilibrium in the money market. Suppose that the supply of money shifts to M'. The interest rate will decline to i_1. Note that in the lower interest rate levels, increases in the money supply will tend to produce smaller and smaller decreases in the interest rate. Keynes termed the infinitely elastic portion of the liquidity preference curve as the **liquidity trap**. When interest rates are at the liquidity trap level, the public prefers to hold money rather than securities. Remember that at lower interest rates, the chance of an increase in interest rates (fall in bond prices) tends to outweigh the chance that a further decline will occur in rates. In other words, it is best to hold money with a zero return than bonds that have a good chance of falling in value. In the Keynesian system, the important implication of the liquidity trap is that there is a point where monetary policy is ineffective in stimulating investment and, hence, pushing income back to the full employment level.

Linkages Among Money, Interest, Investment, and Income in the Simple Keynesian System[1]

The Keynesian income-expenditure theory is a theory of income and a theory of money. Unlike the classical approach, which stressed that money affected only prices, the Keynesian framework provides for changes in the money supply to affect output via its effect on interest rates and, hence, investment and income. However, Keynes' discussion of the liquidity trap and the zealousness of some of his interpreters to consider the liquidity trap as a general case rather than

1. The word "simple" is used because we have omitted from our discussion most of the secondary determinants and many qualifications applicable.

a special case, led many economists to conclude that "money didn't matter" in the Keynesian explanation. The consensus among modern Keynesian economists is that the liquidity trap is a special case associated with depression periods and that changes in the money supply do have an impact on income.

Figure 11-9 contains three quadrants that show the linkages between i, I, and Y. At i_o, I_o investment will be forthcoming, which yields Y_o income or GNP. At this point, $I_o = S_o$. If, for example, the money supply decreases to M', then the interest rate will rise to i_1, investment will fall to I_1, and income will decline to Y_1; savings will fall to S_1; and equilibrium is established at $I_1 = S_1$.

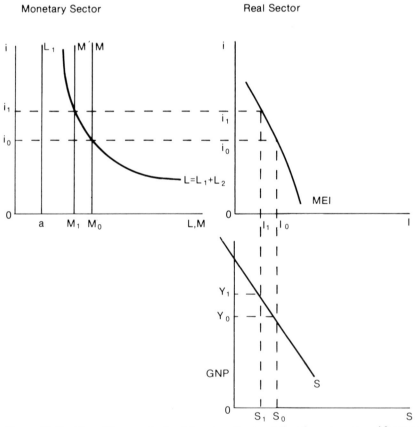

Figure 11-9 How Changes in the Monetary Sector Affect Investment and Income

Summary of Variables in the Simple Keynesian Framework

Figure 11-10 contains a summary of the variables in the simple Keynesian framework. This diagram will assist you in thinking through several "paths of causation." Here are several.

1. Increases in money supply:
$$M_s \uparrow\ i \downarrow\ I \uparrow\ Y \uparrow$$

2. Decrease in money supply:
$$M_s \downarrow\ i \uparrow\ I \downarrow\ Y \downarrow$$

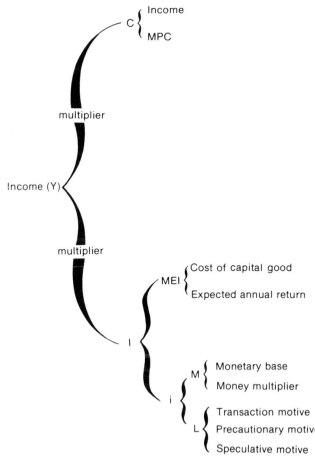

Figure 11-10 Summary of Variables in the Simple Keynesian Framework

3. Public becomes more uncertain about future:
$$L \uparrow \quad i \uparrow \quad I \downarrow \quad Y \downarrow$$

4. Congress accelerates depreciation allowances:
$$MEI \uparrow \quad I \uparrow \quad Y \uparrow$$

As we wind down our discussion of the linkages in the Keynesian system, it is appropriate to point out that there are three dimensions involved in the study of cause and effect relationships in any field: (1) direction, (2) magnitude, and (3) timing. In the examples above, all we did was specify **direction**. This is an accomplishment in itself given that economics is not blessed with constants as are some of the physical sciences. Economics, however, does have its statements of tendency or principles which have been discovered over the years.

Magnitude refers to the degree of response caused by changing a particular variable. For example, how much do interest rates decline when the money supply is increased? How much does investment increase when interest rates fall? This degree of responsiveness refers to the elasticity of the particular functions, which in these examples are L and MEI. Indeed, the elasticity of these functions are the keys to the success of monetary policy in influencing the economy. Economists have conducted extensive research into the elasticity of the various functional relationships in the Keynesian system.

Timing refers to when the effects of changing a particular variable will be realized. This dimension is as difficult to measure as magnitude. The main difficulty with both is that each dimension varies from period to period. For example, researchers may find X amount of investment stimulated in one period by a given change in interest rates and Y amount in the next period.

The IS-LM Curve Synthesis of the Classical and Keynesian Systems

In 1937, one year after *The General Theory* appeared, Sir John Hicks of Oxford published a synthesis of the monetary and real sectors.[2] This model was popularized by Alvin Hansen of Harvard and today is known as the Hicks-Hansen synthesis. In the simple

2. J.R. Hicks, "Mr. Keynes and the Classics: A Suggested Interpretation," reprinted in *Readings in the Theory of Income Distribution* (Philadelphia: Blakiston, 1946), pp. 461–476.

Keynesian framework just covered we looked at how monetary and real variables are linked. In the Hicks-Hansen synthesis we will establish using one diagram a general equilibrium involving both the monetary and real sectors. In general equilibrium, the supply and demand for money will be equal in the monetary sector and savings and investment will be equal in the real sector.

In Figure 11–11, the **IS curve** shows for different interest rates and income levels all points where $I = S$ in the real sector or commodity markets. It is negatively sloped with respect to interest rates, which means that lower and lower interest rates are associated with higher and higher I and, hence, Y. The higher incomes generate the S to match the I.

There are two important characteristics of the IS curve: slope and position. With respect to slope, the greater the interest elasticity of the MEI curve and the higher the MPC, the flatter the IS curve. If MEI tends to be interest inelastic and MPC is low, then the IS curve will be steeper. With respect to position, any change in the factors underlying the consumption or MEI functions will shift the IS curve. For example, a reduction in federal income taxes will shift it to the right. A tax hike will shift it to the left.

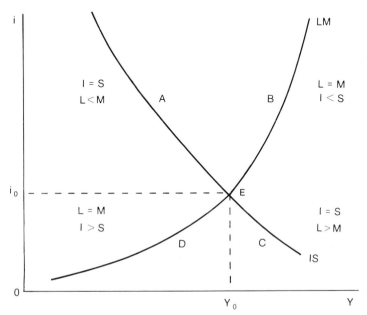

Figure 11-11   General Equilibrium in the Monetary Sector and Real Sector

The **LM curve** shows for different interest rates and income all points in the monetary sector where $L = M$. It is positively sloped with respect to interest rates, which means that higher and higher interest rates are necessarily associated with lower and lower amounts of money demanded. We know that the amount of L_1 balances demanded increases with income. Hence, higher interest rates are needed to pull money from L_2 uses into L_1 uses to support the higher income levels.

Slope and position also are the two important characteristics of the LM curve. With respect to slope, the LM curve will be steeper, the greater is the income elasticity of L_1 (recall that our L_1 curve was infinitely inelastic) and the lower the interest-elasticity of the L_2 curve. In other words, if money demanded for L_1 uses is quite responsive to changes in income and if money demanded for L_2 uses is quite unresponsive to changes in interest rates, then LM will be more steeply sloped.

Looking at Figure 11–11, at the intersection (E) of the IS and LM curves, the equilibrium interest rate is i_o and equilibrium income is Y_o. To demonstrate that E is the equilibrium point, consider point A. It is on the IS curve, so $I = S$. But point A is at a "high" interest rate, well above point D, where $L = M$. Hence, at point A, the quantity of money demanded must be less than the quantity supplied. Therefore, i must fall, which raises I and Y. Only at E are all variables in equilibrium.

Consider point B. It is on the LM curve, so $L = M$. But point B is at a "high" interest, well above point C, where $I = S$. Hence, at point B, I must be less than S. Therefore, Y must fall to E to bring S into equilibrium with I. See if you can explain why points C and D are not general equilibrium points.

Summary

Keynes challenged Say's Law as an explanation of national income. In its place, Keynes devised a simple system of income determination whereby the major components of aggregate demand are summed. Fluctuations in total income are explained by fluctuations in its components.

Consumption is the largest and most stable element of income, and it also depends primarily on income. From the slope of the consumption function, we derive the multiplier, which relates changes in income to changes in any component of aggregate demand.

Investment is the most volatile element of income and depends on the marginal efficiency of investment and the interest rate. To Keynes, the interest rate was the reward for not holding money and was determined by the demand and supply of money. It was through his liquidity preference theory of interest that Keynes integrated monetary and income theory.

The Hicks-Hansen synthesis provides a general equilibrium solution for both the monetary and real sectors through *IS* and *LM* curves.

Questions and Problems

1. Explain and illustrate with a diagram Keynes' law of consumption.
2. Explain how to draw a MEI schedule for the economy.
3. Derive and define the investment multiplier.
4. Explain Keynes' liquidity preference theory of interest.
5. In the Keynesian system, explain how an increase in the money supply affects income.
6. What does an *IS* curve depict? What does an *LM* curve depict?
7. Explain why equilibrium exists at the intersection of the *IS-LM* curves.

Suggestions for Additional Reading

Keynes, John M. *The General Theory of Employment, Interest and Money.* New York: Harcourt, Brace and World, 1936.

Lekachman, Robert, ed. *Keynes and the Classics.* Boston: D.C. Heath & Company, 1964.

Peterson, Wallace C. *Income, Employment, and Economic Growth,* 3rd ed. New York: W.W. Norton & Company, 1974.

12

Modern Theories of the Demand for Money

The demand for money refers to the amount of money that people and businesses wish to hold. This chapter contains an analysis of the major theories of the demand for money that have evolved since Keynes' pioneering liquidity preference theory in 1936.

Earlier in the book we discussed at length the determinants of the money supply. In the next chapter, we shall analyze the transmission and adjustment processes that take place in the monetary and real sectors as a result of changes in the supply and demand for money.

In this chapter, our goals are (1) to review very briefly the role of money in the classical and Keynesian theories, (2) to describe several modern refinements in the Keynesian liquidity preference theory, (3) to discuss money and other forms of wealth, (4) to explore the neo-Keynesian portfolio balances approach to the demand for money, and (5) to outline Milton Friedman's modern quantity theory approach to the demand for money.

Demand for Money: Review and Significance

Review

Before we launch our discussion of modern theories of the demand for money, it would be useful to review the basic ideas in our earlier discussion on the subject. All modern theories of the demand for money are refinements of or represent a logical evolution from the

Fisher transaction and Cambridge cash balances approaches to the quantity theory of money.

To the classical economists, money was a useful commodity because it was a medium of exchange. Money enabled people to overcome the problems associated with barter. Because of a belief in Say's Law, they did not hold that changes in the money supply affected real income. At the full employment level, changes in the money supply affected only the general level of prices (the quantity theory of money). Irving Fisher, in the late 1800s and early 1900s, specified very clearly in his transactions theory the conditions under which the quantity theory was true, namely, full employment and a stable velocity of money. To Fisher, money was used primarily to effect transactions.

Meanwhile, at about the same time, the Cambridge economists formulated a cash balances approach to the quantity theory that focused on why people hold money. To these economists, money's greatest service also was as a medium of exchange, and they related the demand for money for this purpose to the volume of transactions.

Keynes came along in 1936 and extended the cash balances approach. To the transactions motive, Keynes added the precautionary and speculative motives. The latter was the idea that people want to hold money as an asset in lieu of earning assets such as bonds. Keynes held that the demand for money as an asset could become infinitely elastic at low rates of interest (the liquidity trap). This meant that increases in the supply of money would not reduce interest rates further and, hence, not stimulate investment spending enough to push the economy back to the full employment level. Keynes asserted that when the economy is at less than the full employment level, instability in the demand for money (or velocity, in the Fisher tradition) could negate the beneficial effects of an increase in the supply of money. Some of Keynes' followers went a step further and adopted a position that "money didn't matter." It was not until the mid-1950s that money began to make a comeback, thanks largely to the theoretical formulations and empirical investigations of Milton Friedman of the University of Chicago.

Significance

The most important issue in monetary theory today is the extent to which changes in the money supply affect interest rates, income, and prices. At the root of this issue is disagreement among academic and

Fed economists over the nature and stability of the demand for money function. According to many economists, it is the interaction of the supply and demand for money that triggers changes in the financial sector and, later, in the real sector. In general equilibrium, the supply and demand for money are equal. In disequilibrium, interaction between the two forces sets off changes that are felt throughout the economy. Although both the monetary base and the money multiplier are influenced by factors outside the Fed's control, the Fed still has the ability to control the potential money supply within fairly narrow limits over a period of at least one year. The demand for money, however, is determined by the public. Thus, the Fed is in the unenviable position of having less than absolute control over the supply of money, no control over the demand for money, yet responsibility for the consequences of the interaction of the two forces. However, economists are discovering new relationships about the demand for money, so the situation is not quite as hopeless as it might sound.

Refinements to the Keynesian Liquidity Preference Theory

Since Keynes' liquidity preference theory was the predominant theory of the day following publication of *The General Theory*, it was natural to expect that theoretical and empirical research would be concentrated on this theory of the demand for money. Below are some of the major refinements of the three motives for holding money.[1]

Transactions Demand for Money

The Cambridge economists and Keynes in *The General Theory* held that the demand for money was a function of income only. William G. Baumol in 1952 and James Tobin in 1956 showed that transactions demand depended on interest rates. We will present Baumol's analysis and conclusions here. In his example, Baumol assumes that an income recipient is paid once per period, say, per month. However, the funds are spent evenly over the period. Hence,

1. For an excellent discussion of these refinements, see Dwayne Wrightsman, *An Introduction to Monetary Theory and Policy*, 2nd ed. (New York: The Free Press, 1976), pp. 175–182.

the transactor is holding funds at every point during the month except on the last date after the last item is purchased. The question is: What is the optimal amount of transactions balances to hold given that an interest-earning asset can be held, but there is a brokerage fee for making each liquidation of the earning asset? The transactor in this case seeks to minimize his or her costs over the period. Management students will recognize that this demand for transactions balances problem is just an optimal inventory problem.

Assume that an individual spends T dollars in a steady stream over the month, and that he or she obtains funds by liquidating assets. These withdrawals are made in C lot sizes, but the person must pay a brokerage fee of b dollars, and forego an i opportunity cost on the withdrawn funds. The number of withdrawals is T/C, with a total brokerage fee of bT/C.

Since C is spent at a steady rate, the average cash holding is $C/2$, and the annual opportunity cost is $iC/2$. Hence, the total cost of meeting transactions by liquidating assets is

$$\frac{bT}{C} + \frac{iC}{2}$$

The optimal C is found by taking the first derivative of the total cost with respect to C and setting it equal to zero, hence

$$\frac{d\left(\dfrac{bT}{C} + \dfrac{iC}{2}\right)}{dC} = \frac{-bT}{C^2} + \frac{i}{2} = 0$$

Solving for C,

$$C = \sqrt{\frac{2bT}{i}}$$

The average transactions balance, $C/2$, should be one-half of the optimal C:

$$\frac{C}{2} = \frac{1}{2}\sqrt{\frac{2bT}{i}}$$

Thus, the demand for transactions balance is proportional to the square root of the volume of transactions (which also means income and prices), and inversely proportional to the square root of the rate of interest. A numerical example will help to understand Baumol's analysis.

Suppose (1) that an individual's expenditures are $2,000 per month, (2) the liquidation cost is $1.00 per transaction, and (3) the interest rate is 10 percent. Using the formula, we find

$$C = \sqrt{\frac{(2)(\$1.00)(\$2,000)}{.10}}$$

$$C = \$200$$

Thus, ten liquidations will be made in units of $200 each; monthly liquidation costs will be $10; annual foregone interest cost will be $10; and the average cash balance held will be $100.

Using this model, we can show that it would pay to economize on transactions balances if the interest rate rose, say, to 40 percent. The individual would decrease his or her lot size to $100, reduce the average transactions balance to $50, and make twenty withdrawals per month. That's a lot of withdrawals, but the opportunity cost is high not to do so. After studying Baumol's model, you should be able to understand an important reason why, in recent years with interest rates at a relatively high level, the growth rate in M_1 has lagged that of M_2.

Precautionary Demand for Money

The demand for precautionary balances stems from uncertainty regarding future receipts and payments. After our discussion of the refinements to transactions theory, you probably have anticipated that precautionary balances also have an opportunity cost associated with them. In 1966, papers by Edward Whalen, Merton Miller, and Daniel Orr linked the interest rate to the demand for precautionary balances. Given the interest rate, the cost of holding precautionary balances is proportional to the size of the balance. Given the size of the balance, the cost varies directly with the interest rate.

A holder of precautionary balances could reduce his or her uncertainty about future receipts and payments by holding large amounts of cash, but this has a high opportunity cost. At the other extreme, he or she could hold small precautionary balances, but endure higher costs from running out of money. The optimal precautionary balance is one that minimizes these two costs. The size of the optimal precautionary balances varies inversely with the interest rate.

Speculative Demand for Money

In the Keynesian system, the speculative demand for money was inversely related to the interest rate. Savers could choose between two assets: money with no risk and no return and bonds with risk and with a possible return. Keynes' assumption that the public will hold either money or bonds was a useful explanatory device, but it was unrealistic. In the real world, people diversify their portfolio and hold both money and securities.

In 1958 James Tobin demonstrated that changes in portfolio composition caused by efforts to avoid risk also lead to an inverse relationship between the demand for money and the interest rate. Tobin assumes that a portfolio can be distributed between money and bonds. To simplify the discussion, Tobin assumes that the expected interest rate equals the current interest rate, so there is no expected capital gain from holding bonds. The yield on the portfolio then varies proportionately with the amount of bonds held. At one extreme, an investor could hold all bonds and no money. This portfolio would have the maximum income and maximum risk. At the other extreme, an investor could hold all money and have no risk and no income. The degree of risk and income is directly proportional to the amount of bonds in the portfolio; hence, risk and return vary in direct proportion to each other. Investors then know that to have more return, they must assume more risk.

Most investors are "risk averters," not "risk lovers." That is, given a choice, they would not accept risks. However, the prospect of a return causes them to accept risk up to the point where the marginal disutility of the risk is equal to the marginal utility of the return. To illustrate the principle, let's perform a simple financial experiment with an investor. Suppose that we ask an investor how he would diversify his portfolio if the interest return on bonds was 9 percent. He might say, "50 percent in bonds, 50 percent in money." Then, let's ask him how he would weight his portfolio if the interest rate was 11 percent. He might reply, "I would be willing to go 60 percent bonds, 40 percent money." Finally let's dangle a 13 percent yield at him. You can probably see the dollar signs in his eyes, but in the back of his mind a little computer in weighing the additional risk against the return. He finally answers, "Okay, I would be willing to go 65 percent bonds, 35 percent money." Some of you probably have guessed that we have just derived our investor's demand schedule for idle balances, based on his aversion to risk, and it is inversely related to the interest rate. If we ran a simultaneous experiment for all investors, the demand for speculative balances would be a downward sloping curve, much like the L_2 curve in the last chapter. Unlike Keynes' "either-or" condition with respect to money and bonds, Tobin's framework explains the basis for diversification between money and bonds, and shows that normal investor risk aversion provides a good foundation for the inverse relationship between the quantity of money demanded and the interest rate.

Money and Other Forms of Wealth

Analysis of the Keynesian motives for holding money improves our understanding of the demand for money, but most people do not have three little piles of money labeled "transactions," "precautionary," and "speculative." Most people have one pile of money, and the decision as to how much to hold is not a simple money versus bonds decision, but a money versus bonds versus stocks versus real assets versus etc. decision. In recent years, the work of Friedman, Tobin, and others has pointed out that analysis of the demand for money is a part of capital theory or portfolio theory. In general equilibrium, the utility derived from holding money is equal to the utility from holding many kinds of assets. As preparation for consideration of Tobin's portfolio balances approach to the demand for money and Friedman's portfolio type approach in the form of the new quantity theory of money, let's examine the primary characteristics of five major forms of wealth that people hold.

Money

We had a lot of nice things to say about money as an asset in the first chapter, but it would be helpful to review its most important characteristics. First, money is the only asset generally accepted as a medium of exchange for goods and services. Second, unlike all other assets, money's nominal or face value is predictable. Third, because the timing and cost of many purchases is unpredictable, money as a temporary abode for purchasing power gives the holder great flexibility in his or her market activities. Finally, if the value of other forms of wealth is expected to decline, then money has attraction as a short-run or intermediate term asset. As we know, some forms of money, such as savings deposits, yield interest and can be converted into demand deposits or currency very readily. Interest, even at a relatively low rate, increases money's attractiveness as an asset. As shown in Table 12-1, cash comprised 12.9 percent of the total wealth of the top wealthholders in 1972.

Bonds

Bonds are debt instruments issued by corporations and governments. Bondholders receive a fixed interest payment each six months based on one-half of the stated **coupon rate**. For example, a $1,000 bond with a 9 percent coupon rate and maturing in 2009 would yield $45 every six months until maturity. If you buy the bond for $1,000, the **current yield** (interest/price) is 9 percent and the **yield to maturity (YTM)** is 9 percent. YTM is similar to the MEI concept studied in the last chapter and is defined as the rate of discount that will make the sum of the present values of each semiannual interest payment plus the payment of $1,000 at maturity equal to the purchase price of the bond. If you pay $1,000 for a $1,000 bond, then the coupon rate, current yield, and YTM are equal.

Bondholders accept two basic risks: (1) the risk of default on interest and/or principal payments and (2) the money risk, the chance that interest rates might rise (bond prices fall) and the bondholder will lose part of the principal if he or she has to sell before maturity. When general market prices rise, the price of existing bonds must fall to bring their YTMs into line with YTMs or newly issued bonds.

As a form of wealth, bonds are attractive to those who seek an above-average current yield, but are unattractive to those who wish an asset with a predictable value because bond prices fluctuate quite widely over the interest rate cycle and because of the erosion of purchasing power due to inflation. As shown in Table 12-1, between 1953 and 1972 bonds declined from 9.9 percent to 5.8 percent of the personal wealth of the top wealthholders.

Equities

Equities include common stocks and preferred stocks and represent owners' claim on assets and earnings. Common stock, the

Table 12-1

Personal Wealth of the Top Wealthholders,
by Asset Composition: Selected Years, 1953 to 1972

Type of Asset	1953	1958	1962	1969	1972
	Asset Composition (billions of dollars)				
Total assets	$356	$542	$752	$1,581	$2,152
Real estate	82	133	188	428	645
Bonds	36	36	48	85	124
Corporate stock	141	231	326	551	629
Cash	34	46	71	190	278
Notes and mortgages	13	21	30	59	86
Insurance equity	7	11	16	31	42
Other	44	66	74	236	346
minus debts	32	50	83	204	301
Net Worth	324	492	669	1,377	1,852
	Percentage Composition				
Total assets	100.0%	100.0%	100.0%	100.0%	100.0%
Real estate	23.0	24.5	25.0	27.1	30.0
Bonds	9.9	6.6	6.4	5.4	5.8
Corporate stock	39.6	42.6	43.3	34.9	29.2
Cash	9.5	8.5	9.4	12.0	12.9
Notes and mortgages	3.5	3.8	4.0	3.8	4.0
Insurance equity	2.0	2.0	2.1	2.0	2.0
Other	12.4	12.1	9.8	14.9	16.1
minus debts	8.9	9.2	11.0	12.9	14.0
Net Worth	91.1	90.8	89.0	87.1	86.1

Note: Estimates based on Federal estate tax returns showing gross assets of $60,000 or more filed with Internal Revenue Service. Comparability of data is affected by revisions in estimating techniques.

Source: U.S. Internal Revenue Service, *Statistics of Income,* 1962, 1969 and 1972, Supplemental Report, *Personal Wealth.*

most important type of equity, has two types of return: dividends and capital gains. The price of a share of common stock may be viewed as the discounted cash value of expected dividends and appreciation in value of the stock. The rate of discount to apply to this future income depends on the risk or variability associated with this income. The greater the risk, the higher the discount rate and, hence, the lower the share price for an expected stream of income.

In the United States, we have a highly developed financial system that facilitates public ownership of equities. Stocks are traded on the New York and American Stock Exchanges, on several regional exchanges, and in the over-the-counter market. On the New York Stock Exchange alone, value of the shares listed grew from $94 billion in 1950 to $797 billion in 1977, while the average daily trading volume rose from 2 million to 21 million shares. During this period annual dividends on common shares at this exchange grew from $5.4 billion to $36.3 billion.

As shown in Table 12–1, in 1972 equities comprised 29.2 percent of the personal wealth of top wealthholders. For many top wealth-holders, their largest asset is their business. Other wealthholders hold minority interests in many businesses. As a form of wealth, equities offer the opportunity to participate in the growth and profitability of business. Compared with other forms of wealth, the potential return from equities ranges from very great (for example, a share of McDonald's bought when it was offered) to zero (a share in W.T. Grant, for example, bought prior to bankruptcy). All of us have heard rags-to-riches and riches-to-rags stories about equity investments, so it is difficult to generalize about potential returns.

Physical Wealth

Physical wealth includes land, houses, household furnishings, art, antiques, jewelry, cattle, and a myriad of other tangible forms of wealth. Excluded are physical capital owned by businesses because bonds and stocks represent this wealth. For most people, their home is their largest asset holding. In Table 12–1, note that between 1953 and 1972 real estate climbed from 23 percent to 30 percent of personal wealth. Undoubtedly, the appreciation in personal residences is the major factor accounting for the increase in real estate in wealth holdings. Real estate is an attractive form of wealth because its value tends to increase in inflationary times. However, real estate values also have been known to plummet, as they did during the Great Depression.

With respect to other forms of physical capital, most of us have known people who have valuable collections of art, antiques, and other items. Although such items of physical capital tend to appreciate faster than prices in general, they do suffer from poor liquidity. However, "beauty (value) is in the eye of the beholder," which means that the value of tangible physical capital depends on who wants to buy it.

Human Wealth

Human wealth may be defined as the discounted present value of expected wages and salaries. In other words, people have an economic value based on the expected income stream that they can generate. As we saw in Chapter 11, in 1978 compensation to employees accounted for 76.4 percent of national income. Thus, it is possible to say that for most people, their greatest form of wealth is themselves. People add to their human wealth through education and training. The Bureau of the Census estimates that over a work life period from age 18 to age 64, the average college graduate will earn $234,000 more than the average high school graduate. If you think of studying for the next exam as a wealth-creating activity, it may help you overcome the loss of utility associated with your inability to pursue your favorite leisure-time activity.

Neo-Keynesian Portfolio Balances Approach to the Demand for Money

Tobin's 1958 work was a refinement to Keynes' liquidity preference theory and made money depend on risk aversion in a two-asset world of money and bonds. In the 1960s Tobin and others added further realism to the liquidity preference theory by developing a portfolio balances approach to the demand for money and other assets. According to this theory people do not hold just money or bonds but a portfolio of financial assets including equities, short- and long-term government debt, and other securities. Investors attempt to allocate wealth among the different forms so as to equalize the interest return, yield, or utility from each asset in the portfolio. Thus, the portfolio theory is a theory of asset choice. Money is one of these assets; hence, the portfolio balances approach also is a theory of the demand for money.

In the portfolio balances approach, the demand for an asset, including money, varies directly with its own yield, but varies inversely with the return on substitute assets. For example, if bond yields increased, other things being equal, the quantity of bonds demanded would

Figure 12-1. James Tobin (*Courtesy of the American Economic Association*)

increase. On the other hand, if the yield on bonds fell, the quantity demanded would decrease. Thus, the quantity of money demanded would decrease if the return on one or more other assets increased, but the quantity demanded would increase if the return on one or more other assets decreased.

You might picture a supply curve and demand curve for each asset, including money. Any time the supply or demand for any asset changes, it sends a rippling effect out to all other individual sets of supply and demand curves. This means a change in the supply or demand for any financial asset affects the quantity of money demanded. It also means that the demand for money depends on many interest rates, not just one interest rate, as Keynes held in his liquidity preference theory.

The portfolio balances theory has a powerful implication for monetary policy. That is, a change in the relative supplies of any asset in the portfolio is capable of affecting interest rates and, hence, the real sector. Portfolio balances theorists agree that money is an important asset, but it is just one among many assets held. Thus, the neo-Keynesians are unimpressed with the monetarist argument that changes in the money supply are the most important variable affecting movements in interest rates, income, and prices.

Friedman's Modern Quantity Theory of Money

The Keynesian revolution and its implication that "money does not matter" almost banished the quantity theory to a place John Kenneth Galbraith calls "the museum of irrelevant ideas." As discussed earlier, Keynes agreed with the quantity theory conclusion about the effect of increases in the money supply on prices at the full employment level. However, he argued that at less than the full employment level of income, instability in the demand for money would tend to negate changes in the supply of money and possibly render monetary policy ineffective as an approach to economic stabilization. To the Keynesians, this meant that **fiscal policy**, the use of taxing and spending powers by the federal government to influence aggregate demand, had to be the principal means of influencing employment, income, and prices.

Figure 12-2. Milton Friedman (*Courtesy of the American Economic Association*)

However, Friedman and other economists at the University of Chicago continued their research into the nature and stability of the demand for money and the impact that changes in the money supply have on the key economic variables. In 1956 Friedman published a paper, "The Quantity Theory of Money—A Restatement," which outlined a new approach to the quantity theory of money. In 1963, Friedman and Anna Schwartz published a monumental study, *A Monetary History of the United States, 1867–1960*, which showed that changes in the money supply were the most important determinant of fluctuations in income and prices during the period covered. These and other similar studies were largely responsible for sparking a rejuvenation of research in monetary economics. Since 1956, literally hundreds of papers have reported on results of empirical investigations of the demand for money and the impact of the money supply on the real sector. For his contribution to the analysis of money, his study of monetary history, and his work on the permanent income hypothesis, Friedman was awarded the Nobel Prize in Economics in 1976.

According to Friedman, all versions of the quantity theory rest on the distinction between the real demand for money and the actual amount available to be held. The **real demand for money** represents the amount of money that people wish to hold. The **nominal supply of money** is the actual amount of money provided by the central bank. As we shall see in the next chapter, it is discrepancies between the real demand for money and nominal supply of money that lead to changes in the financial and real variables. In his analysis of the demand for money, Friedman distinguishes between ultimate wealthholders, who hold money as part of their wealth, and businesses, who view money as a type of capital good that enables them to carry out normal production and distribution activities.

Demand for Money by Ultimate Wealthholders

Individuals are the ultimate wealthholders. Their major forms of wealth include money, corporate bonds and equities, and physical and human wealth. After money is seen as a form of wealth, the question is: What determines how much money will individual wealthholders want to hold? Friedman set forth the following real demand for money equation for individual wealthholders:

$$\frac{M}{P} = f(y,\ w,\ r_m,\ r_b,\ r_e,\ \frac{1}{P}\frac{dP}{dt},\ u)$$

where

$\dfrac{M}{P}$ = real demand for money

y = expected real income

w = fraction of wealth in human form

r_m = expected rate of return on money

r_b = expected rate of return on bonds

r_e = expected rate of return on equitities

$\dfrac{1}{P}\dfrac{dP}{dt}$ = expected rate of change in prices, hence, expected rate of return on real assets

u = other factors besides income that might affect the utility attached to the services of money.

Expected real income. According to Friedman, expected real income is a major determinant of the demand for money. Whereas the Cambridge economists believed that the real demand for money increased proportionately with increases in real income, Friedman's research showed that over the 1870–1954 period, the demand for real cash balances rose 1.8 percent for each 1 percent increase in real income. This means, of course, that the income elasticity of demand was 1.8. Friedman concluded from this finding that money was in the nature of a "luxury" item.

Friedman also found that the demand for money was not constant with respect to income over the cycle. When measured against actual income, the real demand for money tends to fall during expansionary periods but rise during recessions. However, when measured against real income, the real demand for money tends to rise during expansions and fall during recessions.

In place of real income, some economists prefer to use wealth in the demand for money equation. After all, wealth is the source of all income. Wealth (W) may be estimated by capitalizing the expected stream of income (Y) at an appropriate discount rate (r). Hence,

$$W = \frac{Y}{r}$$

As pointed out earlier in Table 12-1, cash holdings, as a percentage of wealth, rose between 1953 and 1972.

Fraction of wealth in human form.   An important difference between the new quantity theory and the portfolio balances approach is Friedman's inclusion of human wealth in total wealth. Of course, for most people human wealth is the most important source of income. The conversion of human wealth into nonhuman wealth is not as easily done as the exchange of bonds for stocks. Thus, it is argued that the higher the ratio of total wealth in human form, the higher the percentage of total wealth people will want to hold in money form.

Expected rate of return on money.   Time and savings deposits yield interest, so it is to be expected that the higher the yield, the greater will be the demand for real cash balances. On the other hand, service charges are levied on demand deposits; hence, the higher these charges, the lower will be the demand for real cash balances.

Expected rate of return on equities and bonds.   Keynes, of course, stressed the importance of the interest rate as a determinant of the demand for money. Since publication of *The General Theory*, numerous empirical studies covering different time periods, employing different methods, and performed in several different countries have verified the inverse relationship between interest rates and the real demand for money.

Expected rate of change in prices.   The higher the expected rate of change in prices, the smaller the demand for real cash balances. When prices are expected to rise, people prefer to hold physical wealth that tends to rise in line with the general increase in prices. Again, empirical studies have found in different countries and for different time periods an inverse relationship between rates of inflation and the demand for real balances. An extreme example of this occurred during the German hyperinflation in the early 1920s. People were paid several times a day and given time off from work so that they could convert money into goods before the next price increase.

Other factors.   There are many other factors that affect the demand for real cash balances, but they are difficult to quantify. Friedman felt that the expected degree of economic instability was a determinant of the demand for real cash balances. The chance of war might raise the real demand for money. The increase in the educational level of the population might raise the overall demand for money. On the other hand, a greater proportion of young people in the population might decrease the real demand for money. The decline in the self-sufficient farm population might increase the demand for money. Perhaps you can think of other factors.

Demand for Money by Business Enterprises

Business enterprises view real cash balances just like any other asset that aids in their production and distribution activities. Money is listed on the balance sheet along with raw material, inventory, machines, land, and other productive resources. The importance of money to business enterprises is underscored by the fact that they own better than 60 percent of all bank IPC demand deposits. IBM alone has $4 billion in cash assets and, if incorporated as a bank, would rank twenty-sixth in size.

The determinants of the business demand for real cash balances are somewhat different than for an individual. The first item in the business real demand for money equation should be a variable that measures the amount of "work" that money must do. Economists call this a **scale** variable. Friedman, however, is unsure about which variable to use: total transactions, net value added, net income, total capital in nonmoney form, or net worth. Empirical studies have not answered the question because of the lack of available data. From observation we know that business cash balances are directly related to size, but there are significant economies involved as per Baumol and Tobin's transactions theory.

The division of wealth between human and nonhuman form would not be very relevant in the business demand for money function. However, the rate of return on money would be significant. Bank service charges are much higher on business checking accounts; however, unlike personal accounts, business accounts receive an interest credit for deposit balances up to, but not greater than, the amount of the service charges. Hence, the rate of return on money, whether negative or positive, has an impact on business demand for real cash balances.

The rate of return on alternative financial or physical wealth, of course, has a significant effect on the real demand for money by businesses. If the rate of return on alternative assets rose, then the demand for money would decline. The rate of interest on loans from all sources is important because it represents a direct charge for obtaining real cash balances.

Finally, under the heading of "other variables" Friedman cites expectations regarding economic stability as an important determinant of the business demand for real cash balances. These expectations would be conditioned by such items as the direction of monetary and fiscal policy, the threat of an oil embargo, and international conditions.

Aggregate Real Demand for Money

The aggregate real demand for money is the sum of all demands for money by individuals and business enterprises. All of the variables cited have some effect on the aggregate real demand for money. However, the level of real income is the most important determinant of the total real demand for money. Over time, the level of real income in this country continues to grow as the level of population, productivity, capital, and technology advances. Therefore, the real demand for money continues to grow, and the Fed must accommodate this growth. If the Fed oversupplies nominal dollars when the economy is at the full employment level, then inflation will ensue just as predicted in the crude quantity theory. If it supplies too few dollars relative to the real demand for money, then income will fall.

Thus, an important part of the Fed's research efforts must involve estimating the demand for money. As of yet, economists are unable to forecast accurately the real demand for money. Friedman and others in the monetarist school hold that the demand for money is a stable function of a number of variables. But they do not contend that it is a constant. Like Keynes, neo-Keynesians believe that the demand for money is very unstable. The stability of the demand for money is at the root of the monetarist-Keynesian debate about monetary policy. We will have more to say about this in the next chapter.

Summary

In Keynes' liquidity preference theory, the demand for transactions and precautionary balances was a function of income. Speculative or idle balances depended on the interest rate. Several refinements to Keynes' basic framework have improved our knowledge of the demand for money. First, Baumol and Tobin showed that transactions balances also depended on the interest rate. Second, Whalen and

Miller and Orr demonstrated the same relationship for precautionary balances. Finally, Tobin showed that the inverse relationship between speculative balances and the interest rate could be explained by normal investor aversion to risk.

Today, there are two main approaches to the demand for money: the portfolio balances approach of the neo-Keynesians and Friedman's modern quantity theory of money. The portfolio balances approach shows that money is just one of several types of financial assets, with the demand for money a direct function of its own utility or yield, but inversely related to all other interest rates. A change in the demand or supply of any other financial asset affects the demand for money.

The modern quantity theory holds that the real demand for money for ultimate wealthholders is a function of expected real income; the fraction of wealth in human form; the rates of return on money, equities, and bonds; the expected change in price levels; and "other variables." The demand for real cash balances by business depends largely on how much "work" money must perform and what interest rates are on alternative assets. Businesses tend to view money as a productive asset and not as a form of wealth to hold in the long run.

Questions and Problems

1. Why is the demand for money an important variable?

2. Using Baumol's model make up and solve an original problem to show that higher interest rates encourage people to economize on transactions balances.

3. Explain how the inverse relationship between the demand for money and interest rates can be explained by investors' aversion to risk.

4. List and describe briefly the pros and cons of the various forms of wealth.

5. Explain briefly the neo-Keynesian portfolio balances approach to the demand for money.

6. List and explain briefly the variables outlined by Friedman as important determinants of the real demand for money.

Suggestions for Additional Reading

Baumol, William J. "The Transactions Demand for Cash: An Inventory Theoretic Approach." *Quarterly Journal of Economics* (November 1952), pp. 545–556.

Gordon, Robert J., ed. *Milton Friedman's Monetary Framework*. Chicago: The University of Chicago Press, 1974.

Laidler, David W. *The Demand for Money*, 2nd ed. New York: Harper & Row, Publishers, 1977.

Miller, Merton H., and Orr, Daniel. "A Model of the Demand for Money by Firms." *Quarterly Journal of Economics* (August 1966), pp. 413–25.

Tobin, James. "Liquidity Preference as Behavior Towards Risk." *Review of Economic Studies* (February 1958), pp. 65–86.

———. "Money, Capital, and Other Stores of Value." *American Economic Review* (May 1961), pp. 26–37.

Whalen, Edward L. "A Rationalization of the Precautionary Demand for Cash." *Quarterly Journal of Economics* (May 1966), pp. 314–324.

13

Channels of Monetary Influence: Relative Price Effects and Wealth Effects

The term "channels of monetary influence" describes (1) portfolio adjustments that take place in the financial sector in response to a change in the money supply, (2) the transmission mechanism between the financial and real sectors, and (3) the adjustment process in the real sector as the economy seeks an equilibrium level. Very simply, the channels of monetary influence refer to how money affects the economy. The primary goal of the Fed is to stabilize the economic (real) sector, and monetary policy is its only tool to accomplish this objective. Yet, as we have stated several times before, neither the Fed nor anyone else for that matter knows precisely the process by which money affects income, employment, and prices. Friedman has said that the channels of monetary influence are so complicated that any attempt to describe them in detail is foolhardy.

With Friedman's caveat in mind, our specific goals in this chapter are (1) to provide an overview of the channels of monetary influence; (2) to outline three of the most important explanations of the channels of monetary influence: the traditional Keynesian approach, the portfolio balances or neo-Keynesian approach, and the modern quantity theory or monetarist approach; and (3) to investigate the wealth effects that take place in response to a monetary change.

288

Overview

The question of how money affects the economy has inspired mountains of research, but is still unresolved. In the last chapter we discussed the demand for money, which is probably the most significant aspect of the total issue as to how money affects the economy. However, there are other parts to the problem, such as the transmission process between the financial and real sectors and the adjustment mechanism in the real sector. Much of the **monetarist-Keynesian debate** that you probably have heard about has to do with the channels of monetary influence. However, with respect to the basic explanatory framework, monetarists and Keynesians agree on a number of points. They part company primarily over interpretation of empirical findings and on the conduct of monetary policy.

Before we proceed to a discussion of the major portfolio adjustment processes, it would be helpful to have an overview of the channels of monetary influence. Figure 13–1 contains a chart that summarizes the monetary transmission process. All that we want to do now is sketch the overall process and introduce some terms that will be used shortly. So hold your questions about the specifics of the process.

The transmission process begins with monetary disequilibrium, usually caused by a change in the supply of money. This sets off two major types of effects in the financial sector: (1) relative price effects and (2) wealth effects. A **relative price effect** is the impact on other financial or real assets and/or total spending caused by a change in the price (yield) of one class of financial or real asset held in the portfolio. The word "relative" means that the price or yield on one type of asset changes, while others remain constant, at least initially. Changes in relative prices are also called **substitution effects**. If the yield on one asset, say, bonds, decreases then other financial assets appear to offer higher yields, thereby causing people to tend to substitute the higher-yielding asset in their portfolio for the lower yielding asset.

A **wealth effect** is the impact on other financial or real assets and/or total spending caused by a change in the value of money balances or other wealth such as stocks. For example, if the value of your stock portfolio increased $100,000, you would experience a wealth effect and perhaps rush out and buy a new car.

Thus, the prevailing thought among monetary economists is that changes in relative prices and wealth effects are the two primary

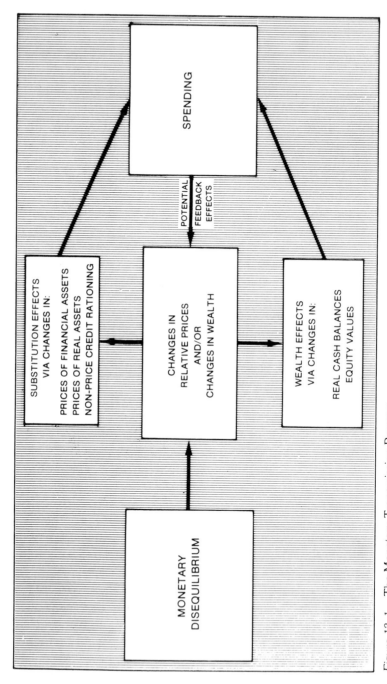

Figure 13-1. The Monetary Transmission Process

Source: Roger W. Spencer, "Channels of Monetary Influence: A Survey" Federal Reserve Bank of St. Louis, *Review,* November 1974, p. 8.

mechanisms by which monetary changes are transmitted to the real sector. In the sections ahead, we shall describe how these mechanisms work and link with the real sector and the adjustments that take place in the real sector. Relative price effects are the primary transmission mechanism in the traditional Keynesian approach, the portfolio balances approach, and the modern quantity theory approach. It is very important to understand that each of these three explanations are types of portfolio balances approaches. That is, all involve an analysis of portfolio adjustments in the financial sector caused by monetary disequilibrium. With respect to wealth effects, a few economists have contended that this is the primary channel of monetary influence. A majority opinion probably would be that wealth effects reinforce relative price effects.

Traditional Keynesian Approach

Chapter 11 was devoted to the Keynesian income-expenditure approach. We explained the equilibrium condition where planned I must equal planned S and showed how Keynes integrated the financial sector with the real sector via the interest rate-investment relationship. Figure 11-9 contains a three-quadrant diagram that links the financial and real sectors. It all seemed to work nicely in the diagram, but now let's describe in more detail the portfolio adjustments and transmission process underlying the curves and diagrams.

Let's begin from a position of monetary equilibrium with the demand and supply of money equal. Now suppose that the Fed increases reserves through open market operations. At this instant, the banking system has more excess reserves than it wishes to hold. Banks then attempt to substitute loans and investments for excess reserves in their portfolios. In the process of making new loans and investments, the money supply expands. Banks seeking to make loans and purchase securities tend to push the interest rate down (security prices up).

The initial increase in the money supply will be held primarily by two groups: (1) financial investors who sold the securities to the Fed and (2) capital investors who just received bank loans and have projects with MEIs equal to or greater than the new lower interest rate. Financial investors want to hold larger money balances at lower interest rates essentially because of increasing risks associated with higher security prices. At the new lower rate, financial investors are satisfied, at least temporarily. Capital investors, however, are not satisfied. They do not wish to hold money but spend it on newly produced capital goods with MEIs greater than the interest rate. This act of spending on investment goods is the link between the financial and real sectors.

Spending by capital investors for investment goods represents income to the capital goods manufacturers, who, in turn, will spend most of it for raw materials, salaries and wages, rent, interest, and taxes. Of course, a portion will be saved. Income created by the spending of capital goods manufacturers will generate additional spending and saving. This process will continue through many rounds until total consumption expenditure is several times larger than the initial change in investment. This is the **investment multiplier** in action.

As shown in Figure 13-1, there are potential feedback effects from the increase in income in the real sector on the demand for transactions and precautionary balances. At higher levels of income, more L_1 balances will be needed, and they will have to come from L_2 balances. This will push the interest rate part of the way back toward the equilibrium level that prevailed prior to the monetary disequilibrium. This increase in interest rates will tend to reduce the level of investment and income below what they would have been without the feedback effects.

After all feedback effects have played out, the net effect of the increase in money supply will be to reduce the equilibrium level of interest rate and increase the equilibrium level of income. All of the increase in the money supply will be distributed between L_1 and L_2 balances. Thus far, we have indicated the **direction** of the change in the key variables. The **magnitude** of the change in income depends on (1) the elasticity of the L_2 function because this determines the initial decrease in the interest rate; (2) the elasticity of the MEI function because this determines the responsiveness of investment spending to the change in interest rates; (3) the elasticity of the C function because this determines the size of the multiplier; and (4) elasticity of the L_1 function because this determines the magnitude of the feedback effects.[1] What are numerical coefficients for these elasticities?

---

1. **Elasticity** means the degree of responsiveness in the dependent variable to a change in the independent variable. The greater the elasticity, the greater the responsiveness. For example, if a section of the MEI curve is elastic, this means that a given percentage increase in the interest rate produces a larger percentage increase in investment spending.

Economists do not know precisely. They vary from period to period and with a myriad of other factors. Because of these uncertainties, Keynesians prefer to rely on fiscal policy to induce changes in C and/or I or change G directly. What about the **timing** dimension? When will the feedback effects play out? Econometric models indicate that it takes several years for an initial surge in the money supply to work itself out fully.

Portfolio Balances or Neo-Keynesian Approach

In the portfolio balances approach, money is just one of several forms of wealth.[2] People allocate wealth among the different forms up to the point where the yield or benefit from each asset is equal. The demand for each asset varies directly with its yield or benefit and inversely with the yield or benefit from all other assets. In the portfolio balances approach, there is not one, but many interest rates—one representing each imperfectly substitutable asset with different risk-return characteristics. Portfolio balances theorists contend that a change in the money supply or the supply of other financial assets can have an effect on total spending.

Let's trace how a change in the money supply affects the economy. First, assume equilibrium in the financial and real sectors. In the financial sector, this means that interest rates, yields, or benefits on all assets are equal. In the real sector, planned I and S are equal and aggregate demand and supply are equal. Suppose that the Fed reduces the reserve ratio on demand deposits. This creates excess reserves for the banking system. In bank portfolios there is an imbalance of excess reserves. To restore portfolio equilibrium, banks will attempt to substitute additional loans and securities for excess reserves. In the process, they create money in the hands of the people.

Let's pause a moment and analyze what might be a typical portfolio adjustment to the increase in money balances. For illustrative purposes, assume that prior to the reduction in the reserve rate John Q. Bigbucks had the following balance sheet:

2. Much of the discussion in this section is adapted from Wrightsman, pp. 192–203.

Bigbucks' Balance Sheet (before r_d decreased)			
Money	$ 200,000		
Apartments	1,000,000	Net worth	$1,000,000
Bank loans	–200,000		
Total	$1,000,000	Total	$1,000,000

To simplify the analysis, note that we have made Bigbucks' bank debt a negative asset. Thus, if Bigbucks borrows more, his negative asset will become a larger negative number and his money balances will increase. Bigbucks reads the *Wall Street Journal* and learns that the Fed has reduced the reserve ratio on demand deposits. Having excelled in a money and banking course many years ago, he knows that bank lending ability has increased. He reasons that loan rates will decrease; hence, in his portfolio, he wants to reduce his negative asset (increase borrowing) because the interest rate on it is less. This is like selling a security that has risen in price (yield fallen).[3] So he calls his banker and requests a $100,000 loan—$90,000 for a new duplex and $10,000 of additional money to hold. Bigbucks believes that these adjustments will restore his portfolio balance.

Because of Bigbucks' excellent financial condition, credit rating, and large balances, the local bank readily grants his request. After the loan, here is what Bigbucks' balance sheet looks like:

Bigbucks' Balance Sheet (after loan)			
Money	$ 300,000		
Apartments	1,000,000	Net worth	$1,000,000
Bank loans	–300,000		
Total	$1,000,000	Total	$1,000,000

Bigbucks considers his portfolio temporarily imbalanced. Because of the decrease in loan rates, he decreased his holdings of that negative asset. However, when this happened, this meant that both the benefit

3. As a clarification, suppose that Bigbucks had $100,000 of maturing T-bills. If the yield on newly issued T-bills was lower, he might not replace this security in his portfolio. Hence, he would reduce a positive asset from +$100,000 to zero. Similarly, if Bigbucks raises bank loans from –$200,000 to –$300,000, he also reduces an asset (that is, he moves left on the numerical spectrum).

or utility of holding money and the return on apartments was higher than the new loan rate. Bigbucks' demand for these assets increased by the same amount as the decrease in his negative asset.

After Bigbucks builds the duplex his new equilibrium balance sheet will appear as follows:

Bigbucks' Balance Sheet (after purchase of apartments)			
Money	$ 210,000		
Apartments	1,090,000	Net worth	$1,000,000
Bank loans	–300,000		
Total	$1,000,000	Total	$1,000,000

In the real world there will be many investors doing the same thing that Bigbucks did: decreasing negative assets (loans), adding to money balances, and acquiring real assets. Of course, some of the initial increase in money balances will be used to purchase bonds and stocks, but let's not complicate the analysis by introducing these assets. The principles discussed also would apply to a multi-asset portfolio.

Returning to the transmission process, we find that as investors bid for real capital assets, such as duplexes, their price tends to rise and, hence, yield falls. For example, the more you pay for a duplex, the lower will be the MEI. However, spending to build duplexes and for other capital assets increases income for capital goods manufacturers who, in turn, buy raw materials and pay salaries and wages, interest, rent, and taxes. Just as with the liquidity preference approach, investment sets off the multiplier process that raises the equilibrium level of income.

In sum, portfolio balances theorists hold that an increase in the money supply at less than full employment level of income will generate portfolio adjustments that stimulate investment and increase income. This conclusion is the same as the traditional Keynesian approach, but the means to get there are different. More assets and interest rates are involved. Unlike the traditional Keynesian approach where financial investors and capital investors are considered as different groups, portfolio theorists lump all wealthholders into one group. It is more realistic to consider that the same profit-maximizing principles govern both types of investors, and that both will seek to hold larger money balances after the increase in money supply. A radical implication of the portfolio balances approach is that a change in the supply of any other asset can affect interest rates and income. An increase in the supply of any asset creates a portfolio imbalance and leads to an increased demand for capital assets and an expansion of income. Even more controversial is the portfolio balances conclusion that, depending on the substitution effects, an increase in the supply of one asset and equal decrease in another asset may lead to a change in income in the opposite direction.

Professor Dwayne Wrightsman of Dartmouth hypothesizes a situation where the government sells $2 billion in bonds to the public and uses half of the proceeds to purchase an old apartment building for a public housing project.[4] If money and bonds are close substitutes for each other, then the public will buy the bonds with only a slight increase in interest rates on the obligations. However, if apartments are not considered close substitutes for money and bonds, then the demand for apartments will not decline very much because of the slight rise in bond rates. If the decrease in the supply of apartments is greater than the decrease in demand for them, then the imbalance will raise the price of apartments and **stimulate** production in the real sector. Traditional Keynesians would have projected a decrease in production and income because a reduction in the money supply (due to the open market sale of bonds) causes the interest rate to rise and investment to fall. It is this implication that causes many economists to question the absolute assertion by Friedman and other monetarists that the money supply is the most important determinant of fluctuations in money income. It also brings into question whether the Fed can use the money supply and interest rates as indicators or targets for monetary policy. At this point, you should have a better understanding of what Friedman meant when he pointed out the complexities of describing how a change in the money supply (or now other assets) affects the economy.

The Modern Quantity Theory Approach

Professor Milton Friedman is the chief architect of the modern quantity theory, which he says is not a theory of income or prices, but a theory of the demand for money. Friedman points out that all

4. Wrightsman, pp. 198–201.

changes in money income can be traced to changes in the supply or demand for money. However, this is a tautology and, hence, proves nothing. To Friedman, the modern quantity theory is not this tautology, but an empirical generalization that the demand for real cash balances is quite stable and changes only very slowly or is the result of events caused by changes in the supply of money. Friedman concludes that changes in money income and prices almost invariably are the result of changes in the supply of money.

Friedman's explanation of how changes in the supply of money affect the economy is a type of portfolio adjustment approach as are the traditional Keynesian and portfolio balances approaches. We will begin the explanation by assuming a position of equilibrium between the real cash balances that the public wishes to hold and the supply of money as determined by the Fed. The demand for real cash balances depends on all the factors in Friedman's equation discussed in the last chapter, while the supply of money depends on the money multiplier and the monetary base. Assume that the Fed purchases securities through open market operations. This causes a portfolio imbalance between excess reserves and other bank assets and induces the banking system to make new loans and investments. In the process of lending, the quantity of nominal dollars held by the people becomes greater than the demand for real cash balances. The public then will attempt to get rid of the excess balances through expenditures for consumer goods, repayment of debts, and purchase of stocks, bonds, and other financial assets. Expenditures and outlays are receipts to others who also find that their nominal money balances now exceed their real demand for money. These people also attempt to get rid of their excess money balances through spending, financial investing, and debt repayment. In the course of spending for consumer goods and services, prices are bid up, which encourages manufacturers to expand output and expand productive capacity. Investment also is stimulated by the decline in interest rates caused by the increase in the money supply. This is the short-run Keynesian liquidity effect.

Friedman's transmission process does not stop here. After a lag, the increase in the money supply causes interest rates to reverse course and rise because of the income effect and price effect. A higher level of income raises the demands for L_1 balances, which pushes interest rates up. This is the **income effect** on interest rates. In addition, higher prices raise the inflation premium in interest rates. To the monetarists, nominal interest rates are composed of a real rate and an inflation premium. The real rate reflects the underlying productivity of capital. Inflation premiums come into interest rates because of pressure from both the supply and demand sides of the market. When lenders expect prices to rise, they will demand an inflation premium in the stated rate in order to compensate for expected price increases and ensure a real return on their funds. When borrowers expect prices to rise, they will attempt to obtain additional funds ahead of the anticipated price increases. They hope to benefit from the expected inflation by repaying their loans with cheaper dollars. Of course, this increase in the demand for funds also tends to put upward pressure on interest rates. This is the **price effect** on interest rates. Many years ago, Gibson, an English financial writer, called attention to the direct relationship between changes in the level of interest rates and prices. Keynes was so impressed with the data that he labeled the relationship the **Gibson Paradox**. Irving Fisher, in an essay written in 1896, is credited with development of the income and price effect concepts.[5]

The higher interest rates just discussed cause the demand for real cash balances to decline, a factor which reinforces the original expansion of income and prices. This additional surge in income and prices is sometimes called the **overshoot effect** because income and prices tend to overshoot their equilibrium values. The overshoot effect is analogous to the feedback effect mentioned earlier.

Equilibrium will be restored when the demand for real balances equals the supply of money available to be held. Even though the nominal supply cannot change, the initial excess in money supply will be eliminated either by a reduction in real quantity held through price increases and/or by an increase in the real demand for money caused by increases in output (income).

Conversely, if the Fed reduced the nominal money supply below the real demand for money, then people would attempt to build up their cash balances through balance sheet adjustments and reduced spending. This leads to lower prices and output. Lower prices will raise real cash balances, while lower output will reduce the demand for real balances. Income and/or prices must fall until the demand for real cash balances equals the new nominal supply of money.

In Friedman's scheme of things, money is one of many wealth forms. All of the adjustments described represent rearrangements of assets

5. Irving Fisher, "Appreciation and Interest," American Economic Association (Evanson, Ill.: Northwestern University, 1896), pp. 75–76.

and/or liabilities through buying, selling, lending, or borrowing activities and/or through use of current income and expenditures. Friedman points out that the traditional Keynesian liquidity preference approach emphasized the first adjustment, while the crude quantity theory stressed the second. He contends that the modern quantity theory approach to the transmission mechanism emphasizes both adjustment processes. Friedman also underscores the point that it may take many months for all adjustment processes to work themselves out.

Wealth Effects

Wealth effects are the second channel of monetary influence. Relatively few economists believe that wealth effects are the primary channel of monetary influence. However, most would agree that wealth effects reinforce relative price effects. We shall look at two wealth effects: the real cash balance, or Pigou effect, and the equity effect.

Real Balance, or Pigou Effect

In *The General Theory* Keynes held that the economy may settle at an equilibrium point at less than the full employment level. Moreover, the liquidity trap concept precluded monetary policy from lifting the economy back to full employment. In 1941 Alvin Hansen, one of Keynes' chief followers in this country, took Keynes' less than full employment equilibrium condition and developed a stagnation thesis which expanded on Keynes' idea. Obviously conditioned by the Depression experience, Hansen painted a bleak picture with respect to economic growth and claimed that the economy may be permanently stagnated. Disturbed by Hansen's thesis, A.C. Pigou in 1943 challenged the idea that the economy might be in equilibrium at less than the full employment level. Pigou demonstrated that with falling prices and an unchanged money supply, the value of cash balances would rise, and this would stimulate consumption, reduce saving, and push the economy back to full employment. The impact of a change in the real value of money balances on consumption is known as the **real balance** or **Pigou effect**. An important implication of the Pigou effect is that even if interest rates were at the liquidity trap level and the MEI schedule was interest inelastic, that is, investment was not very responsive to a given change in *i*, an increase in real cash balances could stimulate output and income.

Theoretically, the real balance effect is a powerful concept. However, empirical verification of it is lacking. Economists challenge the idea on theoretical grounds because they do not believe that prices are flexible in a downward direction. Nevertheless, the real balance effect is important because it indicates that the Fed should not let actual money balances fall during periods of depression or recession or rise during periods of inflation. No matter how small, price declines working through the real balance effect will help to push the economy in the direction toward full employment. Conversely, price increases reduce real balances and set in motion a negative real balance effect that will tend to depress consumption and reduce the rate of inflation. To benefit from the negative real balance effect, the Fed must resist the temptation to accelerate growth of the money supply. Otherwise, the negative real balance effect will be offset.[6]

Equity Effect

The **equity effect** is the impact on consumption spending caused by a change in the market valuation of common stocks. According to this theory, higher common stock values induce higher consumption, and vice versa. Lloyd Metzler in 1951 was probably the first economist to have an equity effect in his model. Franco Modigliani of MIT, and one of the leading neo-Keynesians, advanced an equity channel in a paper published in 1963. There is an equities-consumption channel in the large Federal Reserve Board-MIT econometric model of which Modigliani is a primary architect. In 1969, Frank de Leeuw and Edward Gramlich reported that in the FRB-MIT model the equity channel accounted for 45 percent of the entire monetary influence on total spending. This is impressive evidence of the strength of the equity channel.[7]

In 1971 Tobin and Walter Dolde stressed the importance of wealth effects. They considered the "two most recognized channels of monetary influence on consumption: (A) changes in wealth and

6. Some economists would prefer to increase the money supply during an inflationary period in hopes of avoiding the decline in income and employment that result from a negative real balance effect caused by the price increase.
7. Frank de Leeuw and Edward M. Gramlich, "The Channels of Monetary Policy," *Federal Reserve Bulletin* (June 7, 1969), p. 48.

Figure 13-2. Trading floor of the New York Stock Exchange (*Photo by Edward C. Topple*)

interest rates, (B) changes in liquidity constraints."[8] Wealth changes were primarily associated with capital gains (the equity effect). Their liquidity effect referred to the cost of converting nonliquid assets into liquid form in a world of imperfect capital markets. The level of the cost of conversion (a relative price) either inhibits or encourages conversion of illiquid into liquid assets and, hence, affects consumption.

8. James Tobin and Walter Dolde, "Wealth, Liquidity and Consumption" (Boston: Federal Reserve Bank of Boston, in *Consumer Spending and Monetary Policy: The Linkages*, 1971), p. 100.

Summary

The channels of monetary influence may be classified as (1) relative price effects or (2) wealth effects. A relative price effect is the impact on total spending caused by a change in the price or yield of one type of financial or real asset. A wealth effect is the impact on total spending caused by a change in the value of money balances or other wealth such as stocks. Changes in relative prices generate substitution effects in a portfolio of assets that lead to changes in spending. Wealth effects lead to changes in spending because of a change in the total value of the portfolio, not because of a rearrangement of assets within the portfolio (the relative price effect).

There are three primary relative price explanatory frameworks: (1) the traditional Keynesian approach, (2) the portfolio balances or neo-Keynesian approach, and (3) the modern quantity theory or monetarist approach. All approaches have these common characteristics: (1) they view money as a form of wealth whose demand is determined like the demand for any other asset, (2) all view monetary changes as working themselves out by portfolio adjustments, and (3) all consider that changes in the money supply can affect income and prices. However, only the modern quantity theory emphasizes that money is a unique asset and the primary cause of changes in income and prices.

In the traditional Keynesian approach, an increase in the money supply lowers the interest rate. This leads to an increase in investment, which, working through the multiplier, leads to an increase in income. Two important questions in this approach are the elasticity of the demand for money schedule and the elasticity of the investment schedule.

According to the portfolio balances approach, an increase in the money supply *may* lead to substitution effects, which may cause investors to purchase more real capital, which generates an increase in income. However, depending on the nature of the substitution effects, a change in one asset may lead to a change in income in the opposite direction.

In the modern quantity theory approach, an increase in the money supply causes an imbalance between the nominal money supply and the demand for real cash balances. People attempt to spend their excess balances, which leads to increases in output and prices.

The real balance effect is the impact of a change in the real value of money balances on consumption. For example, if prices fall, real balances will increase, and people will attempt to get rid of their excess balances, thereby causing spending to increase. The equity effect is caused by a change in the market valuation of common equities. There is evidence in a large FRB-MIT econometric model that a change in equity values has an impact on consumption.

Questions and Problems

1. Define (a) relative price effect and (b) wealth effect.
2. Trace the effects of an increase in the money supply through the traditional Keynesian framework.
3. Trace the effects of an increase in the money supply through the portfolio balances or neo-Keynesian framework.
4. What are the radical implications of the portfolio balances theory for monetary policy?
5. Trace the effects of an increase in the money supply through the modern quantity theory framework.
6. What is the Gibson Paradox?
7. Explain the real balance or Pigou effect.
8. What is the equity effect?

Suggestions for Additional Reading

Brainard, William C., and Tobin, James. "Pitfalls in Financial Model Building." *American Economic Review* (May 1968), pp. 99–122.

Brunner, Karl, and Meltzer, Allen H. "The Place of Financial Intermediaries in the Transmission of Monetary Policy." *American Economic Review* (May 1963), pp. 319–354.

De Leeuw, Frank, and Gramlich, Edward M. "The Channels of Monetary Policy." *Federal Reserve Bulletin* (June 1969), pp. 472–491.

Friedman, Milton. "A Theoretical Framework for Monetary Analysis." *The Journal of Political Economy* (February 1971), pp. 15–32.

Modigliani, Franco. "The Monetary Mechanism and Its Interaction with Real Phenomena." *The Review of Economics and Statistics* (February 1963), pp. 72–107.

Spencer, Roger W. "Channels of Monetary Influence: A Survey." Federal Reserve Bank of St. Louis, *Review* (November 1974), pp. 8–26.

Tobin, James, and Dolde, Walter. "Wealth, Liquidity and Consumption." Federal Reserve Bank of Boston, *Consumer Spending and Monetary Policy: The Linkage* (June 1971), pp. 94–144.

Wrightsman, Dwayne. *Monetary Theory and Policy,* 2nd ed. New York: The Free Press, 1976.

5

Monetary Policy

14

The Domestic Goals of Monetary Policy

The domestic goals of monetary policy are (1) reasonable price stability, (2) low levels of unemployment, and (3) a satisfactory rate of economic growth. In our system of government, national economic goals are determined by the people through the political process. Every two years, the people choose among candidates advocating various positions on economic issues. Every four years, we vote for a president and, more likely than not, we cast our ballot for the candidate whose position and philosophy on the various economic goals more closely approximates our own. The political process not only reveals the specific economic goals, it prioritizes them. If the majority of the people favor reasonable price stability over low levels of unemployment, candidates espousing the position will tend to be elected.

The primary aims of this chapter are to discuss each of the major national economic goals. In this regard, we will examine the meaning and measurement of each goal, the past record of achievement, the causes of inflation and unemployment and the determinants of economic growth, the adverse effects of inflation and unemployment and the need for economic growth, and the future prospects.

Twice Congress has passed legislation to formalize the nation's economic goals. Therefore, it seems appropriate to begin the chapter with a brief look at these acts.

The Full Employment Acts

The Full Employment Act of 1946

For those who did not experience the Great Depression, it is difficult to imagine that the Great Depression really lasted as long as it did, from 1929 to 1940. The rate of unemployment hit 25 percent in 1933, but it was 15 percent in 1940! With its entry into World War II, the United States "shot" itself out of the Great Depression.

After the war, most economists predicted and the general public feared that our nation would slip back into an economic depression. Reflecting the public's sentiment, Congress passed the historic Employment Act of 1946, which pledged the federal government's efforts to prevent another economic collapse. Below is the key section in the act:

> It is the continuing policy and responsibility of the Federal Government to use all practicable means consistent with its needs and obligations and other essential considerations of national policy, with the assistance and cooperation of industry, agriculture, labor, and state and local governments, to coordinate and utilize all its plans, functions, and resources for the purpose of creating and maintaining, in a manner calculated to foster and promote free competitive enterprise and the general welfare, conditions under which there will be afforded useful employment opportunities, including self-employment, for those able, willing, and seeking to work, and to promote *maximum employment, production, and purchasing power.* [Italics added.]

Following the war and to everyone's pleasant surprise, the economy did not sink into a depression. Rather, spurred by pent-up demand for consumer goods, the economy after a brief respite was able to overcome the decline in government spending and expand until the 1948–1949 recession hit.

Full Employment and Balanced Growth Act of 1978

For three decades the Employment Act of 1946 has been a basic policy making guide for the president, Congress, and the Fed. Since 1946 monetary and fiscal policies have been used to facilitate and stimulate economic prosperity. However, the double-digit inflation of

1973; the 1973–1975 recession, the most severe downturn since the Great Depression; and the inflation that persisted during and after the recession all served notice of fundamental difficulties in the economy. To deal with these problems Congress passed the Full Employment and Balanced Growth Act of 1978, or the Humphrey-Hawkins Act, as it is popularly known. This act amends and strengthens the Employment Act in three essential areas: (1) it explicitly identifies national economic priorities and objectives; (2) it directs the president to establish, and the Congress to consider, goals based on those priorities and objectives; and (3) it creates new procedures for the president, the Congress, and the Fed to improve the coordination and development of economic policies.

Specifically, the act sets forth two primary goals: (1) "the fulfillment of the right to full opportunities for useful paid employment at fair rates of compensation of all individuals able, willing, and seeking to work" and (2) "reasonable price stability."

The act further stipulates that in the president's first *Economic Report* published under the act, the goal for unemployment for 1983 should be 4 percent for workers aged 16 and over and 3 percent for workers aged 20 and over. The act also requires that the goal for the rate of increase in consumer prices in 1983 should be 3 percent.

In addition to the basic objectives of lower unemployment and inflation, the Humphrey-Hawkins Act listed four other economic aims for policymakers to take into account during the coming years. These secondary goals are

1. encouraging the growth of investment and capital formation.
2. reducing the share of federal spending in the nation's output.
3. balancing the budget.
4. improving the competitive position of the US economy in the world, while promoting fair and free international trade and a sound and stable international monetary system.

In addition the Full Employment and Balanced Growth Act directs the president to establish and Congress to consider numerical objectives based on the above primary and secondary economic goals. The president is required to set annual numerical goals for key indicators over a five-year period for employment, unemployment, prices, production, real income, and productivity. Goals for the first two years of the five-year period are considered short-term objectives, and the president is required in his budget to recommend levels of spending and receipts consistent with them. Goals for the final three years are medium-term goals, and projections of spending and receipts consistent with them are to be included in the president's budget.

The Full Employment and Balanced Growth Act also created new procedures and requirements for the president, the Congress, and the Federal Reserve to improve the coordination and development of economic policies. Each year the president is to present a program for achieving the goals that he has set. As a matter of general guidance the act requires that the government should rely as far as possible on growth in the private sector to meet the nation's employment and income goals. At the same time, the act calls the president's attention to various government programs for dealing with unemployment, inflation, inadequate capital formation, and other problems. Table 14-1 contains the nation's economic goals for the 1979-1983 period. The act authorizes no new programs to assist in achieving the goals set forth.

To improve the coordination of fiscal and monetary policies, the act requires the Federal Reserve Board to make semiannual reports to Congress on its objectives and plans with respect to monetary policy.

Table 14-1
Economic Goals, 1979-1983

Item	1979	1980	1981	1982	1983
	Level, fourth quarter[2]				
Employment (millions)	97.5	99.5	102.6	105.5	108.3
Unemployment (percent) ...	6.2	6.2	5.4	4.6	4.0
	Percent change, fourth quarter to fourth quarter				
Consumer prices	7.5	6.4	5.2	4.1	3.0
Real GNP.................	2.2	3.2	4.6	4.6	4.2
Real disposable income	2.8	2.3	4.4	4.4	4.0
Productivity[1]	.4	1.1	1.8	2.0	2.0

[1]Based on total real GNP per hour worked.
[2]Seasonally adjusted.

Source: 1979 Economic Report of the President, p. 109.

In these reports the Fed Board is required to comment on the relationship between its objectives for monetary policy and the president's short-term economic goals.

The policies of the president and the Fed Board will be considered jointly by the Congress. The act directs the Joint Economic Committee of Congress to review reports from the president and the Federal Reserve Board, together with submissions from the committees of Congress, and to offer its findings regarding the economic situation to the Budget Committee in each House prior to the development of the First Concurrent Resolution on the Budget. Four hours during the debate on that resolution in each House will be reserved for debate on economic policies and goals and specific budgetary plans for achieving economic objectives. Through this process of reports and debates, the new act aims to improve economic decisions by providing better ways of arriving at them and better information on which to base them. Let's turn now to a consideration of the major domestic economic goals.

Reasonable Price Stability

Meaning and Measurement

Many economists believe that inflation is the nation's number one economic problem. **Inflation** simply means a persistent rise in the general level of prices. It does not mean a rise in the price of one good or service because underlying supply or demand schedules change.

There are three primary measures of inflation: (1) the consumer price index (CPI), (2) the producer price index (PPI), and (3) the GNP deflator. The **CPI** is published by the Bureau of Labor Statistics (BLS) and measures the average changes in the cost of a fixed, or constant, "market basket" of approximately 400 consumer goods and services purchased by urban wage earners and clerical workers (80 percent of the civilian noninstitutional population). Weights in the market basket reflect the relative importance of the items purchased, such as food, housing, entertainment, and medical care. The items in the index are described by detailed specifications to ensure that, as far as possible, the same quality is priced each time, and that differences in reported prices are measures of price change only.

The **PPI** (formerly the wholesale price index) also is published by the BLS and is based on approximately 2,800 commodity price series.

Prices used in constructing the index are collected from sellers, if possible, and generally apply to the first significant large-volume commercial transaction for each commodity, that is, the manufacturer's or other producer's selling price, the importer's selling price, or the selling price on an organized exchange or at a central market. The weights used in the index are values of net shipments of commodities as derived from the industrial censuses of 1972 and other data.

The **GNP deflator** is published by the Department of Commerce in connection with its estimates of GNP. This index is the most comprehensive index of prices because it measures price changes for all goods and services in GNP, including the cost of government services.

The Record

Inflation is a worldwide problem. As shown in Table 14–2, between 1972 and 1977 the median annual rate of inflation in twenty-five industrialized countries was 11.5 percent; during the same period, the annual rate in the United States was 7.1 percent. Thus, in relative terms, our country's inflation record looks rather good, but in absolute terms most people would agree that a 7.1 percent annual inflation rate is unacceptable. The worst inflation has occurred in South America, where annual rates above 25 percent are common. In Chile, Uruguay, and Argentina the value of money in 1977 was less than 1 percent of its value in 1967.

Let's turn to the long-run record of inflation in this country. Figure 14–1 shows the CPI and the index for food for the 1913–1977 period. Figure 14–2 shows producer prices for industrial commodities and farm products for the 1913–1977 period with an inset for the 1800–1977 period. Looking first at the long-run picture in the inset, note that generally the periods of sharpest inflation occurred during and/or following wars—the War of 1812, the Civil War, World War I, World War II, the Korean War, and the Vietnam War. After the first three wars, prices retreated substantially. However, following WW II, prices have continued upward and accelerated sharply during and after the Vietnam War.

Turning to Figure 14–1, note that consumer prices increased slowly but steadily from 1951 to 1965. Since this last date, however, the CPI has more than doubled, with the steepness of the increase similar to the World War I and World War II patterns.

World Currencies: A Depreciation Tally, 1972-1978

	Industrialized countries Indexes of value of money (1967 = 100) 1972	1977	Annual rate of depreciation of money '67-'72*	'72-'77*	1978†
Switzerland	81	62	4.2%	5.3%	1.3%
West Germany	84	64	3.4	5.4	2.7
Luxembourg	83	55	3.7	7.9	3.0
Austria	81	56	4.1	7.1	3.5
Netherlands	75	49	5.7	7.9	3.7
Japan	76	41	5.4	11.5	3.9
Belgium	82	52	3.9	8.8	4.6
United States	79	55	4.4	7.1	6.5
Ireland	69	33	7.0	13.9	6.7
Portugal	67	27	8.0	16.4	7.5
Australia	81	44	4.1	11.6	7.6
Norway	74	48	5.7	8.5	7.6
United Kingdom	73	34	6.2	14.0	7.9
Canada	83	54	3.8	8.2	8.2
France	76	47	5.3	9.3	8.3
Finland	77	39	5.2	12.6	8.5
South Africa	81	47	0.4	13.6	9.1
Denmark	74	45	5.7	9.8	10.5
Sweden	78	50	4.8	8.8	10.6
Italy	83	39	3.8	13.9	11.1
Yugoslavia	59	26	9.9	15.3	11.2
Greece	88	42	2.5	13.9	11.7
New Zealand	73	39	6.2	11.5	11.8
Spain	75	35	5.5	14.3	16.2
Turkey	61	24	9.5	17.0	37.5
Median rates			5.2	11.5	7.9

	Less-developed countries Indexes of value of money (1967 = 100) 1972	1977	Annual rate of depreciation of money '67-'72*	'72-'77*	1978†
Panama	87	60	2.7%	7.3%	2.3%
India	84	53	3.5	8.9	3.2
Malaysia	94	65	1.2	7.3	4.2
Costa Rica	83	51	3.6	9.4	4.8
Singapore	95	59	0.9	9.0	5.0
China (Taiwan)	80	44	4.3	11.4	6.2
Venezuela	89	62	2.4	7.1	6.4
Paraguay	85	50	3.1	10.3	6.6
Philippines	66	35	7.9	11.9	6.6
Bolivia	81	31	4.2	7.1	7.4
Thailand	90	55	2.2	9.3	8.3
Indonesia	30	10	21.3	19.3	8.8
Kenya	89	50	2.3	11.0	10.9
Ecuador	73	36	6.0	13.0	11.1
South Korea	58	28	10.4	13.4	11.6
Iran	85	42	3.2	13.0	13.3
Mexico	81	35	4.0	15.6	15.2
Jamaica	74	35	5.9	14.1	15.7
Colombia	64	22	8.4	19.3	18.8
Brazil	39	10	17.2	23.4	27.5
Peru	66	23	8.0	19.3	29.0
Chile	22	‡	26.1	73.6	31.4
Uruguay	14	‡	32.1	41.9	32.2
Israel	71	17	6.6	24.7	33.7
Argentina	33	‡	19.9	58.8	66.5
Median rates			4.3	13.0	10.9

*Compounded annually.   †Based on average monthly data for 1978 compared with corresponding period of 1977.   ‡Less than 1.

Source: Citibank, *Monthly Economic Letter* (October 1978). p. 7.

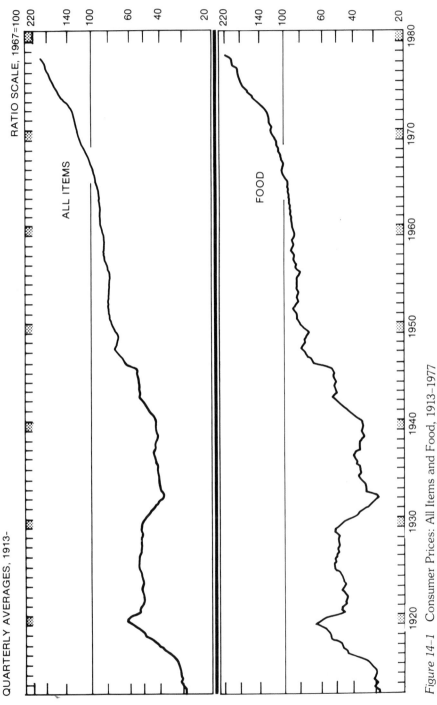

Figure 14-1 Consumer Prices: All Items and Food, 1913–1977

Source: Board of Governors of the Federal Reserve, *Historical Chart Book.*

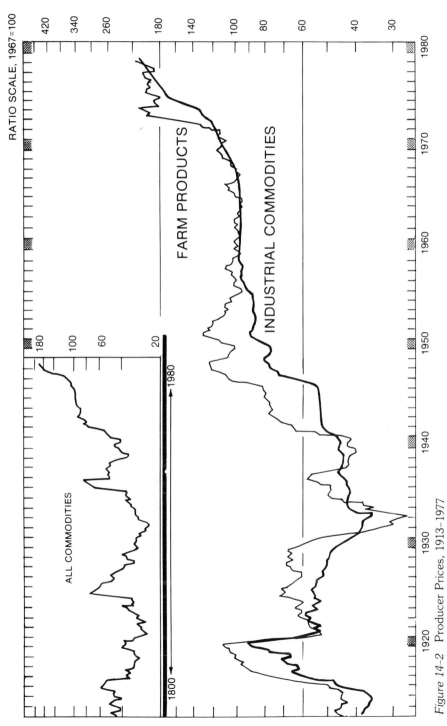

Figure 14-2 Producer Prices, 1913–1977

Source: Board of Governors of the Federal Reserve, *Historical Chart Book.*

Figure 14-3. A sample of prices in the early part of the twentieth century (*Courtesy of the Woolworth Company Archives*)

Moving to Figure 14–2, note that the PPI has exhibited much more volatility. The period of greatest price stability was the period between the end of the Korean War in 1954 and the escalation of the Vietnam War in 1965. In the 1970s, the PPI more than doubled.

Theories of Inflation

Since the end of World War II, economists have analyzed extensively the problem of inflation. A number of explanations have been offered for the persistent inflation that has plagued the economy. The two primary theories that have emerged are the demand-pull theory and the cost-push theory. Most economists would ascribe to the view that no one theory fully explains inflation. There are times when one theory appears more applicable than others. Then there are times when forces contained in both theories seem to be behind the sustained increase in prices. Finally, most economists would agree that there is still much to be learned about the inflationary process.

Demand-pull theory.   The **demand-pull theory** is the traditional theory of inflation. According to this theory, inflation is caused by excess demand (spending) relative to the available supply at the existing level prices. Frequently, this process is described as "too much money chasing too few goods." Both the traditional Keynesian and the modern quantity theory approaches hold that inflation is the result of excess demand.

In the Keynesian income-expenditure theory, inflation is caused by an excess of aggregate demand at the full employment level of output. The Keynesian explanation also holds that increases in aggregate demand at below the full employment level may pull up prices somewhat as well as stimulate output. According to the Keynesians any factor that can create excess demand is a potential cause of inflation. For example, investment spending, an important component of aggregate demand, can increase because of an increase in the money supply, a decrease in taxes on business profits, accelerated depreciation allowances, or just a more optimistic set of expectations. Inflation also could result from an increase in government spending or a shift in the consumption function.

According to modern quantity theorists, inflation is a monetary phenomenon. Their studies of inflation in many countries have shown that a sustained change in the rate of growth of the money supply causes a similar change in the rate of inflation. Figure 14–4 shows the relationship between money growth and inflation in the United States from 1954 to 1977. The specific hypothesis underlying this chart is that the rate of inflation in a quarter is directly related to the rate of monetary growth in the current and prior twenty quarters.[1]

1. John A. Tatom, *"Does the Stage of the Business Cycle Affect the Inflation Rate?" Federal Reserve Bank of St. Louis, Review* (September 1978), pp. 10–12.

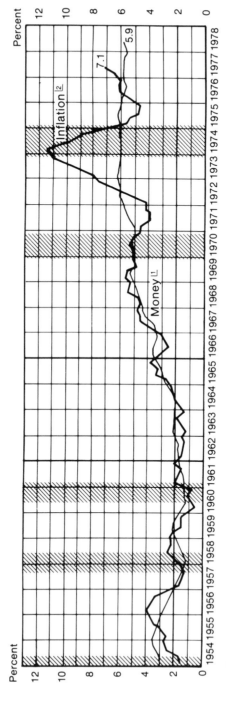

Shaded areas represent periods of business recessions.

[1] Twenty-quarter annual growth rate of m_{1}.

[2] Four-quarter annual growth rate of the GNP Deflator, ending four quarters in the future.
Latest data plotted: Inflation-2nd quarter 1977; Money-2nd quarter 1978

Figure 14-4 Money Growth and Inflation in the United States, 1954–1977
Source: John A. Tatom, "Does the Stage of the Business Cycle Affect the Inflation Rate?"
Federal Reserve Bank of St. Louis, *Review* (September 1978), p. 9.

In essence, the chart shows that the inflation rate had tended to equal the trend rate of growth in the money supply. Temporary developments such as weather and strikes do influence the inflation rate from quarter to quarter. The large deviations in the inflation rate in the 1971–1975 period are explained by special events. In 1971–1973, the errors reflect the existence and removal of wage and price controls. The bulge in prices in late 1973 through early 1975 reflects the large increase in price of energy resources due to previously unused monopoly power.

According to modern quantity theorists, inflation is caused by an increase in the rate of growth in the money supply. People will attempt to spend the excess nominal dollars, which leads to an increase in output and prices. However, the output component of total spending is determined by growth in labor and capital resources whose long-run growth is fairly constant. Hence, a change in the growth rate of money tends to be reflected fully in the inflation rate.

Cost-push theory.   The **cost-push theory** holds that inflation stems from the exercise of market power by business and/or labor groups, or it may be caused by higher import prices or higher taxes. Under this theory firms in some industries have the power to push up their prices even in the face of weak demand. In addition, unions may ask for wage increases in excess of productivity gains. Businesses then raise their prices to cover the higher wage costs. It would be an error to blame unions solely for this increase when it actually was businesses that raised prices. It is alleged also that higher import prices and taxes provide the impetus for inflation when they raise the costs of businesses that possess market power and can raise prices.

The main implication of the cost-push theory is that traditional monetary and fiscal policies are not effective against inflation with origins on the supply side. A tight money policy would exacerbate the unemployment problem. However, some economists advocate increasing the rate of monetary growth to validate the increase in costs.

Effects of Inflation on the Distribution of Wealth and Income

Wealth is the source of income, so our analysis of the effects of inflation on wealth and income may be considered under one heading. The effects of inflation on the distribution of wealth and income depend on whether the inflation is anticipated or unanticipated, the form in which wealth is held, and on the ability of individual wealth owners to demand and receive income payments that match the inflation rate. For example, if inflation is anticipated, interest rates tend to rise to reflect an inflation premium. However, if the increase in rates is not enough to cover the inflation rate, then wealth is transferred from creditors to debtors. The same analysis applies with respect to other income shares—wages and salaries, rents, profits, and dividends. If property owners anticipate inflation and competitive conditions allow them to raise rents proportionately with the inflation rate, then their share of income will not change.

However, in this country the experience is that inflation has tended to redistribute wealth and income. Market interest rates at times have not risen enough to fully reflect the inflation rate. Moreover, many debt contracts such as home mortgage loans have fixed interest rates. Under such conditions, wealth has been transferred from creditors to debtors. As a group, homeowners have been a primary beneficiary of the redistribution of wealth brought about by inflation.

With respect to those that depend on wages and salaries for the bulk of their income, some groups benefit while others lose. Those people in occupations that cannot get wage and salary increases at least equal to the inflation rate or those under labor or employment contracts that do not allow cost of living increases see their relative income share fall. Many teachers and retirees do not receive annual pay adjustments equal to the inflation rate. On the other hand, most people and employees have become so aware of inflation that the annual cost of living adjustment is an expected event.

The effect of inflation on business profits depends on the pattern of cost adjustments. If a firm's costs lag, then profits tend to increase in inflationary times. If costs rise proportionately or more than proportionately, then profits will hold up only if the firm has enough market power to increase prices at a rate to match cost increases. Dividends are a function of profits, so the effect of inflation on this income source will depend largely on what happens to profits.

Future Prospects

In spite of the lofty goals of the Full Employment and Balanced Growth Act of 1978, most economists are deeply concerned about the future prospects for inflation in this country. This worry stems basically from their doubt about the resolve of Congress, the President, and the Fed to deal with the problem of inflation. They see growing market power on the part of big business and big labor. They see a dwindling supply of low-cost raw materials and sources of energy. As stated earlier, our economic goals are determined through the political process, and when the people decide that inflation must be defeated, it will. However, if the cost of reducing the inflation rate is more unemployment, then the people may hesitate to urge the attainment of a lower rate of inflation.

Low Levels of Unemployment

Meaning and Measurement

Most people would say that the attainment of low levels of unemployment is the most important national economic objective. Let's look briefly at the concept of unemployment and how it is measured.

The basic source of labor market information is the monthly survey data collected by the Bureau of Census for the BLS. The Census Bureau surveys about 50,000 randomly selected individuals, and the

Figure 14-5. Unemployment line in Detroit, December 1974 (*Reprinted by permission of Newsweek*)

BLS then constructs various labor market and employment measures. First, the **civilian labor force** comprises all civilians classified as employed or unemployed according to definitions shown below. The **total labor force** also includes the armed forces. **Employed persons** comprise (1) all civilians who, during the survey week, did any work for pay or profit or worked fifteen hours or more as unpaid workers in a family enterprise and (2) all persons who were not working but who had jobs or businesses from which they were temporarily absent for uneconomic reasons (illness, bad weather, vacation, labor-management dispute, etc.). **Unemployed persons** comprise all civilians who had no employment during the survey week, who made specific efforts to find a job within the previous four weeks (such as applying directly to an employer, or to a public employment service, or checking with friends), and who were available for work during the survey week. Persons on layoff from a job or waiting to report to a new job within thirty days also are classified as unemployed. All other persons, 16 years old and over, are "not in the labor force." The **unemployment rate** is the percentage of the civilian labor force that is seeking work but does not have a job. The **employment rate** is the percentage of noninstitutionalized population between 16 years of age or older that is employed.

The Record

Figure 14-4 shows trends in the civilian labor force, total employment, and the unemployment rate. In 1978, the total civilian labor force climbed above 100 million people. Of this total, 94 million were employed and 6 million were unemployed. Over 63 percent of the population was in the labor force.

As shown in Figure 14-6, between 1948 and 1978 the civilian labor force climbed by over 40 million people, while employment rose by 36 million. The ability of the economy to absorb such a large percentage of the new entrants in the labor force is evidence of a strong and growing economy.

The media and many economists tend to look first at the unemployment rate and not the positive achievement cited above. In the bottom panel of Figure 14-6, the unemployment rate has risen in each of the five postwar recessions: (1) 1948–1949, (2) 1953–1954, 1957–1958, (3) 1960–1961, (4) 1969–1970, and (5) 1973–1975. For several months in 1975, the unemployment rate climbed over 9 percent, the highest

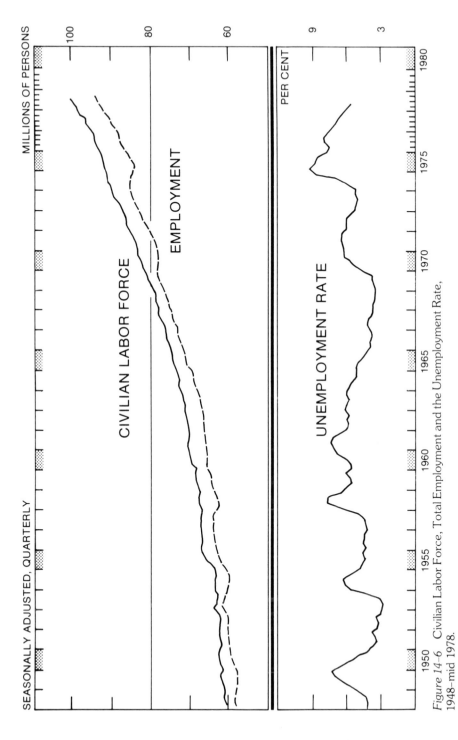

Figure 14–6 Civilian Labor Force, Total Employment and the Unemployment Rate, 1948–mid 1978.

Source: Board of Governors of the Federal Reserve, *Historical Chart Book.*

rate in the postwar period. The failure of the unemployment rate to decline rapidly during the subsequent recovery was cited by proponents of the Humphrey-Hawkins Act as evidence of the need for greater government monitoring of our national economic goals.

A number of economists have argued that the current concept of the unemployment rate overstates the "true" situation. Geoffrey Moore, director of business cycle research at the National Bureau of Economic Research, pointed out that during ten "full employment" years (1947–1948, 1951–1953, 1956, and 1966–1969), 55.7 percent of the working age population 16 years and over were employed; those unemployed comprised 2.1 percent of the working population.[2] In November, 1977, Moore found that 4.3 percent of the working age population were unemployed; however, 57.8 percent were employed. During the "full employment" years, 2.5 percent of the working population were in the armed forces, while in November, 1977, only 1.3 percent were in uniform. Moore argues that if the nation was employing a larger percentage of its population in 1977 when the unemployment rate was 7 percent than it was in 1956 or in any other year when the unemployment rate was 4 percent, then it would appear that there was fuller employment in 1977 than in earlier years.

Another reason for the belief that the current concept of unemployment overstates the true situation is that recent expansion of the unemployment insurance program requires that applicants must remain in the labor force to receive benefits even though they may not be seriously looking for work. Such behavior tends to give the unemployment rate an upward bias.

Causes of Unemployment

There are four basic types of unemployment, each caused by a different set of circumstances. When unemployment rises during a recession because of insufficient demand for national output, this is called **lack-of-demand unemployment**. The relationship between unemployment and aggregate output is known as **Okun's Law**.[3]

The second type of unemployment is **structural unemploy-**

---

2. Geoffrey H. Moore, "Toward 'Full Employment,'" Morgan Guaranty Trust Company, *Morgan Guaranty Survey* (January 1978), pp. 5–6.

3. Arthur M. Okun, "Potential GNP: Its Measurement and Significance," American Statistical Association, *Proceedings of the Business and Economic Statistics Section*, 1962, pp. 98–104.

ment, which is caused by an imbalance between the types and location of the jobs available and the types and location of the jobs demanded by the labor force.

Third, there is **frictional unemployment**, which is caused by the usual resignation and job shifting that take place in the labor market. Some people anticipate not working for a while, knowing that there is a job available for their skills, and simply do not look for a job.

Finally, **seasonal unemployment** stems from the seasonal pattern of work in a particular industry or area. Some people may be able to find work in other industries or areas, but this is not always possible.

Of course, the appropriate monetary policy prescription to deal with unemployment depends on the cause of unemployment. During recessions, the bulk of the unemployment is because of lack of demand. As we shall discuss in Chapter 16, Keynesian-activists prefer massive doses of government spending and tax cuts to deal with lack of demand unemployment. Monetarists prefer to prevent this type of unemployment by eliminating instability in the money supply. During periods when lack of demand unemployment declines, other types of unemployment also tend to decline somewhat. However, because of their very nature, these other types of unemployment cannot be reduced significantly by acceleration of aggregate demand. Retraining and job information programs are most ineffective in assisting those who do not wish to work.

Effects of Unemployment

Unemployment has disastrous effects on the specific individuals involved and on everyone in the economy. The unemployed lose the benefits of their labors in the current period and jeopardize themselves and their children in the future if provision for food, medical care, and education is lacking. There is no way to measure the short- and long-run psychological wear and tear that unemployment causes. The loss of dignity associated with being unemployed may be as great a burden on the unemployed as the economic loss.

For the economy as a whole, unemployment reduces the quantity and range of goods and services that everyone can enjoy, not only in the short run, but also in the long run. The Great Depression demonstrated clearly the importance of the interdependence within the economy. Sales, profits, and employment at your firm depend on other people's economic means to purchase from you. The goods that we consume must be produced. Moreover, think of the future production that is lost because unemployment leads to reduced investment in physical capital and in human beings.

Future Prospects

Future prospects for achieving low levels of unemployment are clouded. On the optimistic side, Say's Law as a long-run proposition is still true. The act of production does create income equal to the value of the production. Employment will increase if more goods and services are demanded. Our knowledge of the macro- and micro-economic policies to deal with unemployment are imperfect, but improving. Moreover, the federal government's commitment to reduce unemployment was underscored recently in the Full Employment and Balanced Growth Act of 1978.

On the negative side, the problem of finding adequate energy sources creates uncertainty in the business environment which discourages investment and expansion of employment. Some government policies such as high taxes, inadequate depreciation allowances, onerous red tape and reporting requirements, and overregulation are not conducive for business expansion and growing employment. Moreover, the slowdown in the growth rate of labor productivity in this country opens the way for foreign imports, at least as long as we can buy them. In other words, employment grows in other countries, but stagnates in ours. Most of these negative aspects of future employment prospects cannot be dealt with by the Federal Reserve. However, the Fed can make a great contribution by creating a non-inflationary environment that encourages business investment, and, hence, greater employment.

Satisfactory Rate of Economic Growth

Meaning and Measurement

Economic growth refers to output or the capacity to produce output. The most commonly used measure of economic growth is **GNP**, gross national product, which is the money value of the goods and services produced in a year. However, GNP is a money value concept that reflects not only quantities of real goods and services but also price increases. Therefore, **GNP in constant dollars** is better than GNP in current dollars as a measure of economic growth. GNP in constant dollars may be growing but, if population is growing more rapidly, then individual economic welfare will decline. Hence, **per capita GNP in constant dollars** provides a good measure of individual welfare. Finally, per capita GNP in constant dollars does not reflect the effort to produce this output. Therefore, **output per manhour** measures labor productivity, which is an essential factor underlying growth in GNP.

The Record

Figure 14-7 (top panel) shows the growth in GNP in current and constant dollars from 1947–1977. During this period GNP in current dollars rose from $400 billion to over $2 trillion. In constant 1972 dollars, GNP climbed from slightly less than $500 billion to over $1.3 trillion. Note the slow growth in constant dollar GNP since 1972 even though GNP in current dollars accelerated. This divergence shows clearly that most of the growth in current GNP is illusory.

The lower panel shows the quarterly growth rate in real GNP. The erratic quarterly pattern in real growth stands out as do the recession periods, especially the 1973–1975 drop.

Figure 14-8 shows the growth in real GBNP since 1900. The annual trend value is 3.1 percent over better than three-quarters of a century. Since the beginning of the century real GNP increased from $50 billion to over $1.3 trillion.

Figure 14-9 contains per capita GNP from 1900. The severity of the 1921 recession and the Great Depression as well as the post-World War II adjustment are apparent. Only four postwar recessions seem to stand out: (1) 1953–1954, (2) 1957–1958, (3) 1969–1970, and (4) 1973–1975. Economists call the 1973–1975 recession the most severe since the Great Depression. Yet, it seems miniscule when compared with the Depression decline.

Finally, Figure 14-10 shows output per manhour, which measures productivity. Since the Depression, productivity has had an annual trend value of 2.9 percent. However, since 1972 the productivity growth rate has declined sharply. This is attributed to a number of factors including the influx of inexperienced workers (mainly women) into the labor force, the decline in rate of new capital investment, the decline in the willingness of people to work, and the increase in the

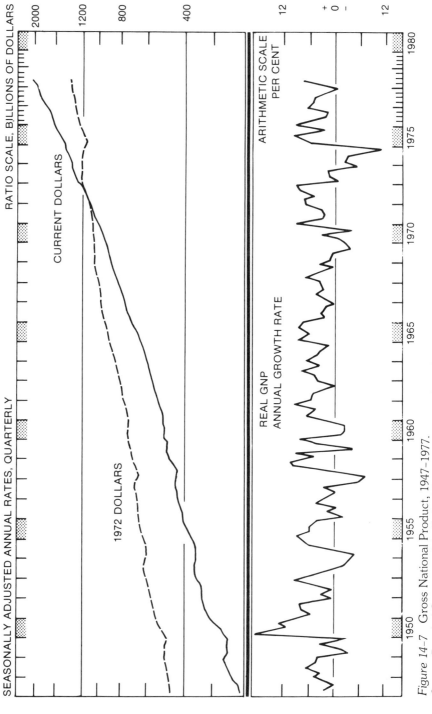

Figure 14-7 Gross National Product, 1947–1977.
Source: Board of Governors of the Federal Reserve, *Historical Chart Book.*

Annually; trend, growth rate

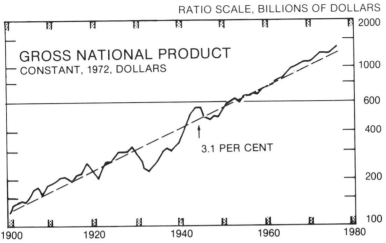

Figure 14-8 Growth in Real GNP, 1900–1977.

Source: Board of Governors of the Federal Reserve, *Historical Chart Book.*

number of paid holidays and vacations. Many economists believe that the decline in productivity is one of our most serious economic problems because our ability to solve the problem of inflation and provide an adequate standard of living for all depends largely on productivity.

In sum, our long-run record of economic growth has been impressive. However, the record also shows that real growth has slowed considerably in the 1970s and, as will be discussed later in this chapter, this trend has serious implications for economic welfare.

Determinants of Economic Growth

Economic growth depends on growth in the quantity and quality of our human resources, physical capital, raw materials, energy sources, managerial ability, and technology. Not to be overlooked is the willingness of the people to work hard, which is a factor underlying labor productivity. Our rate of population growth has declined, but through education and training programs, we can make our available labor force more productive.

Our rate of physical capital growth has declined in recent years. Some economists blame high taxes, overregulation, outdated de-

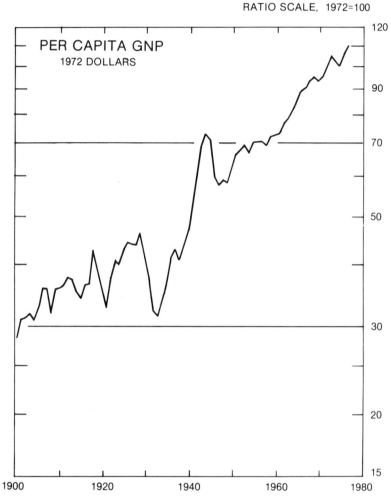

RATIO SCALE, 1972=100

Figure 14-9 Per Capita GNP, 1900–1977.

Source: Board of Governors of the Federal Reserve, *Historical Chart Book.*

preciation allowances, and an uncertain business climate for this. More capital investment improves labor productivity, makes US goods more competitive in world markets, and helps to defeat inflation by increasing productive capacity.

The nation's problems in the energy area are well known. Germany, the Scandinavian countries, and Switzerland have about the same standard of living as the United States but use half the energy to accomplish this. In the past our economic growth has been achieved

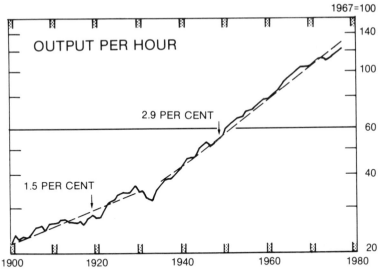

Figure 14-10   Output Per Manhour, 1900-1977

Source: Board of Governors of the Federal Reserve, *Historical Chart Book.*

with the inefficient use of energy. In the future, growth must be achieved with relatively less energy, hence, energy technology must improve.

Finally, America's "aces in the hole" are the ability of its business managers and its vast strength in technology. If we are to achieve adequate economic growth in the future, our ability in management and technology probably hold the key to achieving this goal.

Why We Need Economic Growth

Adequate economic growth is needed (1) to absorb new entrants into the labor force, (2) to improve the overall standard of living and quality of life, and (3) to enable the nation to have an adequate national defense.

Entrants into the labor force include young people seeking work for the first time, adults, such as women who previously have not been a member of the labor force, and reentrants. Between 1960 and 1977, the population's participation rate in the labor force increased from 59.2 percent to 61.8 percent. During this period, the participation for females climbed from 37.1 percent to 47.8 percent. A growing economy is vital to provide jobs for all those who wish to work.

There are many unfilled needs in the economy. Not all of our citizens have adequate food, shelter, or medical care. The ability of people to provide for their own needs and for government to provide for those unable to provide for themselves is enhanced in a growing economy. When the pie grows, the size of all slices in the pie tends to increase.

Finally, a strong national defense is necessary for physical survival. The burden of taxing the people to provide for an adequate national defense is lessened in a growing economy.

Future Prospects

Our economic growth prospects are clouded for the same reason that the unemployment picture is hazy. Expanded capital investment, growth in labor productivity, and improved technology, especially energy technology, hold the key to economic growth. The Federal Reserve's role is to provide an environment conducive for these growth elements to flourish. Other arms of the government could assist by reducing taxes and providing programs that encourage investment in human beings, physical capital, and the development of technology.

Summary

Congress in 1946 and 1978 passed Employment Acts as evidence of their commitment to the nation's economic health. Unlike the 1946 Act, the Full Employment and Balanced Growth Act of 1978 specified quantitative goals of 4 percent and 3 percent for unemployment and inflation in 1983. These are ambitious goals, and many economists doubt that they are attainable within the current regulatory and economic environment.

Reasonable price stability is an important goal because unanticipated inflation causes a redistribution of wealth and income. The two primary theories of inflation are demand-pull and cost-push. Most Keynesians and monetarists would ascribe to the demand-pull theory, with the latter contending that inflation is primarily a monetary phenomenon. However, at times cost-push forces do tend to account for general price increases. Monetarists would argue that in the long run, such price increases cannot stick unless validated by an increase in the monetary supply.

Low levels of unemployment are an economic goal because the people dislike the bad effects of unemployment on those that are unemployed and everyone in the aggregate. Of the four types of unemployment, lack-of-demand unemployment is the most responsive to increased aggregate demand.

A satisfactory rate of economic growth is vital for absorbing entrants into the labor force, improving the standard of living, and making it possible to have an adequate national defense without undue burden. Economic growth depends primarily on adequate capital investment, improved labor productivity, and improved technology. The Fed's role in the achievement of low levels of unemployment and satisfactory economic growth is to provide a monetary environment conducive for these growth determinants to flourish. But it must do so in a manner that does not generate inflation.

Questions and Problems

1. Discuss briefly the background and aims of the Full Employment Act of 1946.
2. Outline the primary and secondary economic goals in the Humphrey-Hawkins Act.
3. Explain briefly (a) demand-pull inflation and (b) cost-push inflation.
4. Explain the effects of inflation on the distribution of wealth and income.
5. List and describe briefly the four basic types of unemployment.
6. Why is continued economic growth important?

Suggestions for Additional Reading

Burger, Albert E. "Is Inflation All Due to Money?" Federal Reserve Bank of St. Louis, *Review* (December 1978), pp. 8–12.

Butler, Larry. "The Relation Between Income Growth and Unemployment." Federal Reserve Bank of San Francisco, *Economic Review* (September 1974), pp. 12–23.

Carlson, Keith M. "Estimates of the High-Employment Budget and Changes in Potential Output." Federal Reserve Bank of St. Louis, *Review* (August 1977), pp. 16–22.

Dewald, William G., and Marchon, Maurice N. "Monetary Growth, Inflation, and Unemployment: Projections Through 1983." Federal Reserve Bank of Kansas City, *Economic Review* (November 1978), pp. 3–17.

Francis, Darryl R. "The Origin and Impact of Inflation." Federal Reserve Bank of St. Louis, *Review* (December 1975), pp. 18–22.

Gordon, R.J. "The Theory of Domestic Inflation." *American Economic Review* (February 1977), pp. 128–134.

Haley, Sharon M. "Behind the Unemployment Rate." Federal Reserve Bank of Richmond, *Economic Review* (October 1973), pp. 10–16.

Helbling, Hans H., and Turley, James E. "A Primer on Inflation: Its Conception, Its Costs, Its Consequences." Federal Reserve Bank of St. Louis, *Review* (January 1975), pp. 2–8.

Humphrey, Thomas M. "The Concept of Indexation in the History of Economic Thought." Federal Reserve Bank of Richmond, *Economic Review* (November/December 1974), pp. 3–16.

———. "Some Current Controversies in the Theory of Inflation." Federal Reserve Bank of Richmond, *Economic Review* (July/August 1976), pp. 8–19.

Lovati, Jean M. "The Unemployment Rate as an Economic Indicator." Federal Reserve Bank of St. Louis, *Review* (September 1976), pp. 2–9.

McElhattan, Rose. "Estimating a Stable-Inflation Capacity-Utilization Rate." Federal Reserve Bank of San Francisco, *Economic Review* (Fall 1978), pp. 20–30.

Smith, Sharon P. "An Examination of Employment and Unemployment Rates." Federal Reserve Bank of New York, *Quarterly Review* (Autumn 1977), pp. 14–18.

Spencer, Roger W. "Inflation, Unemployment and Hayek." Federal Reserve Bank of St. Louis, *Review* (May 1975), pp. 6–10.

Tatom, John A. "Economic Growth and Unemployment: A Reappraisal of the Conventional View." Federal Reserve Bank of St. Louis, *Review* (October 1978), pp. 16–22.

Zell, Steven P. "Recent Development in the Theory of Unemployment." Federal Reserve Bank of Kansas City, *Monthly Review* (September/October 1975), pp. 3–10.

15

International Goals of Monetary Policy

In Chapter 14, we discussed at length the major domestic goals of monetary policy. However, we live in an increasingly interdependent world. All of the nations of the free world depend on one another for goods and services, and most of these nations hold dollars as an important part of their international reserves. Therefore, our competitive position in world markets and our role as the world's banker are of such importance that the Fed must consider them in the formulation of monetary policy.

In this chapter, our objectives are (1) to discuss briefly the nature and significance of our international economic goals, (2) to describe the nature and determination of exchange rates, (3) to analyze the nature and significance of our international transactions, and (4) to examine the role of dollars, gold, and SDRs in the evolution of the international monetary system.

Our International Economic Goals: Nature and Significance

As mentioned above, we live in an increasingly interdependent world. The United States depends on the Mideast for oil, and the

Mideast depends on us for manufactured goods of all types. Japan depends on the United States for agricultural commodities and many other products, and we look to Japan for consumer electronic items and a large percentage of our economy cars. The US economy must have oil and other raw materials if it is to operate at a level that provides an adequate standard of living for its people. In turn, our agricultural commodities, computers, and aircraft are vital to the survival, growth and development of most of the countries in the free world.

Aside from the goods and services aspect of our interdependent world, much of the free world uses dollars as a medium of exchange and as an important part of its international reserves. Foreigners generally prefer dollars to other currencies because of their confidence in the United States. This confidence stems from our industrial capacity, which far exceeds that of any country in the world, including Russia; from our military strength; and from our system of laws, institutions, and government, which are committed to the protection of the rights and freedoms of our citizens and foreigners who hold deposits in our banks, own domestic corporations, and hold private and US government securities.

In the course of our economic development, the United States' demand for goods and services such as oil from the Mideast, automobiles and consumer electronics from Japan, and travel in foreign countries has grown at an exceptional rate. In addition, American businesses are represented in every corner of the free world either through direct investments or the purchase of securities. Moreover, the US government has had a policy of providing grants and military aid to the free world in an attempt to accelerate economic development and improve the defense posture of other nations.

To pay for these goods and services, investments, and foreign aid, we have used income from goods and services and investments and incurred a large amount of debt to foreigners. In addition, we have seen the foreign exchange price of the dollar decline as the supply of dollars kept outpacing the demand for dollars. In recent years, it has become increasingly obvious that we cannot indefinitely continue to build up debt to foreigners or watch the exchange price of the dollar plummet.

At some point foreigners will become very reluctant or cease to accept private or public debt as an asset because of one or more of the following risks: (1) the risk of default, (2) the risk of a fall in the foreign exchange price of the dollar, which reduces the value of the debt and interest, and (3) the risk that inflation will reduce the real yield on the debt and undermine the purchasing power of the principal. If we become unable to purchase needed oil, raw materials, and other items, this will have a disastrous effect on our ability to produce and, hence, on economic welfare. Moreover, if the foreign exchange price of the dollar drops because of an adverse supply and demand interaction, then it would take more dollars to buy foreign goods and services. This raises the cost of purchasing necessary goods and services and, thus, pushes up the costs of domestic products. Proponents of the cost-push theory of inflation blame higher import prices for much of our recent inflation and the fall in the foreign exchange price of the dollar.

What all this amounts to is that because of the anticipated limit on foreigners' willingness to accept debt and the increasing reluctance of both US citizens and foreigners to watch the foreign exchange price of the dollar fall, we must improve our competitive position in world markets. In recent years, the amount of money spent for foreign merchandise, services, and paid out in the form of pensions and grants overseas has exceeded the amount that we have received for merchandise and services sold, investment income, and other items. The difference has been made up by foreigners accepting the private and public debt of this country. In sum, we must achieve a more reasonable balance between money spent for goods and services and money received for goods and services. This does not mean that we have to buy less than foreigners buy from us; it just means that there must be a closer balance than has been achieved in recent years. We will have more to say about this later in the chapter.

Because of the increasing influence of the international economy on the domestic economy, the Full Employment and Balanced Growth Act of 1978 explicitly recognized several international goals for our economy. This act calls on policymakers to work for an *improvement in our trade balance* as well as our competitive position in world trade. At the same time, the act calls for the *promotion of fair* and *free international trade and a sound and stable international monetary system*. These goals, of course, become objectives for monetary policy. Let's turn to the determination of exchange rates which are so important to the achievement of our international goals.

Foreign Exchange Rates

Nature of Exchange Rates

Within the fifty states, dollars are fully accepted for goods and services. If you walk into a McDonald's in New York, California, or Texas, you can exchange dollars for hamburgers and a soft drink. However, if you wish to purchase a Mercedes, you would like to pay in dollars but the manufacturer in Germany wishes to be paid in marks because he has to pay for steel, labor, and other expenses in marks. Hence, before the dealer in America can acquire the Mercedes, he must exchange dollars for marks. Then he can pay the manufacturer as he wishes. The price of another country's currency in terms of your own is called **the exchange rate**. If on the date that the dealer paid for the Mercedes, one deutsche mark (DM) equals fifty cents, then to buy a $20,000 Mercedes, the dealer first must buy DM 40,000 in the foreign exchange market.

Suppose that three months later, DM1 = $.54, then the cost of purchasing DM 40,000 would be $21,600. If the cost of the Mercedes in DM had risen also, then the cost of the car in dollars would have been even higher. Thus, you can see that the chance that the DM might rise adds an element of uncertainty to the purchase of foreign goods. The dealer not only has to anticipate price increases, but also changes in the exchange rate.

The Foreign Exchange Market

The foreign exchange market comes into being because exporters have foreign funds to exchange for domestic money, and importers have domestic funds that they wish to exchange for foreign funds. The large New York banks are the primary institutions making a market in foreign exchange. Importers like the Mercedes dealer could purchase marks from one of these banks, while on the same day an exporter might be selling marks that he had received from a sale. Purchases and sales of foreign exchange for immediate delivery take place in the **spot market**.

Suppose that the dealer places an order for delivery of so many Mercedes in 90 days at a set price. In order to **hedge** the risk that the exchange rate might rise in the interim, he could buy an equivalent amount of marks 90 days **forward**. This means that he has bought the right to have someone deliver marks to him at a stated rate in 90

Figure 15-1. Irving Trust Company's foreign exchange trading desk in London
(*Courtesy of the Irving Trust Company*)

days. On the supply side of the market might be an exporter who expects to receive marks in 90 days. He is concerned that the mark might slip in value and wipe out some of his profit on the sale. The exporter could sell marks 90 days forward and hedge his risk that their exchange value might fall.

Besides exporters and importers, there are speculators in the forward market who have various expectations of future exchange rates. For example, those that are "bullish" on marks, that is, they expect marks to appreciate, would buy forward contracts. Those that are "bearish" on marks, that is, they expect marks to depreciate, would sell contracts forward. The action of many exporters, importers, and speculators tends to stabilize exchange rates.

Determination of Foreign Exchange Rates

Under the gold standard. For most of the nineteenth century and up to 1933, most countries were on the gold standard, which meant that each country defined its monetary unit in terms of gold, and agreed to redeem its paper currency in gold. Under the gold standard, if the dollar was defined as 1/20 ounce of gold and the pound was defined as 3/20 ounce of gold, then the pound would be worth $3. Because both currencies were defined in terms of gold, they were related to each other. If the cost of shipping 3/20 ounce of gold between the two countries was 2¢, then the cost of pounds can never exceed $3.02 per pound nor be less than $2.98. In other words, the exchange rate can only fluctuate between the very narrow limits of $2.98 = £1 and $3.02 = £1. If the rate exceeded $3.02, a US importer could take $3.00 to the US Treasury, obtain 3/20 ounce of gold, ship it to England, and exchange it at the British Treasury for £1. Thus, there is no reason for the importer to pay more than $3.02 for £1.

By similar reasoning, a British importer will never accept less than $2.98 for his pound. He too can take his pound to the British Treasury, obtain 3/20 ounce of gold, ship it to the US Treasury, and exchange it for $3.00. Thus, by linking the monetary unit to gold, the gold standard tended to produce **stable exchange rates**, as in the example where fluctuations would be within $2.98 and $3.02. Stable exchange rates reduced considerably the exchange risk faced by exporters and importers.

While stable exchange rates were a positive feature of the gold standard, a strong negative aspect was that it limited a nation's ability to pursue policies to stabilize the domestic economy. When the United States entered the Great Depression, it began to lose gold. The Fed was torn between (1) a policy to raise interest rates to keep gold from flowing to other nations that had higher rates and (2) a policy to lower interest rates to stimulate the domestic economy. By 1933, the United States and most other countries abandoned the gold standard in order to pursue expansionary domestic policies.

Under the Bretton-Woods System.   In 1944, the major nations of the world (except Russia) met at Bretton-Woods, New Hampshire, to create the International Monetary Fund (IMF), the International Bank for Reconstruction and Development (World Bank), and plan other aspects of the international monetary system. The purpose of the IMF was to provide short-term credit to debtor nations and engage in the cooperative management of foreign exchange rates. The World Bank was to provide long-term credit for sound investment projects to aid in postwar reconstruction and development. Also out of the conference came a system of **pegged exchange rates** whereby nations tied their currency to gold or to a strong currency like the dollar. This system was supposed to create relatively stable exchange rates and permit countries to pursue appropriate domestic policies. Nations that experienced balance of payments[1] difficulties could borrow gold and other currencies from the IMF. For example, if England ran a deficit, it could borrow dollars to pay its obligations and repay them later when the problem was resolved.

Under the Bretton-Woods system, nations were not to devalue their currency unless they consulted with the IMF. **Devaluation** means a reduction in the gold content of the monetary unit. For example, in 1934, the United States devaluated the dollar by reducing the gold content from 1/20.67 ounce of gold to 1/35 ounce of gold. Several times between 1946 and 1971, England reduced the foreign exchange value of the pound in order to shore up its sagging export sector. The basic problem with the Bretton-Woods system of managed pegged exchange rates was that it was not set up to allow for fundamental changes in demand, productivity, and costs that were bound to develop among nations. Nations like Germany and Japan, after they got back on their feet, began to develop large balance of payments surpluses. This was good for jobs and profits, but it also put pressure on prices because of the increase in aggregate demand. For example, the mark was undervalued relative to other currencies. The simple solution to the problem would have been to let the mark appreciate under the natural forces of supply and demand. This would have made German exports more expensive and set in motion market forces to produce a new equilibrium level.

Then there was the problem of the United States with its overvalued dollar. Chronic balance of payments deficits had produced a glut of dollars on the world market. Again, the simple solution would have been to let the foreign exchange value decline. This would have raised the cost of imports, reduced the cost of exports, and led to a resolution of the problem.

Another difficulty with managed pegged exchange rates accompanied by periodic devaluations was that it created obvious profit opportunities for speculators betting on an upward revaluation of the

---

1. A nation's **balance of payments** is the record of transactions between its residents and foreign residents over a specified period such as a year. If the flow of funds out of a country due to imports and capital exports exceeds the inflow, the nation was said to have a balance of payments deficit. Under the gold standard, these deficits required the transfer of gold. Under the Bretton-Woods system, deficits could be made up with gold or other currencies held or borrowed from the IMF. Under the floating rate established in 1971, the concept of the balance of payments became obsolete because there are no deficits or surpluses.

undervalued currencies. Speculators would purchase the under-valued currencies and sell the overvalued currencies. This action put additional pressure on the governments to unpeg the rates and fulfill the speculators' expectations.

Managed floating exchange rates.   From 1946 to 1971, the Bretton-Woods system struggled to keep exchange rates stable. Finally, in 1971, the Bretton-Woods system succumbed to the many pressures, and exchange rates were allowed to float and find their equilibrium level. Under a **floating or flexible exchange rate system**, rates are determined by the forces of demand and supply. Underlying the demand schedule for, say, yen would be our demand for Japanese automobiles, consumer electronics, and other items. Behind the supply schedule would be Japanese demand for our exports such as agricultural goods and a myriad of industrial and consumer products. If our demand for Japanese goods increased, this would tend to push the foreign exchange price of the yen upward, which would make the cost of Japanese goods and services more expensive and the cost of American goods and services less expensive. In theory, the mechanism of floating exchange rates provides a way for imbalances in the foreign exchange market to work themselves out without a country having to resort to domestic policies that adversely affect employment and income. A disadvantage of floating exchange rates is that uncertainty about future rates does create a burden for exporters and importers. However, as explained earlier, the forward market permits hedging activity which eliminates such uncertainty.

Since 1971 governments have been unwilling to permit "clean" floating exchange rates free of government intervention and stabilization activity. Periodically, governments have entered the market to buy weak currencies and sell strong currencies. The Fed has been very active since 1962 with currency swaps with other countries to stabilize the foreign exchange price of the dollar and other currencies on world markets. Following the precipitous fall of the dollar in 1977 and 1978, President Carter and the Fed announced on November 1, 1978, a massive $30 billion program to support the dollar. Because of intervention such as this, we are said to have a managed or "dirty" floating exchange rate system.

How have exchange rates reacted under the managed exchange rate system? Table 15-1 shows foreign exchange rates for the major world currencies for January, 1971, before rates floated, and for 1977

Table 15-1

Foreign Exchange Rates: Selected Periods, 1971–1978
(in U.S. cents per unit of foreign currency)

Country/Currency	January 1971	Annual Average 1977	Annual Average 1978
Australia/dollar	111.82	110.82	114.41
Austria/shilling	3.87	6.05	6.90
Belgium/franc	2.01	2.79	3.18
Canada/dollar	98.83	94.11	87.73
Denmark/krone	13.36	16.66	18.16
France/franc	18.12	20.34	22.22
Germany/deutchemark	27.50	43.09	49.87
India/rupee	13.27	11.41	12.21
Ireland/pound	240.58	174.49	191.84
Italy/lira	.16	.11	.12
Japan/yen	.28	.37	.48
Mexico/peso	8.01	4.42	4.39
Netherlands/guilder	27.82	40.75	46.28
Norway/krone	14.21	18.79	19.08
Portugal/escudo	3.50	2.62	2.28
South Africa/rand	139.81	114.99	115.01
Spain/peseta	1.43	1.33	1.31
Sweden/krone	19.37	22.38	22.14
Switzerland/franc	23.23	41.71	56.28
United Kingdom/pound	240.58	174.49	191.84

Source: Board of Governors of the Federal Reserve, *Federal Reserve Bulletin.*

and 1978. As may be seen, the mark, Swiss franc, and yen have appreciated sharply. Appreciation in the mark and yen is a major cause of the sharp increase in the cost of German and Japanese automobiles and other products.

In conclusion, managed floating exchange rates are working quite well. It is difficult to imagine the degree of disruption that might have occurred following the quadrupling of oil prices in 1973 and 1974 if we had not had floating exchange rates to absorb much of the external shock. Floating rates have allowed the United States and other countries to pursue macroeconomic policies with primary regard for domestic economic goals. Another aspect of this point is that nations have been able to set internal policies independent of the macroeconomic policies of other countries. On the other hand, some economists point out that floating rates have not eliminated balance of payments disequilibria; they have not allowed total policy independence; they have not prevented inflation; and they have introduced major new elements of instability and uncertainty to financial markets. All of these criticisms have some truth to them, but behind each of these problems lie more fundamental factors, such as excessive monetary growth and external shocks like the oil price increase. Let's turn now to an examination of the international transactions that shape the supply and demand for the dollar.

US International Transactions

Meaning and Measurement

A country's **international transaction accounts** (balance-of-payments) are the records of transactions between its residents and foreign residents over a specified period such as a year. Transactions are recorded according to the principles of double-entry bookkeeping. A debit entry is used to record an increase in assets or a decrease in liabilities, while a credit entry is used to show an increase in liabilities or a decrease in assets. In a complete system of international transaction accounts the sum of the debits always equals the credits. In other words, the system of international accounts or balance-of-payments always balances. A summary of our international transactions for 1978 is shown in Table 15-2.

There is no requirement that the sums of the two sides of a *selected number* of international transaction must balance. For example, exports do not necessarily have to equal imports. Under a system of fixed or pegged exchange rates, a nation whose outflow of funds for imports, services, foreign securities, and the like exceeded its inflow from similar items was said to have a balance-of-payments deficit. To settle this deficit, it had to transfer international reserves in the form of gold or foreign currency to the nations owed. Of course, if inflows exceeded outflows, the nation would have a surplus and would be the recipient of international reserves. Under fixed or pegged exchange rates, a balance of payments deficit would indicate pressure on the foreign exchange price of the currency. Under the floating exchange rate system the concepts of deficit and surplus do not have much meaning. Imbalances in the demand and supply of the dollar caused by imbalances in the demand and supply for goods, services, investments, and other items are reflected primarily in changes in the foreign exchange price of the dollar. This does not mean that imbalances between exports and imports are not of concern. Congress showed its concern by including international goals in the Humphrey-Hawkins Act. As pointed out earlier, if the dollar falls in value, this increases the cost of imports and leads to inflation. In keeping with floating exchange rates, official US government statistics do not show a balance of payments deficit or surplus. All data are shown under the heading "US International Transactions." With this background in mind, let's analyze a few examples to see how international transactions are recorded.

Suppose that IBM ships a computer to a German company with payment to be made in 90 days. The sale is recorded as a credit to "merchandise exports" (line 1 in Table 15-2) to reflect the reduction in a US asset. The payment is recorded as a debit to "nonbank-reported claims" (line 19) to reflect the increase in this kind of asset held by US residents.

Suppose that a US oil company imports oil with payments made with balances held in foreign banks. This purchase is recorded as a debit to "merchandise imports" (line 2) to reflect the increase in assets and the payment as a credit to "bank-reported claims" (line 18) to reflect the decrease in US private assets abroad.

Let's examine Table 15-2 in more detail. Although we no longer measure a balance-of-payments deficit, there are combinations of accounts within the US International Transactions that are of considerable interest.

First, there is the **merchandise trade balance**, which is derived by computing the net excess of debits or credits in the merchandise accounts. As shown in Table 15-2, in 1978 debits exceeded credits by $34.1 billion. Oil comprised 18.5 percent of the nation's merchandise imports.

Second, by including the net excess of military transactions, investment income, and service income, we can compute the **balance on goods and services**. The debit balance in 1978 indicates that the US received more real resources (goods and services) from other countries than it transferred to them. Net investment income, the largest item in this category, offset more than half of the negative merchandise trade balance and reflected the return on US capital and financial investment.

Third, the **balance on current account** is the net excess of

Table 15-2

US International Transactions, 1978
(millions of dollars)

Items	Debits (−)	Credits (+)	Excess of Debits (−) or Credits (+)
I. *Current Account*			
1. Merchandise exports		141,844	
2. Merchandise imports	175,988		
3. *Merchandise trade balance*			−34,144
4. Military transactions, net		531	
5. Investment income, net		19, 915	
6. Other service transactions, net		2,814	
7. *Balance on goods and services*			−10,885
8. Remittances, pensions, and other transfers	2,048		
9. Government grants	3,028		
10. *Balance on current account*			−15,961
II. *Capital Accounts*			
11. Change in US government assets other than official reserve assets, net (increase −)	4,657		−4,657
12. Change in US official reserve assets (increase −)			872
13. Gold	65		
14. SDRs		1,249	
15. Reserve position in IMF		4,231	
16. Foreign currencies	4,543		
17. Change in US private assets abroad (increase −)			−54,963
18. Bank-reported claims	33,957		
19. Nonbank-reported claims	2,256		

Table 15–2 (cont.)

US International Transactions, 1978
(millions of dollars)

	Items	Debits (–)	Credits (+)	Excess of Debits (–) or Credits (+)
20.	US purchase of foreign securities	3,389		
21.	US direct investment abroad, net	15,361		
22.	Change in foreign official assets in the US (increase +)			33,967
23.	Other US government securities		24,063	
24.	Other US government obligations		656	
25.	Other US government liabilities		2,810	
26.	Other US liabilities reported by US banks		5,043	
27.	Other foreign official assets		1,395	
28.	Change in foreign private assets in the US (increase +)			29,293
29.	US bank-reported liabilities		16,860	
30.	US nonbank-reported liabilities		1,676	
31.	Foreign private purchases of US Treasury securities		2,248	
32.	Foreign purchase of other US securities, net		2,899	
33.	Foreign direct investments in the US, net		5,611	
34.	Statistical discrepancy		11,449	11,449
	Net Balance	245,292	245,292	0

Note: Totals do not necessarily add due to rounding.
Source: US Department of Commerce.

Figure 15-2. Imports arriving in New York

debits or credits in the accounts for goods, services, and unilateral transfers in the form of remittances, pensions, and government grants. Because total debits must equal total credits, the balance on current accounts must equal the balance on the remaining, or capital, accounts. Thus, the current account balance is an approximation of the change in the net claims of US residents on the rest of the world. Since the balance on current account was $16 billion in 1978, it meant that foreigners increased their net claims on the United States by this amount.

In reviewing the capital accounts, we see that US private assets abroad increased by $55 billion; however, foreign official and private assets in the United States rose by $63.3 billion. It is important to note that, in spite of the large debit balance on current account, the change in US official reserve assets was quite small.

Analysis of Table 15-2 enables us to understand better the interdependence of financial transactions. Money spent for imports is likely to show up as money spent for our exports or as investment income or an increase in foreign official private assets in the United States. Money spent for imports is not lost; by the very nature of double-entry bookkeeping, it also has to show up as a credit somewhere in the accounts.

The Record

Table 15-3 contains a summary of US international transactions from 1960-1978. As shown in this table, net merchandise trade turned negative in 1971 for the first time during the postwar period. In 1978, net merchandise trade reached a record negative balance of $34.1 million. Figure 15-3 shows very dramatically the adverse turn of events in the net merchandise trade and current accounts in the 1970s. In 1976 net military transactions became positive for the first time in the postwar period as amounts spent by foreigners in the United States for defense items exceeded the amount spent by the United States in the rest of the world. It is interesting to note that between 1970 and 1978, foreign private and official investment in US assets was almost equal to the change in US private and official assets in the rest of the world: $271.3 billion to $277.2 billion. This underscores the points made earlier that even though the United States merchandise trade balance may be negative, this just means that the nation must be importing capital or financial assets.

Explanation of Excess Demand for Foreign Real and Financial Assets

There are two explanations for the recent excess demand for foreign real and financial assets: (1) monetary and (2) nonmonetary.

Monetary explanation. Economists who hold the theory that changes in the money supply are the primary determinants of change in output and prices also assert that excessive monetary growth is the main reason for the excess demand for foreign assets and the declining foreign exchange price of the dollar. According to this explanation, if the actual money supply in the United States is greater than the

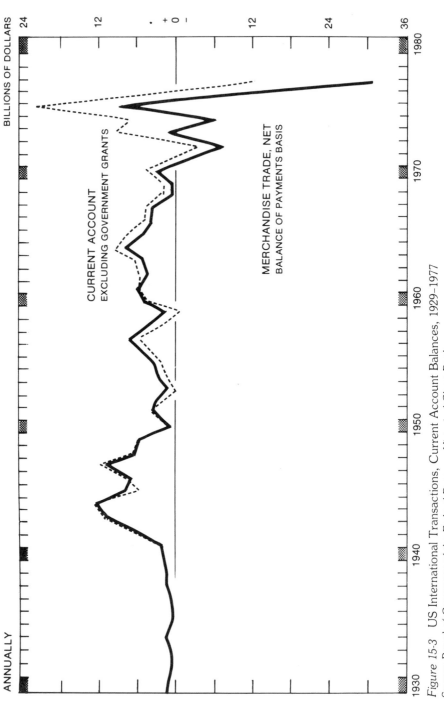

Figure 15-3 US International Transactions, Current Account Balances, 1929–1977
Source: Board of Governors of the Federal Reserve, *Historical Chart Book.*

Table 15-3

US International Transactions—Summary: 1960 to 1978
(billions of dollars)

Year	Merchandise trade balance	Military transactions balance	Net investment income	Net travel and transportation receipts	All goods and services balance	Current account balance	Foreign assets in US, net	US assets abroad, net	US official reserve assets, net (end of period)
1960	$ 4.9	$-2.8	$ 3.4	$-1.0	$ 5.1	$ 2.8	$ 2.3	$-4.1	$19.4
1965	5.0	-2.1	5.4	-1.3	8.3	5.4	.7	-5.7	15.5
1966	3.8	-2.9	3.6	-1.3	4.5	1.6	3.3	-5.5	14.9
1967	3.8	-3.2	4.0	-1.8	4.4	1.3	6.9	-8.0	14.8
1968	.6	-3.1	6.0	-1.5	3.6	.6	9.9	-11.0	15.7
1969	.6	-3.3	6.1	-1.8	3.4	.4	12.7	-11.6	17.0
1970	2.6	-3.4	6.2	-2.0	5.7	2.4	6.4	-9.3	14.5
1971	-2.3	-2.9	7.3	-2.3	2.3	-1.4	23.0	-12.5	12.2
1972	-6.4	-3.6	8.2	-3.0	-2.1	-6.0	21.7	-14.5	13.2
1973	.9	-2.3	12.0	-3.1	10.8	6.9	18.7	-22.8	14.4
1974	-5.3	-2.1	15.5	-3.1	8.9	1.7	34.7	-34.7	15.9
1975	9.0	-.9	12.8	-2.5	23.1	18.4	15.6	-39.4	16.2
1976	-9.4	.3	15.9	-2.2	9.4	4.3	37.0	-50.6	18.7
1977	-31.1	1.3	17.5	-3.0	-10.6	-15.3	50.9	-34.7	19.3
1978	-34.1	.5	19.9	-3.3	-10.9	-16.0	63.3	-58.7	18.6

Source: US Department of Commerce.

amount that the public wishes to hold in real terms, the people will spend the excess balances until monetary equilibrium is restored. This will tend to increase the price of domestic real and financial assets. Economic units will react by decreasing their demand for domestic real and financial assets in favor of foreign real and financial assets. Domestic suppliers of these assets will attempt to sell more at home and less abroad. At the same time, foreign economic units will decrease their demand for US assets and attempt to sell more of their assets here. All of these factors serve to stimulate an outflow of funds and discourage an inflow. Under a system of floating exchange rates, the foreign exchange price of the dollar will fall concomitantly and set off forces to counteract the negative merchandise trade balance and the increased demand for foreign assets. Any attempts by the government to prop the exchange rate will frustrate the adjustment process and exacerbate the imbalance. Of course, the monetarist prescription to cure imbalances in international transactions is to curb excessive monetary growth.

Nonmonetary explanation. Nonmonetary explanations of the negative merchandise trade balance and other imbalances in international transactions focus on specific accounts and problems within the United States and other economies. Most of these nonmonetary explanations should be familiar because they are frequently cited on the "nightly news" and on the front page of the daily newspaper as causes of our international economic problems.

First, the inflation in the domestic economy has made US goods more expensive relative to those of other countries.

Second, our foreign and military aid programs have been very generous over the years. However, a large percentage of these grants are spent in the United States.

Third, the large overseas investment by American businesses is often cited for the pressure on the foreign exchange price of the dollar. However, part of this investment generates demand for the future.

Fourth, economies overseas did not recover as rapidly from the 1973–1975 recession as did the US economy. This has reduced export demand below what it would have been.

Fifth, some countries have erected discriminatory trade barriers against American products, which, of course, have an adverse effect on exports.

Sixth, improvements in productivity in Western Europe and Japan have reduced the need for many US goods. Moreover, goods from these areas have displaced US goods in many other world markets. Both developments augur against a positive US merchandise trade balance.

Seventh, as stated earlier, oil imports account for a large percentage of US imports. After 1973, oil prices quadrupled, and this action raised the cost of US imports significantly.

Finally, the recent decline in the foreign exchange price of the dollar has made our currency less attractive to foreigners as an official international reserve and as a store of value for private interests.

Future Prospects

At this juncture, prospects of improvement in the merchandise trade balance do not look as favorable as we might like. Monetarists would argue that stable monetary growth in line with real growth in the economy would do much to bring inflation under control. Stable monetary growth would slow down the growth of imports. A reduced rate of inflation and slower growth in imports would strengthen the dollar on foreign exchange markets. Higher unemployment is the primary risk of gearing down growth in the money stock.

Nonmonetarists would argue that the solution to our current international imbalances lies in fundamental changes in the economy. Besides reducing the rate of inflation, productivity must be increased in order to make our goods more competitive on world markets. Domestic sources of energy must be developed to reduce the dependence on foreign oil. Other nations must be encouraged to reduce discriminatory barriers to our exports.

In conclusion, it is necessary to remember that imports and exports, capital inflows and outflows, and, for that matter, all international inflows and outflows are interdependent. Our international goal is not a gigantic merchandise trade surplus, but a more reasonable balance than we have had in recent years. The United States does not have an infinite amount of international reserves to use in propping the dollar; therefore, some fundamental changes are necessary. Does the United States have the resolve to make the necessary internal adjustments, including bringing the rate of monetary growth down? It is possible that it does not. Few people are aware of the consequences of not eliminating the disequilibrium. Until more people are, meaningful changes will not be made.

The Fed's role in the achievement of our international goals is critical. The Fed must provide for a rate of monetary growth that causes the inflation rate to recede and allows for capital investment to expand in order to promote an improvement in productivity. However, the reduction in the inflation rate must be attained without the creation of an unacceptable rate of unemployment.

Dollars, Gold, and SDRs in the Evolution of the International Monetary System

Transition from Dollar Shortage to Dollar Glut

Following the end of World War II, the nations of western Europe and Japan immediately began to rebuild. They had a great demand for US industrial goods and agricultural commodities and had no productive capacity to earn the needed dollars. At the prevailing exchange rate, the quantity of dollars demanded was far greater than the quantity supplied. That is, there was a shortage of dollars. Thanks to the Marshall Plan and other foreign aid and military aid programs, the United States poured billions of dollars into the reconstruction of the war-torn nations. The fruits of these efforts began to pay off as rebuilt productive capacity began to turn out goods and services. This reduced the need to import from the United States and led to increased foreign exports.

For a while foreigners were willing to accept dollar claims on the United States because they knew that they could exchange dollars for gold at any time. By the 1960s, the dollar shortage had turned into a dollar glut as foreigners turned in dollars for gold at a record rate. By 1970, the US gold stock had dropped from a peak of $24 billion in 1947 to $10 billion. On August 15, 1971, President Nixon ordered a halt to the conversion of dollars into gold and instituted a 10 percent surcharge on most imports. From this date until December, the dollar floated against other major currencies.

The Smithsonian Agreement

In December, 1971, members of the Group of Ten major industrial countries met at the Smithsonian Institution in Washington and reached an agreement to depreciate the dollar relative to the mark, yen, and other major currencies. Members also agreed to widen the band for exchange rate fluctuations from 1 percent to 2-1/4 percent.

The United States agreed to remove the 10 percent surcharge on imports. Also, it devalued the dollar by increasing the gold price from $35 to $38 per ounce. This was almost a meaningless move because the United States already had a policy of not exchanging dollars for gold.

Managed Floating Exchange Rates

The new exchange rate ranges set at the Smithsonian lasted until early 1973, when speculation against the dollar caused a sharp drop in its value. In February the United States again raised the dollar price of gold, this time to $42.22 an ounce. In February and March of 1973, the major countries of the world gave up trying to defend the Smithsonian parities and allowed their currencies to float. Since this time, the United States has been under a managed floating exchange rate system with frequent government intervention in foreign exchange markets to stabilize the value of the dollar. Interestingly, in January, 1976, the IMF at its meeting in Kingston, Jamaica, gave official blessings to the increased exchange rate flexibility in effect for nearly three years.

The Role of Gold

Gold once was the premier international reserve. To be sure gold still comprises an important part of international reserves, but SDRs, dollars, and other key currencies now make up the majority of official reserve assets. In early 1976, the IMF proposed to refund to member nations part of its gold holdings and to sell another part to aid less developed countries. Besides this official note, gold is still considered an excellent store of value by many people throughout the world. In the free market, the price of gold fluctuates in response to supply and demand. This price reached over $425 per ounce in 1979 as inflationary pressures mounted. Gold has been around for thousands of years in private hoards, and it is likely to continue in this role for eons to come. Fortunately, in recent years nations have eliminated the possibility of gold having a pronounced influence on income, employment, and prices.

The Role of SDRs

As the volume of international transactions grew in the post-World War II period, there was an urgent need for international reserves to grow. Gold could not fill this need because of the limited amount mined each year that is not sold for commercial uses. Reserve growth in the form of dollars held by foreign monetary authorities proved to be unsatisfactory largely because it led to a loss of confidence in the dollar. In 1969, the IMF introduced SDRs as a means to supplement the supply of international reserves. SDRs are nothing more than bookkeeping entries that participating governments have agreed to accept as legal tender in settling international accounts. The value of an SDR is defined in terms of currency as the value of a "basket" containing 40 US cents and specified quantities of fifteen other major currencies. The first issue of SDRs took place during the 1970–1972 period. In March, 1979, the United States held $2.7 billion of SDRs plus $11.5 of gold, $1.1 billion in the IMF, and $6.4 billion of convertible foreign currencies.

The IMF at its Jamaica meeting also proposed that SDRs become the principal reserve asset in the international monetary system. With the IMF forced into a subordinate position in the transition to floating exchange rate systems, it remains to be seen if the nations of the world will accept an expanded role for SDRs.

Summary

The US international economic goals are to improve our merchandise trade balance and to promote fair and free international trade and a sound and stable international monetary system. Achievement of these goals must be in a world with managed floating exchange rates and with the dollar comprising the bulk of the international reserves held by foreigners.

From 1946–1971, exchange rates were pegged under supervision of the IMF. However, chronic deficits in the US balance of payments undermined this system. In 1971, the dollar was depreciated relative to the mark, yen, and other major currencies. Finally, in 1973, under pressure from persistent deficits and foreign speculation, the dollar was allowed to float, not cleanly, but with frequent government intervention to stabilize its foreign exchange price.

If free to float, exchange rates are determined by the forces of demand and supply. The demand for dollars reflects primarily other nations' demand for our goods, services, and financial assets; the supply of dollars reflects primarily our demand for other nations' goods, services, and financial assets. In recent years, the US merchandise trade balance has had a large deficit. This imbalance together with a growing unwillingness to hold dollars have been largely responsible for sharp declines in the foreign exchange price of the dollar.

There are two major explanations for the international imbalances: (1) the monetary explanation, which focuses on excessive monetary growth, and (2) the nonmonetary explanation, which stresses problems in specific accounts such as excessive dependency on foreign oil and overgenerous military and foreign aid programs. Appropriate policies to remedy the international imbalances depend on which explanation is more correct. The monetary approach would emphasize curbing excessive monetary growth, while the nonmonetary approach would focus on policies to curb imports directly and stimulate exports.

Our present international monetary system featuring managed floating exchange rates is much more able to absorb external shocks such as the 1973 oil price hike. More important, it will lessen the need to expand international reserves in the form of gold and SDRs to accommodate expanding world trade.

Questions and Problems

1. Discuss the nature and significance of our international economic goals.
2. Discuss the international monetary system that originated at Bretton-Woods.
3. What are the pros and cons of floating exchange rates?
4. Define (a) merchandise trade balance, (b) balance on goods and services, and (c) balance on current account.
5. Why do international transactions always balance?
6. Outline (a) the monetary and (b) the nonmonetary explanations of our recent excess demand for foreign real and financial assets.
7. Discuss the evolution of the postwar international monetary system.

Suggestions for Additional Reading

Coombs, Charles A. *The Arena of International Finance.* New York: John Wiley & Sons, 1976.

Fieleke, Norman S. *What Is the Balance of Payments?* Boston: Federal Reserve Bank of Boston, 1976.

Kubarych, Roger M. *Foreign Exchange Markets in the United States.* New York: Federal Reserve Bank of New York, 1978.

Solomon, Robert. *The International Monetary System, 1945-1976, An Insider's View.* New York: Harper & Row, Publishers, 1977.

Throop, Adrian W. "Decline and Fall of the Gold Standard." Federal Reserve Bank of Dallas, *Business Review* (January 1976), pp. 1-11.

16

Alternative Strategies for Monetary Policy

The last two chapters set forth the domestic and international goals of monetary policy. This chapter deals with alternative monetary strategies to achieve these goals. Economists in the Fed and the academic community have devoted much of their research efforts to the analysis and evaluation of the various monetary strategies. It is encouraging to report that because of these research efforts, our understanding of the monetary policy process has improved considerably.

In this chapter, we shall (1) discuss the priorities and possible conflicts involved with the national economic goals, (2) analyze the natural rate of unemployment and accelerationist hypotheses to achieve these goals, (3) examine the impact of the rational expectations hypothesis on Phillips curve analysis and its challenge to traditional Keynesian stabilization policy, (4) explore the issues in the monetarist and Keynesian debate, and (5) outline the Fed's current strategy for monetary policy.

Economic Goals: Priorities and Conflicts

Before we turn to an examination of alternative monetary strategies, it would be helpful to review very briefly the evolution of priorities among our economic goals and then discuss some possible

359

conflicts that have arisen among several of these goals. These priorities and conflicts have had a great bearing upon the choice of a monetary strategy.

Historical Perspective on Priorities

Of the significant events in our history, the Great Depression has had the greatest influence in shaping the priorities in our national economy. The fear of unemployment similar to what we experienced in the Depression has made the achievement of low levels of unemployment the number one economic goal for most of the post-World War II period. The employed, unemployed, and many federal government agencies lobby for this goal.

On the other hand, except for the flare-up right after World War II and at the inception of the Korean War, inflation has been a problem only since 1965. Although inflation adversely affects the vast majority of the public, the public does not lobby with the same fervor for price stability as it does low levels of unemployment. However, a number of economists contend that inflation is a far more serious problem than unemployment, and its defeat should be given top priority.

Aside from economists, few people argue for economic growth as a national goal, even though growth is the means to absorb new workers into the labor force, and is the source of more goods and services to satisfy human wants. Therefore, growth tends to rank third on the list of national economic goals.

Finally, our international economic goals of improved competitiveness and the promotion of free trade are not understood by most people. They cannot see how their personal lives are affected by international economic conditions. However, as explained in the last chapter, our individual economic welfare is shaped more and more by international economics. The impact of the acceleration in foreign oil prices and other products has a very real effect on all of us. For most of the post-World War II period, it seems clear that our international economic goals have ranked last in terms of need for action.

Thus, if surveyed, the American public probably would rank our economic goals in the following manner:

1. low levels of unemployment
2. reasonable price stability

3. satisfactory rate of economic growth
4. improvement of international competitiveness and promotion of free trade and international stability

For all practical purposes, the two most important goals are low levels of unemployment and reasonable price stability. If we achieve low levels of unemployment, we usually have achieved a satisfactory rate of economic growth. Moreover, most economists would agree that if we achieve reasonable price stability, we make our goods more competitive in world markets. Hence, the important questions become: Can the nation simultaneously achieve low levels of unemployment and reasonable price stability? If not, what is the trade-off, if any, between the two objectives?

The classical economists, of course, would contend that the economy tended toward full employment and that inflation could be controlled with monetary policy. Traditional Keynesians would tend to view inflation as a problem caused by excessive aggregate demand at the full employment level. For all of these economists, inflation and unemployment usually could not exist simultaneously.

The Phillips Curve Trade-Off: Full Employment vs. Price Stability

In 1958, Professor A.W. Phillips of the London School of Economics published a pioneering study that apparently demonstrated that inflation could coexist with unemployment.[1] As shown in Figure 16-1, Professor Phillips fitted an empirical curve to a statistical scatter diagram of time series data for annual percentage rates of money wage changes and unemployment for the British economy over the 1861–1913 interval.[2] The resulting curve was downward sloping, indicating an inverse relationship between two variables. When unemployment was low, money wages tended to rise rapidly. However, when unemployment was high, wage changes tended to be low.

1. Much of this part and the next is based on Thomas M. Humphrey, "Changing Views of the Phillips Curve," Federal Reserve Bank of Richmond, *Monthly Review* (July 1973), pp. 2–13.
2. Economists soon transformed the wage-unemployment relationship into a price-unemployment relationship by assuming that the rate of change in prices was equal to the difference between the rate of change in money wages (w) and changes in man-hour productivity (q), that is, $p = w - q$. In other words, the inflation rate was equal to the cost-of-living adjustment factor in wage increases.

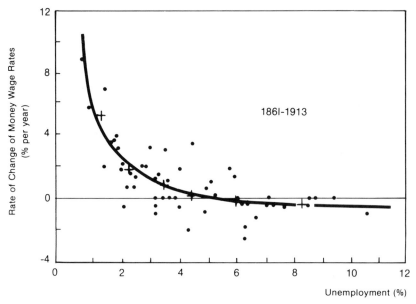

Figure 16-1 The Original Phillips Curve

Source: A.W. Phillips, "The Relation Between Unemployment and the Rate of Change of Money Rates in the United Kingdom, 1861–1957," *Economica,* 25, No. 100 (November 1958), p. 285, as reprinted in Thomas M. Humphrey, "Changing Views of the Phillips Curve," Federal Reserve Bank of Richmond, *Monthly Review* (July 1973), p. 2.

The policy implication of the original Phillips curve was that it was impossible for the monetary authorities to attain zero inflation and full employment. The two goals appeared to be incompatible and conflicting. More of one objective could be obtained only at the cost of less of the other. In the 1960s, it was often said that the Phillips curve offered the Fed a "menu" of feasible policy choices between the two problems of inflation and unemployment. Also, the Phillips curve trade-off pointed out the need for new programs such as job training and retraining to shift the curve toward the origin.

Doubts About the Phillips Curve

Up until the late 1960s, the Phillips curve was largely accepted by economists even though there was not a convincing statistical relationship between inflation and unemployment in the United States. However, as shown in Figure 16–2, after 1969, inflation and

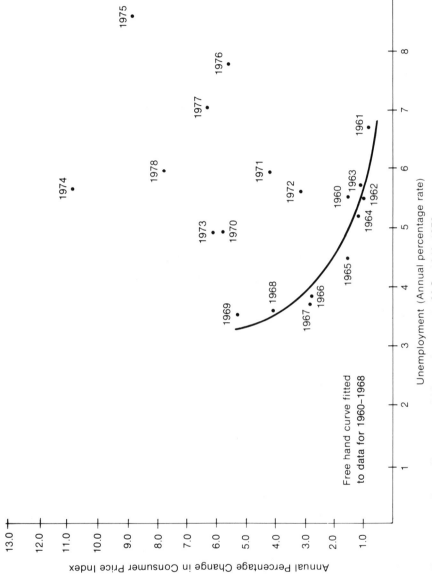

Figure 16-2 Price Changes and Unemployment in U.S., 1960–1978

unemployment rates depart significantly from the pattern established from 1960 through 1969. It appeared that escalating inflation was required to keep unemployment fixed in place.

Moreover, statistical studies showed that the dispersion of observations around the fitted Phillips curve required introduction of many other variables, such as the rate of change of unemployment, lagged changes in the cost of living, indexes of the dispersion of unemployment across separate labor markets, trade union membership, job vacancy rates, and corporate profits to improve the statistical fit. These findings suggested that there might be not one Phillips curve but rather numerous families of short-run Phillips curves corresponding to the many other variables (shift parameters) cited above that influence the inflation-unemployment relationship. In other words, the Phillips curve shifted over time in response to changes in these other variables.

The Natural Rate of Unemployment and Accelerationist Hypotheses

After it became apparent that the Phillips curve did not offer policymakers a certain trade-off between inflation and unemployment, economists began to search for the dominant variables underlying the relationship. Two innovations were introduced to explain the absence of a certain trade-off: the natural rate of unemployment and the accelerationist hypotheses.[3]

The Natural Rate of Unemployment

In his 1967 Presidential Address to the American Economic Association, Professor Milton Friedman argued that there is no permanent trade-off between inflation and unemployment because in the long run real variables such as unemployment are determined independently of nominal variables such as inflation. There are trade-offs in the short run, but they stem from unanticipated inflation. However, in the long run, there are no inflationary surprises; and the

---

3. This section is adapted from Thomas M. Humphrey, "Some Recent Developments in Phillips Curve Analysis," Federal Reserve Bank of Richmond, *Monthly Review* (January/February 1978), pp. 15–23.

rate of inflation is fully anticipated and realized. If actual unemployment is temporarily reduced by a surge in aggregate demand, it will return to its **natural rate**, which is defined as that rate of unemployment at which expected inflation equals actual inflation and where the real wage rate is at its equilibrium level. For the actual rate of unemployment to decline below the natural rate, there must be unexpected inflation. Thus, the difference between actual and expected inflation, that is, unexpected inflation, is the trade-off for the difference between the actual and natural rates of unemployment. When unexpected inflation disappears, so does any "excess employment" above the natural rate of unemployment.[4] This analysis implies that the Phillips curve is a vertical line at the natural rate of unemployment. In sum, there is no long-run trade-off between inflation and unemployment. Moreover, the natural rate of unemployment is compatible with any rate of inflation provided that it is fully anticipated.

The Accelerationist Hypothesis

A corollary of the natural rate hypothesis is the **accelerationist hypothesis**, which holds that because there is no long-run trade-off between inflation and unemployment, attempts to peg the rate of unemployment below the natural rate will produce ever-accelerating inflation. According to this theory, actual inflation must be kept ahead of expected inflation in order to prevent unemployment from returning to the natural rate. Accelerationists contend that the public formulates inflationary expectations based on past inflation, with the most recent experience given heavier weight. Expectations are adjusted based on an error-learning mechanism. When actual inflation turns out to be different than expected inflation, the public will revise their expectations by a fraction of the error. Such revisions will continue until the expectational error is eliminated. Accelerationists point out that this expectational lag may be exploited to peg unemployment below the natural rate only at accelerating rates of inflation. Because the public is constantly closing the gap between actual and expected inflation, actual inflation must continually be accelerated to stay one step ahead of the policymakers. In other words, accelerationists imply that the long-run trade-off is between

---

4. Later in this chapter, we will discuss the mechanism by which the actual and natural rates of unemployment diverge.

excess demand and the rate of acceleration of inflation, not the excess demand and inflation rate itself, as in earlier Phillips curve formulations.

Figure 16–3 illustrates the phenomena just described. A long-run Phillips curve (L) is shown at unemployment rate U_o along with a family of short-run Phillips curves $(S_o \ldots S_4)$. The position of each short-run Phillips curve depends on the expected rate of inflation. For example, curve S_o corresponds with an expected inflation rate of 2 percent.

Beginning at point A, suppose that policymakers engineer an increase in aggregate demand. Initially, product prices rise more rapidly than money wages (W). This divergence causes real wages (W/P) to fall. This decline in real wages induces employers to expand production and employment, thereby lowering unemployment to U_1. The economy moves along curve S_o from point A to point B. Inflation rises from 2 percent to 6 percent. Initially, workers were fooled by the surge in prices and did not anticipate that inflation would erode their real wages. But workers soon begin adjusting for their miscalculations and adjust expectations to the actual inflation rate of 6 percent and incorporate these expectations into wage bargains. As the gap between anticipated and unanticipated inflation closes, so does the difference between the rates of increase between inflation and money wages. Money wages begin to catch up with price increases, thereby raising the real wage rate back to the level existing before the stimulus. The increase in real wages causes employers to reduce employment. The economy then moves from point B to point C, where inflation is 6 percent. In the long run, inflation is fully anticipated and will be incorporated in all wage demands. The old real wage is reestablished and both money wages and inflation are at higher levels than originally. If policymakers attempt again to push the actual employment rate below the natural rate, then the economy will move along path CDE to an even higher inflation rate.

There are two policy implications of the natural rate and accelerationist hypotheses. First, policymakers can peg either the inflation rate or the unemployment rate, but not both. If they peg unemployment, inflation accelerates. If they peg inflation, unemployment will return to the natural rate. Of course, this conclusion is contrary to the original Phillips curve which depicted a trade-off between inflation and unemployment.

The second policy implication is that policymakers could choose

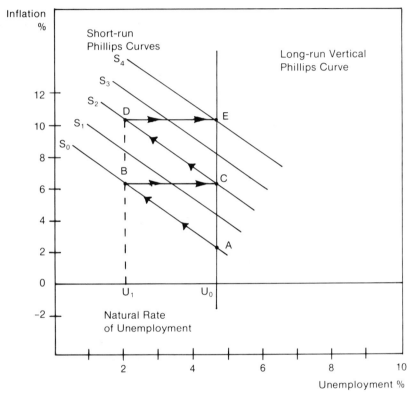

Figure 16-3 The Natural Rate and Accelerationist Hypotheses and Short- and Long-run Phillips Curves

among alternative transitional adjustment paths to the desired steady-state rate of inflation. If they wish to move to a lower inflation rate, they must lower inflationary expectations. To do this, they must create slack capacity in the economy, thereby causing the actual inflation rate to fall below the expected rate. The speed of the adjustment depends on the degree of slack. Thus, policymakers could choose a path of quick adjustment with high unemployment for a short period or a path of slow adjustment with lower unemployment for a longer period.

The accelerationist adaptive expectations/error learning scheme has been criticized as a misrepresentation of how inflationary expectations are formed. Critics doubt that inflationary expectations are formulated solely from a weighted average of past inflation and independent of current information on growth in the money supply, announced price increases, and government taxing and spending plans. Many economists point out that it is inconsistent for inflationary expectations to be formed independent of the manner in which inflation is actually generated in the economy. Because of this inconsistency, it is claimed that inflationary expectations based only on past inflation will be systematically wrong and, hence, ceased to be used. Rational economic units will seek a more accurate method of formulating inflationary expectations. This need brings us to the rational expectations approach to Phillips curve analysis and monetary policy.

The Rational Expectations Hypotheses and Phillips Curve Analysis

The Nature and Importance of Rational Expectations

The term **rational expectations** is simply an assumption that people make economic decisions in a way that tends to take into account *all* available information bearing significantly on the future consequences of their decisions.[5] Moreover, they tend to use that information in a way so as not to repeat past mistakes. This informa-

5. Much of the discussion in this section is based on "Rational Expectations—Fresh Ideas that Challenge Some Established Views of Policy Making," Federal Reserve Bank of Minneapolis, *Annual Report, 1977*, pp. 1–13.

tion includes, among other things, knowledge about past monetary policy and monetary strategies that might be taken when economic signals begin to change. In effect, the concept of rational expectations says that people appraise the future and attempt to bring all available and anticipated knowledge and information into the decision-making process about future economic events that affect their welfare.

Stated this way, there should not be anything startling about the rational expectations idea. One of the basic assumptions in the study of individual and business decision making is that people are rational and seek to maximize individual welfare and profits for the businesses that they run. Can you imagine a consumer, businessman or businesswoman, investor, or union leader who would not attempt to apply the concept of rational expectations as it was just defined? Yet economists who developed the idea point out that monetary policy as it is currently formulated achieves its effects only if people *fail* to act in their own best interests. When the decision-making process is recast to assume that people apply rational expectations, policy no longer has the same effects.[6]

It is well recognized that people's belief about the future affects their decisions today. Both employers and employees look to the future when an employment contract is negotiated. The Philadelphia Phillies would not have offered Pete Rose $800,000 a year if they had not anticipated that Pete would boost attendance and team run production. People buy a home based on expected income. General Motors schedules car production based in part on its expectation for monetary and other government policies and their impact on future car sales. Consumers, businessmen and businesswomen, and investors have a myriad of commercially available newsletters, reports, and services to aid them in their decision making. The point is that people rationally attempt to consider all information, past and future, as they make economic decisions.

Implications of Rational Expectations Hypothesis for Phillips Curve Analysis

The rational expectations hypothesis has some radical policy implications. It implies that monetary policy based on feedback control

6. The concept of rational expectations originated with John F. Muth. However, Robert E. Lucas of the University of Chicago and Thomas Sargent and Neil Wallace of the University of Minnesota are largely credited with demonstrating the importance of the concept in explaining the business cycle and in the formulation of a monetary strategy.

rules, that is, those that define the Fed's response to changes in the economy, cannot influence real variables such as employment and output even in the short run. This is because people already have anticipated the policy action and incorporated it into their expectations and decisions. To have an impact on real variables, policymakers must be able to create a divergence between actual and expected inflation. This follows from the proposition that inflation affects real variables only if it is unanticipated.

With respect to Phillips curve analysis, the rational expectations approach denies the existence of an exploitable trade-off between inflation and unemployment, even in the short run. Thus, it denies the accelerationist notion of a short-run lag between expected and actual inflation which is the basis for pegging unemployment temporarily below the natural rate. Hence, under the rational expectations hypothesis, there are no short-run Phillips curves; there is only a vertical line at the natural rate.

The Rational Expectations Challenge to Traditional Keynesian Stabilization Policy

By traditional Keynesian stabilization policy we mean counter-cyclical monetary and fiscal policies designed to influence aggregate demand. To review briefly, the Great Depression spawned Keynes' *General Theory*, which provided the theoretical justification for active governmental efforts to manage aggregate demand. The primary aim of these efforts was to prevent unemployment, but the other economic goals have been important objectives on other occasions. The essence of traditional Keynesian stabilization policy is that government must make active use of monetary and fiscal policy to stimulate the economy if unemployment is high or to reduce the level of economic activity if inflation is high.

The rational expectations approach holds that when people's expectations are formed "rationally," Keynesian-activist policies will be frustrated. The rational expectations view of the policy process holds that for activist policies to work, people must behave in ways that are inconsistent with their best interests.

For example, suppose that the Fed increases the money supply in order to reduce unemployment below the natural level. Businesses will expand output and, in the process, increase employment. According to the rational expectations view, workers are fooled into taking jobs because they do not perceive future price increases which will reduce real wages. For monetary policy to be effective, workers must be shortsighted about future inflation. Why else would they take jobs promising lower pay in the future?

The rational expectations criticism of this process is that traditional monetary or fiscal policy will not work if workers expect the future inflation. Moreover, they contend that workers might be fooled once, but not repeatedly.

Rational expectations economists also challenge the fundamental Keynesian notion that an increase in the money supply can temporarily depress interest rates and, hence, stimulate investment. Will lenders be fooled into believing that the Fed's action will not eventually lead to higher inflation? If they believe that inflation will not accelerate, then they will commit funds. But the expectation of inflation causes lenders to demand an inflation premium in interest rates. If interest rates rise by the full amount of the expected inflation, as the rationalists argue, all costs will rise proportionately to the expected price increase; there will be no exploitable profit opportunities.

Criticism of the Rational Expectations Hypothesis

Because of its radical conclusions which yield no constructive role for activist monetary or fiscal policy, rational expectations has elicited much criticism. The principal assumption attacked is that of perfect rationality. Critics still maintain that expectations basically are nonrational or, at best, formulated after a long learning period. Critics also challenge the assumptions that policy is foreseen and anticipated correctly, that prices are flexible, and that costless information is available to the degree claimed by rationalists. At this juncture, these criticisms have not blunted the provocative challenge to the proponents of activist monetary and fiscal policy.

Policy Implications of the Rational Expectations Hypothesis

If the goals of traditional Keynesian activist policy are unattainable, what strategy should policymakers follow? Rationalists contend that policymakers should focus on inflation and announce that their goal is to attain a rate of increase in the general level of prices at some low average rate of growth. This in itself would be a "surprise," but, according to rationalists, it would not raise unemployment because the general price level impact would be built into future expectations. Given the above goal, policymakers also should work to eliminate uncertainty about future inflation. This would contribute greatly to expanded investment, long-term steady economic growth, lower unemployment, and greater international stability.

In conclusion, the rational expectations hypothesis is one of the most important new ideas in economics. It is causing policymakers to rethink their policy processes, and, of course, this is beneficial. Preston Miller, an economist at the Minneapolis Federal Reserve Bank, in his summary of a seminar series on the rational expectations and natural rate hypotheses, asserted that this type of model is "really the only game in town."[7]

The Monetarist-Keynesian Debate

In Part IV on monetary and income theory and especially in Chapters 12 and 13 dealing with modern theories of the demand for money and the channels of monetary influence, we compared monetarist and Keynesian views primarily on theoretical issues. With respect to the monetarist-Keynesian debate, Franco Modigliani of MIT, in his 1976 presidential address to the American Economic Association, stated:

> There are in reality no serious analytical disagreements between leading Monetarists and leading non-Monetarists. Milton Friedman was once quoted as saying, "We are all Keynesian, now," and I am quite prepared to reciprocate that "we are all Monetarists"—if by monetarism it is meant assigning to the stock of money a major role in determining output and prices.
>
> . . . In reality the distinguishing feature of the Monetarist school and the real issues of disagreement with non-Monetarists is not monetarism but rather the role that should probably be assigned to stabilization policies.[8]

Of course, not all monetarists and nonmonetarists would agree that there is as much agreement on theoretical issues as Modigliani implies.

7. Preston Miller, "Epilogue" in *A Prescription for Monetary Policy: Proceedings from a Seminar Series* (Minneapolis: Federal Reserve Bank of Minneapolis, 1976), p. 99.
8. Franco Modigliani, "The Monetarist Controversy or Should We Forsake Stabilization Policies?" *American Economic Review* (March 1977), p. 1.

Moreover, the two schools do disagree to a great extent about the appropriate role for stabilization policies and many other topics across the spectrum of economics.

Our concern with this debate stems from its great influence on the Fed's formulation of monetary policy. Naturally, Fed policymakers are going to be concerned with current thinking and research in monetary theory and policy. As we shall see later in this chapter, the Fed's current strategy for monetary policy reflects both monetarist and Keynesian influences.

Monetarist Propositions

Earlier in the book, monetarism was defined as that school of thought which holds that money is the most important variable affecting nominal income and prices. This is fine as a first approximation, but monetarists ascribe to many other ideas. Professor Thomas Mayer of the University of California at Davis compiled a list of monetarist propositions.[9] Here is his list.

Monetarist Propositions

1. The quantity theory of money, in the sense of the predominance of the impact of monetary factors on nominal income.

2. The monetarist model of the transmission process.

3. Belief in the inherent stability of the private sector.

4. Irrelevance of the allocative detail for the explanation of short-run changes in money income, and belief in a fluid capital market.

5. Focus on the price level as a whole rather than on individual prices.

6. Reliance on small rather than large econometric models.

7. Use of the reserve base or similar measure as the indicator of monetary policy.

8. Use of the money stock as the proper target of monetary policy.

9. Acceptance of a monetary growth rule.

9. Thomas Mayer, et al. *The Structure of Monetarism* (New York: W. W. Norton & Company, 1978), p. 2. Of course, not all monetarists ascribe to all propositions in Professor Mayer's compilation. Reprinted by permission.

10. Rejection of an unemployment-inflation trade-off in favor of a real Phillips curve.

11. A relatively greater concern about inflation than about unemployment compared to other economists.

12. Dislike of government intervention.

As you can see, this list of propositions is far ranging and covers many facets of monetary economics. Most of these propositions are used below to outline the monetarist strategy for monetary policy.

The Monetarist Strategy for Monetary Policy

Monetarists advocate that the Fed use the money supply as a target for monetary policy. By target, we mean the essential financial variable linked with final economic goals. Justification for use of the money supply as a target stems from monetarist studies that show that every major and minor cycle since 1867 has been preceded by a monetary change, which monetarists argue caused the change in nominal income, employment, and prices. To control the money supply, monetarists urge control of the reserve base. Recall that the framework for monetary control described in Chapter 8, $M_1 = mB$, specified that the Fed could control M_1 by control of B, provided that m was relatively stable.

With respect to the money supply target, monetarists advocate a **fixed growth rule**. That is, they want the money supply to grow at a rate of about 3 to 5 percent, year in and year out. This rate is in line with growth in those variables that determine real income.

Monetarists justify on several grounds the fixed growth rule over the Keynesian-activist recommendation that monetary policy be conducted on a discretionary basis. First, they point out that knowledge about how changes in the money supply affect the economy is imperfect. They contend that policymakers do not know enough about cause-and-effect relationships to tinker with the money supply on a discretionary basis.

Second, monetarist studies have shown that there is a variable lag between changes in the money supply and changes in nominal income, employment, and prices. That is, sometimes changes in the money supply begin to affect nominal income after only six months, while at other times it may take twenty-four months. Moreover, these effects in the real economy still are being felt to a small degree as late as five years after the initial monetary change. Because of the variable lag and long-run effects of monetary change, monetarists contend that discretionary monetary policy tends to superimpose the effects of one monetary change on the effects of the next one. This produces an exaggerated and sometimes distorted impact on the real variables. For example, the Fed might increase the money supply and no discernible effects would be apparent in the short run. It might react by letting the money supply rise further. It is entirely possible that the effects of the second increase would occur quickly and at the same time the effects of the first increase would occur. The result may be excessive monetary stimulus and inflation. Because of the variable and long-lag effects of a monetary change, monetarists contend that a fixed growth rule would work best and avoid the problem just cited.

Third, monetarists hold that a fixed growth rule for money would stimulate investment because it would eliminate uncertainty about the future financial environment and reduce the rate of inflation. Any tendency for unemployment to rise during the transition to a lower fixed rate of monetary growth would be offset by the expansion produced by the increase in investment.

Finally, monetarists reject the idea that there is a long-run trade-off between inflation and unemployment. Since in the long run employment is determined largely by real factors, monetary policy should concentrate on control of inflation. Because inflation is largely the result of excessive monetary growth, it follows that a low-level fixed growth rule for money would reduce the rate of inflation.

Keynesian Propositions

Virtually every economist could say with Friedman, the leading monetarist, that "We are all Keynesians," because of the universal acceptance and use of the Keynesian national income accounting framework and terminology. However, the essence of Keynesianism is that because the economy tends toward an equilibrium level at less than the full employment level, government must stimulate the economy through active use of fiscal policy and other measures. Because Keynesianism has its origin in the Great Depression when unemployment was the overwhelming problem, Keynesian economists rank low levels of unemployment as the principal national economic goal. In this regard, it also is important to point out that Keynesians tend to be short-run rather than long-run oriented. If unemployment rises, they would prescribe an immediate policy to deal with it rather than view it as a temporary aberration on a long-run trend. To support this view, they cite Keynes' dictum: "In the long-run we are all dead."

Below is a list of Keynesian propositions, many of which, as you can see, are just diametrically opposite from the tenets of monetarism.

Keynesian Propositions

1. Acceptance of the quantity theory of money as a meaningful proposition only at the full employment level.
2. The Keynesian model of the transmission process.
3. Belief in the inherent instability of the private sector.
4. Belief that allocative detail is important in the short run, that is, output effects precede price effects, and belief in an imperfect capital market.
5. Focus on the aggregate income level rather than the aggregate price level.
6. Reliance on large rather than small econometric models.
7. Use of the interest rate as the indicator of monetary policy.
8. Use of money market conditions as the proper target for monetary policy.
9. Rejection of a monetary growth rule.
10. Acceptance of an unemployment-inflation trade-off.
11. A relatively greater concern about unemployment than about inflation as compared with other approaches.
12. Acceptance of the need for government intervention through active use of fiscal policy and regulatory measures.

Keynesian Strategy for Monetary Policy

Keynesians prefer fiscal policy to monetary policy because they believe that it affects aggregate demand more quickly and with more certainty. They doubt the stimulative potency of monetary policy because of uncertainty about its ability to reduce interest rates and, in turn, the responsiveness of investment to any reduction in interest rates. Moreover, Keynesians hold that changes in the velocity of money tend to offset much of the stimulative effects of a change in the money supply.

In spite of these problems, Keynesians do not wish to foresake monetary policy totally. In his 1976 presidential address to the American Economic Association cited earlier, Franco Modigliani stated:

> Nonmonetarists accept what I regard to be the fundamental practical message of the *General Theory*: that a private enterprise economy using an intangible money *needs* to be stabilized, *can* be stabilized, and therefore *should* be stabilized by appropriate monetary and fiscal policies.[10]

Modigliani pointed out that instability is generated from demand shocks and from a newer type of disturbance—supply shocks. Examples of these shocks are "war and peace, and other large changes in government expenditure, foreign trade, agriculture, technological progress, population shifts and what not. The clearest evidence on the importance of these shocks is provided by our postwar record with its six recessions."[11]

Keynesians or nonmonetarists would use monetary policy to supplement fiscal policy in order to offset or soften the blow of these exogenous shocks. If aggregate demand was insufficient to bring about full employment, their monetary strategy would be to increase the rate of growth in money supply in order to try to reduce interest rates and stimulate investment. In the case of supply shocks such as the 1973–1974 oil price increase, the Keynesian strategy would be to increase the money supply to accommodate the exogenous inflationary shock. This would help relieve some of the pressure on the real sector caused by a sudden increase in costs. According to Keynesians, such a supply shock in the face of a fixed-growth rate rule would only exacerbate unemployment.

Conclusion

For at least twenty-five years the monetarist-Keynesian debate has provided a healthy stimulus to research in monetary economics. It has increased greatly our understanding of how the economy operates and, specifically, how changes in the money supply affect income, employment, and prices. Yet, there is still much to be learned about

10. Modigliani, p. 1.
11. Modigliani, p. 11.

Figure 16-4.   Franco Modigliani (*Courtesy of the American Economic Association*)

the monetary process. Monetarism was dead following the Great Depression. The burden of proof that "money matters" was really on the monetarists, and they rose to the occasion. Led by Milton Friedman, monetarist studies have demonstrated to the satisfaction of everyone, including Keynesians, that money is important. As we shall see in the next section, Fed policymakers have adopted several monetarist propositions. However, Keynesians are unwilling to grant unqualified acceptance of most monetarist propositions. So the debate will go on!

The Federal Reserve's Current Strategy for Monetary Policy

Monetarist or Keynesian?

Based on our discussion in the last section, it should be apparent that if monetarists were in charge of monetary policy their strategy would be to implement a fixed-growth rule for the money supply. If

Keynesians were in charge, they would have a strategy of discretionary changes in the money supply to attempt to offset demand and supply shocks and to control interest rates and influence money market conditions.[12] At this point, an obvious question is: Are Fed policymakers monetarists or Keynesians? The answer is a few are strongly monetarist, a few are strongly Keynesian, and the majority believe that there are merits to each prescription for monetary policy. As a result of this division of opinion, the current Fed policy reflects both monetarist and Keynesian influences.

It has not always been this way. From 1951, when the Fed was freed from its obligation to support the Treasury's goal of keeping interest rates on government debt low, until 1970, when the Fed began to use money supply measures to define the general outlines of its policy objectives and to guide open market operations between meetings, it was clear that the central bank's strategy was basically Keynesian in orientation. Monetary policy was aimed at controlling interest rates and stabilizing money market conditions to achieve our national economic goals. The incorporation of monetary aggregates into the Fed's objectives was an explicit acknowledgment of the significance of monetarist research findings and their implications. With this discussion as background, let's examine how monetary policy is currently formulated.

The Fed's Formulation of a Monetary Strategy

As explained in Chapter 9, open market operations are the most important technique of monetary control. When we speak about the formulation of monetary policy, in essence we mean the formulation of open market policy.

Basically, the FOMC follows four steps in policy formulation:[13]

1. Consideration of economic forecasts for four quarters into the future.

---

12. We did not discuss what portfolio balance theorists might prescribe for monetary policy because at this juncture they are not sure themselves what it should be. Recall from Chapters 12 and 13 than an implication of their theory is that money is not a special asset in the portfolio and that changes in any assets might affect the real sector through relative price effects.

13. William Poole, "The Making of Monetary Policy: Description and Analysis," Federal Reserve Bank of Boston, *New England Economic Review* (March/April 1975), pp. 21-30.

2. Selection of long-term (twelve-month) growth ranges for the monetary aggregates (M_1, M_2, M_3, and commercial bank credit).

3. Selection of short-term (two-month) growth ranges for M_1 and M_2 consistent with the longer-term growth ranges for the monetary aggregates.

4. Selection of a target range and specific target for the federal funds rate that might be associated with the short-term growth ranges for M_1 and M_2.

Let's examine these steps in more detail. The first two steps may be considered the Fed's long-term strategy, while the latter two steps comprise its short-term strategy.

Long-term strategy. The policy process begins at the FOMC with the staff presenting its consensus forecast for GNP, prices, employment, and other long-run targets for the coming year.[14] These forecasts are revised three or four times annually and are updated monthly. The consensus forecast is a combination of the econometric forecast and the staff's judgmental forecast. The econometric forecast is made using the Fed's version of the SSRC-MIT-PENN (SMP) econometric model. The staff's judgmental forecast often is more accurate than the econometric forecast. Differences between the two forecasts are reconciled, and the consensus forecast is prepared.

Next, the staff develops a number of alternative long-run scenarios of economic activity for evaluation by the FOMC. Then alternative trajectories of monetary growth are fed into the model to produce a consistent set of monetary, GNP, employment, and price estimates. The FOMC then evaluates these alternative scenarios and selects its long-term growth ranges for the monetary aggregates. Publication of these goals has taken on great importance in recent years.

In response to House Concurrent Resolution 133, the Fed chairman began reporting quarterly to Congress its long-term objectives for the monetary aggregates. The substance of this resolution was made law in November, 1977, with the passage of the Federal Reserve Reform Act of 1977. Moreover, the Full Employment and Balanced Growth Act of 1978 requires the Fed to establish ranges for monetary growth

14. This discussion of long- and short-run strategy is based in part on Raymond E. Lombra and Raymond G. Torto, "The Strategy of Monetary Control," Federal Reserve Bank of Richmond, *Economic Review* (September/October 1975), pp. 3-14.

and to assess the relationship of its plans for monetary growth to the short-term goals in the president's Economic Report. Table 16–1 contains the FOMC's long-term goals for growth of the monetary aggregates and the actual growth for the period of March, 1975, through 1979 III. Figure 16–5 shows in graphic form the Fed's record with respect to these goals in 1978.

Short-term strategy.   The FOMC's short-term strategy involves selection of the two-month growth ranges for M_1 and M_2 that are consistent with the long-term growth ranges. The staff presents a set of alternative growth rates in the money supply along with associated growth rates for bank reserves and a range and level for the federal funds rate. In the Fed's current strategy, the Manager of the Open Market Account varies the federal funds rate within the specified range in order to achieve the chosen short-term paths for M_1 and M_2. If the monetary aggregates begin to increase at a rate above the upper side of the growth range, then the manager can raise the federal funds rate by making reserves less plentiful to the banking system.

The practice of using the federal funds rate in conjunction with control of the monetary aggregates draws much criticism from monetarists. They point out the inconsistency of having as targets both the federal funds rate and monetary aggregates. Their argument is that to keep the monetary aggregates on target, the Fed sometimes will have to miss the federal funds rate target and vice versa. For example, suppose that the money supply begins to grow too rapidly. If the Fed reduces the availability of reserves, then normally the federal funds rate is going to rise. Similarly, suppose that the federal funds rate rises above the target. If the Fed increases the availability of reserves, the money supply probably will increase at a rate above the specified ranges.

Conclusions

As it stands now, neither monetarists nor Keynesians are particularly happy with the Fed's current monetary strategy. It seems that the Fed has one foot in each camp and is trying to please both schools of thought. Part of the Fed's ambivalence stems from the present standoff in monetary theory between monetarists and Keynesians, and it greatly affects the Fed's formulation of a monetary strategy. Monetarists are convinced of the need to make the money supply the only target of monetary policy. To them, all the Fed has to do is use its

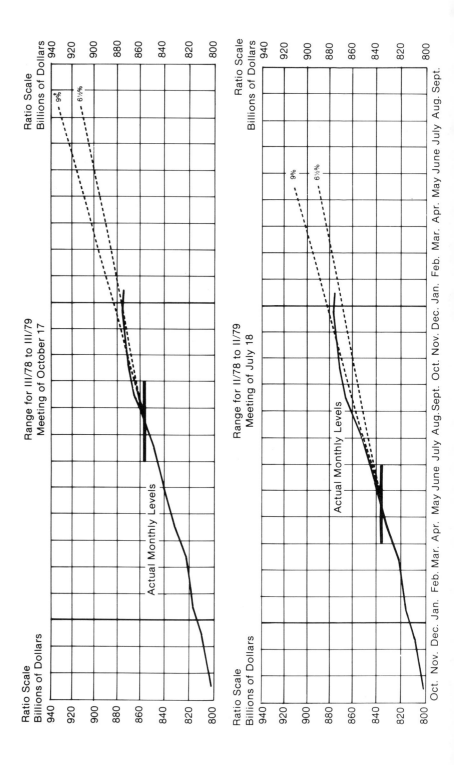

Ratio Scale
Billions of Dollars

Range for III/78 to III/79
Meeting of October 17

9%

6½%

Actual Monthly Levels

Ratio Scale
Billions of Dollars

Range for II/78 to II/79
Meeting of July 18

9%

6½%

Actual Monthly Levels

Oct. Nov. Dec. Jan. Feb. Mar. Apr. May June July Aug.Sept. Oct. Nov. Dec. Jan. Feb. Mar. Apr. May June July Aug. Sept.

383

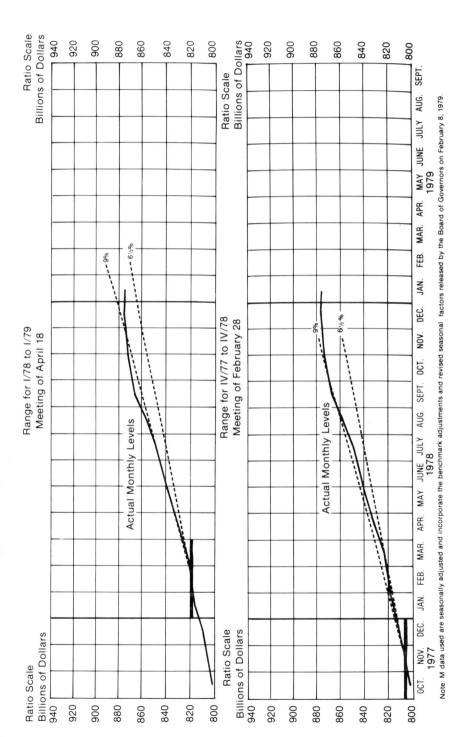

Figure 16-5 FOMC's Twelve-Month Ranges for M_1 Announced during 1978

Source: Federal Reserve Bank of St. Louis. *Review.* (March 1979), p. 9.

Table 16-1

FOMC's Annual Growth Ranges for Monetary and Credit Aggregates, March 1975–1979 IV

Period	Month established	M_1	Actual	M_2	Actual	M_3	Actual	Adjusted bank credit proxy / Bank credit	Actual
March 1975 to March 1976	April 1975	5 to 7½	5.3	8½ to 10½	9.7	10 to 12	12.3	6½ to 9½	3.2
June 1975 to June 1976	June 1975	5 to 7½	4.4	8½ to 10½	8.8	10 to 12	11.3	6½ to 9½	3.2
1975-II to 1976-II	July 1975	5 to 7½	5.4	8½ to 10½	9.6	10 to 12	12.0	6½ to 9½	3.1
1975-III to 1976-III	October 1975	5 to 7½	4.6	7½ to 10½	9.3	9 to 12	11.5	6 to 9	3.7
1975-IV to 1976-IV	January 1976	4½ to 7½	5.8	7½ to 10½	10.9	9 to 12	12.7	6 to 9	4.3
1976-I to 1977-I	April 1976	4½ to 7	6.5	7½ to 10	11.0	9 to 12	12.8	6 to 9	5.0
1976-II to 1977-II	July 1976	4½ to 7	6.8	7½ to 9½	10.8	9 to 11	12.5	5 to 8	5.8
1976-III to 1977-III	November 1976	4½ to 6½	8.0	7½ to 10	11.1	9 to 11½	12.7	5 to 8	11.4*
1976-IV to 1977-IV	January 1977	4½ to 6½	7.9	7 to 10	9.8	8½ to 11½	11.7	7 to 10	11.3*
1977-I to 1978-I	April 1977	4½ to 6½	7.7	7½ to 9½	8.8	8½ to 11	10.5	7 to 10	11.3*
1977-II to 1978-II	July 1977	4 to 6½	8.2	7 to 9½	8.6	8½ to 11	10.0	7 to 10	12.0
1977-III to 1978-III	October 1977	4 to 6½	8.1	6½ to 9	8.6	8½ to 10½	9.6	7 to 10	11.9
1977-IV to 1978-IV	February 1978	4 to 6½	7.3	6½ to 9	8.5	7½ to 10	9.4	7 to 10	11.3
1978-I to 1979-I	April 1978	4 to 6½		6½ to 9		7½ to 10		7½ to 10½	
1978-II to 1979-II	July 1978	4 to 6½		6½ to 9		7½ to 10		8½ to 11½	
1978-III to 1979-III	October 1978	2 to 6		6½ to 9		7½ to 10		8½ to 11½	
1978-IV to 1979-IV	February 1979	1½ to 4		5 to 8		6 to 9		7½ to 10½	

*The Board of Governors of the Federal Reserve System ceased publication of the credit proxy in August 1977. Bank credit growth is given as a guide thereafter.

Source: Federal Reserve Bank of New York, Quarterly Review, Spring, 1979 and Board of Governors of the Federal Reserve, Federal Reserve Bulletin. 1978-IV to 1979-IV February 1979

policy instruments, primarily open market operations, to control the monetary base, which, in turn, determines the money supply, provided the money multiplier is stable. To the Keynesians, the Fed should use interest rates and money market conditions as targets for monetary policy. With appropriate discretionary use of the monetary instruments, exogenous demand and supply shocks may be neutralized and the nation will achieve its economic goals. In sum, monetary policy will continue to evolve and reflect new developments in theory. Spurred by the need to achieve our economic goals, it is clear that the Fed will continue to refine and improve its monetary strategy.

Summary

For the first two decades following World War II, low levels of unemployment and price stability were viewed as trade-offs. This trade was embodied in the famous Phillips curve. In the late 1960s and early 1970s, the natural rate of unemployment and accelerationist hypotheses called into question whether unemployment and inflation really were trade-offs. The two hypotheses implied that efforts to peg unemployment below the natural rate can be achieved only by generating ever-increasing rates of inflation. Unemployment would remain below the natural rate only until the public's expectations about inflation had caught up with actual inflation.

In the 1970s, the possibility of temporarily pegging the unemployment rate below the natural rate received another jolt with the development of the rational expectations hypothesis. This theory held that people take into account all information, including governmental forecasts and anticipated policy actions, in formulating their expectations about inflation. The radical implication of the rational expectations hypothesis is that there is not even a temporary trade-off between unemployment and inflation. Thus, under this assumption, the Phillips curve is a vertical line at the natural rate of unemployment.

The monetarist-Keynesian debate concerning monetary theory, empirical results, the appropriate strategy for monetary policy, and other issues has raged for years. At present, the two schools seem to be in pretty much agreement on major theoretical issues, but are a long way from an accord on the other issues. With respect to monetary policy, monetarists favor a fixed-growth rule for money, while Keynesians prefer discretionary monetary policy.

Finally, the Fed's current monetary strategy is eclectic; it has both monetarist and Keynesian aspects. If further research on the concept of rational expectations substantiates its earlier conclusion, then Fed policy may tilt more monetarist than it is today because rational expectations supports the concept of a fixed-growth rule to stabilize prices.

Questions and Problems

1. How would you prioritize our economic goals? What is your rationale for these rankings?
2. Explain the changing views of the Phillips curve concept.
3. Define natural rate of unemployment.
4. Explain the accelerationist hypothesis.
5. Explain the nature, importance, and policy implications of the rational expectations concept.
6. Outline the monetarist strategy for monetary policy.
7. Outline the Keynesian strategy for monetary policy.
8. Is the present Fed strategy monetarist or Keynesian? Explain.
9. Distinguish between the Fed's short-run and long-run strategies.

Suggestions for Further Reading

Federal Reserve Bank of Minneapolis. *A Prescription for Monetary Policy: Proceedings from a Seminar Series.* Federal Reserve Bank of Minneapolis, December 1976.

Friedman, Milton. "The Role of Monetary Policy." *American Economic Review* (March 1968), pp. 1–17.

Holmes, Alan R. "The Strategy of Monetary Control." Federal Reserve Bank of New York, *Monthly Review* (May 1976), pp. 124–135.

Humphrey, Thomas M. "Changing Views of the Phillips Curve." Federal Reserve Bank of Richmond, *Monthly Review* (July 1973), pp. 2–13.

———. "Some Recent Developments in the Phillips Curve Analysis." Federal Reserve Bank of Richmond, *Economic Review* (January/February 1978), pp. 15–23.

Lombra, Raymond E., and Torto, Raymond G. "The Strategy of Monetary Control." Federal Reserve Bank of Richmond, *Economic Review* (September/October 1975), pp. 3–14.

Mayer, Thomas. *The Structure of Monetarism.* New York: W.W. Norton & Co., 1978.

Modigliani, Franco. "The Monetarist Controversy or, Should We Forsake Stabilization Policies?" *The American Economic Review* (March 1977), pp. 1–19.

Modigliani, Franco, and Papademos, Lucas. "Monetary Policy for the Coming Quarters: The Conflicting Views." Federal Reserve Bank of Boston, *New England Economic Review* (June 1976), pp. 2–35.

Nelson, Clarence V. "Rational Expectations—Fresh Ideas That Challenge Some Established Views of Policy Making." The Federal Reserve Bank of Minneapolis, *Annual Report* (1977), pp. 1–13.

Poole, William. "The Making of Monetary Policy: Description and Analysis." Federal Reserve Bank of Boston, *New England Economic Review* (March/April 1975), pp. 21–30.

Sargent, Thomas J., and Wallace, Neil. *Rational Expectations and the Theory of Economic Policy: Arguments and Evidence.* Federal Reserve Bank of Minneapolis, December 1977.

———. *Rational Expectations and the Theory of Economic Policy.* Federal Reserve Bank of Minneapolis, June 1978.

17

History of Monetary Policy: 1941-Present

We have reached the end of the journey. Over the last sixteen chapters, we have discussed the concept of money, how banks create money, how the central bank controls money, how changes in the money supply affect the economy, and, in the last part, the goals and alternative strategies for monetary policy. The primary purpose of this last chapter is to examine the record of monetary policy since the inception of World War II.

Specific objectives of this chapter are to (1) examine the Fed's role as it accommodated World War II finance and dealt with six postwar recessions, (2) review the famous 1951 "accord" between Treasury and the Fed, (3) analyze the "bills only" and "operation nudge" policies of the 1950s and 1960s, (4) discuss the "credit crunches" of 1966 and 1969–1970, and (5) outline Fed policy in the 1973–1975 recession and during the subsequent recovery.

Monetary Policy: 1941-1951

Accommodation of War Finance

On December 8, 1941, one day after the attack on Pearl Harbor, the Fed announced that "The System is prepared to use its powers to assure that an ample supply of funds is available at all times for financing the war effort and to exert its influence toward maintaining conditions in the United States Government security market that are satisfactory from the standpoint of the government's requirements." The Fed kept its promise.

First, during the four-year war period, 1942 to 1945, tax receipts were $127.1 billion, while government debt rose $220.2 billion. To finance this debt expansion, the Fed created $22 billion in new reserves through purchase of government securities. This injection of reserves enabled the banking system to increase its holdings of government securities from $21.8 billion to $90.6 billion with an accompanying increase in bank deposits from $71.2 billion to $150.2 billion. The increased money supply gave other institutions and the general public greater ability to purchase and absorb the expansion of government debt.

The second function performed by the Fed in war finance was to peg interest rates at very low levels. This action had two important effects: (1) it kept the interest cost of the war low and (2) it encouraged the public to buy government debt without fear that the price would fall if market interest rates were allowed to rise as happened after World War I. In March and April, 1942, the Fed and the Treasury reached an agreement that the Fed would stabilize or peg interest rates on Treasury issues at the following levels: 3/8 of 1 percent on T-bills; 7/8 of 1 percent on Treasury certificates of indebtedness; 2 percent on intermediate-term bonds; and 2-1/2 percent on long-term bonds. Given the present high level of interest rates, these rates are difficult to imagine. However, one of the few beneficial effects of the Great Depression was that the very low rates created by the Depression enabled our country to finance its biggest war very cheaply.

The Fed pegged interest rates by purchasing securities any time the price fell below par value, and the record shows that it was successful in keeping rates stabilized during the wartime period. However, by its pledge to purchase securities at par, the Fed shifted control of bank reserves to the commercial banks and the public. Any time these holders wanted to sell, the Fed had to buy, thereby creating reserves. Under ordinary circumstances, continual monetization of government debt and the subsequent creation of money leads to serious inflation. The only reason this did not occur during the war period was the use of price and wage ceilings and direct control of production, distribution, and use of output. As a result of these controls, between

1941 and 1945, consumer prices rose at an annual rate of only 5.1 percent.

The Postwar Inflation: 1946-1948

The relatively low inflation rate during the war, of course, did not reflect the repressed inflation that was present. Between the end of 1941 and the end of 1945, total bank deposits rose at an annual rate of 20.5 percent. Moreover, the stock of liquid assets in the form of government securities rose sharply. When the war ended, consumers were well armed with liquid assets and were ready to unleash their pent-up demand for goods and services. In response to public pressure, the government began to relax controls. This combination of circumstances caused consumer prices to rise 8.5 percent in 1946 and 14.4 percent in 1947. Wholesale prices climbed 14.4 percent in 1946 and 22.8 percent in 1947.

The Fed, however, was powerless to stop inflation because of its commitment to the Treasury to peg interest rates and to "maintain orderly conditions" in the securities market. Between the end of 1945 and the end of 1947, banks sold $21.4 billion of government securities and increased total loans outstanding by $12 billion. Member bank reserves rose by 20 percent between 1945 and 1948, thanks largely to a $3.3 billion increase in the gold stock. With its hands tied because of its obligation to the Treasury, the Fed became an "engine of inflation."

The 1948-1949 Recession

Postwar consumer prices peaked in 1948, and the economy slipped into its first postwar recession in November, 1948, which lasted until October, 1949. This recession has been characterized as an "inventory recession" because a sharp reduction in inventory accumulation was the primary cause of the decline. Unemployment, which averaged 3.8 percent in 1948, climbed to 5.9 percent in 1949. The Fed's major moves to counter the recession were three one-half percentage point reductions in the reserve ratios applicable to demand deposits.

The Treasury-Federal Reserve Accord of 1951

By early 1950, the economy was in an upswing again. When fighting broke out in Korea in June, 1950, consumers began to hoard goods in anticipation of the possibility of World War II type shortages. Between June and December, 1950, wholesale prices spurted 11 percent, while consumer prices rose 5 percent. However, the Fed's ability to deal with inflation was severely limited by its commitment to peg interest rates. Tension between the Fed and the Treasury over this issue had been building for some time. On August 18, 1950, the Fed Board approved an increase in the discount rate from 1-1/2 percent to 1-3/4 percent, and the FOMC adopted a general policy of making reserves less readily available. As one participant in the action later wrote: "The August, 1950 decision reflected the Federal Reserve's belief that the facts of the economic situation and the general economic program of the government demanded that it break out of that pattern."[1] Within one hour of the Fed's announcement, the Treasury announced its September-October refunding of $13.5 billion in 1-1/4 percent 13-month notes. With the discount rate and other short-term rates above 1-1/4, the Treasury's announcement was designed to put the Fed on the spot to uphold its commitment to support the securities market. The Treasury's sale of the issue was a failure, and the Fed had to purchase nearly 80 percent of it to make sure that the Treasury would not have an embarrassing redemption.

During the following months, the dispute between the Treasury and the Fed spilled over into Congress, which held hearings on the matter. President Truman became involved in trying to settle differences between the two agencies and invited the FOMC to the White House on January 31, 1951. Following this meeting, the president and the FOMC issued conflicting reports on what happened at the meeting. According to a White House press secretary, the Fed had pledged to the president that it would continue to support the government securities market. In a carefully worded letter to the president on February 7, 1951, the FOMC in effect questioned the President's interpretation of the meeting, but pledged to work out with the Secretary of Treasury a program "which will safeguard and maintain public confidence in the values of outstanding government bonds and which, at the same time, will protect the purchasing power of the dollar."[2]

Over the next month the Fed and Treasury began serious negotia-

---

1. Allan Sproul, "The 'Accord'—A Landmark in the First Fifty Years of the Federal Reserve System," in Federal Reserve Bank of New York, *Essays in Domestic and International Finance* (New York: Federal Reserve Bank of New York, 1969), p. 18.
2. Sproul, p. 19.

tions to settle the dispute. Finally, on March 4, 1951, the following joint announcement by the secretary of the Treasury and the chairman of the Fed Board and of the FOMC was released to the press:

> The Treasury and the Federal Reserve System have reached full accord with respect to debt management and monetary policies to be pursued in furthering their common purpose of the government's requirements and, at the same time, to minimize monetization of the public debt.

The "accord" ranks as one of the most significant events in the Fed's history because it freed the Fed to practice monetary policy in a manner consistent with the achievement of national economic goals. However, the Fed did not abandon altogether its commitment to the Treasury and to orderly conditions in the government securities. Since the accord, the Treasury has ensured that Treasury issues are absorbed into the market in an orderly manner. After the accord, interest rates began to rise and, except for brief declines associated with recessions, have been in a long uptrend ever since.

Monetary Policy: 1952–1961

The Bills Only Policy

Free from its nine-year pegging obligation, the Fed turned its attention to how best to conduct open market operations. Representatives from the securities industry made a strong case to a special Fed subcommittee that the FOMC limit its open market activities to short-term securities and not to enter the long-term market except to correct disorderly conditions. The subcommittee found that the long-term government securities market lacked "depth, breadth, and resiliency." **Depth** meant that any substantial deviation in price above or below the existing market price would uncover significant numbers of market participants that would allow an orderly adjustment in price. **Breadth** meant that there was a wide variety of market participants, for example, ranging from large institutions to small individual buyers. **Resiliency** meant the market had the ability to bounce back from movements caused by sudden surges from either the demand or supply side. The subcommittee pointed out that FOMC activity in the long-term end made it difficult for dealers to take positions for fear of losses that might be caused by the Fed raising interest rates. However, this problem did not exist in the short-term end because it had "depth, breadth, and resiliency." At any rate, the Fed accepted the subcommittee's recommendation and adopted in 1953 the **bills only policy** for the conduct of open market operations. Essentially, this meant that except for extreme market situations, the FOMC would confine its open market purchases and sales to securities with a maturity of less than one year. Technically, the bills only policy really was a "bills mostly" policy because the guidelines did permit dealing in notes and bonds with less than one year of maturity remaining.

Over the next eight years, the bills only policy was criticized on the grounds that it reduced the effectiveness of open market operations; therefore, the central bank could not make its maximum contribution toward monetary and economic stability. Keynesian economists were particularly critical of bills only because it had only a delayed influence on long-term rates, which, of course, they deemed to be the relevant rates. Also, by continuing to supply reserves through purchases of bills, the FOMC placed downward pressure on short-term rates and, hence, encouraged the outflow of short-term capital, which exacerbated the US balance of payments.

The 1953-1954 Recession and Recovery

In July, 1953, the economy entered its second postwar recession. Like the 1948-1949 recession, this one was caused by inventory disinvestment. The recession ended in May, 1954, although the peak in unemployment of 6.1 percent did not occur until September, 1954. Throughout most of 1954, the FOMC readily expanded reserves through open market purchases. Moreover, between June 16 and August 1, 1954, the Fed Board reduced reserve ratios on demand deposits by one percentage point for member banks. In February, the discount rate at all reserve banks was reduced from 2 percent to 1-3/4 percent and in April and May was reduced further to 1-1/2 percent.

By late 1954, business activity was in a strong upward swing. In 1955, the automobile industry sold more cars than ever before in its history. Moreover, the level of gross private domestic investment in 1956 was 34.7 percent above the 1954 total. Because of the increase in aggregate demand, the rate of unemployment fell from 5.5 percent in 1954 to 4.4 percent in 1955 and remained slightly below this level over the next two years.

As it became apparent that recovery was underway, the Fed began to "lean against the wind" by putting pressure on bank reserve positions through open market sales. In August, 1955, the discount rate was raised to 2 percent and over the next twenty-four months was pushed up to 3-1/2 percent.

The 1957–1958 Recession

The rate of consumer spending and business investment that led the economy out of the 1953–1954 recession could not be sustained. In the spring of 1957, the recovery began to show signs of weakening. The economy officially entered its third postwar recession in August, 1957. The Fed was slow in reacting to the downturn, and it was not until late in 1957 that the central bank shifted to a policy of monetary ease through moderate open market purchases. In November and December, 1957, the discount rate was reduced to 3 percent. More reductions followed in 1958 and by May, all reserve banks had posted a rate of 1-3/4 percent. In addition, between February and April, 1958, the Fed reduced reserve ratios three times. April, 1958, marked the end of this third recession. Nevertheless, unemployment averaged 6.8 percent throughout 1958.

The 1958–1960 Recovery

As it had after the previous recession, economic activity began to expand quite rapidly after the April 1958 trough. In 1959, gross private domestic investment was 25.4 percent above the previous year's level. In 1959, GNP climbed 8.4 percent, and unemployment fell to 5.5 percent, where it remained in 1960.

However, as recovery began to build momentum, the Fed began to apply the monetary brakes. In August-September the discount rate was increased to 2 percent and in October-November it was raised to 2-1/2 percent. In 1959 three more increases carried the discount rate to 4 percent. In 1959, the FOMC began to exert pressure on bank reserve positions through open market sales.

Many economists have criticized the Fed for shifting too quickly to a tight money policy during the recovery from the 1957–1958 recession. Most of the criticism centered around the Fed's apparent over-emphasis of the goal of price stability as opposed to low levels of unemployment and adequate economic growth. It is true that between

1949 and 1959, consumer prices rose only at an annual rate slightly above 2 percent, which is enviable especially in view of the record in the 1970s. However, the failure of the unemployment rate in 1959 to return to the prerecession level was cited by economists as evidence that the Fed had too hard a grip on the monetary reins.

The 1960-1961 Recession

The effects of the Fed's tight money policy were felt in April, 1960, when the economy entered its fourth postwar recession. This recession was a relatively mild one, but unemployment rose to 5.5 percent in 1960 and 6.7 percent in 1961. As economic activity began slowing down, the Fed shifted quickly to a policy of making reserves more readily available through open market purchases. Moreover, on September 1 and December 1, 1960, the Fed Board reduced reserve ratios. The Fed's easy money policy contributed to the economy pulling out of the downturn in February, 1961. The Fed also announced in February that "The System Open Market Account is purchasing in the open market US Government bonds and notes of varying maturities, some of which will exceed five years." This statement was the official end of the bills only policy.

Monetary Policy: 1961-1970

Operation Nudge: 1961-1965

Throughout the 1950s, the nation's balance of payments was in deficit. Most economists felt that the situation would take care of itself, but the outflow of dollars and gold persisted. Ordinarily, if a country runs a payments deficit, the central bank would execute a tight money policy to raise interest rates in order to reduce the outflow of short-term capital and slow down the growth of the economy to retard imports. However, the 1960 downturn in the domestic economy posed a dilemma for the Fed. If it pushed up interest rates, capital outflows would abate, but unemployment would worsen and the economy might suffer a deep recession. To deal with the situation, the FOMC came up with an innovative approach to open market policy that involved the simultaneous sale of short-term securities and purchase of long-term obligations. The objective was to push short-term rates up to retard the outflow of short-term capital and to push long-term rates down to stimulate domestic capital investment. This policy became known as "operation nudge" or "operation twist" because the FOMC was trying to nudge or twist the yield structure of interest rates.

Operation nudge lasted until about 1965. One study by Modigliani and Sutch showed that operation nudge probably had some slight success in pushing short-term rates up and long-term rates down.[3] Between 1961 and 1965, the domestic economy enjoyed a period of sustained economic growth, although the unemployment rate did not fall to the pre-1957–58 recession level until 1965 and capital outflows continued.

The Credit Crunch of 1966

After mid-1965, federal expenditures soared as the United States became involved in the Vietnam conflict. Prior to this escalation, the economy was at or near the full employment level, and the wartime spending led to reduced unemployment and increased inflationary pressures. In October, 1965, as the scale of our anticipated involvement in the Vietnam war escalated, the chairman of the Fed Board, William McChesney Martin, went to President Johnson and told him that the Fed was going to have to take steps to combat mounting inflation. President Johnson, using his famous powers of persuasion, convinced Chairman Martin to delay any tightening moves because he thought Congress would enact tax legislation to finance the war. Such legislation did not materialize. On December 6, 1965, the Fed Board approved an increase in the discount rate from 4 to 4-1/2 percent, raised the Reg. Q ceiling on time deposits to 5-1/2 percent, but left the ceiling on savings deposits at 4 percent. President Johnson severely criticized the Fed's increase in the discount rate as premature and a threat to full employment and his Great Society goals. Many people point to President Johnson's strong and vocal attack on the central bank as a reaffirmation of the need to have a central bank independent of the executive branch.

The increase in the Reg. Q ceilings was designed to let banks compete more effectively for time deposits to fund loan demand. This action worked initially but by mid-1966 short-term interest rates had risen above the Reg. Q ceilings. Banks and especially S&Ls began to

3. Franco Modigliani and Richard Sutch, "Innovations in Interest Rate Policy," *American Economic Review* (May 1965), pp. 178–179.

experience financial disintermediation as savers withdrew funds and invested directly in higher yielding T-bills and other money market instruments. With respect to the banking industry, financial disintermediation reduced the ability of these institutions to meet the mounting business loan demand. Many S&Ls stopped making home loans. To accommodate the loan demand, banks sold securities from their permanent portfolios. This action only served to drive market interest rates higher. By late summer, supply and demand pressures in the financial markets came to a head and created the first of three "credit crunches" that occurred over the next eight years.

The Fed could have alleviated the situation by increasing reserve availability. However, to have done so would have fueled inflationary pressures. Instead, the Fed chose to resist these pressures through a tight money policy. In July the Fed Board raised from 4 to 5 percent the reserve ratio on bank time deposits above $5 million. In September this ratio was hiked to 6 percent. However, the Fed's most significant action was its September 1 letter to member banks which asked them to reduce the expansion of business loans and refrain from dumping municipal securities on the market to raise needed funds. This last action had the municipal securities market in chaos and forced many postponements and cancellations of municipal security sales to finance state and local government capital projects. The Fed backed up its requests with an indication that noncooperating banks might not be accommodated at the discount window. Apparently, banks and potential borrowers got the message because financial pressures soon abated. As evidence of this, the T-bill rate peaked at 5.59 percent during the last week in September but by year end had fallen to 4.75 percent. The September 1, 1966, letter perhaps was the most effective act of moral suasion in the Fed's history.

The Fed's restrictive actions cooled the economy to such an extent that the rate of growth of real GNP was not nearly as robust during the last quarter of 1966 and the first quarter of 1967. This slowdown was classified as a "mini-recession" by some observers; however, it might more accurately be characterized as a needed respite for the economy from its unsustainable pace during previous quarters. In March, 1967, the Fed responded to the slowdown by reducing from 4 to 3 percent the reserve ratios on savings deposits and time deposits under $5 million. In April it approved a reduction in the discount rate from 4-1/2 to 4 percent. These actions along with expansionary open market operations pushed T-bill rates slightly under 3.50 percent by the last week of May. From December, 1966, to December, 1967, M_2 expanded by 9.9 percent. Monetarists, especially, were highly critical of this rapid increase in the money supply and later blamed it for the high rate of inflation in 1969 and 1970.

The Credit Crunch of 1969–1970

In November, 1967, the Fed began to shift to a less expansionary monetary policy. In November, the discount rate was raised to 4-1/2 percent. In March, 1968, the rate was pushed to 5 percent and to 5-1/2 percent in April. In January, 1968, the reserve ratio on demand deposits above $5 million was raised by one-half percentage point. Open market policy also became less expansionary. T-bill rates responded to this pressure and increased from 4.99 percent at the end of 1967 to 5.84 percent by the end of May, 1968.

In June, 1968, Congress finally passed the tax increase that President Johnson wanted three years earlier. It came in the form of a 10 percent surtax on personal and corporate income taxes. This meant that if you owed $5,000 in taxes, the surtax added an extra $500 to your tax bill. The Fed reacted to the tax increase with the claim that it was "too large" and that the economy was in danger of a "fiscal overkill." The Fed felt compelled to offset this action with an expansionary monetary policy from June to November, 1968. As a signal of its intentions, in August the discount rate was reduced from 5-1/2 to 5-1/4 percent.

In December, 1968, the Fed apparently felt that it had been too accommodative. It suddenly switched to a restrictive policy and raised the discount rate back to 5-1/2 percent. In April, 1969, the discount rate was hiked to 6 percent, and the reserve ratio on all demand deposits was raised by one-half percentage point. During this time and continuing to early 1970, open market operations kept pressure on bank reserve positions.

The effects of this tight money policy were readily measurable in the financial markets. The T-bill rate climbed from 5.63 percent in the first week of December, 1969, until it peaked at 8.10 percent in the first week of 1970. Conditions in the credit markets were much like they were in 1966, except that interest rates were at a higher level. The prime rate hit 6 percent in the 1966 crunch, but rose from 6-1/2 percent in early December, 1969, to 8-1/2 percent by June, 1969. Financial disintermediation caused by market interest rates rising

Figure 17-1. William McChesney Martin, Jr., chairman of the Board of Governors of the Federal Reserve System 1951-1970 (*Photo by Fabian Bachrach*)

Figure 17-2. Arthur F. Burns, chairman of the Board of Governors of the Federal Reserve System, 1970-1978

Figure 17-3. G. William Miller, chairman of the Board of Governors of the Federal Reserve System, 1978–1979

Figure 17-4. Paul A. Volcker, chairman of the Board of Governors of the Federal Reserve System, 1979–present

above the Reg. Q ceilings played a big role in producing this credit crunch, which lasted essentially from mid-1969 to mid-1970, when interest rates on government and corporate bonds peaked.

The 1969-1970 Recession

The Fed's tight money policy was largely responsible for our fifth postwar recession, which lasted from December, 1969, to November, 1970. The beginning of this recession marked the end of an economic expansion that lasted ninety-four months and that ranks as one of the longest on record. In relative terms, the 1969-1970 recession was mild. Unemployment rose from 3.5 percent in 1969 to 4.9 percent in 1970. By today's standards, these conditions would be considered full employment.

To combat the slowdown the Fed in early 1970 shifted to a more stimulative open market policy. However, the long-run effects of the 1968 expansionary policy caused interest rates to peak in the midst of the recession. However, it was not until October, 1970, that the Fed reduced the reserve ratio, and this time it was only a one-point drop on time deposits of $5 million or more. Moreover, the Fed did not reduce the discount rate until November, when the rate was dropped by one-fourth percentage point. In December, it was decreased again by a like amount. Apparently, the Fed was slow in switching to a more expansionary policy in this recession because it did not want to duplicate what many economists felt was excessive monetary expansion following the 1966 crunch and the 1968 tax increase.

Monetary Policy: 1971-Present

Monetary Policy: 1971-1973

In 1971 the nation experienced its first merchandise trade deficit since 1919, when international transaction statistics were first kept. This development and the continued outflow of short- and long-term capital placed great pressure on the foreign exchange price of the dollar. As discussed in Chapter 15, President Nixon on August 15, 1971, announced that the United States would no longer convert dollars into gold for foreigners and that the dollar would be allowed to float on international markets. In addition, the President announced a ninety-day freeze on wages, prices, and rents. Freezes in one form or another remained in effect until April, 1974.

Meanwhile, the Fed's expansionary monetary policy begun in the first months of 1970 continued until late 1972. M_2 grew at an annual rate of 11.4 percent in both 1971 and 1972. This monetary expansion coupled with wage and price controls laid the foundation for the price explosion between 1973 and 1975.

In early 1973, the Fed switched to a more restrictive monetary policy. Open market operations kept pressure on bank reserve positions. The discount rate, which stood at 4-3/4 percent at the beginning of 1973, was raised six times during the year and stood at 7-1/2 percent by August. On July 19 the reserve ratios on demand deposits above $2 million were raised one-half percentage point. All of these actions combined to shove interest rates to record highs in 1973 and 1974. In December, 1972, the T-bill rate stood at 5.06 percent; however, by July, 1973, it was at 8.02 percent. The prime rate was 6 percent at the inception of 1973 but on September 10 it hit 10 percent. On July 5, 1975, the prime rate was raised to 12 percent, where it remained until October 7.

The 1973–1975 Recession

The tight money policy in effect since early 1973 and the resulting record interest rates began to slow the pace of business activity as the year progressed. In November, 1973, the economy sank into a recession that turned out to be the longest and most severe of the postwar period. Unemployment rose from 4.9 percent in 1973 to 5.6 percent in 1974 and to 8.5 percent in 1975. There were 3.5 million more people unemployed in 1975 than in 1973. Moreover, inflation increased sharply in 1974 and 1975 as earlier monetary expansion and special factors such as the oil price boost and bad weather in 1974 combined to send prices soaring. In 1973 consumer prices rose by 6.2 percent. However, the CPI rose 11 percent in 1974 and 9.1 percent in 1975.

As mentioned earlier, the peak in interest rates occurred in mid-1974. After midyear, the Fed moved to a more expansionary policy. Of course, this was well past the beginning of the recession, but the sharp inflationary trend persuaded the Fed to continue pressure on bank reserve positions. However, after unemployment began to rise and industrial production dropped sharply in the October to December quarter of 1974, the FOMC increased reserve availability. On December 12, the reserve ratio on demand deposits above $400 million was reduced by one-half percentage point, while the reserve ratio on time deposits with a maturity of more than 180 days was decreased from 5 to 3 percent. Compounding the Fed's problems was the failure on October 8, 1974, of the $3.6 billion Franklin National Bank in New York. This was the largest bank failure in history and greatly shook business confidence.

Interest rates fell precipitously during the last half of 1974. The prime rate fell to 10-1/2 percent by year end. The T-bill rate, which peaked at 8.74 percent in August, stood at 6.49 percent in January, 1975. By the close of 1975, the prime rate was 7-1/4 percent, and the T-bill rate had fallen to 5.5 percent.

In conclusion, the 1973–1975 recession and its high rate of inflation was costly in many ways for the economy. Obviously, unemployment and inflation harmed everyone directly and/or indirectly. But, this recession reduced confidence in the Fed's ability to stabilize the economy. The trade-off between unemployment and inflation did not seem to exist.

Fixing specific responsibility for the recession is not easy, but a number of factors stand out. Perhaps at the top of the list were the problems going back to 1965 created by our involvement in the Vietnam War which led to excess demand and shortages throughout the economy. The Fed's stop-start monetary policy during this period also was a primary cause of the recession and the inflation. Undoubtedly, supply shocks caused by the OPEC oil price increase and other special factors contributed to inflation and the protractedness of the recession. However, with respect to our study of monetary policy, the 1973–1975 recession underscored again the point that monetary instability usually precedes economic instability.

Monetary Policy: 1976 to Present

At this writing in April, 1979, the economy is beginning its fifth year of expansion. Hence, this recovery is one of the longest on record. Throughout most of this period, the Fed has pursued what most economists would characterize as a modestly expansionary monetary policy. Unemployment has remained relatively high by historic standards, and this has caused modern Keynesians to assert that monetary policy has been too restrictive. However, as inflationary pressures continue to mount in 1979, monetarists claim that monetary policy has been too stimulative in the recovery.

Nevertheless, it is encouraging to observe that since the last recession, partly because of Congressional prodding, the Fed has paid much more attention to the monetary aggregates and, as a result, monetary growth has been more stable than in prior years.

In 1977, the Fed began to adopt a gradually less accommodative stance in the area of reserve management. This policy was continued throughout 1978 and into 1979. The discount rate stood at 5-1/4 percent in the first quarter of 1977. From this point it was raised steadily until it stood at 8-1/2 percent in April, 1979. Interest rates bottomed out in the first quarter of 1977 and rose steadily and approached, but did not break, the 1974 highs. From all indications, the Fed's more steady monetary management is going to be successful in bringing the level of inflation and interest rates down to a more acceptable level.

Summary and Concluding Observations

The history of US monetary policy since 1941 reveals many challenges, many accomplishments, yet plenty of room for improvement. During World War II, the Fed facilitated war finance and kept its commitment to the Treasury to stabilize interest rates at prewar levels. From 1946–1951, the Fed continued to peg interest rates but, in so doing, was powerless to stop the sharp postwar inflation fueled by pent-up demand and early relaxation of direct controls. The "accord" of March 4, 1951, between the Treasury and the Fed freed the Fed from the constraint of having to peg interest rates and allowed it to pursue a more appropriate monetary policy to fight inflation.

An overview of our monetary history between 1951 and 1979 reveals five recessions (1953–1954; 1957–1958; 1960–1961; 1969–1970; and 1973–1975). Each of them was preceded by a period of monetary restraint. In each, the Fed switched to a more stimulative monetary policy through the purchase of securities and reductions in reserve ratios and the discount rate. The Fed's greatest mistake throughout the postwar period was its tendency to "overmanage" monetary policy. Often, the Fed superimposed the short-run effects of a new policy on the long-run effects of a previous policy. In spite of this criticism, the economy did manage to avoid a depression of the magnitude of the 1930s experience. The Fed's propensity to "overmanage" came from its adherence to a fundamental Keynesian principle that discretionary policy changes are necessary for economic stabilization. The above criticism is not to imply that some discretionary monetary policy is not necessary. As Modigliani lucidly points out, discretionary monetary policy has an important role to play in dealing with supply shocks such as the 1974 OPEC oil price increase. In such situations the money supply should be increased to permit a nondisruptive adjustment. However, if there is one lesson to be learned from our monetary history, it is that monetary instability leads to economic instability.

Questions and Problems

1. Describe the Fed's role in World War II.
2. What was the nature and significance of the accord?
3. Define and explain the rationale for the "bills only" policy.
4. Define and explain the rationale for "operation nudge."
5. Explain what is meant by the term "credit crunch."
6. In your opinion, does the Fed deserve praise or criticism for its conduct of monetary policy since the accord? Explain.

Suggestions for Additional Reading

Anderson, Clay J. *A Half-Century of Federal Reserve Policymaking, 1914–1964.* Philadelphia: Federal Reserve Bank of Philadelphia, 1965.

Ahearn, Daniel S. *Federal Reserve Policy Reappraised, 1951–1959.* New York: Columbia University Press, 1963.

Friedman, Milton, and Schwartz, Anna Jacobson. *A Monetary History of the United States, 1867–1960.* Princeton, N.J.: Princeton University Press, 1963.

Maisel, Sherman J. *Managing the Dollar.* New York: W.W. Norton & Company, 1973.

Glossary*

accelerationist hypothesis The theory that holds that because there is no long-run trade-off between inflation and unemployment, attempts to peg the rate of unemployment below the natural rate will produce ever-accelerating inflation. (16)

agency obligations The debt of government-sponsored enterprises, federal agencies, and certain international institutions. (6)

automated clearinghouses (ACHs) A system that permits banks to transfer debt and credit items among themselves by electrical impulse rather than by paper. (1)

automatic teller machines (ATMs) Devices that enable a customer to obtain cash or effect other transfers to and from an account by inserting an identification card and entering instructions into the machine. (1)

balance on current account In the international accounts, this represents net excess of debits or credits in the accounts for goods, services, and unilateral transfers in the form of remittances, pensions, and government grants. (15)

balance on goods and services In international accounts, this represents the merchandise trade balance plus net excess of military transactions, investment income, and service income. (15)

bank audit The verification of assets and liabilities. (4)

bank capital The sum of common stock, preferred stock, surplus, and undivided profits. For purposes of measuring capital adequacy, sometimes includes capital notes and debentures. (5)

bank examination Periodic check by the banking regulatory authorities on a bank's compliance with banking laws and regulations. (4)

bank holding company Any company that owns or controls the voting stock of one or more banks. (4)

bank liquidity A bank's ability to meet

*Numbers in parentheses after each item indicate the chapter in which the concept is discussed.

406

deposit withdrawals, maturing liabilities, and legitimate loan requests without delay. (6)

bank reserve equation The framework for taking into account all sources and uses of member bank reserves on the books of the Reserve banks. (9)

banker's acceptance A negotiable bill of exchange on which a bank has written "accepted" as evidence of its guarantee. (5)

banking paradox The apparent inconsistency between the principles of deposit creation for one bank and those for the banking system. One bank can create new deposits in an amount equal to excess reserves; however, the banking system can expand deposits by a multiple of the excess reserves in the system. (2)

barter To exchange goods and services that we have or produce for those that someone else has or produces. (1)

bills-only policy The open market policy that open market operations should be limited to short-term securities and that operations should not be conducted in the long-term market except to correct disorderly conditions. This policy was in effect from 1953–1961. (17)

Board of Governors of the Federal Reserve System Body consisting of seven members who are appointed by the President of the United States and confirmed by the Senate. They have overall supervisory authority over the Federal Reserve System. (7)

branch bank A bank that operates from two or more locations. (4)

Cambridge cash balances approach An explanation of the quantity theory of money framed in terms of people's motives for holding money. (10)

capital notes and debentures (bank) Debt issued by banks or

bank-holding companies to raise funds for loans and other operating purposes. (5)

cash-in-vault Coin and currency held in a bank's vault. (6)

cash-items-in-the-process-of-collection Checks sent by one bank to another bank for payment. (6)

cashier's check An order on the bank to pay deposits on demand that is signed by a bank officer. (2)

central bank A governmental institution charged with the responsibility for management of the money supply and regulation of the commercial banking system. (7)

certificates of deposits (CDs) An interest-bearing bank time deposit with a fixed maturity, evidenced by a written contract and usually issued in denominations of $100,000 or more, although small denominations are common. (5)

certified check A regular check drawn by a customer on his or her bank, which in turn stamps it "certified" as evidence that payment is guaranteed. (5)

checks Orders to a bank to transfer demand deposits to the payee designated by the signer of the check. (1)

classical theory of interest The theory that specifies that the interest rate is determined by the demand and supply of savings. (10)

clearinghouse A meeting place, such as a bank or local Federal Reserve clearing center, where area banks meet to exchange checks drawn on each other. (7)

commercial bank An institution that creates demand deposits in the process of making loans and investments. Also provides time and savings deposits and a myriad of other services. (2)

commercial loan theory of bank lending Prominent theory prior to the Great Depression that specified that a bank should make only short-term, self-liquidating loans. (6)

commercial paper Short-term promissory notes of a bank-holding company or a nonfinancial business. (4)

common stock account (bank) A bank capital account with funds equal to the par value of the stock times the number of shares outstanding. (2)

compensating balances That portion of loan proceeds that the borrower agrees to keep on deposit as implicit compensation to the bank for the loan. (3)

Comptroller of the Currency Official in the Treasury Department responsible for the chartering and regulation of national banks. (7)

consumer and real estate credit controls Specified down payments and maximum maturities on consumer and real estate loans during World War II. (9)

consumer price index The index of prices on a market basket of approximately 400 consumer goods and services purchased by urban wage earners and clerical workers. (14)

correspondent bank A commercial bank that provides services to another bank in return for deposit balances or fees. (2)

cost-push theory The theory that specifies that inflation stems from the exercise of market power by business and/or labor groups, or from higher import prices or higher taxes. (14)

credit The obligation to pay money in the future. (3)

credit risk Chance of nonpayment at maturity. (3)

credit union A cooperative self-help thrift and loan society composed of individuals bound together by some tie such as a common employer. (3)

Culpeper Switch Central switch in the Federal Reserve teletype transfer system that permits transfer of reserve balances from one member bank to another. (1)

currency Coin and paper money. (2)

defensive open market operations Purchases and sales of securities by the Fed to smooth fluctuations in float or other sources and uses of reserves. (8)

deferred availability cash items A Federal Reserve liability account that includes checks that have not been added to the reserve account of the sending bank. (8)

demand deposits Bookkeeping credits (liabilities) that a bank agrees to redeem without prior notice. (5)

demand-pull theory The theory that specifies that inflation is caused by excess demand (spending) relative to the available supply at the existing level of prices. (14)

devaluation The reduction of the gold content of the monetary unit. (15)

direct deposit system A system whereby funds are deposited directly to the credit of the payee at a designated bank or financial institution. (1)

dirty floating exchange rate system A system in which governments intervene in the marketplace to stabilize exchange rates ordinarily determined by the forces of supply and demand. (15)

discount rate The rate charged by the Federal Reserve bank on loans to banks. (9)

discount window The symbolic place at a Federal Reserve bank where a commercial bank may obtain a loan. (9)

dual banking system A system as in the United States whereby two levels of government have the power to charter banks. (4)

Edge Act corporations International subsidiaries of member banks. (7)

electronic funds transfer (EFT) The transfer of funds and securities among depositors, commercial banks, other financial institutions, and the Federal Reserve banks by electronic means. (1)

eligibility requirements Federal Reserve regulations that specify the types of loans or securities that may serve as collateral for loans made by the Federal Reserve banks to a member bank. (9)

equilibrium level of income The level of income where planned investment equals planned savings. (11)

equity effect Impact on consumption caused by a change in the market valuation of common stocks. (13)

Eurodollars Dollar-denominated deposits held in foreign banks or the branches of United States banks located outside the United States. (5)

excess reserves That portion of a bank's legal reserves in excess of its required reserves. (2)

exchange rate The price of another country's currency in terms of your own. (15)

Federal funds sold Excess reserves that banks lend to each other, usually on an overnight basis. (5)

Federal Open Market Committee Body that determines policy with respect to Federal Reserve open market operations. Composed of seven members of the Federal Reserve Board of Governors, the President of the New York Federal Reserve Bank, and four other Reserve Bank presidents. (7)

Federal Reserve notes Paper currency issued by the twelve Federal Reserve banks. (1)

Federal Reserve System The United States central bank. (7)

financial disintermediation The public's withdrawal of funds from financial institutions. Tends to occur especially during periods when rates on money market securities rise above rates payable on deposits, or shares at financial institutions. (9)

financial intermediaries Institutions that acquire funds by creating claims against themselves in the form of deposits and shares and that create credit as they provide loanable funds for borrowers. (3)

fiscal policy The use of the government's taxing and spending powers to influence income, employment, and prices. (7)

Fisher's transactions approach An explanation of the quantity theory of money framed in terms of reasons why the velocity of money is stable. (10)

fixed growth rule for the money supply The policy advocated by monetarists that the money supply should grow at a rate between 3 and 5 percent, year in and year out. (16)

float The difference between cash-items-in-the-process-of-collection and deferred-availability-cash-items on the books of the Federal Reserve. This difference, or float, reflects reserve credit for checks not yet collected. (8)

floating exchange rates Exchange rates determined in the market place by the forces of supply and demand. (15)

fractional reserve system A banking system which requires that banks hold reserves equal to only a percentage of their deposits and other designated liabilities. (2)

Gibson Paradox The theory that specifies that in the long-run there is a direct relationship between changes in the level of interest rates and prices. This is opposed to the Keynesian conclusion that an expansion of the money supply reduces interest rates. (13)

GNP Gross National Product. The money value of the goods and services produced in the economy in a year. (14)

gold certificate A type of money issued by the US Treasury to the Federal Reserve banks. Prior to 1965, gold certificates served as a reserve for member bank reserves and other deposit liabilities. Prior to 1968, gold certificates served as a reserve for Federal Reserve notes outstanding. (8)

gold standard A system whereby each country defines its monetary unit in terms of gold and agrees to redeem its paper currency in gold. (15)

inflation A rise in the general level of prices. (14)

insured bank A bank whose depositors are insured by the FDIC. All member banks are insured banks. (4)

international transaction accounts Records of transactions between a country's residents and foreign residents over a specified period such as a year. (15)

investment The purchase of newly produced capital goods. (11)

investment multiplier The relationship between a change in Y (income) and a change in I (investment). (11)

IS curve Shows for different interest rates and income levels all points where $I = S$ in the real sector. (11)

Keynes' law of consumption "On the whole and on the average, as income increases, consumption will increase but by a lesser amount." (11)

legal reserves Those assets that may be counted for purposes of meeting the Federal Reserve or state reserve requirement. (2)

liability management (bank) The process by which a bank locates and acquires adequate funds from sources with the lowest possible cost. (5)

liquidity preference theory of interest The Keynesian theory that specifies that the interest rate is determined by the demand and supply of money. (11)

liquidity trap The interest elastic portion of the Keynesian liquidity preference schedule. In this sector, increases in the money supply will cause little or no decrease in the interest rate and, hence, stimulate investment and income. (11)

LM curve Shows for different interest rates and income levels all points in the monetary sector where $L = M$. (11)

M_1 Currency and coin outside banks plus commercial bank demand deposits. (1)

M_1+ M_1 plus savings deposits at commercial banks, NOW accounts at banks and thrift institutions, CU share accounts, and demand deposits at MSBs. (1)

M_2 M_1 plus commercial bank time and savings deposits other than negotiable CDs in denominations of $100,000 or more. (1)

M_3 M_2 plus deposits at MSBs and S&Ls and CU shares. (1)

M_4 M_2 plus negotiable CDs in denominations of $100,000 or more. (1)

M_5 M_3 plus negotiable CDs in denominations of $100,000 or more. (1)

marginal efficiency of investment (MEI) The rate of discount which will make the discounted present value of the future net returns equal to the cost of the capital goods. (11)

margin requirements The minimum down payment required to purchase securities on credit. (9)

marginal propensity to consume (MPC) The additional consumption out of each dollar of additional income. (11)

medium of exchange A primary

function of money. As a medium of exchange, money enables the holder to swap goods and services that he or she has produced for the goods and services that others have produced. (1)

member bank A bank that is a member of the Federal Reserve System. All national banks are member banks. State banks have the option of becoming a member bank. (4)

merchandise trade balance In the international accounts, this represents the net excess of debits or credits in the merchandise accounts. (15)

merger (bank) The absorption of one bank by another bank with future operation under only one of the charters. (4)

modern quantity of theory of money The theory that specifies that the real demand for money is a function of expected real income; fraction of wealth in human form; rates of return on money, equities, and bonds; expected change in price levels; and other variables. (12)

monetarism School of thought that stresses that the demand for money is a stable function of many variables and that the money supply is the most important determinant of interest rates, money income, employment, and prices. (10)

monetary base (B) Amount of member bank reserves on the Federal Reserve Bank's books plus currency in circulation. (9)

monetary policy The actual management of the money supply to achieve our national economic goals. (10)

monetary theory That branch of macroeconomics that seeks to discover and explain how the demand and supply of money influence, interest rates, income, employment, and prices. (10)

money Anything commonly used and generally accepted as a medium of exchange and as a unit of account. (1)

money illusion The act of viewing economic values in nominal rather than real terms. (1)

money market mutual fund A fund consisting of CDs and short-term corporate and government securities. This fund pays daily interest and may permit shareholders to redeem shares by writing a check on the account. (1)

money multiplier (m) The ratio of the money supply to the monetary base: $m = M_1/B$. (9)

money risk The chance that market interest rates may rise (security prices fall) thereby causing securityholders to lose principal if the securities must be sold before maturity. (11)

moral suasion The use of speeches, press releases, and directives by members of the Fed Board to influence member bank borrowing, bankers' willingness to lend, and the demand for credit. (9)

municipals Securities issued by states and their political subdivisions. (6)

mutual savings bank A financial institution found primarily in the Northeast that provides time and savings deposits and NOW accounts (in New England and New York) and invests largely in mortgages and corporate bonds. (3)

national bank A bank chartered by the federal government, specifically, the Comptroller of the Currency. (4)

natural rate of unemployment That rate of unemployment at which expected inflation equals actual inflation and where the real wage rate is at its equilibrium level. (16)

nominal supply of money The actual amount of money available to the public. (12)

noninsured bank A bank whose depositors are not insured by the FDIC. (4)

nonmember bank A bank that is not a member of the Federal Reserve System. (4)

NOW account Interest-bearing checking account at banks, MSBs, and S&Ls in New England and New York. Account holders transfer funds with a negotiable order of withdrawal (NOW). (1)

Okun's Law The relationship between unemployment and aggregate output. (14)

open market operations The buying and selling of Treasury securities, agency obligations, and banker's acceptances by the Fed for its own account. (9)

open market policy directives The Federal Open-Market Committee's general instructions to the Manager of the Open-Market Account regarding how to conduct open market operations until the Committee's next meeting. (9)

operation nudge (twist) The open market policy from 1961–1965 involving the simultaneous sale of short-term securities and purchase of long-term obligations to push up short-term rates to retard the outflow of short-term capital and to push down long-term rates to stimulate domestic capital investment.

pegged exchange rates A system whereby nations tie their currency to gold or to a strong currency such as the dollar. (15)

Phillips curve The schedule that shows the trade-off between unemployment and inflation. Higher levels of unemployment tend to be associated with lower levels of inflation, and vice versa. (16)

Pigou effect Impact of a change in the real value of money balances on consumption. (14)

point of sale systems Systems allowing a customer to pay for goods and services at the merchant location by having funds transferred from his or her demand deposit, NOW, or credit card account. (1)

portfolio balances approach The theory that specifies that money is just one of several types of financial assets, with the demand for money a direct function of its own utility or yield but inversely related to all other interest rates. (12)

primary deposit A deposit made in a bank in the form of coin, currency, or checks drawn on other banks. (2)

private noninsured pension funds Financial entities established mainly by corporations to provide retirement and deferred profit-sharing benefits to employees. (3)

quantity theory of money Other things being equal, there is a direct and proportionate relationship between changes in the money supply and the general level of prices. (10)

rational expectations The assumption that people make economic decisions in a way that tends to take into account all available information bearing significantly on the future consequences of their decisions. (16)

real demand for money The amount of goods and services (expressed in terms of money) over which people wish to have command. (12)

real value of money The amount of goods and services that money can command in exchange. (1)

Regulation Q The Federal Reserve regulation that prohibits the payment of interest on bank demand deposits and limits the rate of interest that may be paid on time and savings deposits. (4)

relative price effect The impact on other financial or real assets and/or total spending caused by a change in the price (yield) of one class of financial or real assets held in a portfolio. (13)

remote service units Off-premises electronic teller machines that enable an S&L depositor to obtain funds from his or her savings account. Usually located in supermarkets and airports. (1)

repurchase agreement An agreement with a securities dealer to purchase a given amount of obligations and to resell them to the dealer at a specified time and price. (16)

required reserves That portion of a bank's legal reserves that must be held, given the bank's deposits and other liabilities and the applicable Federal Reserve or state reserve ratios. (2)

reserve requirement Federal Reserve or state regulation relating to the holding of reserves; such a regulation specifies what assets count as legal reserves, the deposits and other liabilities that must be matched by legal reserves, and the applicable reserve ratios. (2)

savings deposits Interest-bearing bank deposits with no set maturity and usually evidenced by a passbook. (5)

Say's Law "Supply creates its own demand" or "the act of production generates exactly enough income to purchase all the goods and services produced." (10)

secondary deposit A deposit that may be created by a bank as it makes a loan or investment. (2)

share draft A checklike instrument that enables a person to transfer funds from his or her interest-bearing account at a CU. (1)

special drawing rights (SDRs) So-called "paper gold" created by the International Monetary Fund as part of an effort to increase international reserves. (8)

state bank A bank chartered by a state government. (4)

structural unemployment Unemployment caused by an imbalance between the types and location of jobs available and the types and location of the jobs demanded by the labor force. (14)

surplus account (bank) A bank's "permanent" retained earnings. (2)

term loan A loan with an original maturity of one year or longer. (6)

time deposit, open account Interest-bearing bank deposits with fixed maturity and evidenced by a written contract. (5)

transaction account A deposit or account on which the depositor or accountholder is allowed to make withdrawals by negotiable or transferable instruments or other similar items for the purpose of making payments to third persons or others. (4)

Treasury bill The shortest term US Treasury obligation. Maturities range from 91 days to one year. (6)

Treasury bonds Coupon issues that pay interest semiannually and have initial maturities in excess of five years. (6)

Treasury notes Coupon issues that pay interest semiannually and have initial maturities ranging from one to ten years. (6)

Treasury tax and loan accounts (TT&L accounts) Treasury accounts at commercial banks used for the deposit of taxes and proceeds from the sale of securities. (5)

undivided profits (bank) The bank capital account to which net earnings are credited. (2)

unemployment rate The percentage of the civilian labor force that is seeking work but does not have a job. (14)

unit bank A bank that operates from only one location. (4)

unit of account A primary function of money. As a unit of account, money facilitates placing economic values on goods and services. (1)

velocity of money The annual turnover of the money supply; the number of times $1 appears to effect transactions during a year (transactions velocity); the number of times $1 appears to buy final goods and services during a year (income velocity). (10)

wealth effect The impact on other financial or real assets and/or total spending caused by a change in the value of money balances or other wealth such as stocks. (13)

wire transfer system An electronic transfer system that enables the Fed to transfer funds and securities among Reserve banks and commercial banks. (1)

Index